I wish to dedicate my first book to the most important person in my life and career, my wife Diana, who has waited for this book longer than anyone else I know.

AN EXPANDED EDITION

NORTHERN BUSH CRAFT

MORS L. KOCHANSKI

First Printed 1987
Expanded Edition 1988 10 9 8 7 6 5

Printed in Canada

The Publisher: **Lone Pine Publishing**

206, 10426 - 81 Ave.
Edmonton, Alberta
Canada T6E 1X5

202A, 1110 Seymour St.
Vancouver, B.C.
Canada V6B 3N3

16149 Redmond Way, #180
Redmond, Washington
USA 98052

Canadian Cataloguing in Publication Data

Kochanski, Mors L.
Northern Bushcraft

Includes index.
ISBN 0-919433-51-0

1. Wilderness survival—Canada, Northern.
2. Outdoor life—Canada, Northern.
3. Taiga ecology—Canada, Northern. I. Title.
GV200.5.K63 1988 796.5 C88-091384-3

Cover Design - Ed Kusiak
Layout - Yuet C. Chan and Ewa Pluciennik
Typesetting - Pièce de Résistance Typographers, Edmonton, Alberta
Printing - Jasper Printing Group Ltd., Edmonton, Alberta
Illustrations - Mors L. Kochanski

The publisher gratefully acknowledges the assistance of Alberta Community Development and the Department of Canadian Hertiage, the support of the Canada/Alberta Agreement on the cultural industries, and the financial support provided by the Alberta Foundation for the Arts.

PREFACE

The purpose of *Northern Bushcraft* is to provide practical information on the more important crafts used in every day bush living in the Northern Forests. This is not simply a manual on wilderness camping or survival, but rather discusses the basic existence skills that allow you to live in the bush on an indefinite basis with a minimal dependence on technological materials and tools.

The major problem in writing a book of this nature is selecting the most relevant material to include when it is possible to expand each chapter into a large book. I continuously asked myself how often I had occasion to use a certain technique. For example, there are many fine fire types described. The one I use nine-tenths of the time is the parallel firelay. The other three that are included I would have occasion to use rarely if I did not instruct Wilderness Living Skills as a livelihood. In my opinion, all the other unmentioned fire types have little to offer over the four chosen ones.

This second edition of *Northern Bushcraft* has given me an opportunity to include thirty-four colour photographs, which illustrate and augment a number of subjects covered in the book. Page numbers are appended to each photo caption for ease of reference.

Mors Kochanski, 1988

ACKNOWLEDGEMENTS

The greatest influence on my career as a student, instructor and writer about wilderness living skills and survival, has been without question, Tom Roycraft of Hinton, whose many years of experience and incisive insights have lent considerable force to my bush knowledge.

Another important person is Don Bright of Edson, with whom I published the *Wilderness Arts and Recreation* magazine. The magazine motivated me to produce a working volume of written material that forms the basis for this and future books.

I am grateful to the publisher Grant Kennedy, who provided the encouragement that resulted in this book becoming available now rather than ten years from now.

CONTENTS

INTRODUCTION

There is no reason why a person cannot live comfortably in the Northern Forests with a few simple, well-chosen possessions such as a pot and an axe. It is also conceivable that with the right knowledge you may live well enough without a pot or axe. The reader may never have to do without these two precious items, tan a moose hide, or build a subterranean winter shelter, but intelligent advice derived from a reliable source may furnish the knowledge that allows you to do a passable job on the first attempt, should the need arise.

Fire is the most useful and important skill in basic bush living, particularly in the cold. It warms and dries, makes water and food safe and transforms any place in the forest into a home. Fire is a passable companion when you are alone, is never boring to watch, and has held our fascination from time immemorial. Possessing the means and the knowledge to light fire at any moment is a prerequisite for living and surviving in the bush. If you are fire's master it is the genie that does your bidding, but if a lack of knowledge limits your ability to master it, fire will be a trying servant that may jeopardize your safety.

A pot is an important possession for heating water, cooking, melting snow, putting out campfires, excavating earth and for collecting berries and other edibles. Drinking adequate amounts of safe water is necessary for maintaining health and reducing fatigue. Giardiasis is apt to be found in the remotest corners of the Northern Forests, a parasite that is easily killed by boiling. Boiling is the most effective and convenient method of cooking in the bush. You may get by without a pot, but it will be sorely missed.

Of the tools useful in bush living, the axe is foremost because of its versatility and durability in cutting firewood, fashioning shelters and other articles useful in daily existence. The knife is the smallest cutting tool that one may carry; small, light and unobtrusive, it is readily available for hundreds of tasks in bush living. Like fire, these tools are a great asset if used safely and knowledgeably, but impose penalties on the ignorant and careless. Using an axe to fall a tree is one of the more hazardous wilderness activities. The saw is the complementary opposite of the axe. It is safer, faster and quieter for such applications as cutting firewood.

Cordage and binding holds most things together in basic

bush living. Without cord you cannot rotate the spindle of the bow drill for making fire or drilling holes, make bow strings, fish lines, nets and snares. Without some form of binding you cannot tie up a twig bundle, lash shelter poles, or build toboggans, sleds and canoes. From a sewing thread made of stinging nettle to a tow cable of grass, cordage-making and its application is an important bush skill.

It is a major accomplishment in the bush to be able to rest and sleep with comfort when on the move. When the weather is mild, a ready-made bed can be found in the dry, organic materials at the base of a large white spruce. When conditions become too cold or wet, a fire will give respite. Under prolonged and adverse conditions, maintaining a fire is hard work because of the large amounts of fuel required. An appropriate shelter helps to keep the weather at bay and captures a fire's warmth with greater efficiency.

The raw materials used in bush living are the locally available plants and animals. The more you know about using these resources the more alternatives you have to adequately meet your daily needs. There is nothing in the bush that does not have a use at some time or other.

There was only enough space to deal with the two most important animals in the Northern Forests, the biggest and the smallest—the moose and the varying hare. The moose is a major source of meat and fabric for clothing and shelter. Where the moose feeds the village, the hare provides the day to day fare.

I did not write this book for old trappers or the people who have lived in the bush all their lives. I have written it for the person who wishes to become more knowledgeable about, and more comfortable in, the bush.

1

FIRECRAFT

When all else fails, fire is the simplest means of providing comfort and warmth against cold and wet in the Northern Forests.

If you were dressed in the old European tradition, with numerous layers of fluffy wool adequate to deal with the bitter cold, you would likely be wearing about nine kilograms or 25 pounds of clothing. If you were unable to dry your clothing out, within five days you would be carrying six kilograms more weight of accumulated frost. The efficiency of your clothing would be so impaired by this frost build up you could die of hypothermia within a week.

When you stop moving in cold weather, the first thought should be to light a fire. Your hands should not be allowed to become so numb that fire-lighting becomes difficult. A simple test of your level of physical capacity is to touch the thumb to the little finger of the same hand. The moment you have any difficulty in doing this **you should light a fire**.

In cold, wet weather when the need is most urgent, fire-lighting is often the most difficult. You may have to exercise strenuously to restore some manipulative capacity to your hands, or in your clumsiness you may drop or break matches while attempting to strike them.

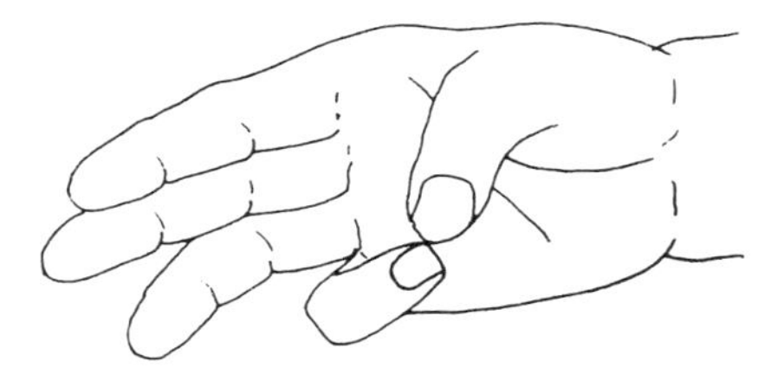

The test for hypothermic incapacity. *If you cannot touch your thumb to your little finger, you should take immediate steps to warm up.*

FIRE-LIGHTING

There are four basic stages in fire-lighting:

1. Ignition. Fire may be started in a variety of ways. The most common methods are matches, the flint and steel, and the bow drill.

2. Establishment. This stage involves using the most effective method to light the required type of fire with the fuel available. Fine and coarse kindlings are ignited, which in turn ignite sufficient fuel of the right quality so the fire will continue to burn even in wind or rain. Establishment is a critical aspect of fire-lighting under adverse conditions as there are often many problems to overcome.

3. Application. There are a number of different fire arrangements that produce the best desired effect, combined with the special properties of the fuels available. There are fires for cooking, warming, drying, repelling insects, signaling and so on.

4. Maintenance and Moderation. A fire can be made to burn at a desired output with a minimum of smoke. Knowledgeable maintenance will allow you long periods between adjustments or stokings.

In a stove, a fine kindling is set on fire (ignition) which in turn ignites coarse kindling, and then a fuel that burns fairly hot (establishment). The fuel should produce a good bed of coals to better utilize a slower burning, perhaps green fuel, for staying power. If the fire is too hot, green fuel may be added or the air supply restricted (moderation). An open fire, being fuel regulated, is more complex to control than one in a stove but the stages remain the same.

IGNITION

Matches

The most common and convenient way to light a fire is, understandably, to use a match. The match flame should be instantly transferred to a combustible material while taking care to protect the flame from any wind. Open-flame methods of ignition are vulnerable to air movements that tend to extinguish a flame while it is small, but help intensify it when it is large.

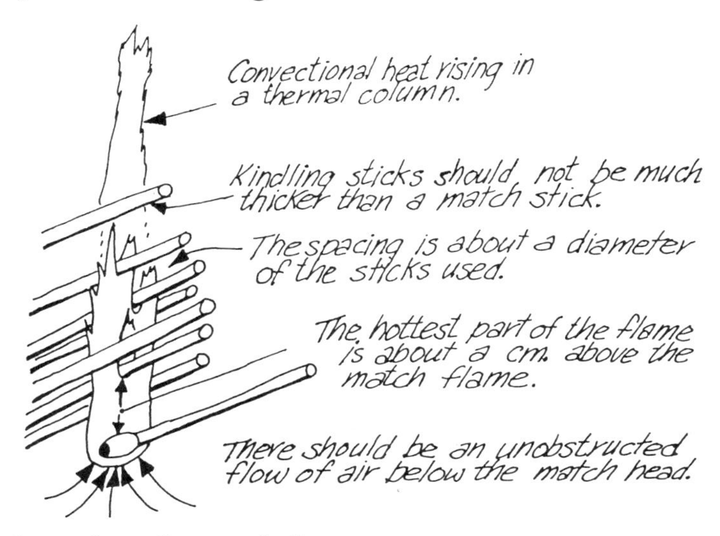

The action of a match flame.

The larger the match, the more time there is to transfer the flame to any kindling, and the better the chance the flame will catch. For example, a large kitchen match will burn for at least the count of 40, one of paper for 15, and a split paper match for five. If you consistently succeed with a split paper match in wet, windy weather, you should never have a problem lighting fires in the bush.

Matches should be carried in waterproof containers in three separate places. First, in your pants pocket (assuming your pants are the last items of clothing to be removed). A second back-up container should be carried elsewhere, possibly in your shirt pocket. The third is a reserve in your pack to replenish the other two sources.

Unprotected matches are ruined by sweat, melted frost build-up in the clothes, rain or from falling into water. A match container should be tested by submersion for ten minutes. The container must be easy to open with wet or numb hands.

Matches should never be carried loose in any pocket. Every year thousands of North Americans suffer severe burns from this habit, with over 50 actually burning to death.

The Flint and Steel

Wind is a major problem when lighting a fire with matches. On the other hand, the flint and steel dispenses with

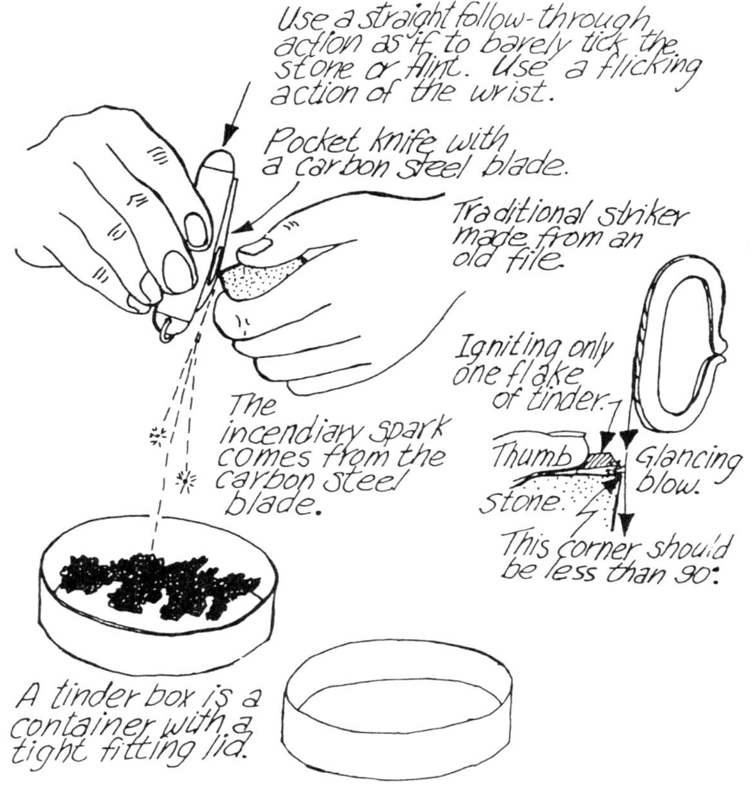

The flint and steel method of fire-lighting.

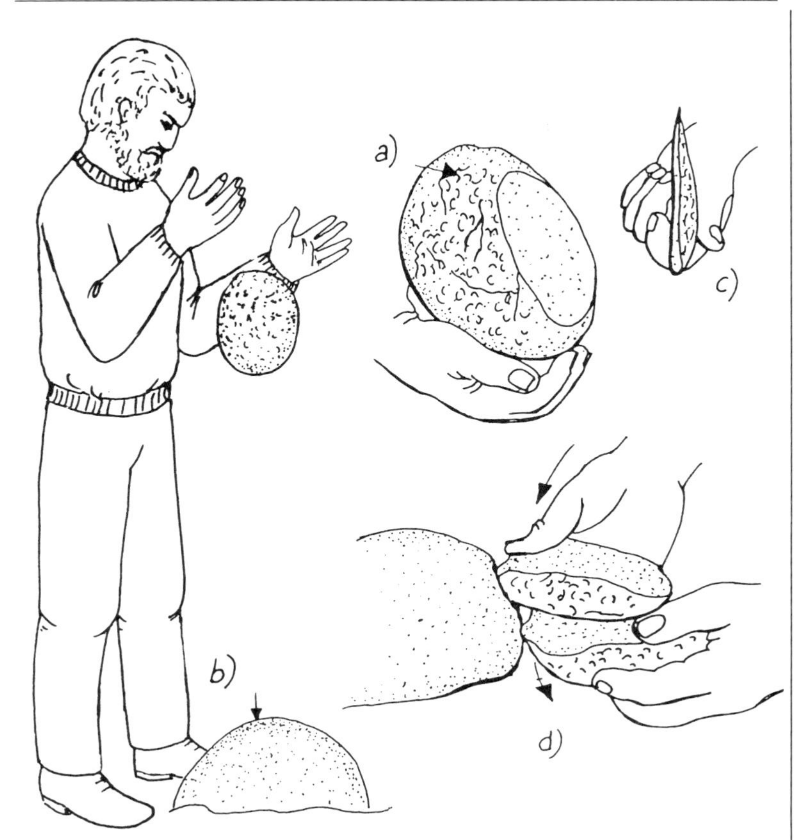

Method of cracking apart a rock to expose a striking surface.

a) Identifying quartzite. Quartzite is a commonly found hard rock that makes a good flint. The best rock displays a surface marked with many crescent-shaped fractures.

b) Cracking a quartzite boulder. Quartzite boulders that are either flat or discus-like are easily cracked when dropped on a larger rock. Spherical or egg-shaped rocks are very tenacious, tending to bounce rather than crack. Rocks that must be thrown to be broken are dangerous and may rebound towards you or the flying shards may cause injury.

c) A quartzite flake. A flake that is knocked off a quartzite boulder is usually sharp enough to be used as a chopper or saw for working wood or as a knife for skinning.

d) Breaking quartzite into small pieces. Once a quartzite boulder is broken in half it is easily fractured into smaller pieces that are more suitable for use as flints. The flints should have sharp edges that can be struck with the steel.

an open flame and uses wind to advantage. Though not as convenient, it is a superior method under all adverse conditions. When you are down to your last ten matches you may choose to conserve them by converting to the flint and steel.

The Flint. Any rock, such as quartzite, that is harder than carbon steel can be used. Wherever rocks are found, some are always hard enough to act as a flint. The rock usually has to be cracked apart to expose a sharp edge to strike against. When the steel is struck against this edge, a fine shaving of metal is produced becoming so hot in the process that it burns.

The Steel. The steel or striker must be of tempered carbon steel to obtain the best sparks. Although many other substances may work, few have the intense fiery focus or incendiary spark like a burning fragment of carbon steel. A natural stone, known as iron pyrite, may be used as a striker or both striker and flint. Two pieces of pyrite may be struck against each other to obtain an incendiary spark. It is difficult to produce sparks from pure iron or stainless steel.

The Tinder. Tinder is a special material that will begin to glow from an incendiary spark. There are three tinders commonly used in the Northern Forests.

1. Synthetic Tinder. Made by charring any vegetable fiber such as cotton, linen or jute. To make a small quantity of cloth tinder, tear out ten strips of old blue jean material a few centimetres wide and 20 centimetres long. Drape the strips across a stick and set the material on fire. As the flame dies down stuff the burning mass into an airtight container. Once the flame subsides and the charred material begins to glow, the lid is put on to exclude oxygen. If no airtight tin or tinderbox is available, two pieces of bark can be used. To make larger quantities tightly roll up and bind a jeans pant leg with wire. Build a fire over the bundle. When it dies down, stuff the glowing mass of cotton into a jam can with a tight-fitting lid.

2. Natural Tinder. Made by extracting the context or cottony substance from the hoof, or false tinder fungus, and boiling it in a slurry made from the powdery-grey ash of a wood fire. The false tinder fungus is usually found on dead birch and occasionally on aspen. It is easy to identify as it looks like a horse's hoof.

3. True Tinder Fungus. Found on living birch trees, it is also easy to identify as it appears already charred. The light-brown interior material is dried to prepare it for use.

Striking the Spark. It takes practice to obtain a good spark. Use a supple flick of the wrist to make a light glancing blow. See how close you can come to the flint with the striker, yet miss it. You know you have a good flint, steel and technique when you can make sparks that strike the ground from a standing height.

Striking into a tinderbox may cause many pieces of the tinder to glow. To ignite one flake, hold it under the thumb above a sharp corner of your flint and strike the spark upward into it.

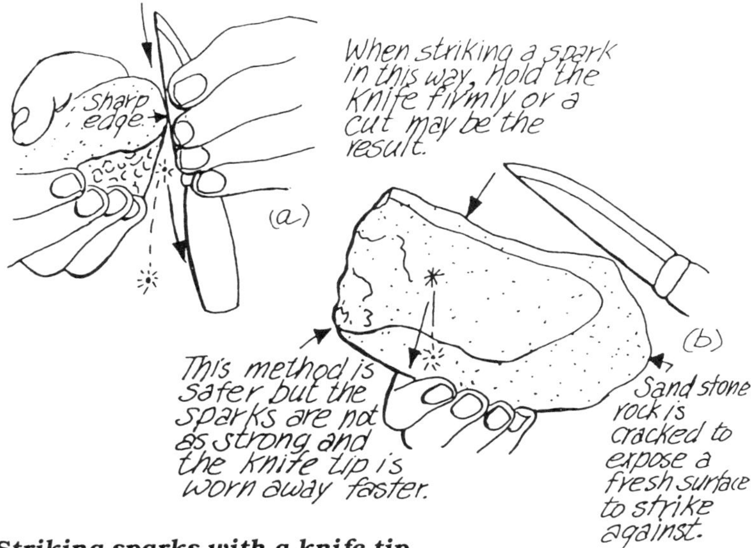

Striking sparks with a knife tip.
a) Striking sparks with the back of a knife. This is the most effective way to strike sparks with the back of a straight knife. It is risky if the blade is not held firmly as the stone is struck.
b) The safest way to use a hunting knife as a striker is to employ the tip of the blade. The sparks are not as intense as those produced with the drill.

Producing Flame. Make a ball of dry material such as grass, inner bark of black poplar or aspen and old man's beard. Place the glowing flakes of tinder in the ball and blow into flame. To keep the smoke out of your face hold the kindling above eye-level and blow up into it. The burning ball of kindling is used to ignite twigs or shavings.

Striking sparks with an axe.

The Bow Drill

Lighting fire by friction is an exacting skill requiring considerable background knowledge. It sharpens one's fire sense and induces a great feeling of accomplishment.

Moisture is a major problem in friction fire-lighting. When fire hazard is high, it is easy to start a fire with a bow drill. You are likely to obtain an ember if there has been no rain for two days, the weather is hot and sunny, and the fire is made in the hottest part of the day (mid-afternoon). Due to the low relative humidity normally found in winter, the bow drill works well, unless there were extensive autumn rains. Laying a board and drill on "dry" ground for a half-hour may cause failure because of the moisture that is absorbed.

Suitable woods. Any dry, firm, non-resinous wood will likely produce an ember. A screeching drill indicates the wood used has a high resin content. The drag created by resin is exhausting to overcome and the powder has a higher

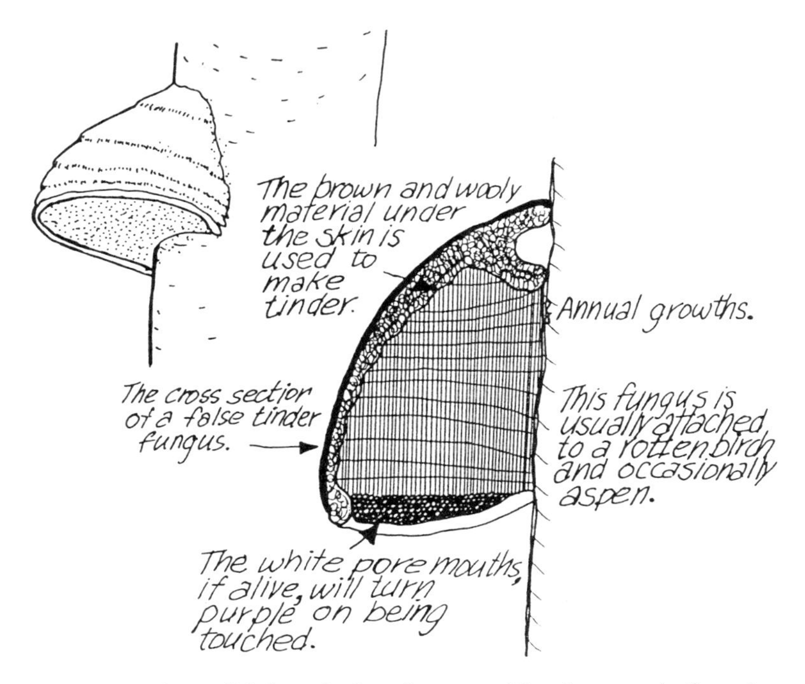

Cross section of false tinder fungus. The fungus is found on dead birch and occasionally on aspen.

ignition point difficult to reach by normal drilling. Wood that is low in resin may not screech but produces a powder composed of tiny rolls, which is a sure indication that it will not work.

Some woods must be sound to work well, while others are best if attacked by a fungus. If the board and drill are from the same piece of wood, and difficulty is encountered, then both pieces should be discarded. The board and the drill must be of the same hardness, or the drill must be the harder of the two, or it will wear away before it can generate the required heat. Aspen, willow and balsam fir work well when both the board and drill are of the same wood.

A superior combination is a punky aspen heartwood board and a dry, weathered wolf willow drill. Aspen and willow are popular because of their availability. Both are easily shaped with a knife or a cracked rock.

Suitable wood is weathered grey, has little bark left on and comes from a protected, sunny location (such as on the

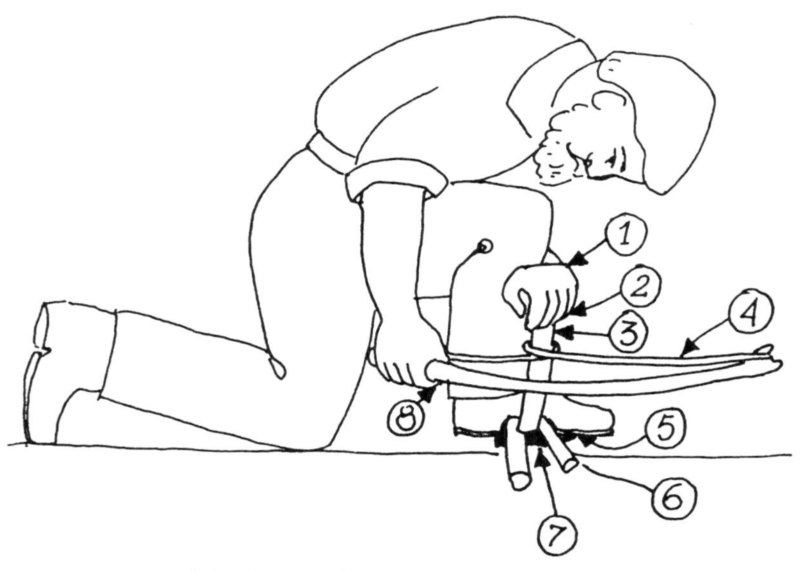

Proper use of the bow drill.
1. The wrist fits snugly against the shin to steady the drill.
2. If you do not bear down enough on the socket you will not make smoke. If you bear down too hard you may become exhausted before you get an ember.
3. Hold the drill vertical.
4. The bow is horizontal and at 90 degrees to the drill.
5. The instep of the foot is close to the drill.
6. The board must be on a firm footing.
7. Kindling.
8. The thumb and fingers are used to vary the tension on the bow string.

south side and close to a big white spruce). It must be vertical with no old man's beard and should be collected well above your height to ensure the minimum of moisture.

Aspen may be found in three suitable forms. The first is firm, in diameters of up to ten centimetres, well-weathered and grey displaying a large check. The second is attacked by a fungus that makes it light and punky and causes the top part of the tree to break off two or three metres from the ground. The third and best board of all, comes from a living aspen attacked by the conk fungus that so weakens the tree internally it falls, usually fracturing into pieces that can be removed without using an axe. This wood is both light and firm, much like balsa.

Drill. A straight drill works best. It should be thicker than the thumb and about a hand span long. The dimensions are not critical as drills a centimetre thick and a few centimetres long or a few centimetres thick and a metre long will work. The larger diameter drill provides more traction and imposes less wear on a weak cord.

Reverse ends often while drilling.
Wood must be dry, firm and hard.
The straighter the drill and the rounder the cross section, the smoother the action.
If the central portion of the drill is larger in diameter than the ends, the bow cord will ride better.
The best woods are: 1. Wolf willow
2. Some Salix

Drill ends should be spherical to parabaloid in shape.

A standard sized drill is about thumb thick but it may range from that of the little finger to twice thumb thickness.

The drill.

Both ends of the drill should be similar in size and symmetry. Initially, sharply pointed ends may seat easier in the socket and fireboard. Switching the ends frequently during drilling is the most effective way to produce an ember. If there is little friction, and the drill wears away rapidly, it is too soft. If there is little friction and the drill and board polish instead of charring, then the wood of both is too hard.

Fireboard. The board should be the source for most of the powder that eventually becomes hot enough to glow spontaneously from the friction of the drill. Only a dry board allows the build-up of temperatures to this ignition point. The board needs only be big enough to be easily held down with the foot.

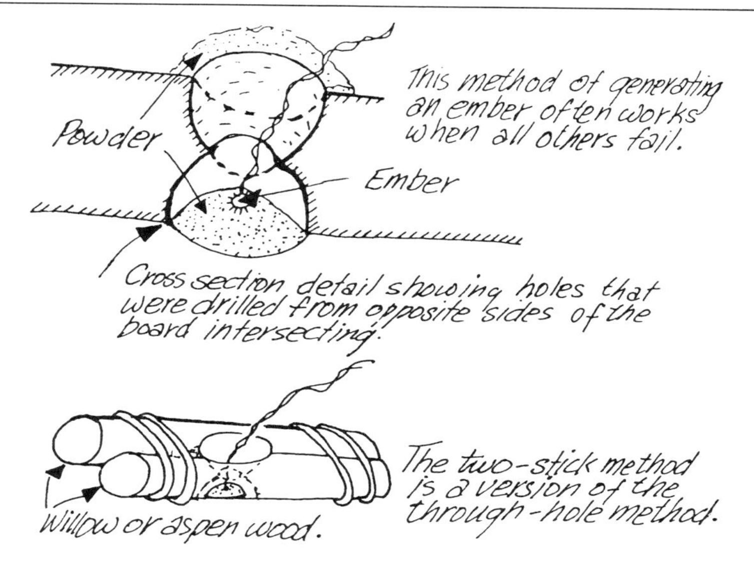

The through hole and two stick methods used with the bow drill.

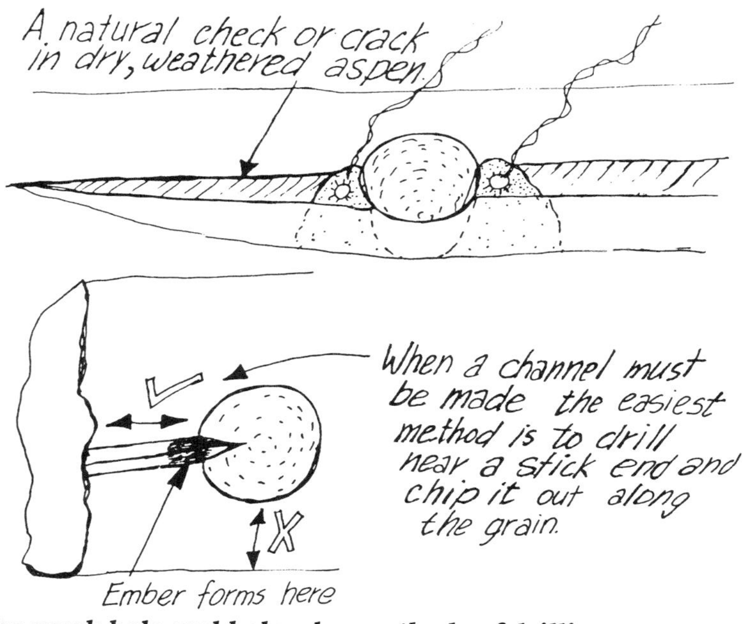

The crack-hole and hole-edge methods of drilling an ember.

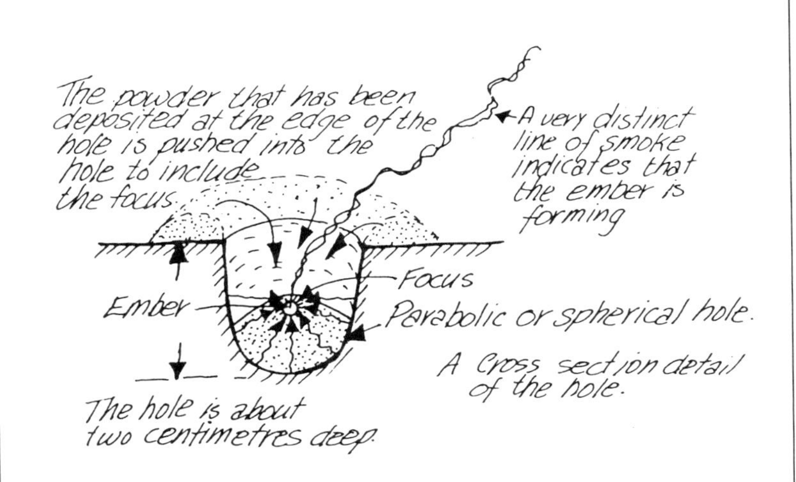

The one-hole method is the fastest method known for producing an ember by drilling.

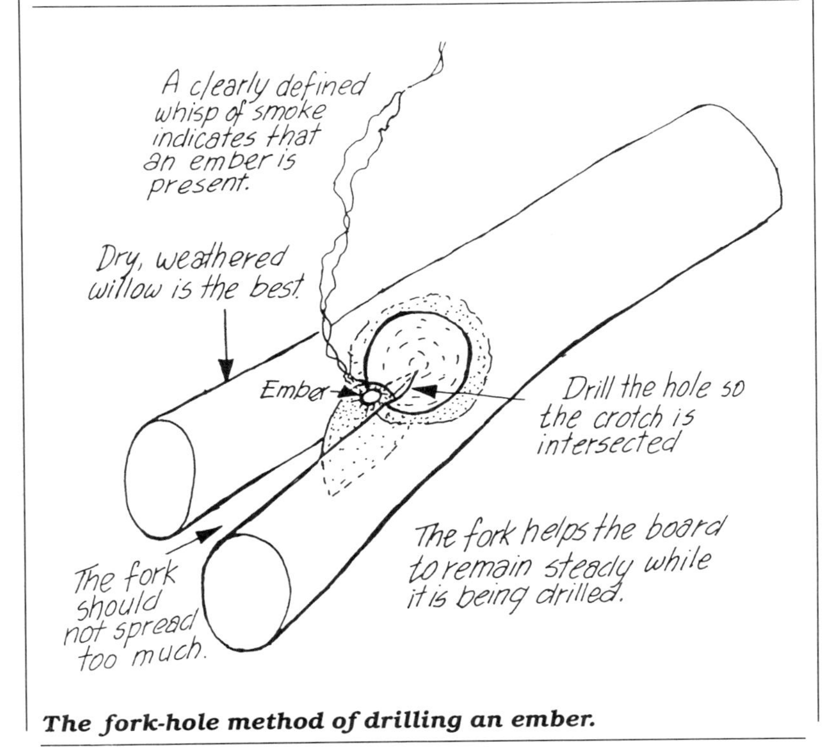

The fork-hole method of drilling an ember.

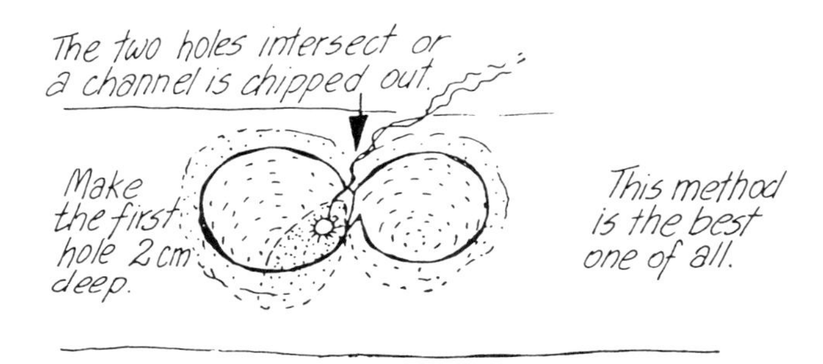

The two-hole method of drilling an ember.

Socket. A socket should be comfortable to hold in the palm of the hand. The diamond depression from both a dry or green "diamond" willow may be quickly made into a socket. One of the best sockets is easily made from the soft, thick outer bark of the black poplar. In a few moments of use it develops an almost frictionless bearing surface. With other sockets the hole may have to be inlayed with something smooth and hard. Green leaves, soap or grease can be used to reduce the frictional drag that is so physically exhausting to overcome. When a lubricant is applied, only one end of the drill can be used for the entire drilling operation.

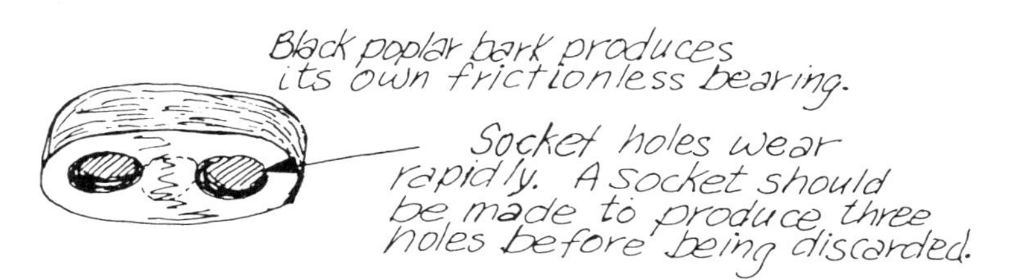

The drill socket.

Bow. The bow is a straight stick that ranges in length from that of the arm, to that of elbow to finger tip. If too flexible, it will not grip the drill and if too rigid, it will rapidly wear out the bow cord. When the bow is held at the ends and bent, it should flex slightly. A dry bow, being lighter and more resilient, is superior to a green one. The tip of the bow may have a fork (if willow) or a hole (if spruce) and the handle should have a hole through which the cord passes snugly so that its tension can be easily adjusted.

The straighter the bow stick the better it works. As it is pulled back and forth it should clatter against the drill. If the cord is too tight the drill will tend to flip out. The tension of the cord can be varied slightly with the thumb and forefinger of the hand working the bow. When the cord is made to take a turn around it, the drill must not be between the cord and the bow.

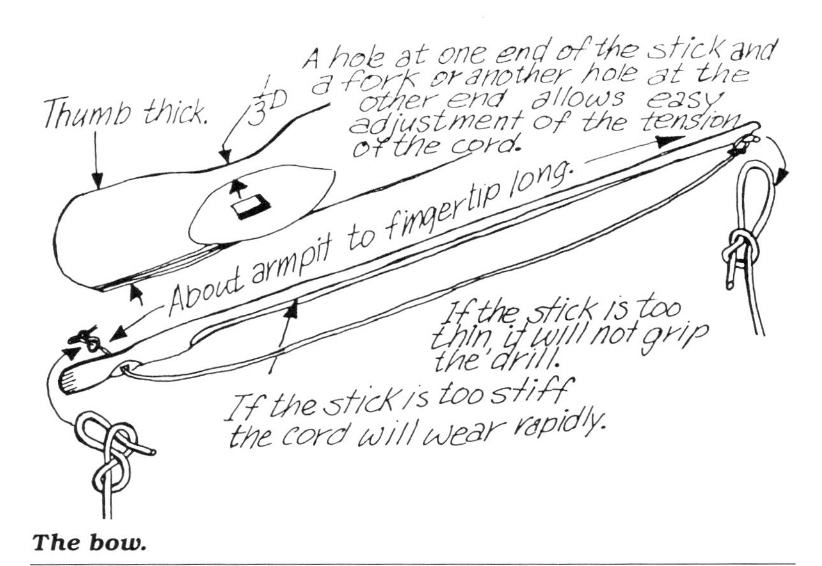

The bow.

It is difficult to find natural materials with which to make a strong enough cord for the bow. Only a few vegetable fibers can withstand the tension necessary to grip and rotate the drill. With two people, a bow is not required. Almost any root by itself is strong enough if one person uses it to rotate the drill while the other steadies the board, drill and socket. (*See* Bindcraft, Chapter 5.)

Preparing the Board and Drill. Sharpen the ends of the drill and make starting holes in the fireboard and socket. In the **edge-hole** method the hole in the fireboard is made near the end of the board, so that the spark is formed outside the edge. Under adverse conditions, especially in strong winds, the **two-hole** method is the most secure for handling the fragile ember.

To drill, take a comfortable position, holding the board steady with the foot opposite to the hand working the bow. The toe or the instep is placed near the hole being drilled and the wrist of the socket hand rests against the shin. If you are not using a lubricant in the socket, switch ends now and again so both ends of the drill maintain a similar size and shape. (A pinch of dry sand will speed up the drilling of the hole.)

All the powder produced is needed to sustain and enlarge the ember. The best powder should be black and fine, resembling instant coffee in texture. If the powder is more brown than black or forms into rolls, then discard the drill and board for something better.

In the two-hole method, when the first hole is about a centimetre deep, the second hole is made to slightly intersect the first. When the two holes are well-established, chip out a good channel between the two. The friction of the drill will grind out powder that will eventually reach the spontaneous ignition point for cellulose. The powder will begin to glow if enough oxygen reaches it through this channel.

Willow is well-suited for the **crotch-hole** method. Drill into the crotch of a closely forked stick so that the powder piles up onto a nest of shredded kindling.

Another method is to drill between two sticks bound together to make the board, with the ember forming through the bottom of the hole.

Sometimes a forked or flat board is turned over and the drilling continued through to the bottom of the previous hole for the **through-hole** method.

An advanced and fast technique is the **one-hole** method. The drill point is made sharp enough to rapidly make a hole two to three centimetres deep by drilling furiously for ten seconds. A parabolic-shaped hole should be produced. The radiating heat from the hot inside surface of the hole converges at its focal point. The powder that accumulates around the edge of the hole is heaped up inside it to include the focal point. It should begin to glow as though a magnifying glass is being directed on it.

Resting Stage. Because it is tiring to prepare the fire-making equipment, and more energy will be needed to produce the glowing coal, take a rest between the two stages. Prepare the fine kindling required for the next stage. Trim the sides of the drill and the hole to create more friction on the drill tips rather than on the sides.

The Ember Stage. Drill vigorously to make a deep hole to contain the ember, then immediately change to the second, more shallow hole that produces the ember, pausing momentarily to chip out a channel between the two. If the drag seems excessive, trim the sides of the drill tip or the shoulders of the drill hole again. Use long, steady strokes to build up the temperature in the hole. If you do not bear down hard enough on the drill you may not produce smoke. If you bear down too hard you may exhaust yourself before obtaining an ember. After a few teaspoons of powder have been produced and the smoke is more pronounced, the drilling is gradually speeded up until you are working as fast as you can.

When you reach the limit of your endurance, stop and look for a thin line of smoke rising from one point in the powder. Dispersed smoke coming from the whole pile indicates the lack of an ember. If an ember is present, fan with your hand to drive more oxygen to it. The use of your hand allows you to catch your breath after the exertion of drilling. Avoid blowing on the ember as the humid air from your lungs may have an adverse affect on the ember. If no ember is produced in 15 minutes of drilling use a different board and drill as there is little hope for success.

Producing a Flame from the Ember. Once the ember is about pea size place a ball of kindling over the hole that contains it. The kindling must be sufficiently frayed to prevent the powder from sifting through. Place a piece of bark on the ball of kindling and hold the bark, kindling and board firmly together. Turn everything over so the board lies on the bark and the ball of kindling. To dislodge the ember give the back of the board a rap with the drill.

Place a second ball of kindling and piece of bark over the ember so it can be handled with the least disturbance. You can dispense with the two pieces of bark if you are careful

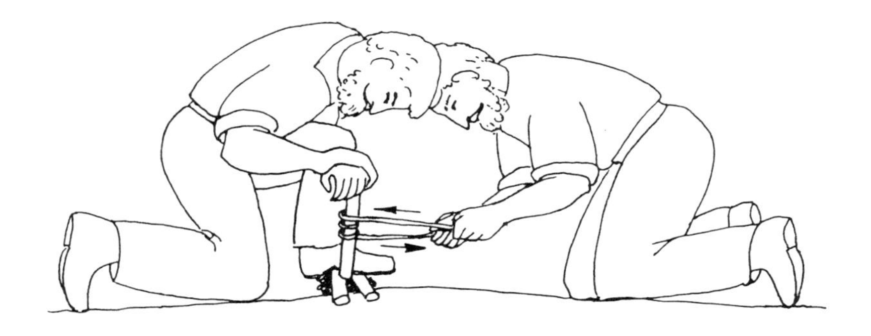

The technique of two persons using the board and drill.

when handling the balls of kindling. Well-frayed grass or fine wood shavings can be substituted for black poplar inner bark.

Either blow the ember into flame, face it into a brisk wind or twirl it at arm's length.

A fire can be made by two people within an hour of starting to look for the required materials and using only cracked rocks as the tools to produce the board and drill.

ESTABLISHMENT

Moisture is a major hindrance in fire-lighting. During evaporation, moisture carries away a great deal of heat and saps the strength of a flame or ember by keeping the kindling cool. As a gram of water requires 540 calories to evaporate, most of the energy of ignition is used drying the fuel.

The cooler and damper air found near the ground can be avoided if the kindling is lit at chest level and then laid down.

Wood size determines how hot and fast a fire will burn. If wood with a surface area of one square metre is split into smaller pieces with a total surface area of ten square metres, these would burn at a greater intensity, to a higher temperature and in less time, but the amount of heat liberated in either case would still be the same.

The Kindlings

A fire is established by the transfer of an ember or flame to a fine fuel or kindling. Kindling should not be confused with tinder (which is a superior form of kindling that glows from an incendiary spark).

Fine Kindlings. Fine kindlings will ignite readily from a glowing piece of tinder as from a flame. This sort of material is scarce in the natural environment.

The inner bark of black poplar is a superior kindling found on trees that have died in the spring, perhaps as a result of forest fire or the work of beaver. No other material in the Northern Forest works as well to enlarge the ember generated by the bow drill.

Dry grass is an excellent kindling found in the winter but

rare in the summer. It excels when used with the flint and steel.

The lichens (*Usnea* and *Alectoria*) commonly known as old man's beard are poor kindlings in wet weather because they absorb moisture from the air. They are most useful in the winter when the relative humidity is low. When dry they burn furiously. They must be used in a fluffy state to work well. Old man's beard is the least objectionable material to dry by body heat if tucked into your shirt above the belt.

Any firm wood of low resin content can be scraped with a sharp knife to produce a fine kindling. Scraped resinous wood works very well with an open flame, but poorly with glowing tinder.

Glowing tinder will cause dry punky wood or charcoal to glow strongly enough to ignite coarse kindling. The glowing tinder is placed between two lumps of charcoal and blown into a large enough ember to easily ignite coarse kindling.

Coarse Kindlings. A coarse kindling is any dry wood as fine as a matchstick that is readily ignited with an open flame or by a *large* quantity of glowing tinder.

Birch bark is well-known for its waterproof properties. Fine shreds are easily ignited by a flame. Like conifer resin, its resinous or oily nature prevents its effective use with tinder.

No matter how wet its surface, the corky outer bark of black poplar can be shaved to expose a dry interior. Fine shavings of the dry bark ignite easily.

Conifer resin is the most important fire-lighting material to use with matches in the Northern Forests. Lumps of pure resin or resin-saturated bark or wood will assist a match in lighting a fire even in the worst of conditions. Like wax without a wick, the resin must be very hot to burn by itself. The wood at the base of the dead lower branches of pines is usually saturated with resin. These branches can be broken off and splintered and used like resin saturated bark.

In pine country, where fine twigs are uncommon, dead pine needles are a passable substitute for birch bark. The needles are waterproof so long as they remain strongly attached to a branch. The needles should be mostly red in color, but some green is allowable. Remove the moisture by slapping the branch against a tree then test on your wrist to see if any remains. (If the needles drop off they must be handled with care and used with moisture remaining on them.)

Tie a large handful of pine branches into a loose bundle. Binding prevents the bundle from springing apart when laid down. The needles will burn poorly if they are too loose or too densely packed together. This important fire-lighting technique should be practiced when an adequate supply of matches is available and should not be attempted for the first time in an emergency.

To ensure a good start to your fire use enough kindling (a good handful) to produce the intensities of heat required to ignite finger-thick wood, which in turn ignites whatever fuel is available. If the kindling is compressed it acts like a solid mass. This prevents any convection heat from working through and, as a result, your fire may die from insufficient heat build-up. As a rule, twigs of match-thickness need a spacing two to five times their thickness.

Fire-Lighting with Twigs

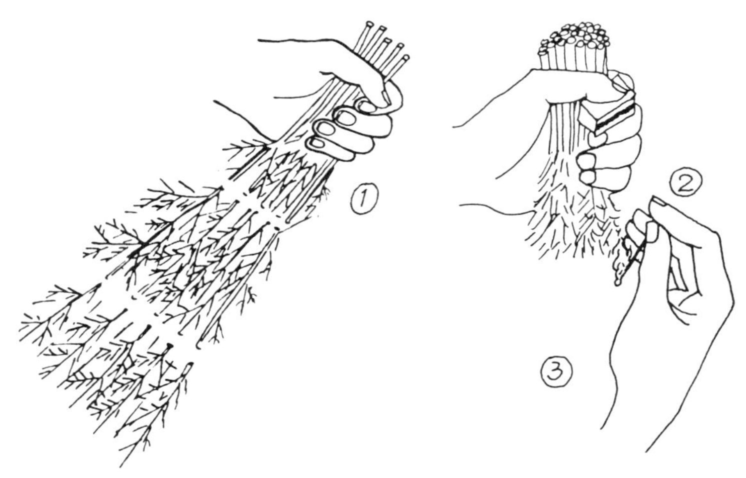

The common method of fire-lighting with twigs.
1. A small handful of dry spruce branches elbow to finger tip long is broken into thirds with the finest twig ends on the bottom.
2. Hold the end of the match between thumb and forefinger, supporting the head with the middle or ring finger to prevent the match stick from breaking.
3. Strike the match and as it flares, move it to the point of ignition, providing additional protection to the flame with the cupped hand. Ignite the finest twigs, which in turn should ignite the larger ones.

Dead twigs on spruce, aspen or willow are easily found. Any fine twigs can be used if they are dry and as thin as a match at their tips. The amount of twigs called for varies according to the needs of the moment. It may be a small handful, used nine-tenths of the time for most fire-lighting purposes; a large handful for an emergency; and a hug of an armful for an intense, hot fire needed to produce a fast signal, or to warm a group of winter hikers or a cold, wet canoeist.

The Common Twig Fire. Gather about five dry spruce branches that are shorter than arm's length and longer than elbow to finger tip. Break the twigs into thirds in an orderly fashion so you can ignite the finest tips first. See how much you can get away with yet still succeed in lighting your fire, assuming you have an adequate supply of matches. Although the common twig fire is adequate for everyday use, it is not foolproof in severe conditions or when you cannot afford to waste any matches.

Emergency Twig Bundle. The most critical factor in this method of fire-lighting is to transfer a match flame as quickly as possible to some combustible material that will help the flame do its work.

The materials for the emergency twig bundle are the same as for the common twig fire. The amount gathered should produce a moderately compressed bundle larger than the circle formed by the thumbs and middle fingers of both hands touching, or over 15 centimetres in diameter. The larger the bundle the more protection afforded the match flame in windy conditions. Avoid old man's beard in wet weather as it is damp and tends to suffocate the match flame rather than enhance it.

Gather the twigs with the butt ends all to one end and flush with each other. The thin ends, which are of various lengths, are folded into the bundle then tied to prevent them from springing apart. The bundle may be tied with cord, grass, roots or two interlocking forks of any pliant shrub.

When lighting a bundle, it is easiest to manipulate it at eye-level. Look for a spot in the thin twig end where the twigs are not too densely packed together or too widely spaced apart. The twigs should be about two or three of their own diameters away from each other. Before the match is lit, a cavity is made where it is to be inserted. In this way you know exactly where to put the match as it flares. The exposed ends ignite more readily if some of the twigs in the cavity are broken.

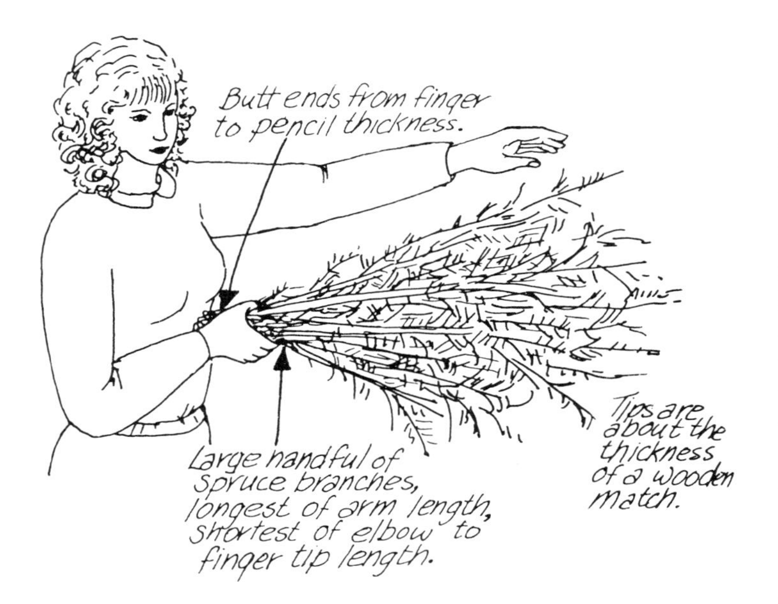

Emergency twig bundle. *The branches used should be shorter than arm length and longer than elbow to finger tip. Note the arrangement of the butts of the twigs. The fine twig ends are folded into the bundle.*

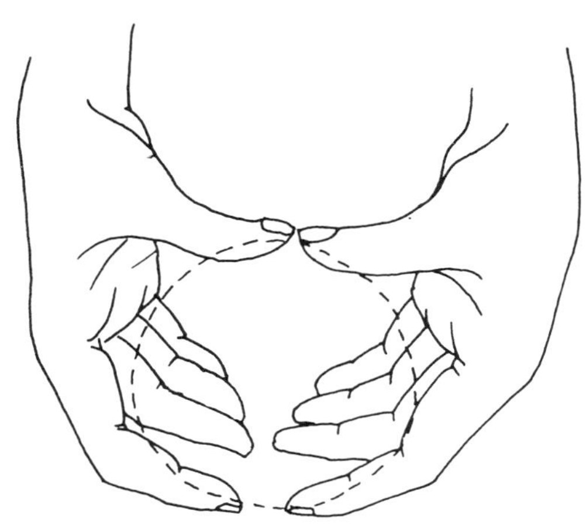

The minimum diameter of a twig bundle. *When squeezing the bundle, you should not be able to touch the tips to the fingers. The bundle should be larger than this and as large as a hug if necessary.*

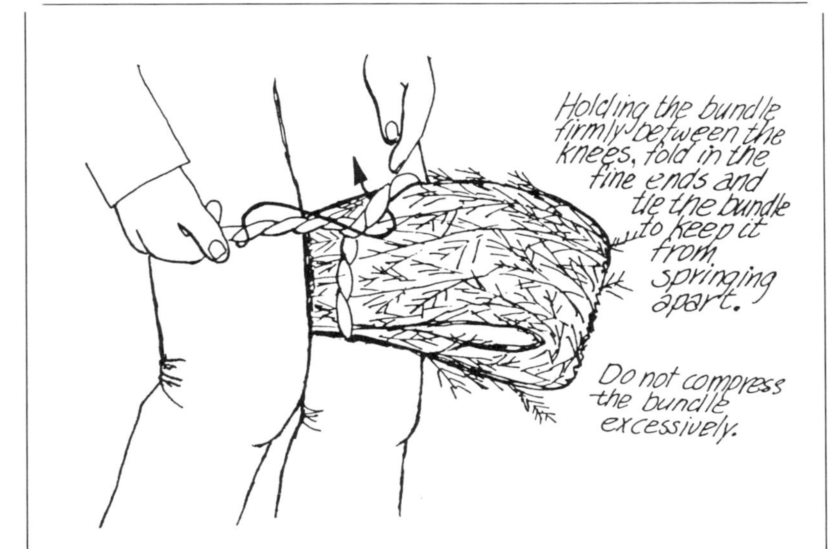

Binding the twig bundle.

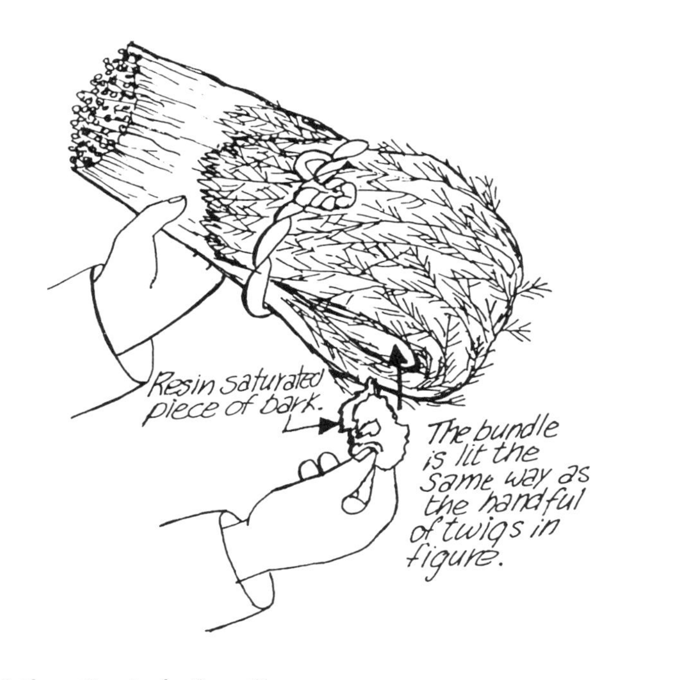

Lighting the twig bundle.

In a strong wind you can make a windproof shelter with your coat in which to ignite the twigs or you may simply turn your back to the wind and hold the bundle in the protection of your coat. Under gusty and variable wind conditions, you may have to turn your body to continue to provide protection. You have about a minute to lay down the burning bundle. This allows you to light it in a protected area some distance from the fire site.

As it burns turn the bundle so the flame engulfs other twigs, and preheats its own fuel. In half a minute, the flame should be well enough established that any wind will intensify it. If there is no wind, and the bundle is damp (as indicated by a dense, white smoke), wave it gently back and forth to keep it burning.

The burning twigs are laid down so that the wind blows the flame into the core of the bundle. Ten finger-thick sticks are added, then two wrist-thick sticks and finally anything less than the thickness of one's leg until the fire is going well. Only then should poor fuel be used.

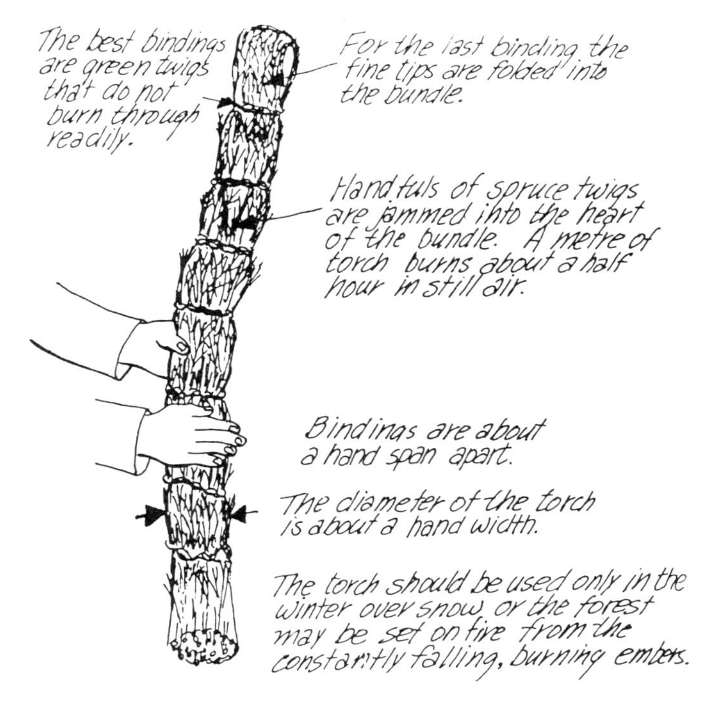

The twig torch.

Using the Bundle in Wet Conditions. Gather twigs that are as dry as possible. Flick violently to remove excess moisture. The bundle may be protected under your coat from further wetting. Search on the lee-side of large tree trunks, such as spruce, for at least a small handful of dry material that can be forced into the thin twig end. This is an appropriate occasion to use conifer resin, or resin-saturated wood from injured conifers or the resin found at the bases of dead pine branches. The resin ignites even if its surface is wet.

The Large Twig Bundle. The large twig bundle is about the size of a hug. Gather the twigs in the same way as for the emergency bundle, but the fine ends are folded in toward the core in small handfuls after the bundle is tied.

The large bundle provides a fast, hot, warming fire for a group. It is totally consumed in a short time, since the largest branches are a finger-thickness or less in diameter.

Feather Stick Fire-Lighting

Kindling from shavings can be made with a sharp knife from any dry, straight-grained, knot-free wood. When naturally-found kindlings are scarce, an axe is advantageous to fall, section and split the shaving wood. Shavings can be made directly on a dry, knot-free standing or fallen tree.

The ideal tree for feathering is dead and well-cured (marked by a deep check and patches of missing bark). The tree should be absolutely vertical to ensure dryness. If the tree can be encircled with the thumbs and middle fingers of both hands then it is too small to stay dry in a prolonged rain.

Split a knot-free section of wood into thumb-thick pieces. If it is raining, the splitting and feathering should be carried out in a stooped position with your back protecting the kindling until it is lit.

The ideal feather stick should be about elbow to finger tip long and as thick as the thumb. The best shavings usually come from the edge of the annual rings on pine and spruce and on the tangent on aspen and willow. The best curls are made with the curved portion of a sharp knife blade. For better control, rest the end of the stick on something solid. Hold the cutting arm straight and make the cut by moving the body instead of bending the elbow. At the end of the cut, the knife blade is used to bend the shavings outwards to

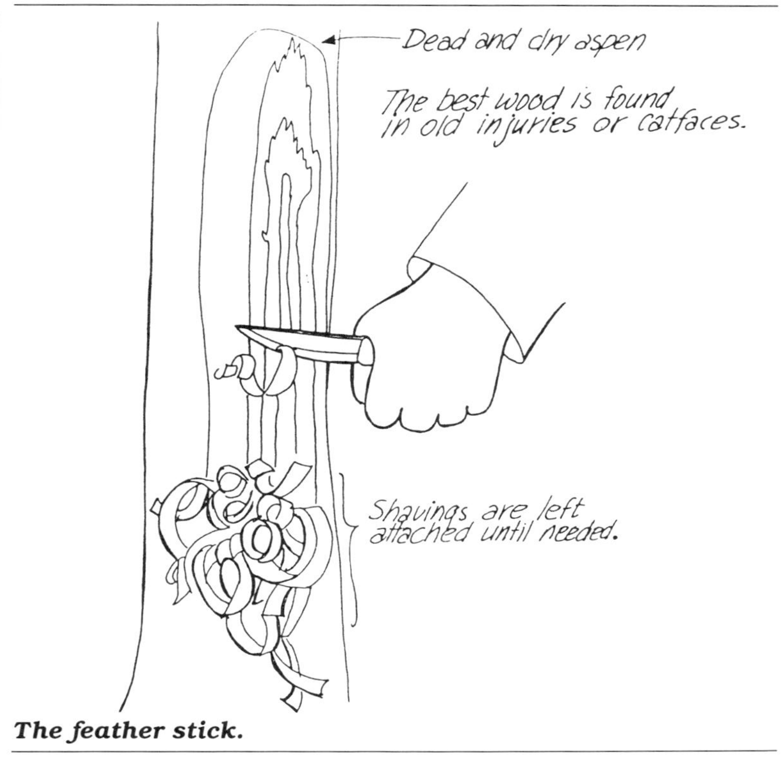

The feather stick.

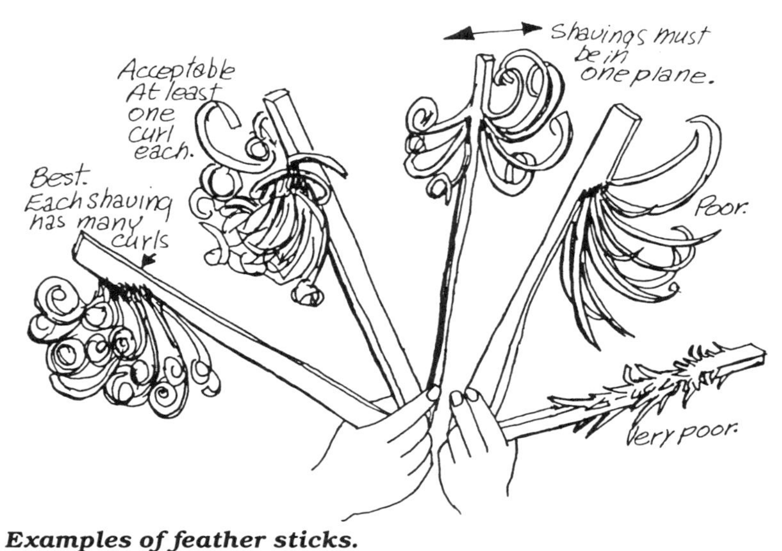

Examples of feather sticks.

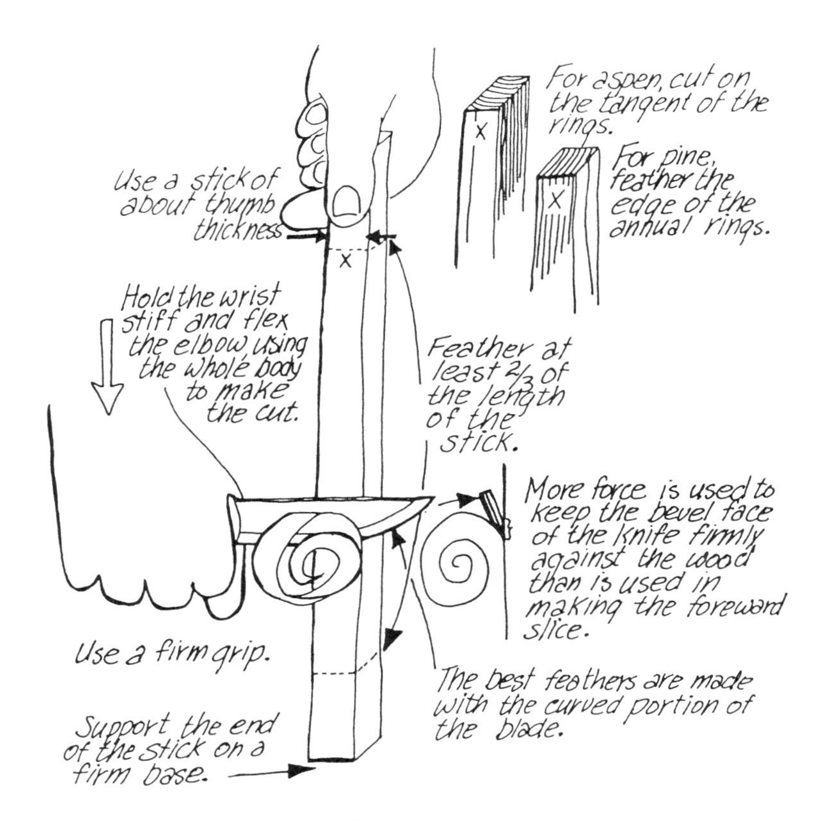

How to make a feather stick.

spread them a little. The shavings should use up two-thirds to three-quarters of the length of the stick. Each shaving should have one or more complete curls as these ignite instantly and resist breaking off when handled. Ideally, the unfeathered portion should burn through before the flame goes out. Trial and error determines what will work the best in each case.

To ensure your fire has a good start, use at least six feather sticks, with two being well made. A teepee arrangement is not as stable as leaning the sticks against a log. Place ten or more finger-thick sticks over the feathers, then two wrist-thick sticks followed by two leg-thick sticks, at which point the fire should be burning well enough to be rearranged into a more parallel configuration.

APPLICATIONS

The Parallel Firelay. The most useful fire for cooking and warming under moderately cold conditions. The fuel is arranged in a parallel fashion and in line with the wind. The standard fire uses fuel of arm span length. The smaller the fire required, the shorter the fuel. When logs can be cut into short lengths, this is the preferred open fire for use inside an enclosed shelter.

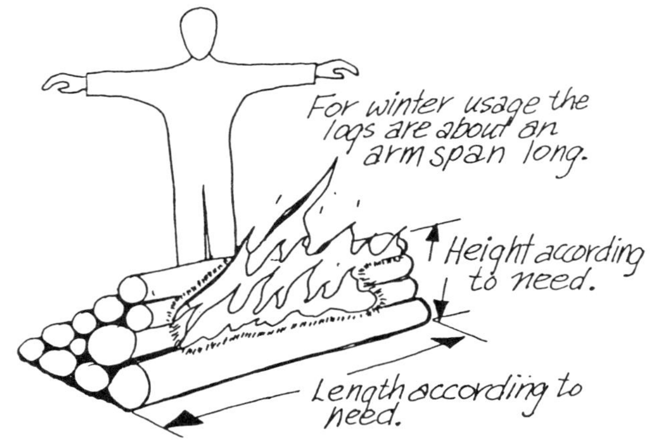

The parallel firelay.

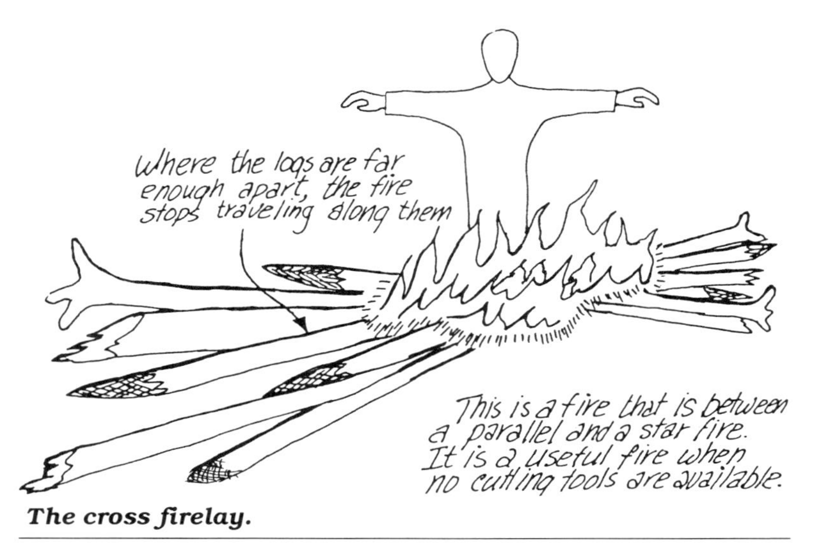

The cross firelay.

When you need cooking coals, wrist-thick willow is piled up to knee height, and allowed to burn down. Small fuel may be added at a constant rate to provide a continuous supply of coals, which are raked over to the upwind end of the fire. Compared to other fire types, the parallel fire uses poor fuel the most efficiently and requires the least adjustment for long burning.

The Cross Firelay. A modification of the parallel firelay useful when there is no axe or saw to cut the logs into arm span lengths for the parallel fire. If the logs are parallel and close enough to each other, a fire at any point in their length can spread to both ends. If the logs are placed at a slight angle to each other, the spread of the fire is confined to the area where the spacing is less than ten centimetres. A useful spread of flame may be achieved in this way, not as wide as the parallel fire, but with a higher sheet of flame.

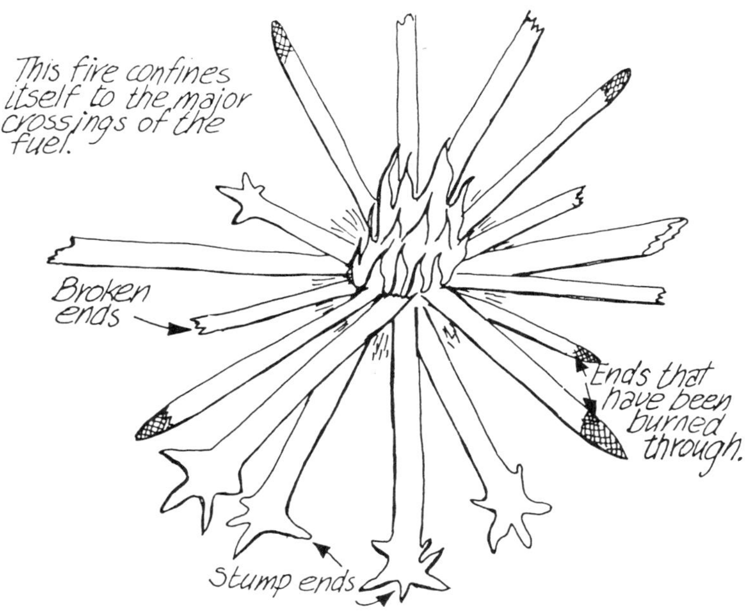

The star firelay.

The Star Firelay. Here, the fuel is crossed like the rays of a star. The fire is confined to a relatively small area where the jumble of sticks cross. As the sticks burn through, cross them again or push the ends into the fire. The tendency of the fire to travel out of the fireplace along logs lying on dry duff is a problem in a shelter. To prevent this, prop up the far ends of the logs.

The star fire is a poor choice for a cold weather use in front of an open shelter. However, it is appropriate for hot weather cooking, for burning long logs into more manageable pieces and as the warming and cooking fire inside a teepee where long logs are used. This type of fire requires good fuel and frequent adjustment to burn at its best.

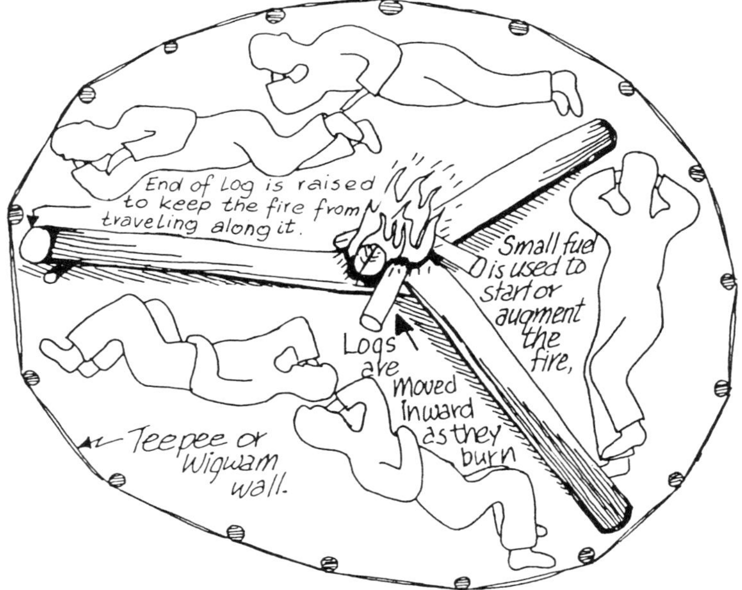

The use of the star fire in an enclosed open-fire shelter.

The Wall-Backed Firelay. A wall is incorporated into one side of a parallel fire. The heat radiating from the far side is mostly re-emitted and partially reflected to provide a greater effect on the near side (for the same amount of fuel). A waist-high wall creates a broad sheet of flame and radiance. Additionally, the wall creates a drawing action so that smoke is better carried overhead. The wall may be made of many materials, the most convenient being green or dry logs. In cold conditions, the burning wall should contribute to both the intensity and endurance of the fire.

For one night, a wall of one log thickness may be made from logs an arm span long. For greater stability in stacking, hew the logs flat both on top and bottom before sectioning. A wall of large logs will stand by itself, but small logs require a brace or two. With a brace log the wall may be leaned slightly forward over the fire so that it will collapse onto it, thereby eliminating a few stoking sessions during the night. In cool weather the wall may be made of green logs, the longest lasting being green black poplar.

Another method for making the wall-backed fire is to stack the logs so that the side next to the fire is as vertical as possible. Depending on the needs of the moment, the logs may

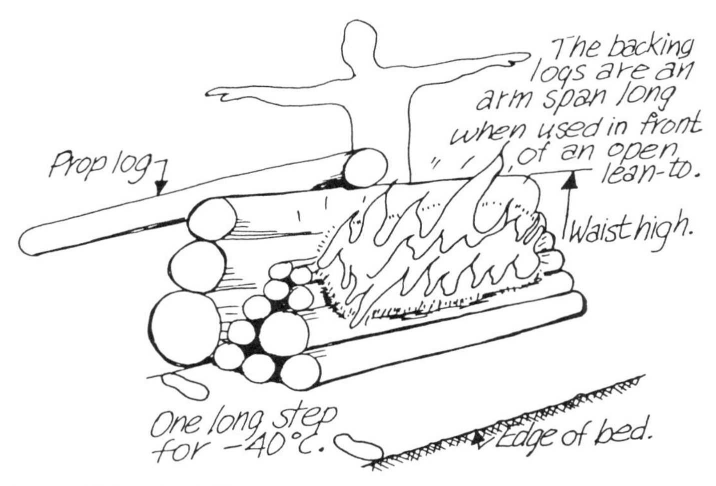

The wall-backed fire.

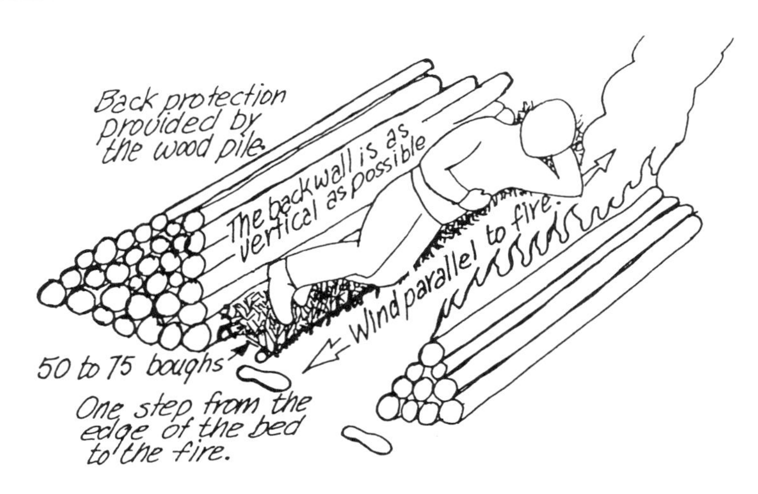

Sleeping between the wood pile and the fire.

be green, dry or a mixture of both. The straighter the logs and the more snugly they are stacked, the more slowly the fire will progress through the wall. This reduces the adjustments required as the fire burns. The colder the weather, the higher the wall up to waist-height. For example, at -60°C it should be waist-high and made only of dry wood. Its burning face should be close to vertical and the fire built against it. The log wall must be parallel to any steady wind, but may vary 15 degrees before problems with smoke and sparks become excessive.

MAINTENANCE AND MODERATION

Fires thrive on attention. Frequent adjustment will keep a fire burning at its best. The adjustment consists of moving together pieces of wood that are too far apart or spreading those that are too close together. A fire tolerates a void under it, but not within it, so these should be collapsed or filled with fuel. Fuel should be put on in time to be adequately dried and preheated. In a heavy rain the amount of fuel piled over a fire may have to be quite large for it to burn properly.

The cure for a smoky fire is often a matter of proper adjustment. If that does not help, excessive smoke is likely due to some inadequacy in the fuel. It may be too green or wet with so much heat being used in drying there is little left over for burning. Putting on dry, finer fuel will burn up more products of inadequate combustion and the improved thermal column will carry the troublesome smoke up and over your head more effectively.

If poor fuel is all you have, start with a hot fire and keep it hot by adding fuel sooner and in larger quantities. With this method even sodden driftwood can be made to burn to a strong intensity.

Once a fire is well-started, most fuels, be they damp, inferior, or green, will burn well if at least three logs of less than ten centimetres thickness are stacked on at a spacing of about one or two centimetres. As long as they are kept close enough together, an inter-reflective action and heat concentration is maintained between them. Green aspen and birch will burn if first split and used on a hot fire, with frequent adjustments for proper spacing. It should be expected that such a fire will be smokier.

Depending on the diameter and quality of the fuel used, a fire may require adjustment from once every three hours to three times an hour. If all you have is wrist-thick wood you may have to adjust the fire every 20 minutes. Over three or four nights you will likely become so accustomed to the routine to hardly remember any stoking, but by morning the fuel pile will be gone. You may stoke your fire from your bed, getting up on occasion to make a major adjustment, or to place large logs on the fire. Small fuel is stacked where it can be reached from your bed, but large logs should be piled in line with your fire and just far enough away so they do not accidentally catch fire.

Amounts of Fuel Required. For an overnight stay at -40°C in an open lean-to, sleeping in your clothes, a spruce 30 centimetres in diameter sectioned into arm span lengths may suffice. If you must gather your fuel without an axe or saw you may need many fires to section your fuel into manageable pieces. Each night you may need a pile as long and wide as you are tall and as high as half your height. Without an axe you may have to move camp as fuel runs out. In a teepee with an open fire, you might only use a third or a quarter of what you would use in an open lean-to. Whereas in an enclosed shelter with a stove, the equivalent of a single day's fuel for an open lean-to would last ten days.

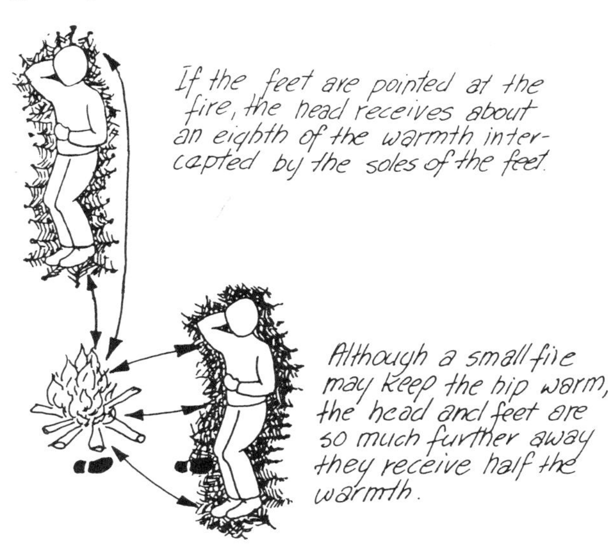

If the feet are pointed at the fire, the head receives about an eighth of the warmth intercepted by the soles of the feet.
Although a small fire may keep the hip warm, the head and feet are so much further away they receive half the warmth.

Inadequacies of a small fire in cold weather.

Determining the Distance to Stay Away From an Open Fire. The most effective and efficient open fire to sleep in front of should be as long as you are tall and big enough to force you to stay a good step away from it. The heat of a large fire forces you to stay beyond the range of normal spark throw. There is less smoke wafting into the face and poor fuel burns more effectively. A fire that is too small may cause you to unconsciously roll towards it while you sleep as you seek more warmth. The result may be damage to your clothing or a burn injury.

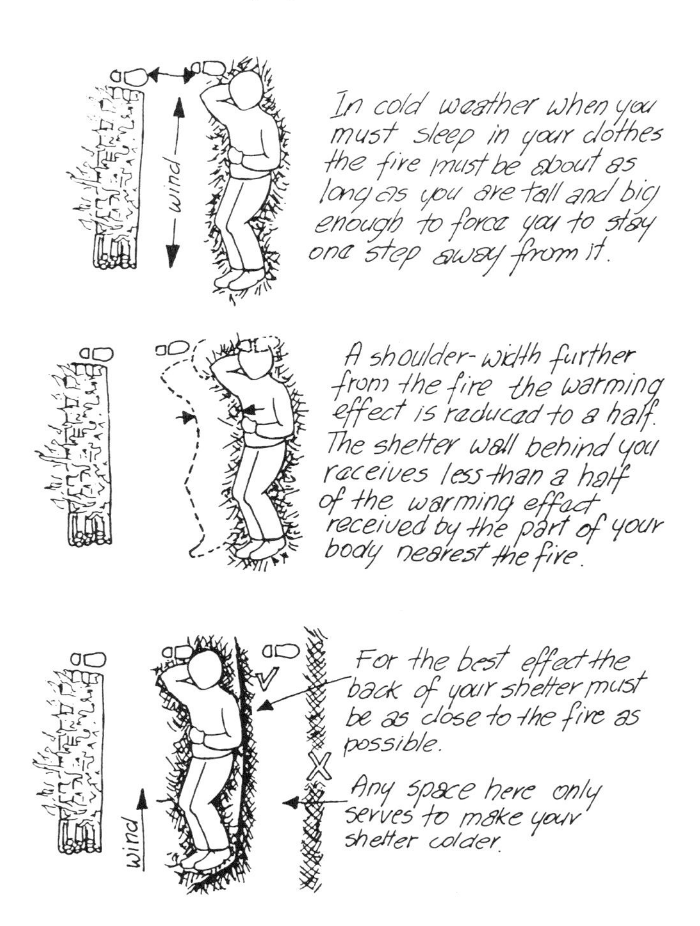

The distance you are from a warming fire is critical to your comfort.

Gathering fuel without tools. Most standing dead wood that can be encircled with the fingers of both hands (about ten centimetres) can be pushed down and broken into manageable pieces. Firewood is also easily gathered from log jams, dense stands of pine, aspen and willow or where beaver have been active. If fallen trees are too heavy to be moved, they may be burned through into manageable pieces. Look for trees that have fallen across each other, or cross them by pushing down standing trees or dragging up fallen ones. Use a star fire to burn them through. Under milder conditions, a cross firelay in front of your shelter can process the wood needed for the night.

CHOOSING A SAFE FIRE SITE

The experienced person develops a *feel* for fire conditions. He or she can sense when extraordinary caution is needed on where to light a fire, how big it should be, how much vigilance has to be maintained over it, and how painstaking the attention in putting it out. A high fire hazard demands care when selecting a safe fire site, as a campfire can spread in moments to become a raging wildfire. Under such conditions a fire should be built on sand or gravel bars, or close enough to a water source to be able to throw water directly on the fire without having to take a step. This also makes it easy to keep the area around the fire soaked down.

The organic layer of soil or **duff** may have to be cleared back for a metre around the fire. Try to find a duff-free area as this saves work and is less disturbing to the environment. If the duff is less than ten centimetres thick, the site quickly reverts to a natural appearance. In this respect, grassy (but not dry) areas and stands of pine or aspen make good sites for open fires.

Thick layers of duff may smolder without being detected. A rodent hole or a root may carry a smoldering fire far enough away so that it is missed when the campfire is put out. Damp or deep duff will smolder, drying a centimetre or so ahead of itself. Such fires can burn unnoticed for years before surfacing to start a forest fire.

Overnight fires on deep moss tend to burn cavities that may take years to regenerate. Such fires require considerable effort to extinguish with certainty. In the winter,

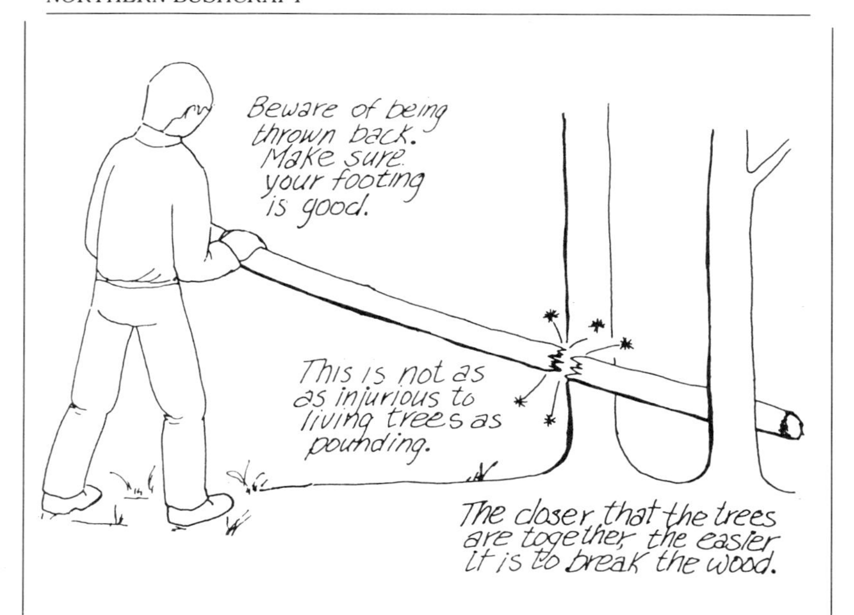

Breaking wood by using leverage and the weight of the body.

Breaking wood by pounding.

when fire caution is relaxed, a ground fire can start that may smolder until the snow is gone and then surface during a dry, windy spell. Heavy rain will not put out a deep ground fire (which may betray its presence by a haze visible only in the early morning after a still night).

Stone Rimmed Fire Places. A common, though unnecessary practice, is to ring open fires with stones. This practice is based on the claim that the stones confine a fire and make it safer, yet many forest fires are in fact traced to such fireplaces. There are, however, justifiable uses of stones in a fire: to store warmth in a closed shelter; to support pots when no other means are available; and, to produce steam for a steam bath or a steam cooking pit. Rocks used without good reason are needlessly defaced and, unless they are scattered after use, leave a permanent marker of the campfire. A stone fireplace also requires more effort to cool, and the stones that are not moved aside can harbour hot spots that may start a forest fire.

Extinguishing Campfires

There are few thoughts that weigh heavier on the mind than the nagging feeling that your fire is not extinguished. The following steps should be followed when putting out a fire.

1. Stop fueling a fire early enough to allow residual fuel to burn up. Use smaller, fast-burning fuel in the last hour before breaking camp.
2. Restack unburned pieces so that mostly ash is left when it is time to put the fire out.
3. Soaking down a fireplace should not be left to the last moment before breaking camp. A light soaking an hour in advance will require a fraction of the water and, you will have a greater assurance that the fire is out if it feels cold when you leave it.
4. Stand a full pot of water in the middle of the fireplace to better use the overflow. Scoop in the ashes and coals until the pot is full. Let everything soak for a moment then transfer the ashes to a heap at one end of the fire base, saving as much water as possible for reuse. Under low fire hazard conditions, the well-soaked ashes may be dispersed about the environment.
5. In following Step 4, half of the fire base should be scraped clean of ashes. The base is now thoroughly soaked

and poked full of holes which allow the water to penetrate better. Keep adding water until the steam stops and you can comfortably poke your fingers into the soil. Shift the ashes over the cooled half and repeat the procedure for the second half.

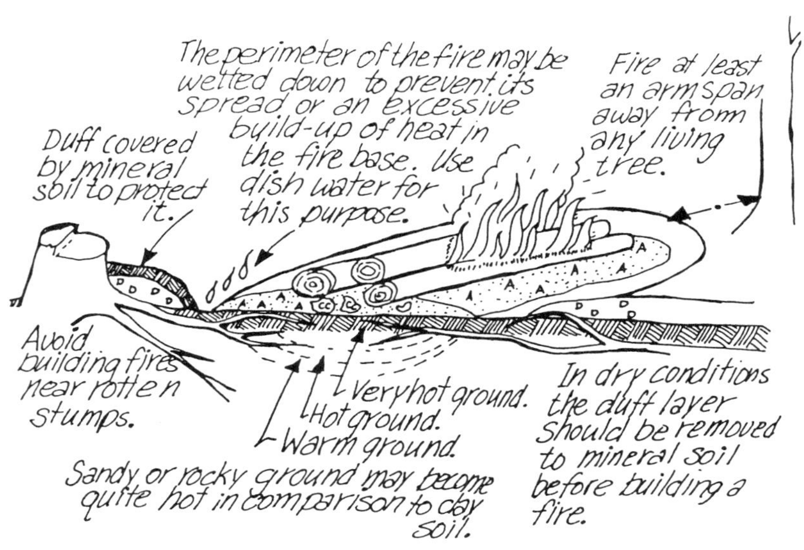

The anatomy of a campfire.

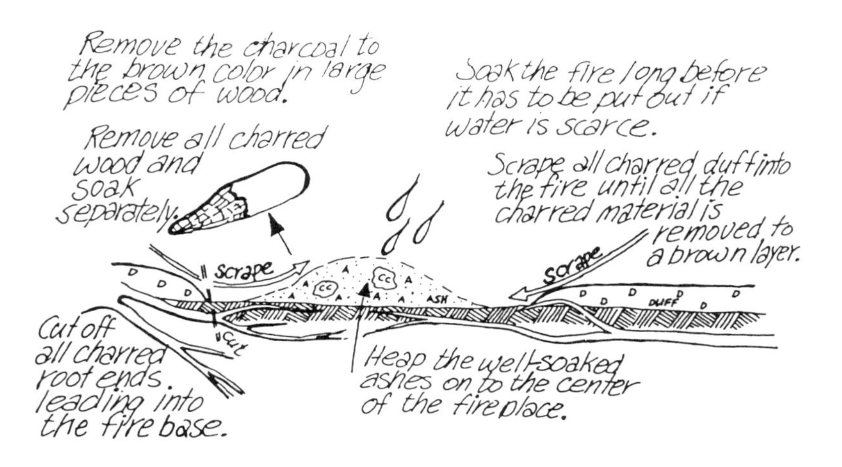

The preliminary steps in putting out a campfire.

6. Heap the well-soaked ashes in the centre of the fire base and poke a deep hole into the mound. Pour water into the hole until it seeps out of the mound.

7. Scrape all charred organic material on the perimeter toward the centre. Cut off all charred root ends entering the fire base.

8. If a shovel is available, drive it into the ground at the border of the fire where the charred duff ceases, and pry it back and forth. Under high fire hazard, this step should be carried out before the fire is made. This cuts any roots leading into the fire base and confines any burning roots to the fireplace. This also allows a better penetration of water into the fire base. Lacking a shovel, use a sharpened pole or stake to punch holes then pour water onto this circle from head-height for better penetration.

9. Pour all dish and wash water around the base of the fire. The soil will stay cooler and the fire will be easier to extinguish. This practice also reduces some of the impact on the soil in the fire base.

10. Extinguishing a fire (without water) built on duff in the summer may take hours and you still cannot be absolutely certain it is out. Fuel should not be added for a few hours prior to extinguishing the fire. Everything combustible should be burned to an ash. Hot spots in the fireplace are scraped out and allowed to cool repeatedly until no more burning is detected. All ash and the remains of the fire are heaped up in the middle of the fireplace and well-covered with mineral soil. Scrape the duff down to the

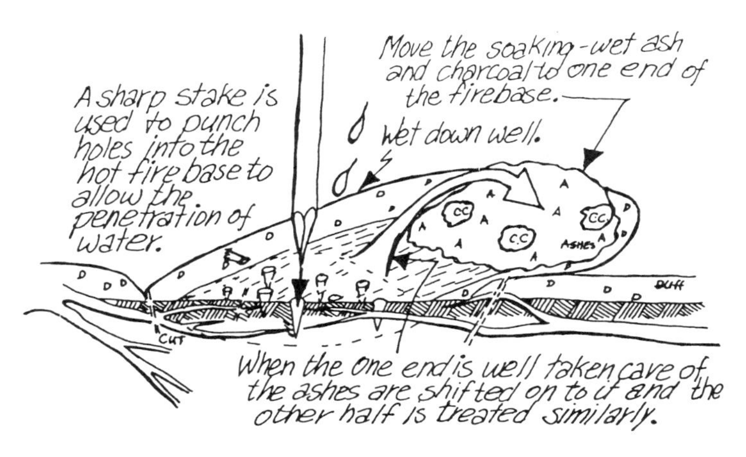

Soaking down the fire base.

mineral soil surrounding the fireplace.

11. A fire built on moss in winter should have any remaining fuel laid out on the snow. All charred materials in the fireplace should be scraped out (with a pot) and spread over the snow.

12. How easily and thoroughly a fire may be extinguished depends primarily on the selection of a proper site. The less organic material in the fire base the better.

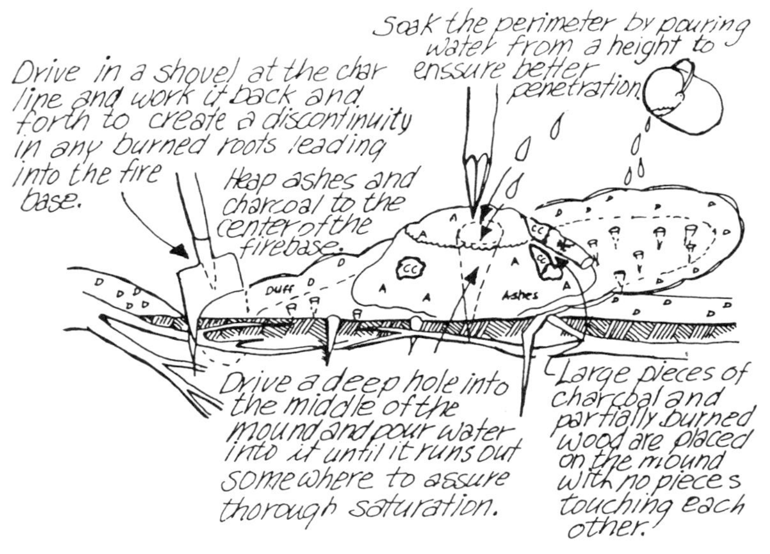

The final steps in putting out a campfire.

METHODS OF SUSPENDING POTS

A fire can be made in minutes, but the means by which a pot may be suspended over it may take much longer to construct. An ideal suspension should be safe to use or else scalds or food loss may result. It should easily raise or lower a pot from simmer to boil to control cooking heat. The mechanism should facilitate shifting of pots over a wide area of the fire. It should allow easy placement or removal of the pots over the fire. The suspension should be readily constructed with materials found at hand.

Quick Rigs

While travelling, when meal time approaches, look for a site with a good source of fuel and the materials with which a quick suspension may be built. Within moments of making the fire, the water to be boiled should be hung from a crude and quickly made suspension with a single height setting that places your pot over the hottest part of the fire. A more versatile rig is constructed by the time the water boils.

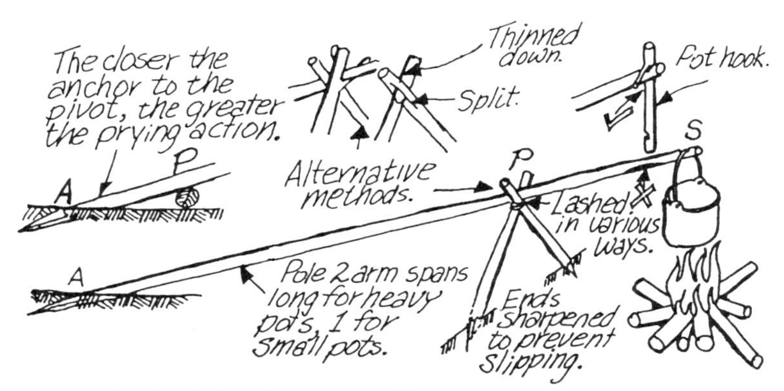

General principles in suspending pots.
The anchor (A) secures the far end of a suspension pole.
The pivot (P) can be adjusted according to the situation.
The suspension (S) is hung.

Most quick rigs consist of three components: the suspension (S); the pivot (P); and, the anchor (A).

The suspension holds the pot or a pot-hook over the fire. This should have a notch to engage the pot handle or pot-hook, which prevents the pot from slipping off the end or down along the pole. On a level pole without a notch, a pot can fall off by simply rotating on its handle. If a suspension pole is too close to the fire it will burn up. A dry pole may burn through in the cooking of one meal. The solution is to place the pole higher and use a pot-hook to lower the pot to the fire. Use the heavy end of the pole at the suspension end as it bends less and takes longer to burn through. Peel the suspension end or charred pieces of bark will continually fall into the pot.

A tripod is useful as a pivot when the ground is either frozen or rocky, or when there is no means to drive posts into the ground. The normal tripod has an inherent tendency for one of the legs to flip up if supporting a heavy load. This is remedied by cutting out the central projection close to the lashing. Tripod lashings must be strong and secure. The legs should be sharpened so they will dig into the ground and not slip outwards. If the far end is firmly anchored, the suspension end of a pole can be raised or lowered to a certain extent by moving the pivot back and forth. The closer the pivot to the anchor, the greater the pull on the anchor. When a fixed anchor is employed, it is the only instance where a bipod can be used. A bipod is stable sideways but not backwards or forwards.

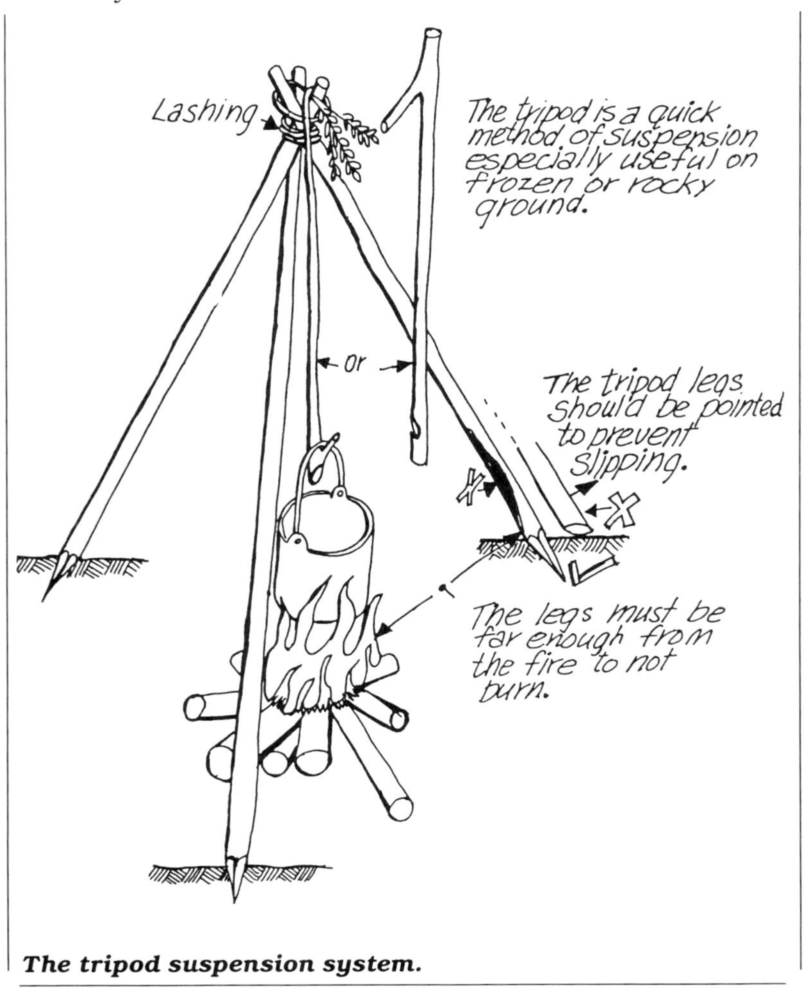

The tripod suspension system.

The anchor that secures the far end of a suspension pole must not release accidently or a scald or loss of food may result.

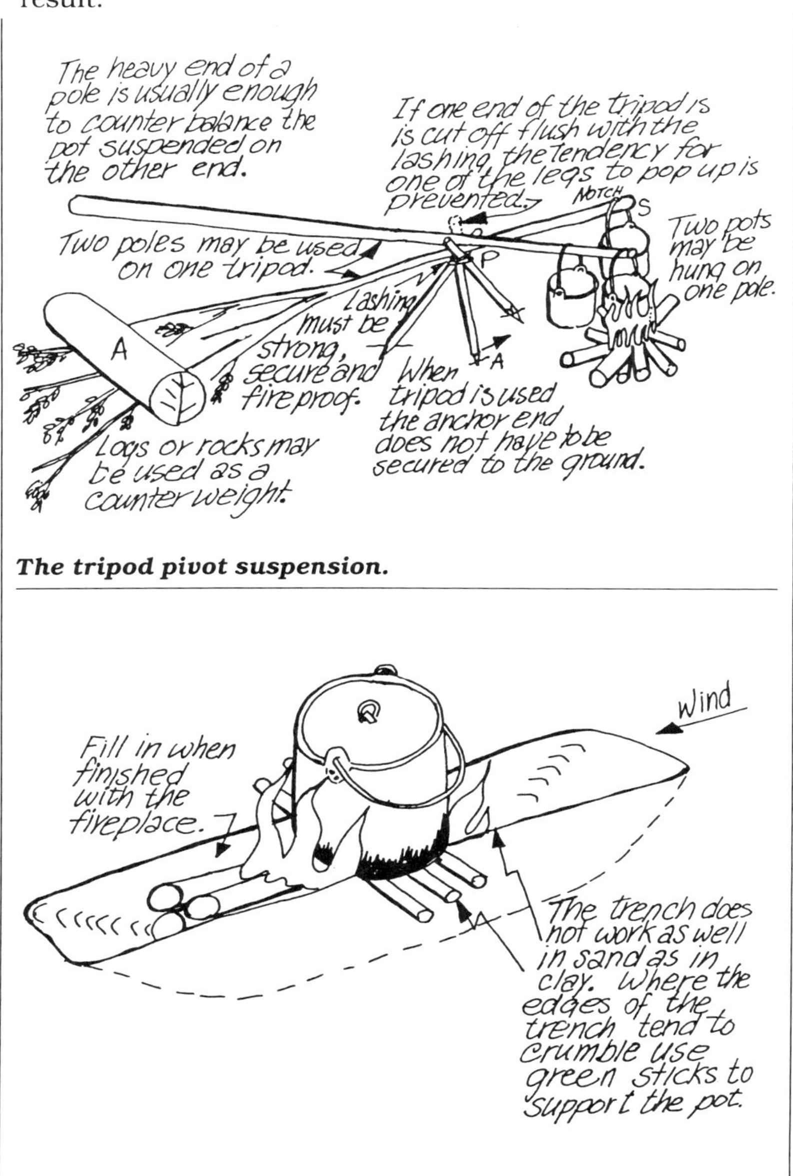

The tripod pivot suspension.

The trench fire.

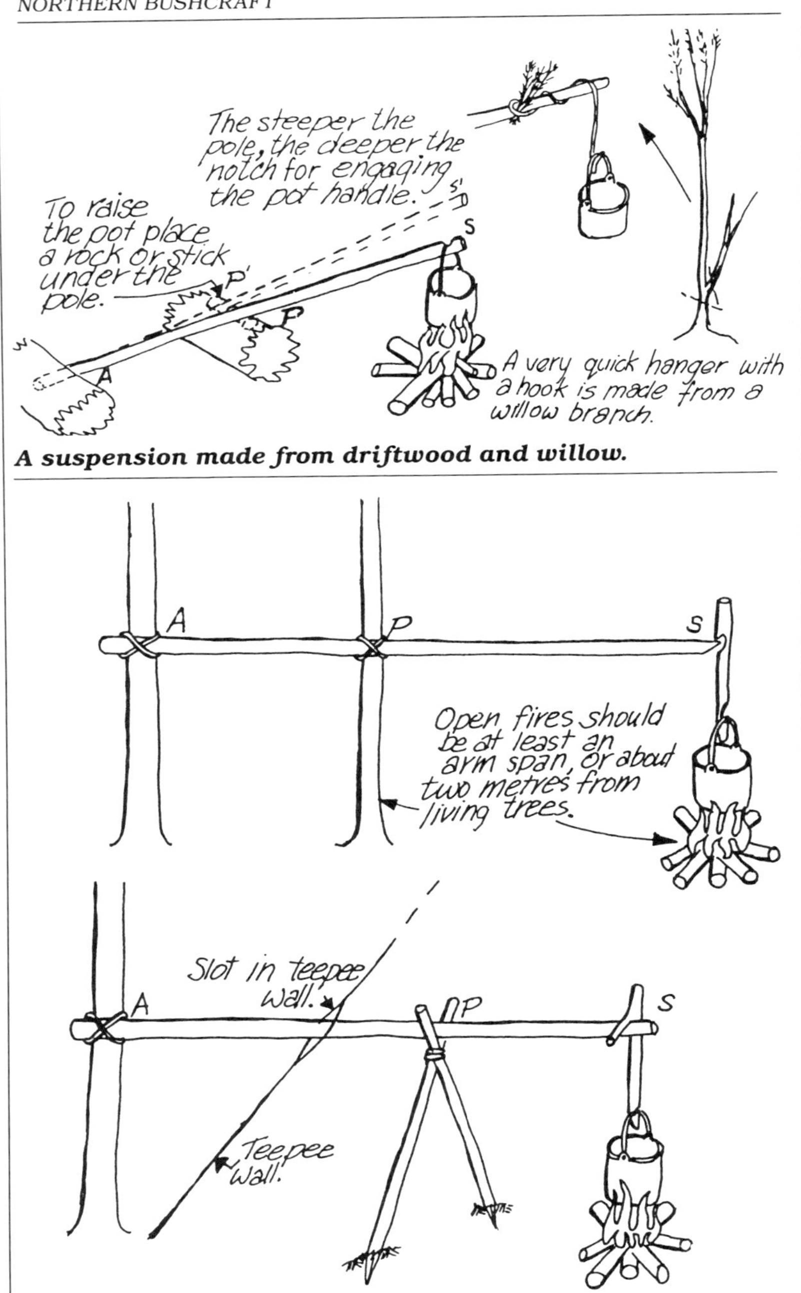

A suspension made from driftwood and willow.

Suspensions using standing trees.

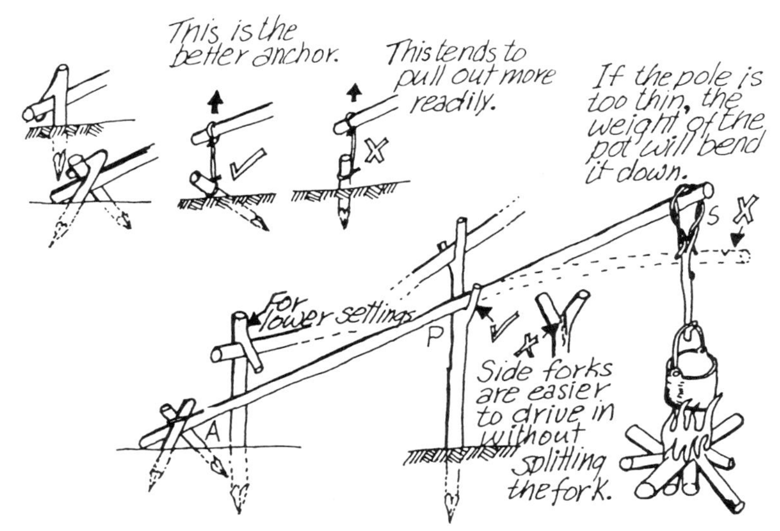

The different anchors that may be employed in suspension systems.

Complex Suspensions

The Australian Cooking Crane. This is one of the few suspensions that fulfills all the requirements needed to hang pots over a fire. This suspension is worth the effort to construct when cooking for large groups staying in one place for a number of meals. It is also useful for suspending a large pot over a small or unstable stove.

1. Prepare from one to four suspension poles about two arm spans long and no less than wrist-thick at the heavy end. Cut a "V" completely around the suspension end as there is no way of predicting which side of the pole will be up.
2. Find the point of balance of one of the suspension poles while holding the suspension end over the centre of your fire. Your pivot bar will be positioned at the point of balance.
3. Erect a pivot bar about as high as the point of your hip. Each suspension pole requires a length of bar equal to the distance from the elbow to the finger tip.
4. The height control cords are now attached. The safest and most effective arrangement is to have the cords coming off both sides of the pole to prevent it from rolling.

The High Bar Suspension. This uses a horizontal bar positioned at head-height. Because the bar is well-above the fire a variety of pot-hooks are employed to lower the pots at the required heights.

A variation of the high bar suspension uses a platform on which to build the cooking fire, thereby saving the cook's back. As well, the smoke will pass over the head more readily.

The Burtonsville Rig. This suspension system is made with straight poles that suspend smaller pots at varying heights.

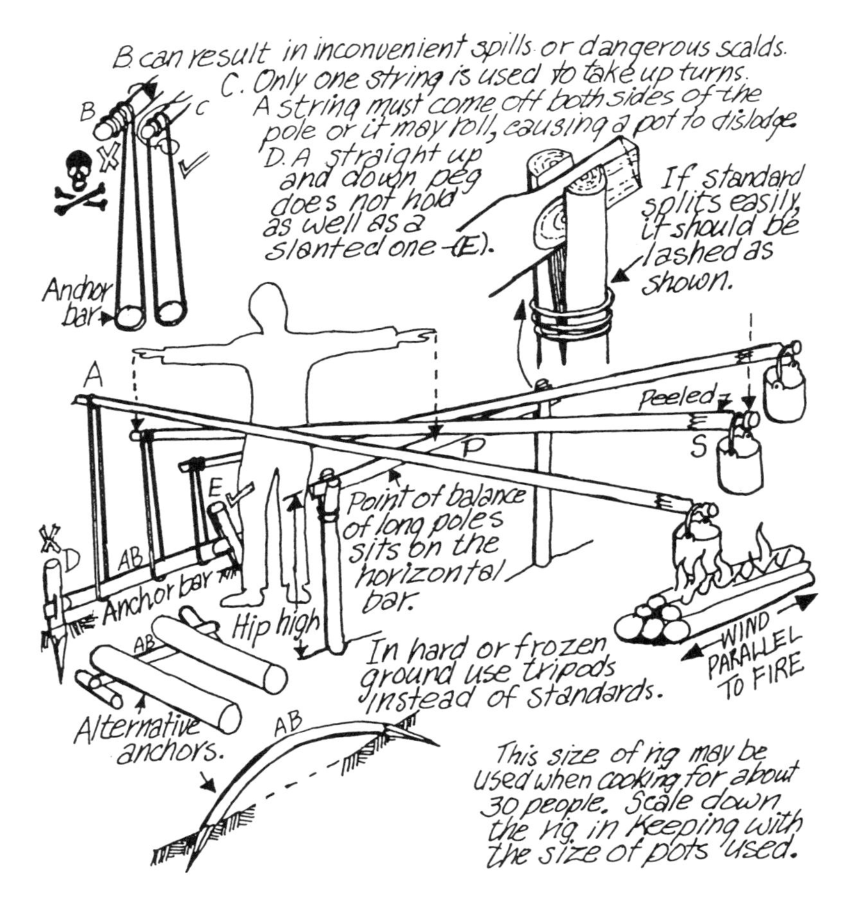

The Australian cooking crane.

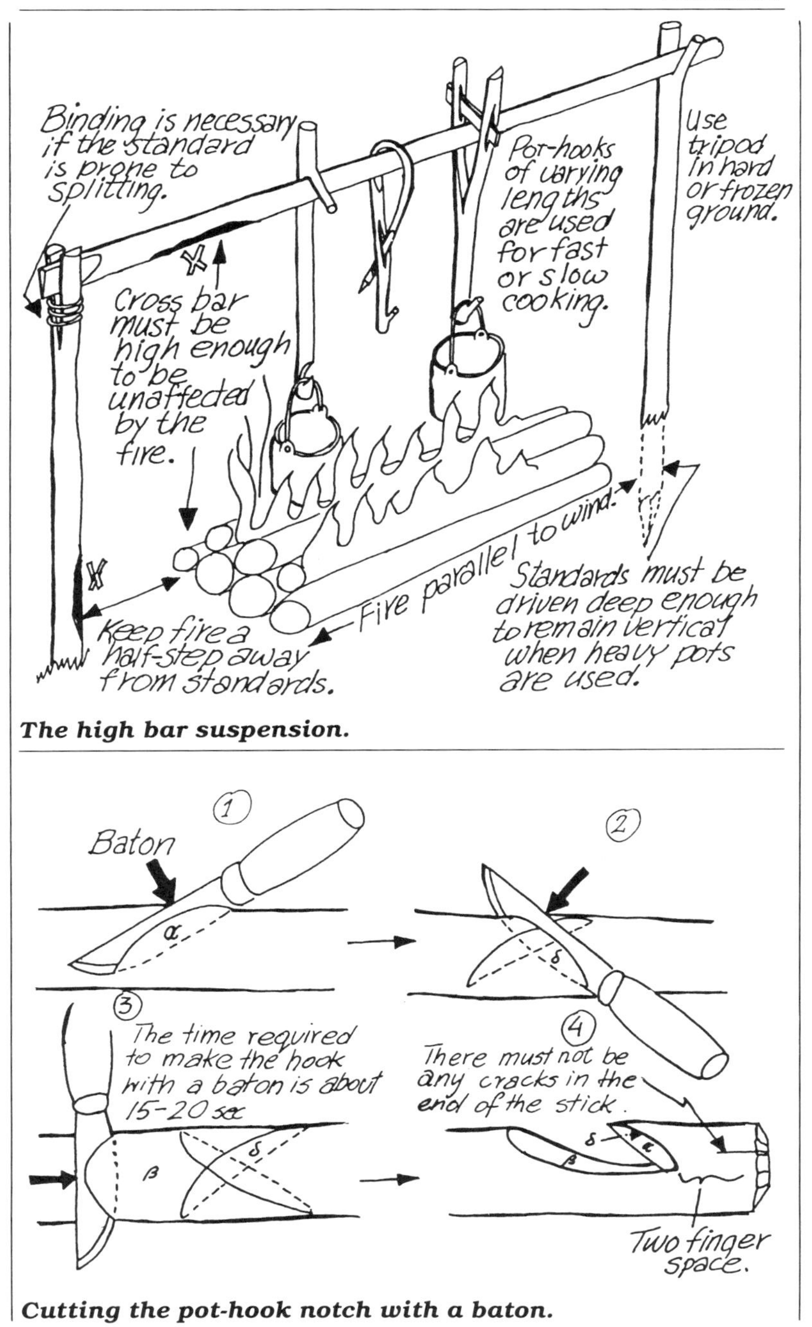

The high bar suspension.

Cutting the pot-hook notch with a baton.

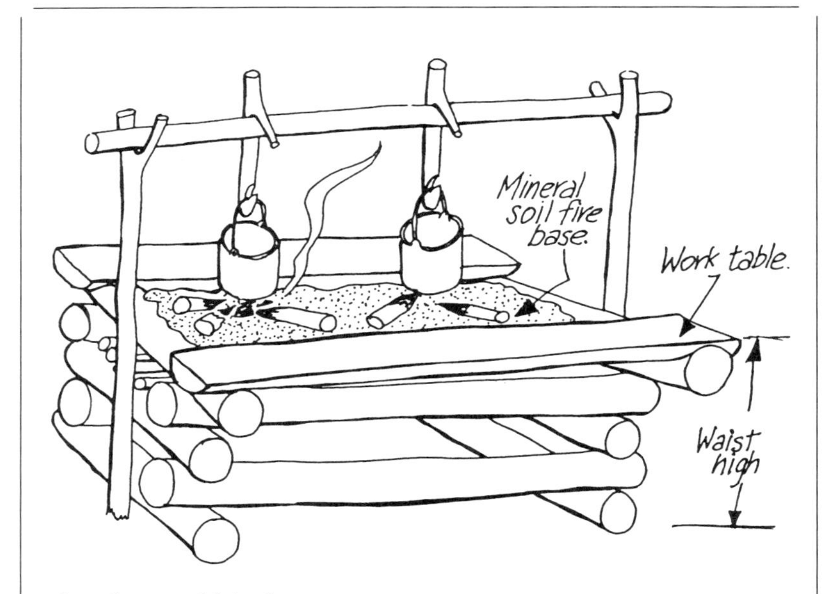

The elevated kitchen.

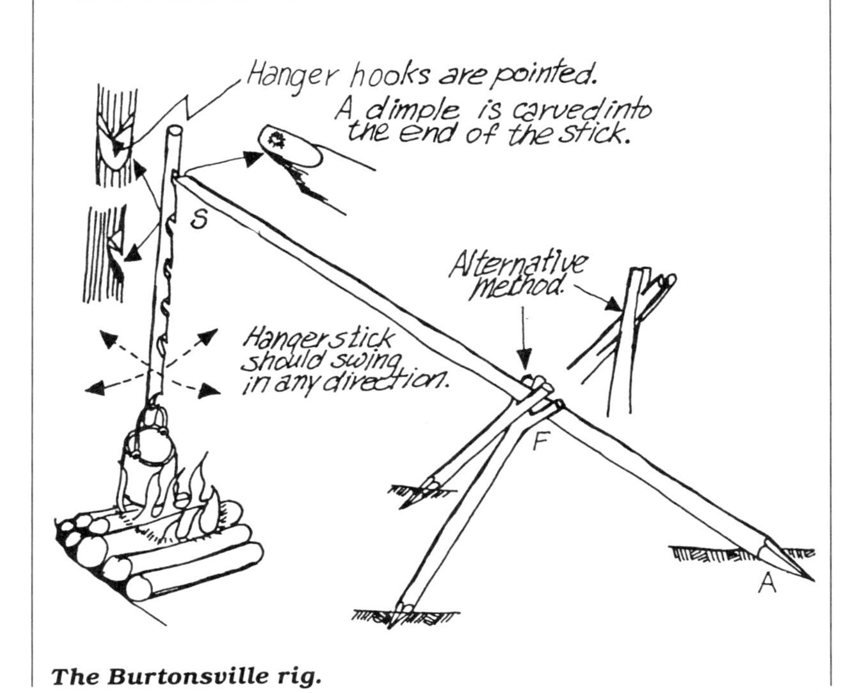

The Burtonsville rig.

OUTDOORS COOKING

Cooking is a compromise between the destruction of nutrients and improved taste and digestibility. Cooking is sometimes necessary to destroy poisonous substances and agents causing disease. Overcooking diminishes vitamins in meat and calories and minerals in vegetables.

Boiling

Boiling is the easiest, most convenient and nutritionally conservative of all the cooking methods. Boiling bursts the fibers and cells of meat and vegetables making them more tender and digestible. Compared to baking, there is less water loss, less fat evaporated, and the cooking water can be used in soups or stews. Boiled food may be less tasty than baked or broiled food, especially without salt or seasoning.

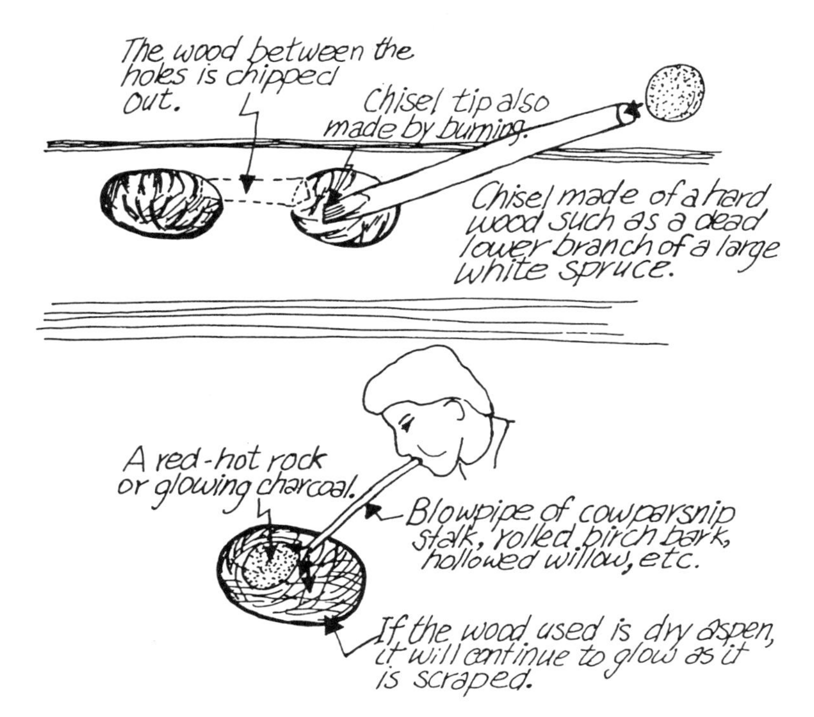

Burning out a cooking container.

For example, a boiled hare may be somewhat bland unless slightly roasted to improve the taste.

Tough meats should be boiled for a short time to extract the flavor and nutrients normally diminished by the necessary long periods of cooking. The stock can be made into soup while the tough meat is cooked until tender in the second water.

Fat meats, especially from aquatic animals such as muskrat, beaver and waterfowl should be boiled only enough to reduce their strong flavor and high fat content as they are likely to be tender. They may be broiled afterwards to enhance their flavor. The valuable fatty stock can be made into soup.

Boiling (100°C) for half an hour should kill all bacteria and parasites, especially in the case of aquatic animals. Carbohydrates of vegetable origin expand through boiling to burst the indigestible cell walls and make the cell contents available. The longer a vegetable is boiled, the more digestible it becomes, but overboiling causes a loss of the desirable

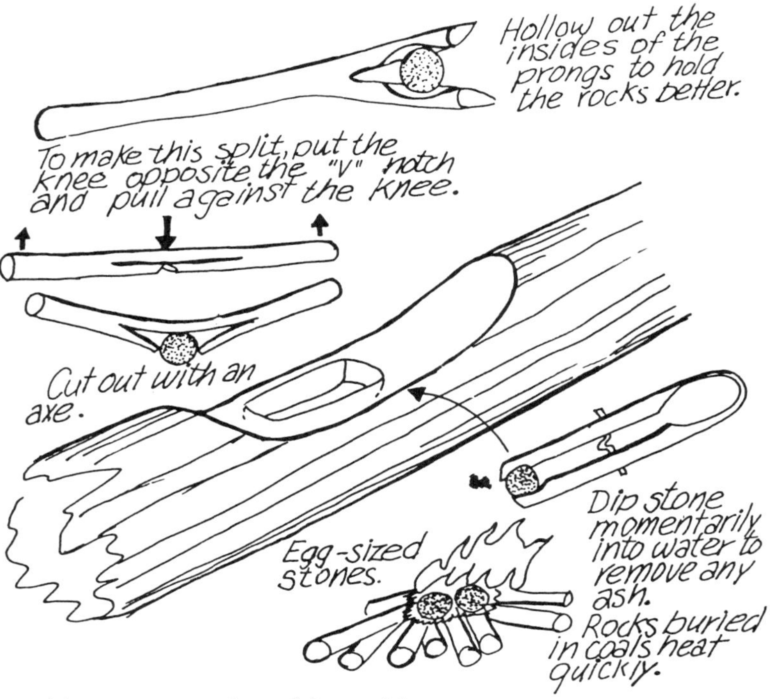

Making tongs and cooking with stones.

constituents in the cooking water. Animal proteins tend to shrink when boiled and become less digestible. If bacteria and parasites were not a problem, meat would be best consumed raw.

The problem with boiling is that a suitable container is needed to hold the water and food while it is being cooked. One method is to use a container of fire-sensitive materials such as wood, bark, conifer roots, hide or the stomachs of large animals. Boiling is brought about by dropping egg-sized, red-hot stones into the cooking water. The boiling utensil used by many Native peoples was a basket woven from spruce roots. Some Native peoples were not particularly impressed with metal pots as they did not fold for transport when camp was moved.

A crude, but functional cooking container can be chopped out of a log in a few minutes. To work the bottom of the container make a chisel out of the base of a dead branch of a large white spruce. When an axe is unavailable, char out a depression in dry aspen wood with hot rocks or charcoal and scrape away the charred material as it glows until the desired depth is obtained. A blowpipe can speed up the process. When a larger container is wanted, burn out two

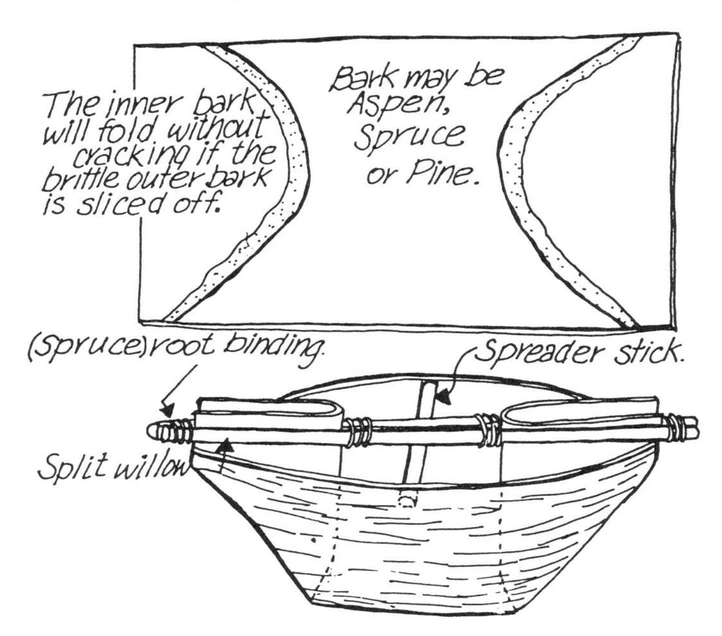

A green bark container for use in cooking with hot rocks.

depressions in line with the grain then chisel out the wood in between with wooden wedges or chisels also made by charring and scraping.

Any bark capable of holding water can be folded to make a crude cooking container. The flexible and foldable birch bark makes the best containers. Stiff barks like those of aspen or black poplar may have to be shaved down at the fold lines to facilitate folding without causing breaks in the bark.

To cook with a green hide, either drape it over four pegs or use it to line a hollow in the ground. The bottom may be protected from the cooking stones with a few flat rocks.

Cooking stone sizes may vary from a hen's egg to that of a baseball. Such stones will heat up quickly and are easy to move with a fork or tongs. Igneous stones are best as they rarely fracture from the heat, unlike sedimentary ones. Stones picked out of the water may explode from internal steam pressure.

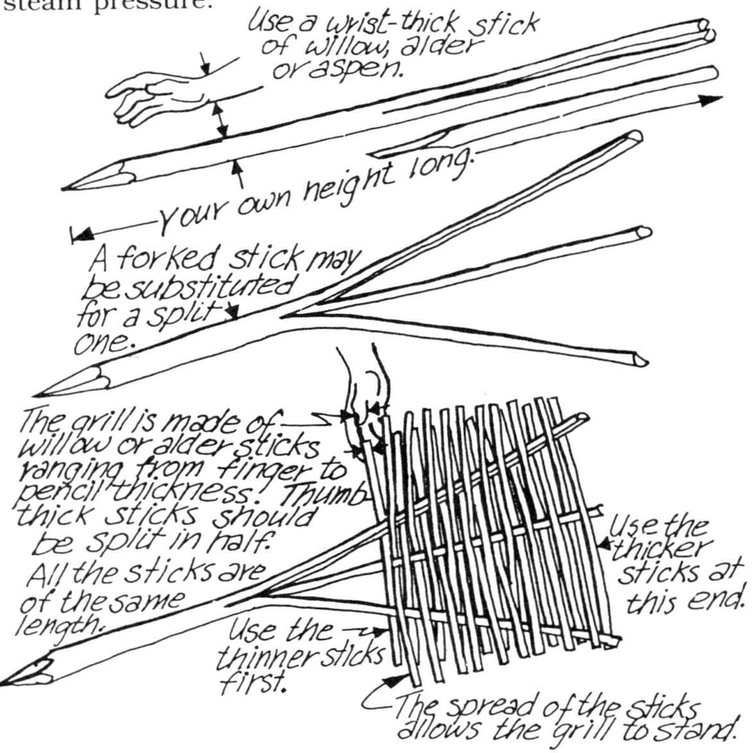

Detail of a grill useful in cooking small game and meat.

Broiling

Broiling or roasting involves exposing food directly to the radiance of a fire or its coals. Broiling is used when no other means of cooking is feasible or, to enhance the flavor of certain meats. Proper broiling requires a high heat to coagulate the surface proteins to seal in the internal juices and then a gentler heat to help cook the interior to avoid a charred outside and a raw inside. Tender meat can be broiled without boiling, however, anything over two kilograms, unless thin enough, may not reach high enough internal temperatures to destroy undesirable bacteria or parasites.

Proper broiling is carried out beside the cooking fire or coals. Broiling directly over coals or flames may deposit some cancer producing by-products of wood combustion on your food.

Small pieces of meat can be impaled on a forked stick. Larger pieces such as fish, grouse or hare should be cut along the backbone, spread flat over a grill and cooked on both sides.

Fish may be gutted by cutting along the backbone, rather than the belly. The scales should be left on. Affix the fish with the scale side down to a disposable green willow grill. The fish is placed directly over the coals so that the scales are charred as the fish cooks through the skin which doubles

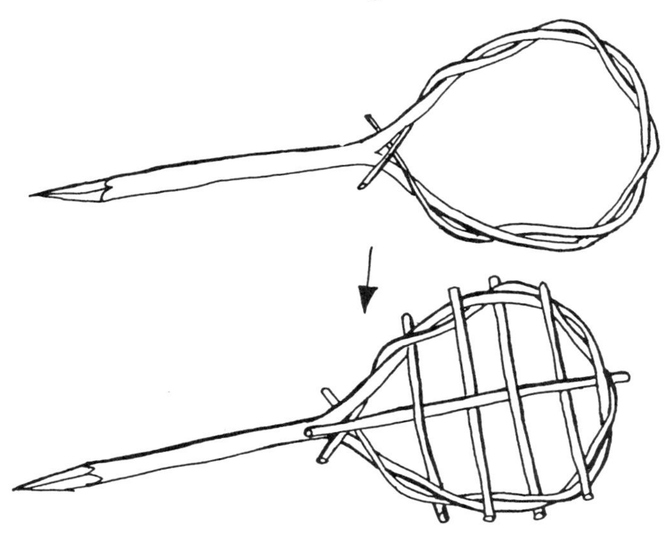

A smaller grill made with a flexible willow fork.

as both a cooking and serving utensil. Unless the fish is very thick, it is cooked on the one side only. Fish low in fat, such as jack, may be basted with fat or oil.

Planking meat is another method of broiling. Wooden pegs are used to pin fish or meat to a split log. Thicker pieces of meat may have to be turned to cook from both sides.

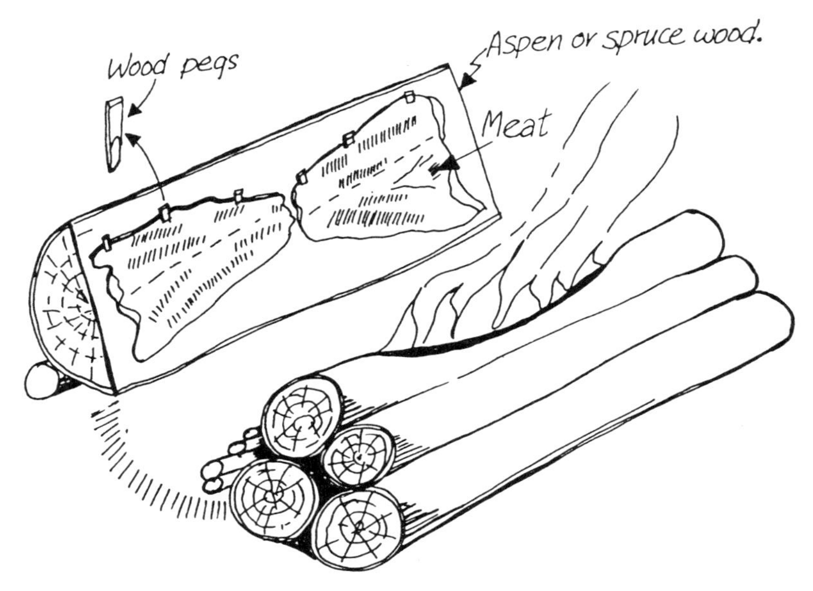

The planking method of cooking fish or meat.

Steaming

The steam pit excels in cooking large pieces of tough meat. A good supply of non-resinous wood such as willow, aspen or alder is required for heating the pit and stones. A good site is a sand bar where you can dig down about 50 centimetres. Sandy soil heats up easily and holds the heat needed for this type of cooking.

First dig a pit with sloped sides to a depth of about 50 centimetres. Build a fire in it with wrist-thick wood piled knee-high. Stones of head size or smaller are then piled on the wood and more fuel is added to cover them well. Have enough stones to make a layer on the bottom of the pit and a second layer over the food to be cooked. Once the stones are glowing and most of the wood has burned up, remove any unburned wood or large embers. Arrange a layer of stones over the bottom of the pit. A thick layer of wet, green foliage such as clover, alfalfa, sedge, fern or alpine hedysarum is laid on the hot stones. Any non-poisonous greens with an acceptable flavor can be used. When greens are not available, a wet cloth can be substituted.

Food can be wrapped in cloth for protection against sand contamination. The food is laid over this foliage and covered with another thick layer of well-soaked foliage. When cooking for six to eight people, eight litres of water should now be added, as adding water later may result in the water contaminating the food with sand. The second tier of hot rocks is arranged over the food. A crudely woven willow mat is placed on top of the rocks and covered with a layer of grass to prevent sand from reaching the food. Additional water is poured around the edges before the pit is covered. Quickly seal with a layer of lightly packed and dampened sand to make the pit steamproof.

The steam pit cannot spoil food through overcooking. The pit can be made up in the morning and opened for supper. Meat must be cooked five hours per kilogram for a minimum of six hours. An average size fish requires an hour. Vegetables can also be cooked in the steam pit. The steam pit is useful when cooking for 40 to 50 people. No cooking utensils are needed and no one has to watch over the cooking. The chance of a bear getting into the food is slight compared to food left to cook on the surface.

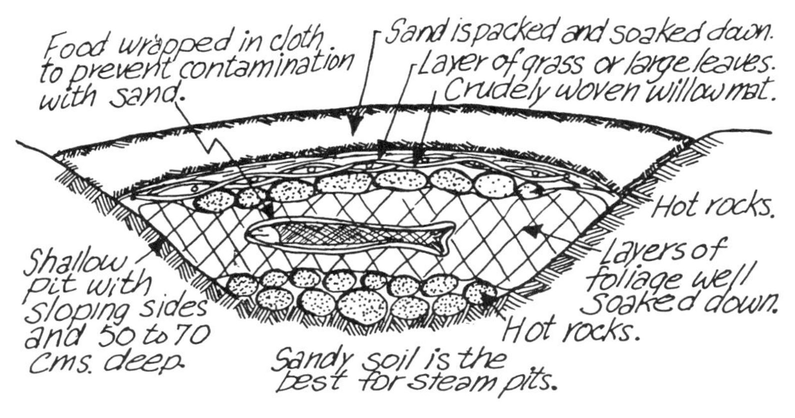

The steam pit.

Baking

Baking involves cooking in an oven with dry heat instead of direct exposure to fire or coals. With a proper oven, baking is very fuel-efficient. Baking is feasible only if you are staying in one place for a period of time because of the time and effort required to build the oven.

A core of kindling and firewood is made for the oven proper. A loose, elongated twig bundle of the required length and diameter for the chimney is stood up against one end of the oven core. Everything is then covered with grass or shrubbery followed by a layer of stiff clay at least 30 centimetres thick. The core is burned out and the oven is ready to use.

A hot fire built in the oven heats the interior. Coals are raked out and the food placed inside. The door and the chimney are blocked off to conserve heat. If a piece of meat is heavier than 1.5 kilograms, baking may not raise internal temperatures sufficiently to kill pathogens. A high fat loss is usually associated with baking.

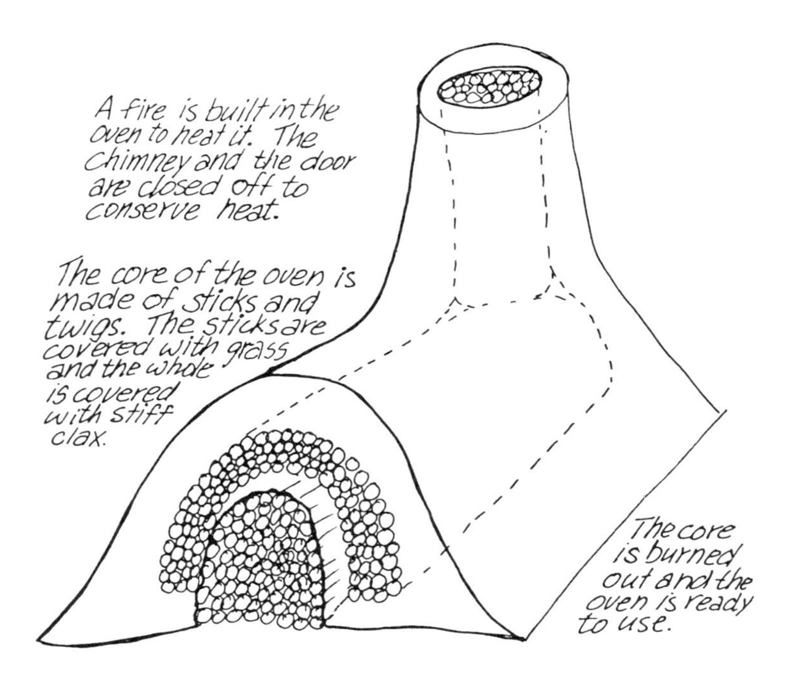

Detail of clay oven construction.

Deep Frying

With deep frying, food is immersed in oil or fat heated to slightly over 200°C (where the fat just begins to give off a pale blue smoke). The food is cooked until golden brown. As cooking takes place very fast, the protein fibers do not harden and the flavor and juices are retained. This is suitable for fish and fry bread, but not for tough meat that should be cooked slowly at a lower temperature.

Frying

Frying is the method of cooking where fat is added to keep food from sticking to a pan or pot. Most foods cooked this way become somewhat indigestible.

Cooking With Coals

Some of the best coals are made from black poplar bark that is two or three centimetres thick. The bark is put on a campfire in a criss-cross fashion. A layer of coals is raked out, a frying pan with a snug lid is placed over them then covered with another layer of coals to bake bannock, cake and pizzas. Another way to produce coals is to use large quantities of finger-thick willow or aspen sticks.

Cooking With a Hot Rock and Insulation

Grouse, chicken or fish may be cooked with a hot rock that will fit into the body cavity. First wash the rock then check that it fits. The red-hot rock is placed into the body cavity and bound in place with twine or wire. Pack in an insulative material such as dry grass or old man's beard. Let sit for about four hours or until the chicken or fish is cool enough to eat.

Making Bannock

Bannock is a form of baking powder bread that is quite popular in wilderness living. This basic recipe is for two people.

1 cup flour
1 moderately heaping teaspoon of baking powder
1/8 teaspoon salt

Mix the ingredients well and make into a stiff dough or runny batter (as needed), by adding from three-quarters to one and a half cups of cold water.

Optional ingredients that will add variety to the basic recipe are a tablespoon of sugar, berries or canned or dried fruit, cheese or cooked meat cut into fine pieces. Without sugar, a bannock browns only slightly.

A bannock from the given recipe requires at least 15 minutes to half an hour to bake properly, depending on the stiffness of the batter. Any bannock that is cooked too quickly will be well done on the outside and raw inside.

One way of mixing the ingredients is to roll down the sides of a flour bag, make a hollow in the centre of the flour and lightly mix in the dry ingredients. Pour the required amount of water into the depression and swirl it about with a stick, finger, or spoon, catching the sides of the depression lightly now and again. Do not rush the job. In a short while the water will take on its full load of flour and can be removed from the bag on reaching the required stiffness. The ingredients can also be mixed in a pot, but first grease the inside by swirling some melted fat in it to help keep the batter from sticking.

Cooking Bannock

1. Bannock on a Stick. Before you start mixing the dough, obtain a green, wrist-thick pole of a good tasting wood like aspen or willow. Peel the portion on which the dough is to be wrapped and place it near the fire to toast. Rotate the pole so it heats up well all around. The hot pole will help make the dough adhere better as well as cook it from the inside while it bakes on the outside. The dough should be stiff enough that a roll of thumb-thickness will hang without breaking. Wrap the dough around the hot part of the pole and pat down to a thickness of about one centimetre, (dough wrapped in the form of a tube as opposed to the popular spiral adheres better). At first, bake fairly close to the coals rotating constantly until the dough firms up or it may rise and drop off in pieces. Next, move it away from the heat so it bakes more slowly, turning it as it browns.

2. Bannock on a Raquet. Here, a stiff dough is stretched to a thickness of not more than one centimetre, and laid on a raquet positioned above some coals at a height where you can barely hold your hand to a slow count of five. Brown each side.

3. Bannock Baked in Ashes. Rake out a good layer of coals and ashes. Be careful to avoid sand as it always adheres to the bannock. Lay down a stiff dough no thicker than a centimetre and cover well with a layer of ash and coals. Leave buried undisturbed for about half an hour.

4. Bannock in a Pot or Frying Pan Without Grease. Stir vigorously as you brown a thin layer of flour on the bottom of your pot. Put a thin layer of stiff dough on the browned flour and suspend the pot at a height where you can barely hold your hand to a slow count of five. Allow the dough to bake on one side for 15 minutes, then turn over.

Set a frying pan on a layer of coals. Once the bottom is cooked, prop the pot or pan in front of a pile of coals to brown the top of the bannock.

5. Bannock in a Pot With a Tablespoon of Grease. Your pot must be thoroughly dry or its bottom will melt from the heat produced should the mixture of steam and smoking fat burst into flame. Heat a tablespoon of fat or oil on the bottom until it barely starts to smoke. Pour in a fairly liquid batter less than two centimetres thick. Spin the pot back and forth so the centrifugal force will make the dough fairly

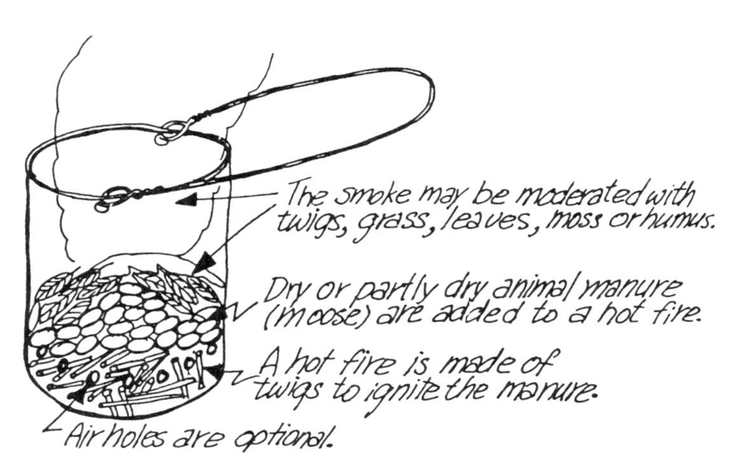

A portable smudge pot useful in repelling mosquitoes and black flies.

thin at its centre. Hang the pot no lower than where you can barely hold your hand for a slow count of five. A lid on the pot will speed up the baking. Bake until the bannock will not sag. The pot is then laid on its side in front of a pile of coals to brown the top half, rotating if necessary to brown the lower half. If the bannock does not adhere to the bottom of the pot, wedge it in place with a stick slightly longer than the diameter of the pot.

6. Fry Bread. Fry bread is bannock that is deep fried. It is the easiest way to make large quantities of tasty bannock to feed big groups. Roll out a stiff dough about one centimetre thick and cut into manageable pieces. If shaped into doughnuts the bread can be fished out of the fat with a stick, otherwise make tongs like those used to pick up hot rocks. Begin cooking the fry bread when a piece thrown into the hot fat comes to the surface by the count of five. It should take about three minutes to cook each side to a golden brown. A raw interior results if the fat is too hot or the pieces of dough are too thick.

2

AXECRAFT

The axe is the most important of the basic bush tools. Outside of fire, little else can contribute more to living comfortably in the wilderness than knowing how to properly use a well-chosen axe.

THE BUSH AXE

There are numerous styles of axe heads available in many weights which can be combined with various lengths of handle. Heads and handles can be modified to create tools that may accommodate the preferences and needs of the individual. The appearance of an axe does not necessarily provide a clue to the quality of its performance as a handsome axe does not always cut as well as an "ugly" looking one.

The larger the axe, the safer it is and the less effort required for its use. The inertia of a heavier axe head is an advantage in cold weather work or in continuous falling. However, heavy axes are unpopular in bush travel because they are cumbersome to carry. The size and weight of a bush axe may be a compromise between the work it will be used for and its portability.

If an axe is uncomfortable to swing, the head may be too heavy. Conversely, if the head is too light, it is more exhausting to use, lacking the inertia of the heavier axe. Ultra-light axes are best suited for experienced users. Their lack of weight requires a stronger swing. It takes a novice a moment to destroy a light axe wielded for years by an experienced person.

Design of the Axe

A blade displaying a slightly convex face, rather than a flat or concave one, releases easily from the cut, throws chips well and is stronger when used with frozen wood. If the face is too convex, the axe blade does not penetrate to maximum depth resulting in a waste of energy. If a blade is too thin, it tends to bind in its cut and requires a particularly annoying tug to free it which also loosens the handle. Change the shape of the blade until enough convex face is achieved to effect release at a maximum depth of cut.

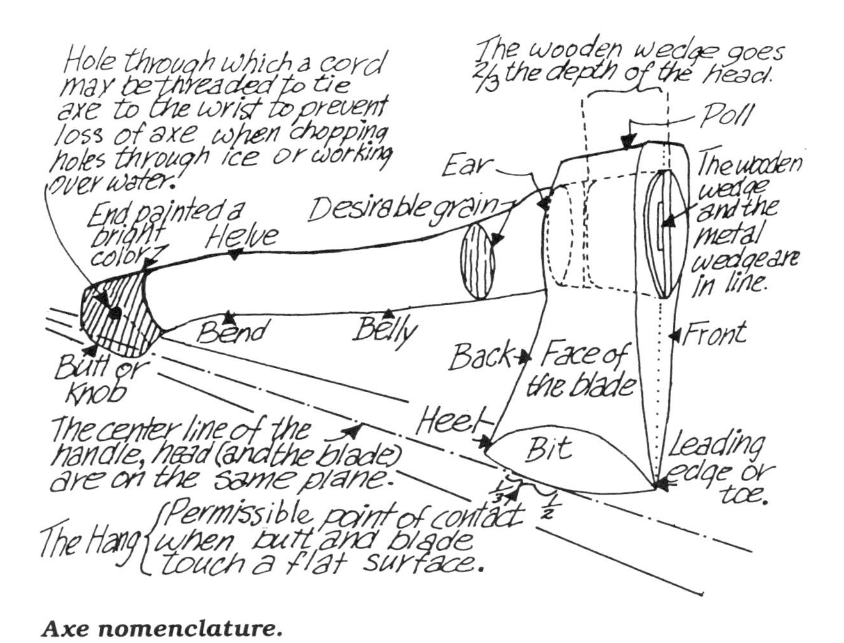

Axe nomenclature.

The heel of the axe blade should be thin enough to set easily into wood that is being split.

A blade 12 centimetres long should bulge out less than a centimetre from a straight line connecting the toe and heel of the blade. A cutting edge greater than 15 centimetres is cumbersome to use.

The eye of the axe is the weakest part. With a small eye, the part of the handle entering the eye may be too thin to have the required strength. With too short an eye, the handle comes loose as there is so little surface of handle in contact with the metal of the eye. A large eye is better providing the metal around it is thick enough not to close, open or crack with use. The metal around the eye is left more malleable than the blade to resist cracking. For this reason, it is easy to distort the eye by pounding the back of one axe with another.

A sensitive user may not want to pound with his axe, but the less fastidious bushwhacker may look upon the axe as being as much a sledge as it is a cutting tool, in which case, a light eye should be avoided. Pounding on the poll with a wooden bat instead of another axe will not distort the eye as much.

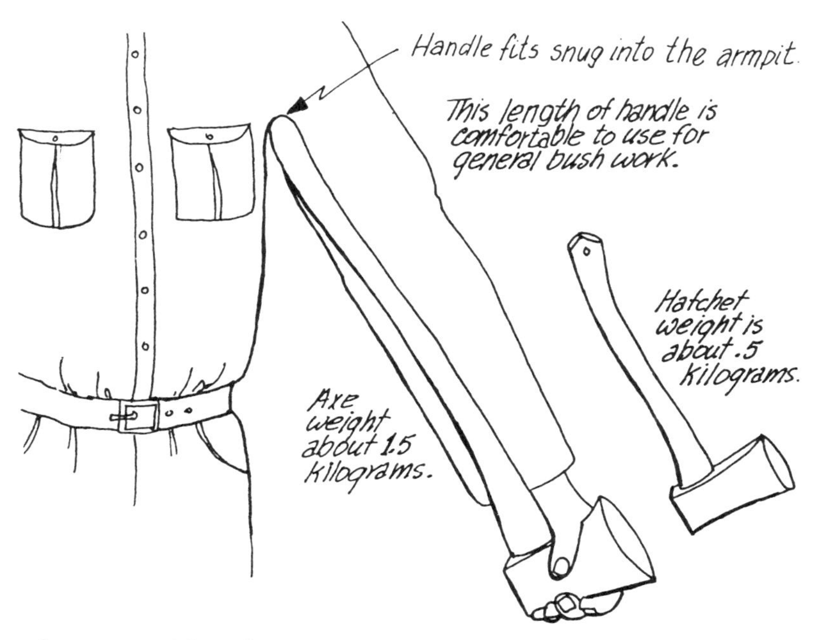

The axe and hatchet.

The temper of the axe blade should be tough but not too hard, or it will be difficult to sharpen with an ordinary file or whetstone. A blade that is too soft will dull easily and wear out faster. A hard-tempered axe is prone to chip when used in very cold temperatures.

A good handle should feel comfortable to the hand, being neither too thin nor too thick. The handle must be slim enough not to jar with hard hits, but not so slim as to flex

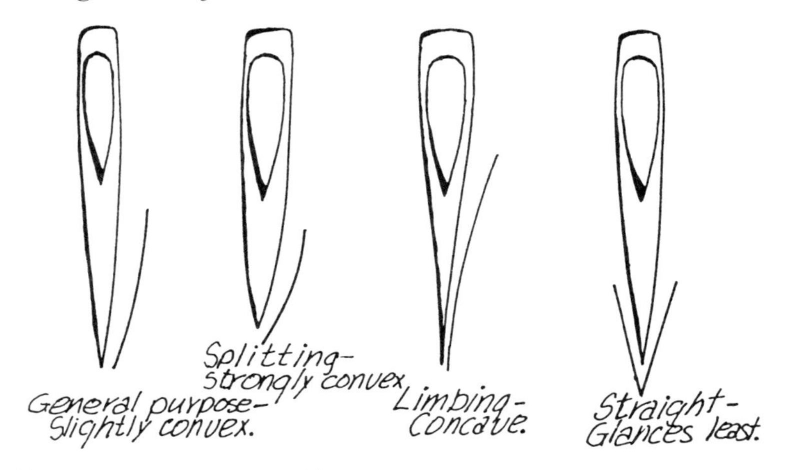

Common axe cross sections.

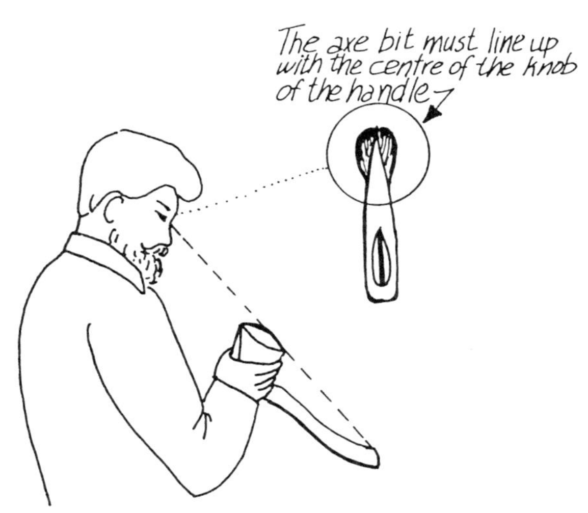

Checking alignment of handle and axe blade.

too easily. If the handle is too round in cross section it is awkward to hold and gives a poor indication of where the leading edge of the blade should be. If too flat it will be tiresome to use if it flexes too much when the blade is pulled from its cut. For a straight handle, the flatness has to be more pronounced to keep the axe from turning in the hand on impact. A good knob signals the hand when the end of the handle is reached.

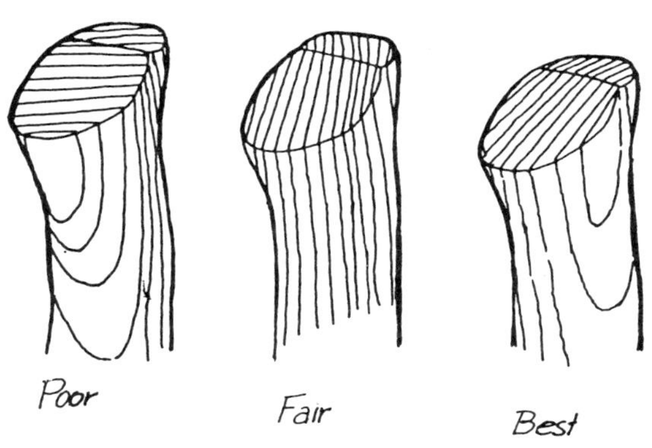

Desirable grain in axe handles.

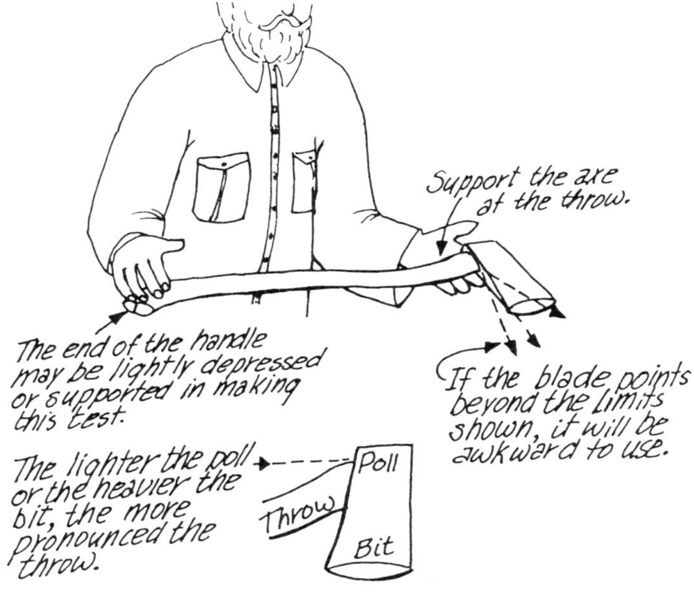

The throw of an axe.

Sight in line with the blade to determine the alignment of the head with the center line of the handle. Some misalignment in the right direction may improve the performance of an axe for some users.

If the knob and the axe blade are both made to touch a flat surface, the blade should make contact from one-third of the way from the heel to the blade's mid-point. This way the weight of the head is fully behind the cutting edge of the blade edge and energy is not wasted through deflection.

The balance is determined by the "throw" of the axe, which is the forward bulge of the handle within 15 to 20 centimetres of the head. If the axe is held at the throw in the flat of one hand and the end of the handle is held up or down by the other hand, the axe head should lie flat or the blade point only slightly upward or downward. The longer the bit, or the lighter the poll, the more throw is required. An axe that exceeds these parameters will feel as awkward to use as a pick.

Sharpening the Axe

The inexperienced and occasional users who are more prone to accidents in the first place, often fail to appreciate the importance of a keen edge. All woodworking tools, including axes, should be sharp enough to shave with for effortless, efficient and enjoyable work. Most new axes require from an hour to half a day of hand sharpening to put them into proper shape. A dull axe is less efficient and more tiring to use. It is also a greater hazard as it glances more readily. An axe should be sharpened on a regular basis, perhaps with every half-hour of use or each time a tree is cut down. A minute spent on sharpening may shorten your chopping time by five minutes.

The first stage of sharpening is the removal of unwanted metal by file, grindstone or coarse whetstone. Coarse grinding tools remove metal the fastest, but leave a rough surface. The second stage produces a finer edge by using a medium whetstone surface. The third stage is a fine edge accomplished with the fine side of a whetstone. The final edge is produced with a hard and smooth stone called a hone which should produce a mirror finish. (Chapter 3 discusses sharpening techniques at greater length.)

A new axe blade may require thinning only once and a file may be used on it again, only if the blade is nicked.

There are files that are specifically made for the axe such as a flat blunt, single cut with second teeth on one side, and double cut bastard on the other. When the teeth are in parallel rows, they are called single cut. Double cut teeth are crossed with a series of similar teeth. The degree of fineness of a file is described as rough, bastard, second cut, smooth and dead smooth. A mill bastard is a small, tough file that leaves a smooth surface and skips least on hard spots. It is more portable than a regular axe file.

Files must be used knowledgeably to provide long service. Files stored together should be wrapped in cloth to prevent the chipping and dulling that results when they come in contact with each other. Protect files from moisture as rust

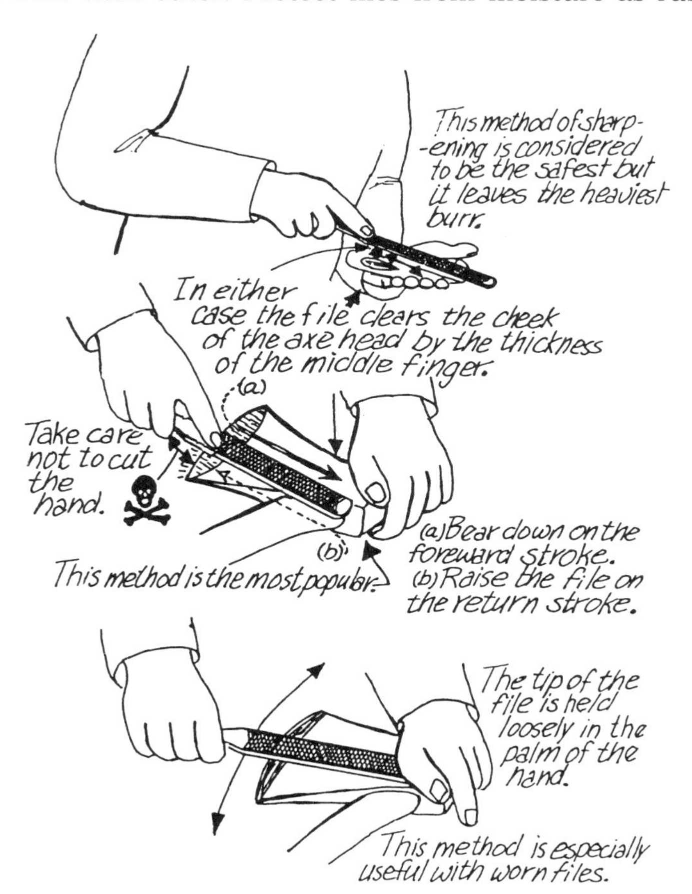

Method of filing an axe.

weakens the teeth. Anything that will clog the teeth such as sap, grease or oil should be avoided. A clean axe may allow your file to last twice as long.

To prolong the life of a new file fill the teeth with blackboard chalk. This reduces clogging, and reinforces the file teeth.

A good handle for tanged files is made from a green birch sapling of a diameter that fits the hand comfortably. The bark is left on to prevent the handle from splitting. The green handle can usually be driven on without pre-drilling. One in four may split. Those that do not, hold well.

When working with a file apply only enough downward force to get a light even cut, as excessive downward force breaks off teeth, especially on the backward stroke. Hold the file handle in the palm, with the forefinger pressing down lightly on the back of the file. On the return stroke, lift the file clear of the work.

Severe nicks may take hours to remove. File out a straight edge in the vicinity of the nick which will regain its curvature with later sharpenings.

Most oldtimers file their axes towards the cutting edge. Perhaps a better blade shape is achieved, or a thinner burr is formed on the edge. On the other hand it is safer to file in the same direction as the cutting edge.

Drawfiling provides a few more sharpenings from a worn out file. The file tip or handle is held in the palm of the hand over the poll of the axe and the other end is worked back and forth.

When travelling light, a whetstone is an appropriate tool for maintaining an axe edge. Most whetstones are made of (synthetic) carborundum. One side is usually medium and the other is fine. The medium side grinds out any file serrations and the fine side grinds out the medium serrations to produce an adequate but rough working edge. This stone is lighter and more compact to carry than a file. A file wears out quickly, but it works much faster.

When properly cared for, a stone may last a lifetime as a fresh surface keeps appearing until the stone is used up. In a year you may wear out many files, each of which is more expensive than a whetstone.

The stone is held about the perimeter with no finger tips protruding over the edges and used in a circular motion so that its whole surface is worn in an even fashion.

An axe can be sharpened with natural stones. Trial and error will quickly establish which stones will work best.

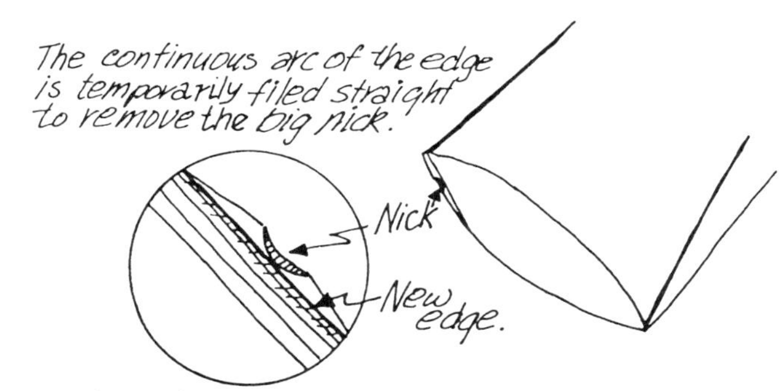

Filing out bad nicks.

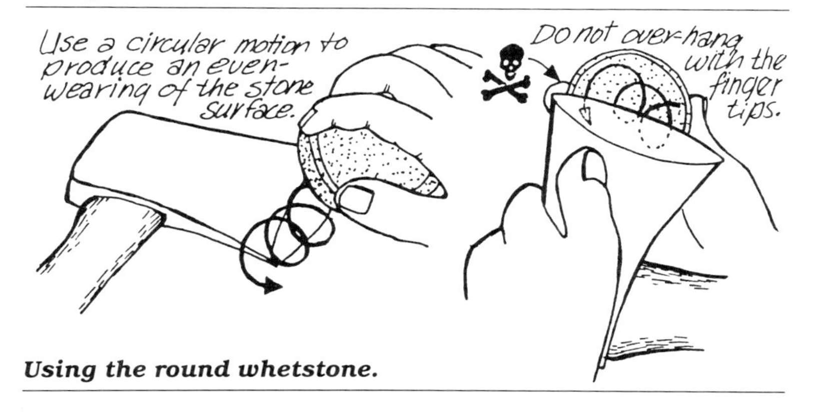

Using the round whetstone.

Replacing an Axe Handle

Removing a broken handle can be a major undertaking. If possible, first pry out any metal wedges. If some of the handle remains it may be thinned down enough to drive it forward through the front of the eye. If inertia-pounding will not do the job, support the head at the poll and at the blade over a V-notch sawn in a sound, upright stump while the handle is hammered through. It may help to dry the wood in the eye to shrink it. If this is done near a fire, be careful not to draw the temper. The axe head should be comfortable to hold at all times. Never burn out the wood in the eye unless you have the expertise and the means to temper steel.

A metal drill bit may have to be used to remove as much wood as possible from the eye. The bit should not cut into the inside of the eye, as the resulting score can cause it to crack.

Second growth hickory makes good axe handles. The wood should be resilient, strong, and straight grained. The strongest handle has a grain that is parallel to the long axis of the handle. Some painted handles may hide poor grain, knots or other flaws.

If a handle is too thick to suit your needs, few tools are as effective as broken glass in shaving it down.

If a replacement has to be carved, it may be simpler to make a straight handle instead of a curved one. There may be little difference between the two, although some claim

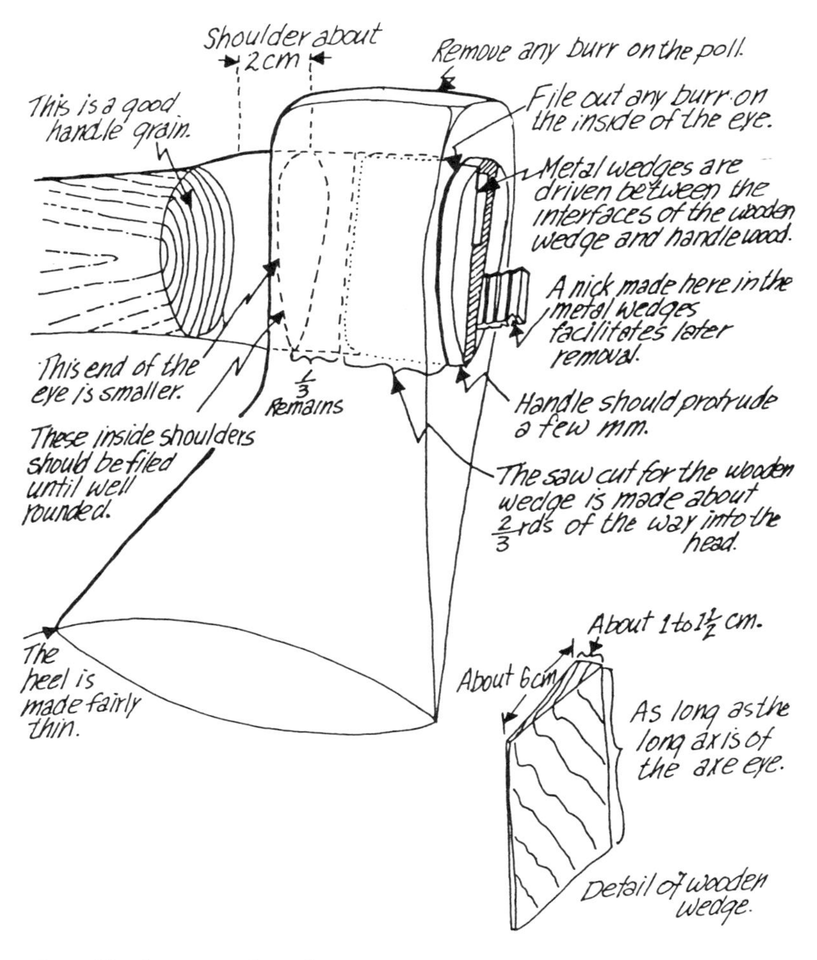

Detail of an axe head.

a straight handle is superior in performance.

Before fitting a new handle, clean and grind all parts of the axe head to perfection. File out any lips, burrs or other irregularities in the eye and on the blade and pole. If the interior of the eye has a lip or if the inside surface is excessively rough it should be filed smooth. The worst lip is generally formed at the front of the eye. The edges at the back of the eye, from which the handle is inserted, should be well-rounded so no sharp corner presses on the wood. This helps prevent a break at this point. The eye is larger at the front end in order to better wedge the head on. If it is difficult to determine which end of the eye is wider, take careful measurements.

Place the axe head on the handle to determine how much wood to trim off, allowing a centimetre extra length. Rasp, carve or shave down the handle with broken glass for a close fit in the eye, taking care to remove an equal amount of wood from both sides so the axe head has the desired alignment with the handle. Fit the handle frequently to make sure you do not remove too much wood for a loose fit.

Saw a slot on the long axis of the handle for two-thirds of the depth that it would fit into the eye. If a vise is available, squeeze the slot closed and resaw it to two-thirds of the slot's depth. Repeat this once more but to one-third the depth to make a slightly tapered slot to accept the wedge.

To drive on the head by inertia-pounding, cut off the point

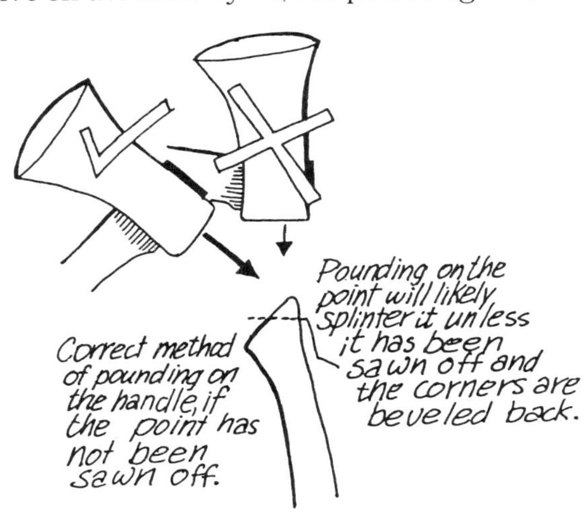

The correct method for driving on the axe head.

of the knob on the handle, bevel the corners to prevent splitting and you can direct your pounding force in line with the handle for the best effect.

The wedge-wood can be any wood that will resist splintering when being driven into the slot. Wedges hold better if soaked in linseed oil. The wedge need not be in one piece but it must extend for the full-length of the long axis of the

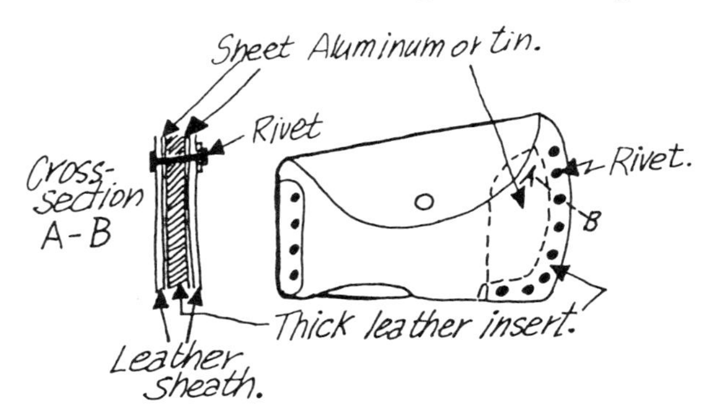

An improved axe sheath.

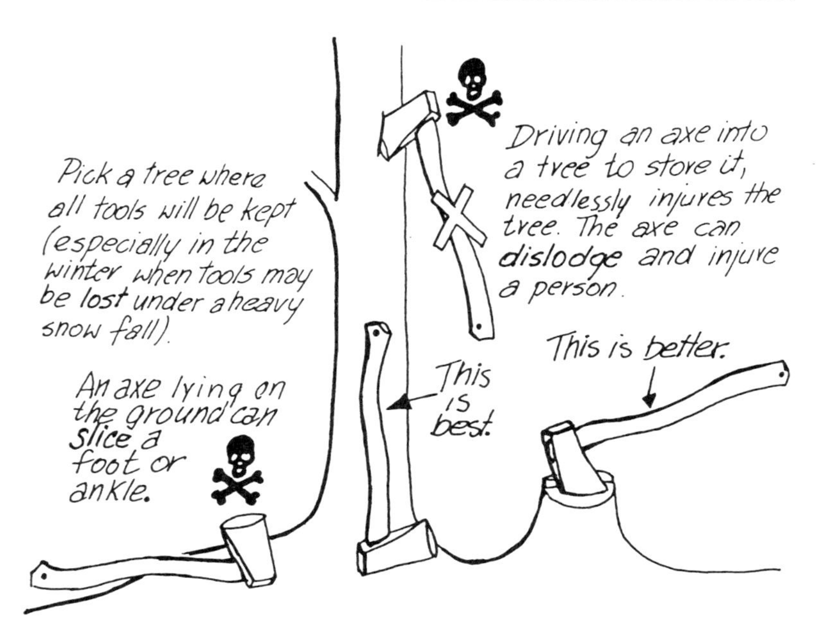

How to store an axe in camp.

eye so that the whole eye is tightly filled with wood. The wedges should be driven in as far as they will go. Trim off any protruding handle and wedge, leaving about half a centimetre. Cutting it flush with the metal of the eye does not allow it to hold as well.

Drive in metal wedges between the interfaces of the wooden wedges and the handle wood instead of crosswise to the long axis of the eye. This spreads the wood outward from the long axis, rather than in line with it, and holds the head on better. The head may be soaked in linseed oil or antifreeze to reduce wood shrinkage and help keep the head on better. Repeated soaking in water to make the wood swell to remedy a loose head weakens the wood so that the head breaks off at the handle.

Axe Sheaths

Never carry an unsheathed axe, but if you must, always be aware of the position of the blade. Carry it at your side with the blade pointing slightly away from you. Should you fall, throw the axe aside a short distance so that you do not cut yourself or anyone near you. Carrying an axe on your shoulder invites a cut to the neck or back, as well as being a hazard to those around you. A sheath protects both you and the axe from unnecessary injury. There are countless instances where people have been severely injured from falling on an axe.

Many commercial sheaths are so poorly designed that the blade cuts through the material with use. The partially exposed blade becomes a hazard to the carrier. Sheaths for belt axes that do not close properly allow the head to push out when you sit or fall backwards and may cause a cut to the forearm. It is wise to have a secure sheath for every axe.

Axe Etiquette

It is poor manners to ask a person for the loan of his axe. It is worse to use it without permission. If you have work that has to be done, ask the axe owner to do it for you. A moment of misuse on your part may mean many hours of work replacing a broken handle or taking out a bad nick. A handle may be bought for a few dollars, but the real cost is the hours of work needed to shape it to perfection.

Safe Axe Use

Safety is a major consideration with axe use. Large or small, the axe is a serious hazard in itself. Using an axe to fall large trees is one of the most dangerous activities in wilderness living. Safe axe use implies that you understand both your tool and the tree you wish to fell. Assured safety depends on the correct knowledge on how to fall the tree, combined with experience and expert guesswork to predict where it will fall. The more experience you have the better your guess and the safer you are.

The best way to learn to use an axe is to work with an experienced person who can provide the training and keep a watchful eye on you until you have become familiar with the hazards of both the axe and the falling tree. Every year many professional forest workers accidentally die at their work. Without a doubt they knew what they were doing, but somehow they missed something on that fatal day. The discipline of axemanship demands that the occasional and professional faller alike must remember many things and be able to recognize a hazard before it causes a fatality.

Axe Size and Safety

The Small Axe. The small camp axe or hatchet with a handle of 30 centimetres can be the most dangerous of all if taken for granted or used without safety principles. The most common injury areas are the knees and the forehead.

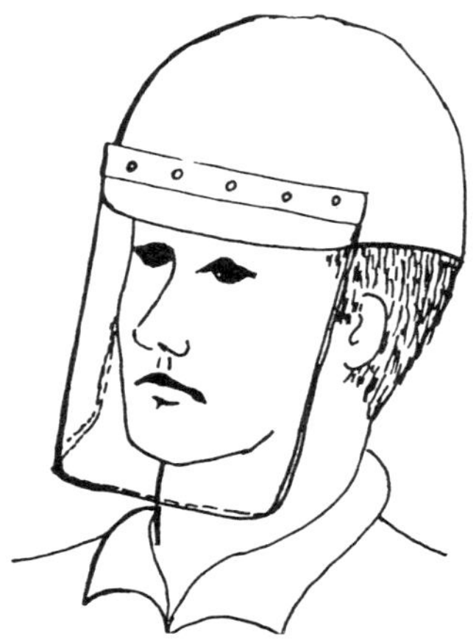

Wear head and eye protection when using an axe.

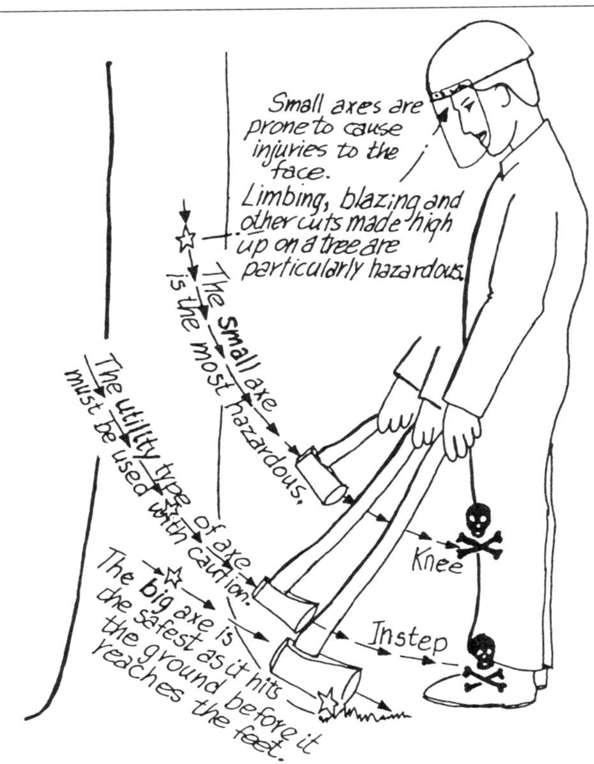

The relative safety of various sizes of axe.

The General Purpose Axe. If you hold the head of this axe in your hand you should be able to fit the end of the handle into your armpit. This is a favorite size for wilderness survivalists, trappers, horse-packers and carpenters. If misused, an axe of this handle length can still cut you in the face, but instead of the knee, it can end up in the instep or make your toes longer or shorter depending on where it hits.

The Large Axe. The full-sized axe with a handle length of about a metre is the safest as it normally deflects into the ground before reaching any part of the body.

Using the Different Sizes of Axe

Camp Axe or Hatchet. The safest way to use this axe is to stand well away from the tree, lean on it with your free hand, and chop as close to the ground as possible. The shoulder and the arm should both participate in the chopping action. At the point in the swing where the axe head is about 30 centimetres from impact, make both the axe head and the hand move forward together by throwing the hand forward in the direction of the swing. This changes the path of the axe head from that of an arc that could deflect towards you to a motion away from you. The axe should bite into the wood at a downward angle of about 30 to 45 degrees. Attempting to chop upward could cause the axe to hit you in the face. The downward angle is exactly the same for both the lower and upper cuts. The resulting stump will look rather ragged, but any other method of cutting will not be any safer or faster.

If the cut is made from a kneeling position, both hands are free to hold the axe. Stay about one or two axe handle

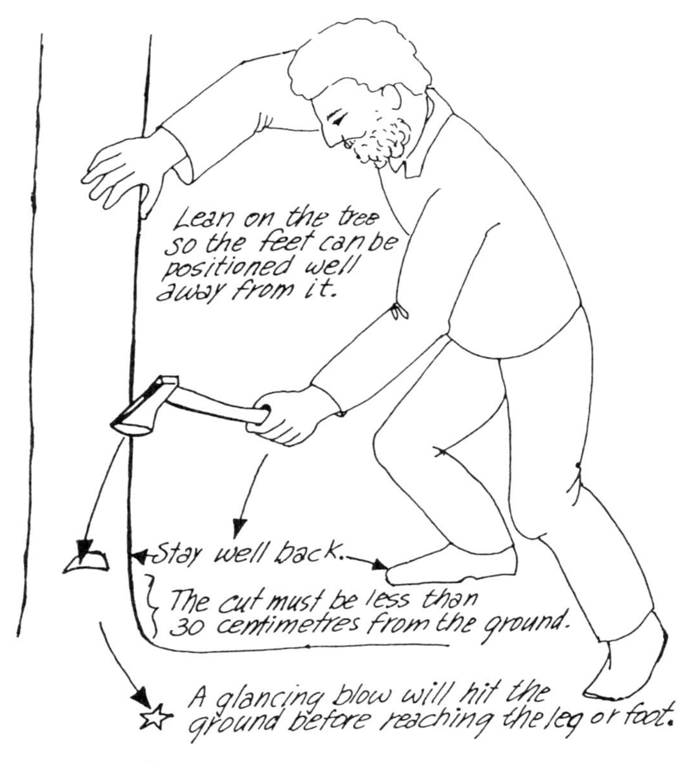

Proper use of camp axe or hatchet.

lengths away from the tree and use the same pre-impact manoeuvre just described.

When limbing a standing tree the parallel action of axe head and hand can serve to make the cut safer because of the greater control of the follow through. By reaching partly around the trunk of the tree, the resulting follow through of the axe head should be off to the side, well away from any part of your body.

The Larger Axes. The safest way to use an axe is to maintain its handle's distance between yourself and the tree, and to chop within 30 centimetres of the ground. In bending the back and reaching in this manner, the deflected axe will have to travel much further to strike the feet, if it does not reach the ground first. For additional safety, the parallel axe head and hand motion should be used as described for the hatchet with both hands on the handle. By the time the axe

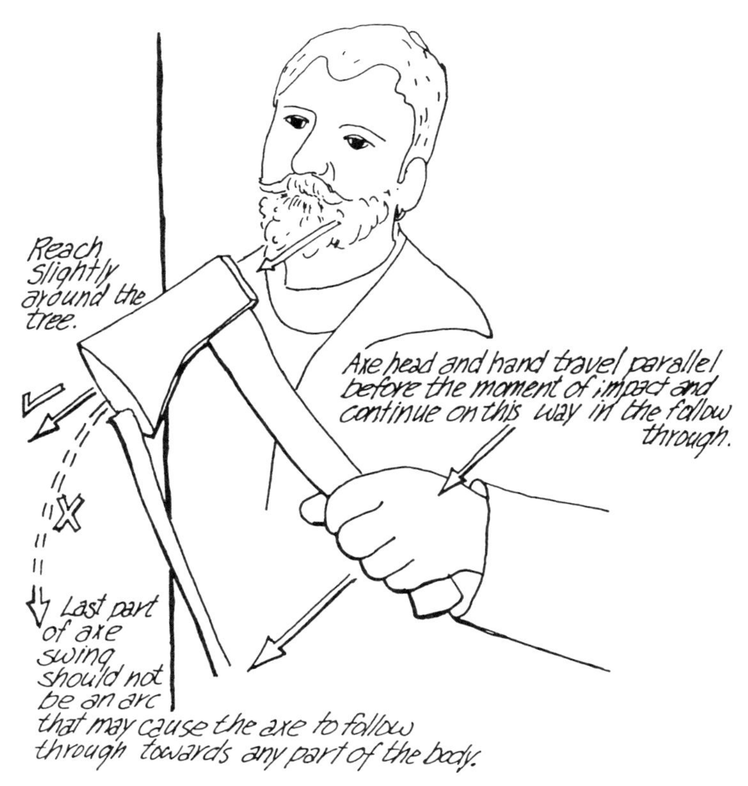

Limbing with a camp axe.

Safe chopping distance and height.

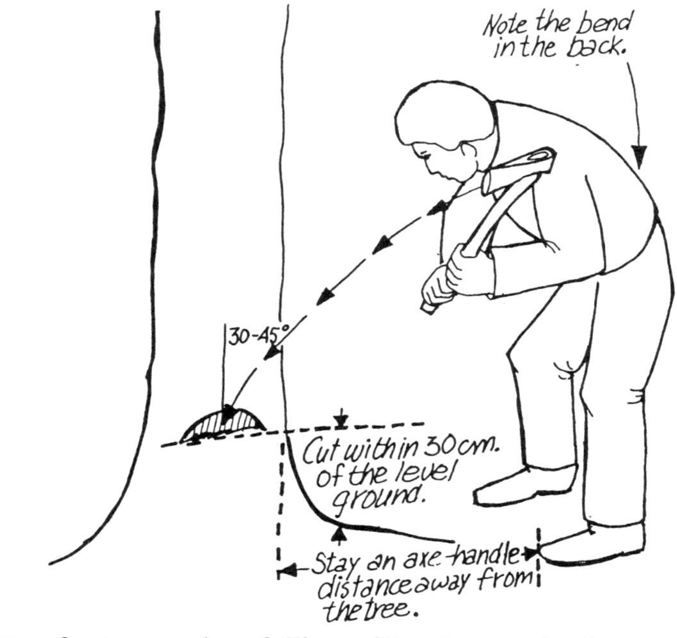

A safe stance when falling with a larger sized axe.

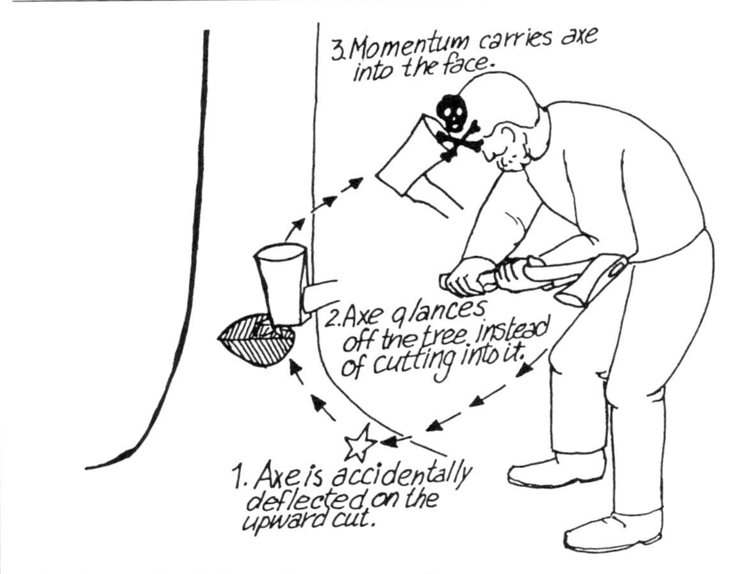

The hazard of chopping upward.

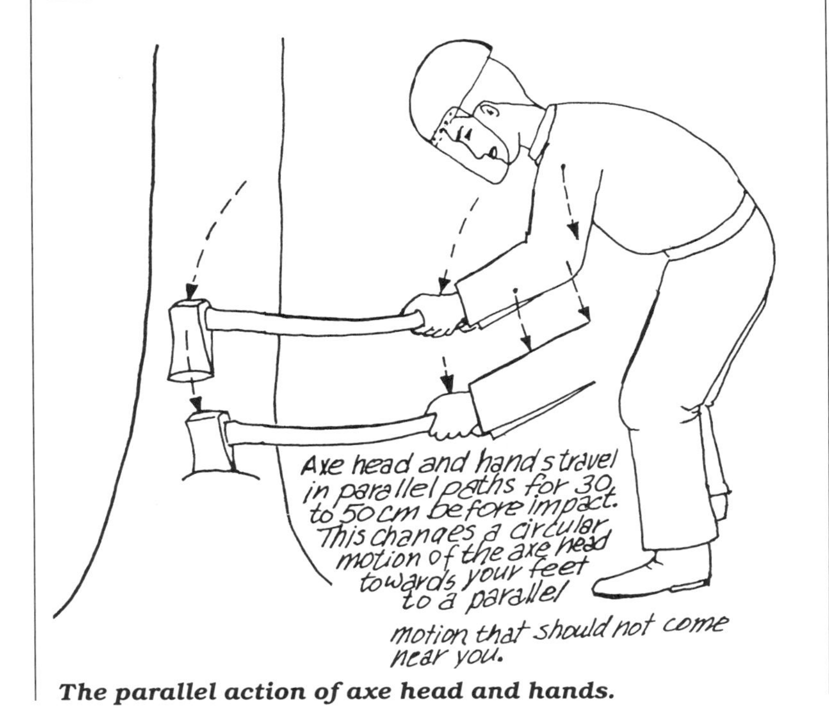

The parallel action of axe head and hands.

stops moving, the handle should end up parallel to the level ground or sticking out at 90 degrees to the trunk of the standing tree.

It is important to keep stumps low. If the point of impact is over 30 centimetres high, a glancing blow may strike the feet. Higher cuts demand caution with respect to this hazardous point.

Axe expertise is largely a matter of coordination. The axe must hit exactly where wanted, at the correct angle, precisely in the previous cut, or effort is wasted in making the same cut over and over again. A mark of competency is producing a few large chips instead of a large amount of small ones.

TREE FELLING

Without experience in tree falling it may be prudent to fall only straight, sound, uncrowded trees under 30 centimetres in diameter that are growing on level ground. Reach around the tree with your right arm and if you cannot touch your left shoulder then the tree is too large to fall without experience. Avoid trees that are crooked, crowded, leaning and those growing on steep slopes until you know what you are doing.

Before you begin, assess the situation and your surroundings. You must have a clear space to work and a sure footing. Always look above you before taking your first swing with an axe. Low branches and brush that may catch the axe should be cleared away. Low overhead branches can spring an axe back into your head or back. A strong axe swing hooked on a low branch can lift your feet clear of the ground and land you flat on your back. When using an axe near camp, always watch out for clotheslines. Clotheslines and woodpiles should be kept well separated.

There are many factors that influence how and where a tree will fall. Unless there is a pronounced lean to the contrary, expect to fall a tree with the wind. A tree is much like a sail—especially an evergreen or a deciduous tree in summer foliage. Trees with heavy branches growing on one side tend to fall in that direction.

A tree of two degrees lean or less can be made to fall in any direction on a still day. An experienced faller, not using

The hazard of falling a crooked tree.

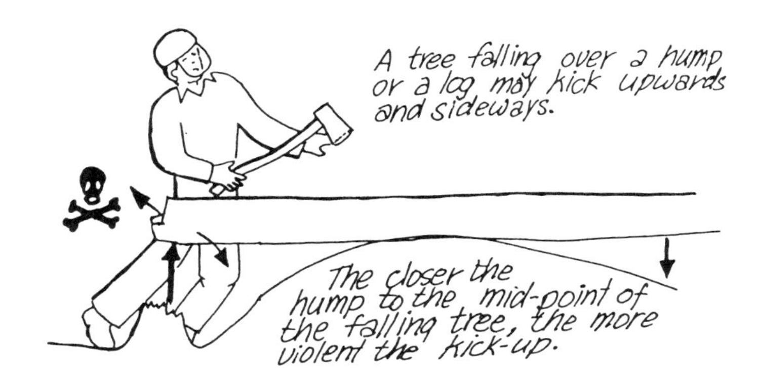

The hazard of falling a tree over a hump.

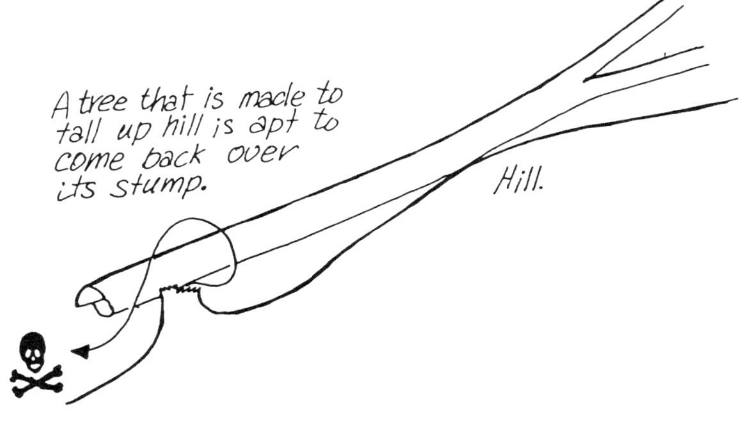

The hazard of falling a tree up hill.

wedges, may fall a tree against a lean of up to four degrees. In the case of a pronounced lean a tree can be made to fall about 70 degrees to either side of its maximum lean. Careless estimation of the lean is the main cause for a tree falling in an unexpected direction. In a critical situation a plumb line should be used from at least two different prospects, 90 degrees apart, to determine the maximum lean.

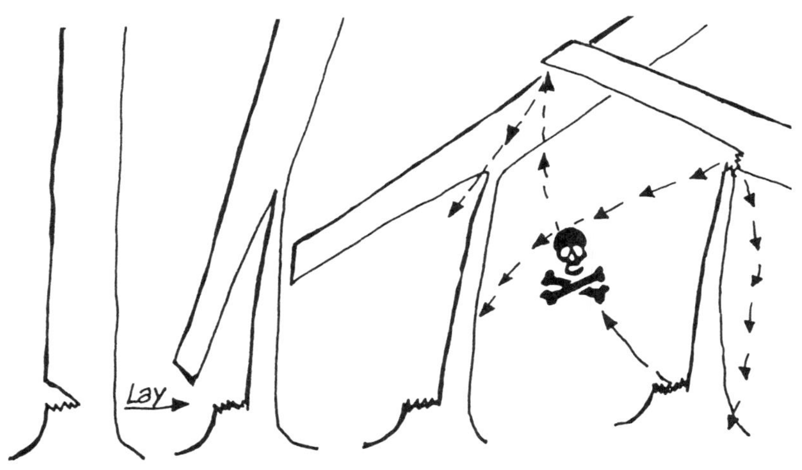

Attempting to fall a tree with little or no undercut may cause the tree to barberchair. Any tree with a pronounced lean is apt to fall in the way illustrated.

The barberchair is considered dangerous as it can happen in an instant catching the faller on the upward swing of the trunk or the highly-raised trunk may spring back and fall on top of him.

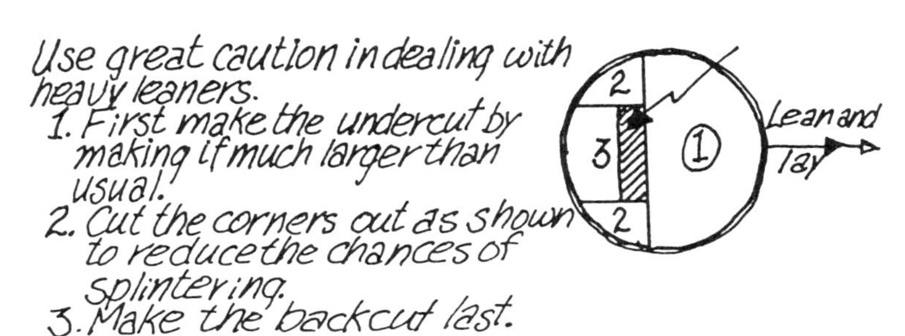

Use great caution in dealing with heavy leaners.
1. First make the undercut by making it much larger than usual.
2. Cut the corners out as shown to reduce the chances of splintering.
3. Make the backcut last.
2
3
①
2
Lean and lay

The barber chair.

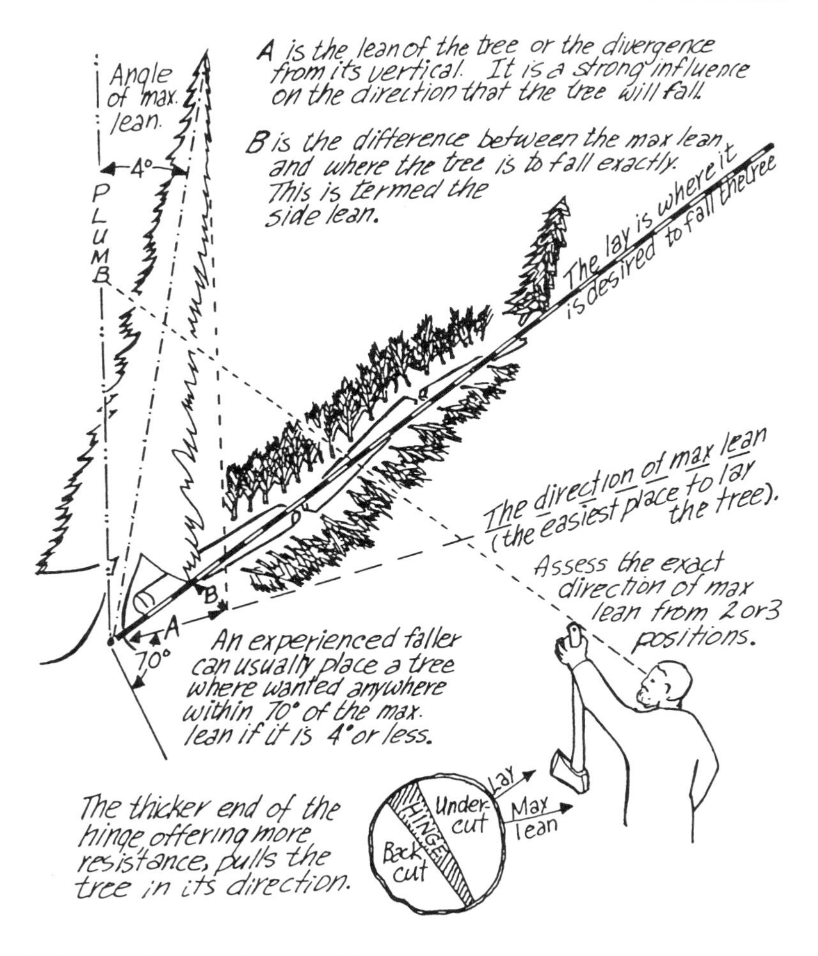

Determining the lay and lean of a tree.

Falling Hazards

Never take anything for granted that concerns a falling tree. The same species of tree may display the same outward appearance, but health, grain, locale and age may determine a unique reaction. Assume that each tree is different and make a careful evaluation of all the problems you might encounter when falling.

First check for the possibility of wood falling from overhead. The vibrations from chopping may cause an unsound top to break off (a habit old dead and fire-killed pines are known for). A suspicious tree should be struck several times with the back of the axe while the tree top is watched carefully to detect any erratic wobble indicating a weakness. Watchfulness will ensure that you are able to side-step anything that falls. At the moment the tree begins to fall, branches or portions of its top or a neighboring one can break off to fall with considerable impact. A wrist-thick branch is big enough to penetrate the skull.

Because of the hazard from falling branches or cones injuring the eyes, one should never look up while chopping without first moving at least five metres away from the tree. Even a pencil-sized branch can cause severe eye injuries.

Every unusual configuration of a tree or terrain may have a hazard associated with it. Trees falling up slope or over a hump may spring back or lash out sideways with crushing force. A tree with a curved trunk, much like the one falling over a hump, may come back over the stump and lash upwards or sideways. As a tree falls, its branches may grab on another and rotate to fall in an unexpected direction—a habit for which trembling aspen is notorious. A hooked small branch at the top of a tree may have a pronounced effect on the direction of fall.

Falling Characteristics of Different Trees

Different species of tree have unique ways of reacting as they fall. For example, the branches of a dense, white spruce tree may cause it to rebound back over its stump. If the flexible birch catches on another tree it may bend beyond its limit of elasticity and on breaking cause pieces of wood to fly in any direction. A falling tree itself may sometimes bend and break a birch sapling to throw broken shards of wood.

The tension in any bent and pinned sapling, particularly birch, must be properly released to avoid personal injury. If cut near the ground the end can lash out with lethal force. A wrist-thick tree bent into a bow can kill if it hits you in the chest or throat. The tension of a bent tree is best released by a partial cut at the central portion of its bend.

White and black poplar often have rotten cores that may cause them to fall sooner than expected or in an unexpected direction. An old injury anywhere on a pine may cause a

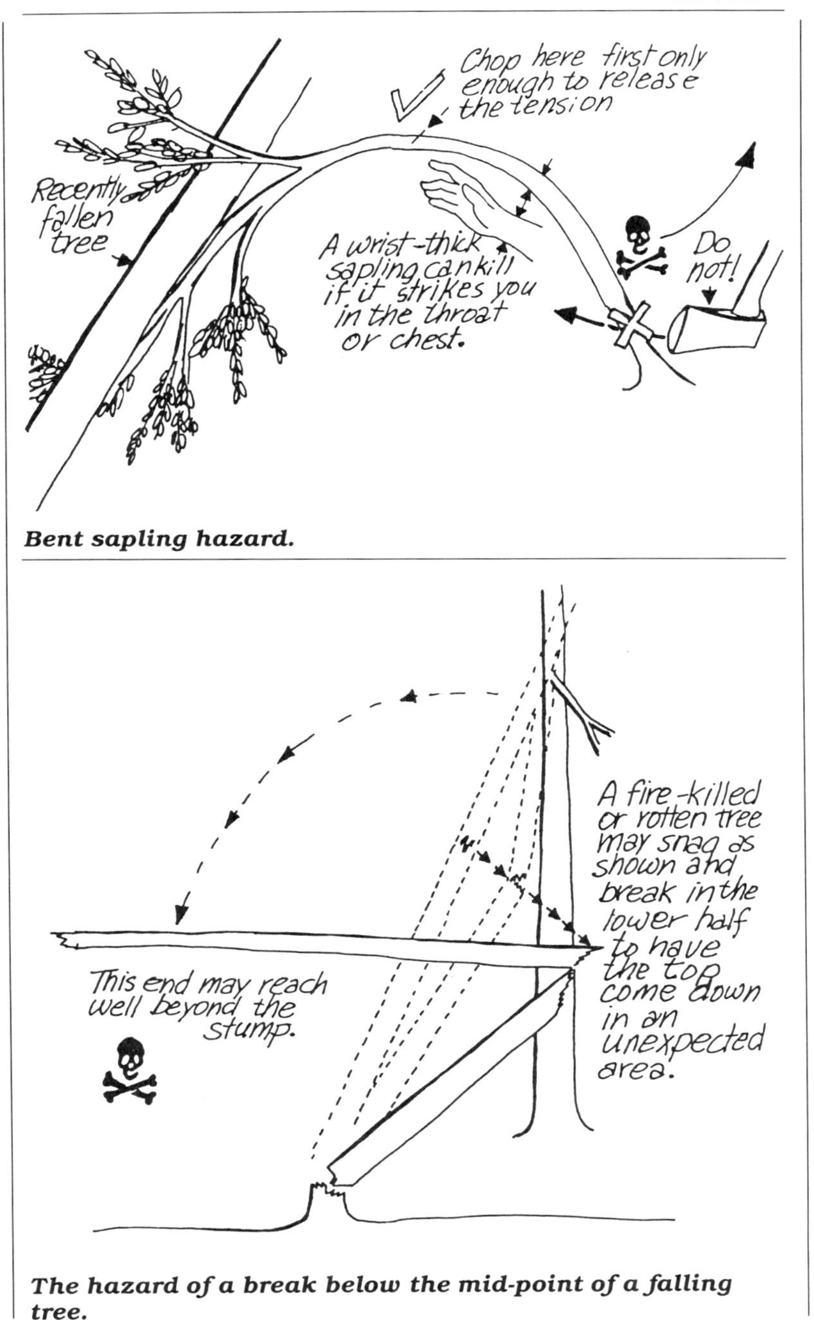

Bent sapling hazard.

The hazard of a break below the mid-point of a falling tree.

weakening rot to progress up and down the trunk from that point. A dry pine can be well on its way in its fall when it snags high up, breaks in its lower half, folds back on itself causing the top to come down violently in the area opposite the direction of fall. Rot in the trunk of a spruce usually starts at the stump and progresses upwards; though not as hazardous as pine, it may still fall unexpectedly.

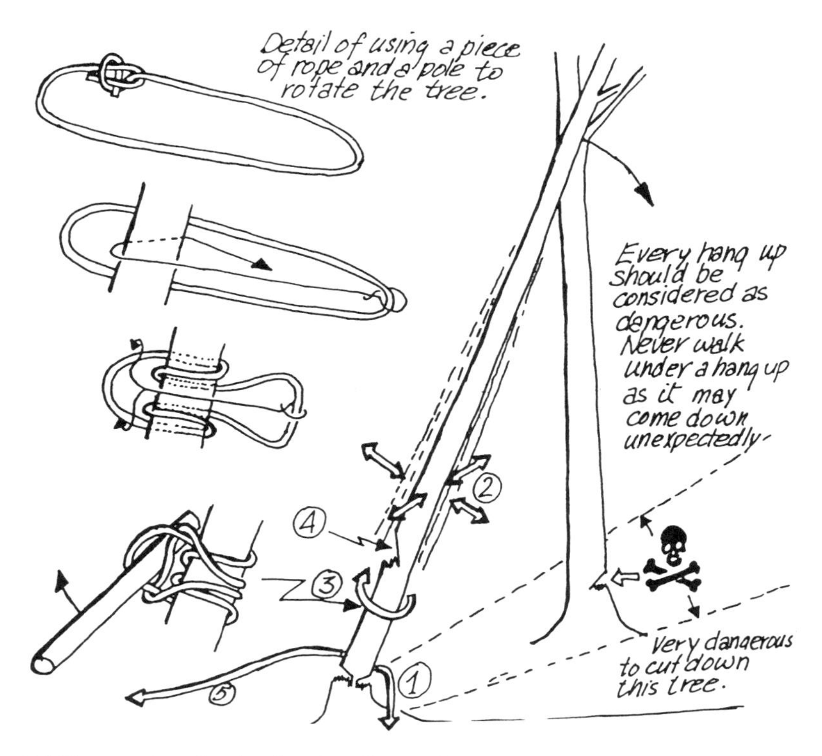

Different Methods for dealing with hang ups.
1. If the tree is freed from its stump, the short fall may dislodge it.
2. Rocking the tree back and forth may dislodge it.
3. Rotating the tree may dislodge it.
4. Chopping out a short section of trunk may help. Use care as the tree may be made to fall in an unpredictable direction.
5. If the tree is light enough it may be freed from the stump and pulled outward to dislodge it. As the tree starts to fall, let go and get clear of it before it hits the ground or you may sustain a severe jar to the arms.

A hung up tree is a hazard that may require close study, caution and experience to bring down safely. As a hang up can be instantly triggered with crushing force, never stand under any part of it. If rocking, rotating or prying does not dislodge it, you may have to chop off sections of trunk a piece at a time until the tree comes down. Cutting down the tree causing the hang up is very dangerous. Felling other trees on the hung up one it will likely result in a greater hang up. This is something an experienced faller will never do.

Falling

1. Determine the direction the tree is to fall.
2. Determine your escape route and clear it. Locate the safe retreat you may use if the tree's actions are not to your liking. Clear away any obstructions near the tree that may interfere with your work.
3. Make the first cut—the undercut—in the direction the tree is to fall. The top part of the cut may be at an angle of 45 degrees and the bottom part is made by using cuts at 45 degrees that move through the wood in increments of a few centimetres. The width of the gap of the undercut is approximately the diameter of the tree. The depth of the undercut

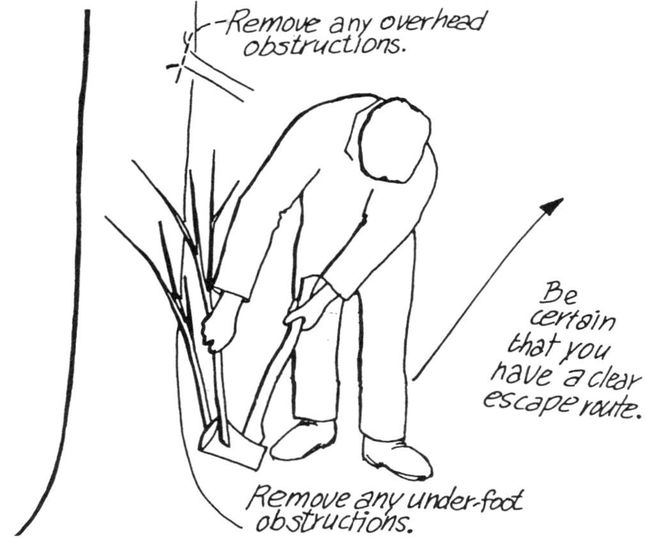

Clear work area and escape route.

may vary from one-third to one-half of the way through the trunk, depending on the soundness of the tree, the degree of lean, the strength of wind and other factors. If the undercut is made too deep, the tree may fall in the opposite direction before the back cut is made, resulting in the notorious and dangerous "barber chair." The cut should be made straight across as a slanted one makes a poor hinge.

4. The back cut is made on the side opposite the undercut and slightly higher. Leaving a few centimetres thickness of wood between the back cut and undercut as a hinge will prevent the tree from slipping off the stump or rotating. If the undercut is not deep enough, or if the back cut is too high above the undercut, the tree may fall in the opposite

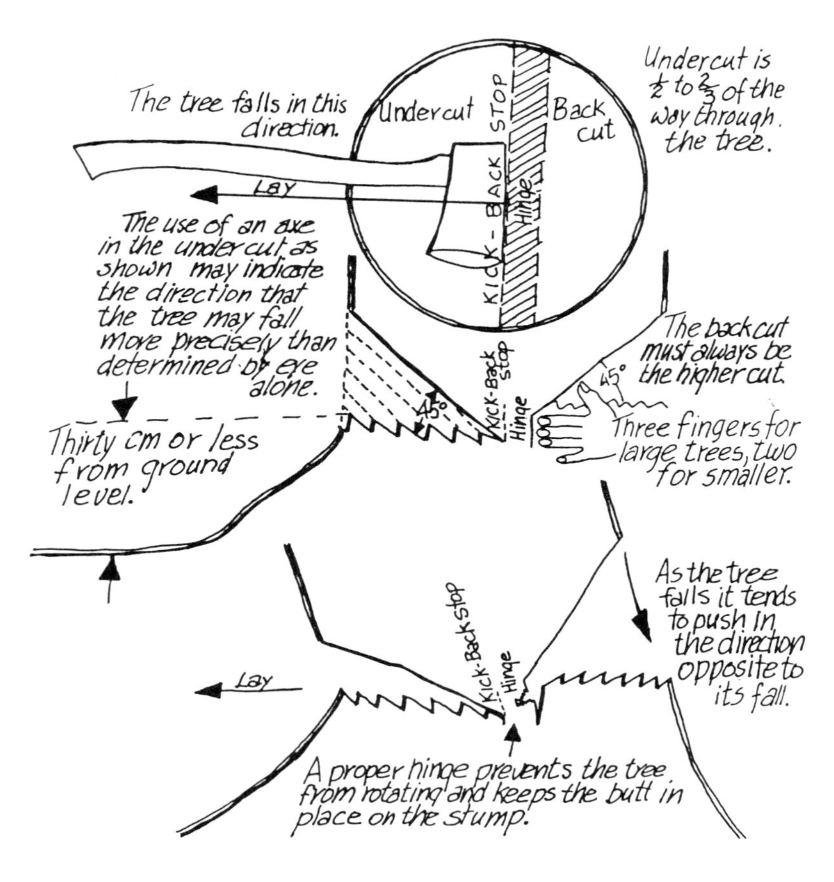

The back cut and the undercut.

direction. The difference in height between the undercut and the back cut may vary with the diameter, the type of tree, whether it is dead or green or whether you have any special effect in mind. A rough measure of the difference would be about two to four finger widths. To fell away from a pronounced lean the hinge is made wedge shaped, when viewed from the top, with the wider part made in the direction the lean is to be shifted. A green tree may fall with a substantial hinge whereas a dry tree tends to fall only when the hinge is relatively thin. (*See* Chapter 4 on felling with the swede saw.)

As the back cut nears completion, the tree may be started on its way with a push to make sure it will fall in the desired direction. From the moment a tree begins to fall watch it closely until it is lying still on the ground so that any erratic or unexpected occurrence may be dodged. Back away from the tree for a distance of at least five metres and stand behind another tree for added protection. Never stand near a tree as it falls because too many dangerous things happen near the stump.

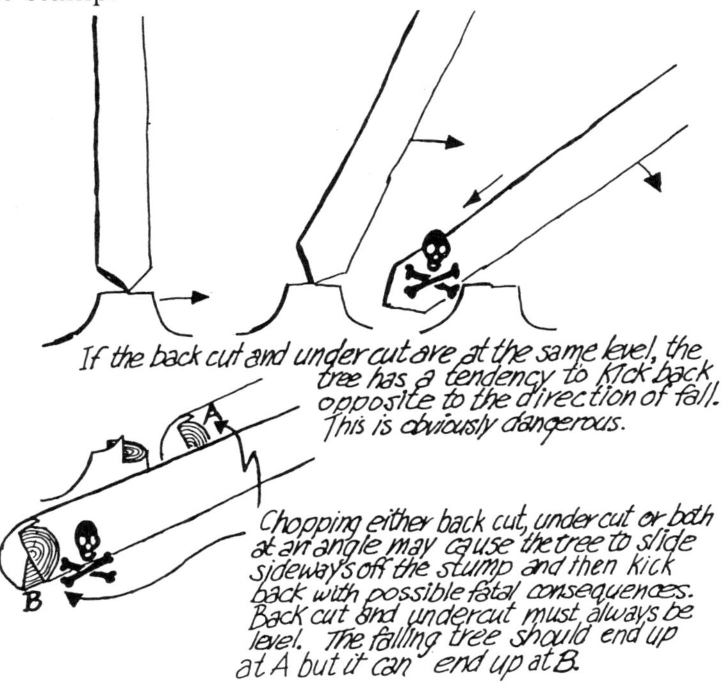

The hazards of an improperly made cut.

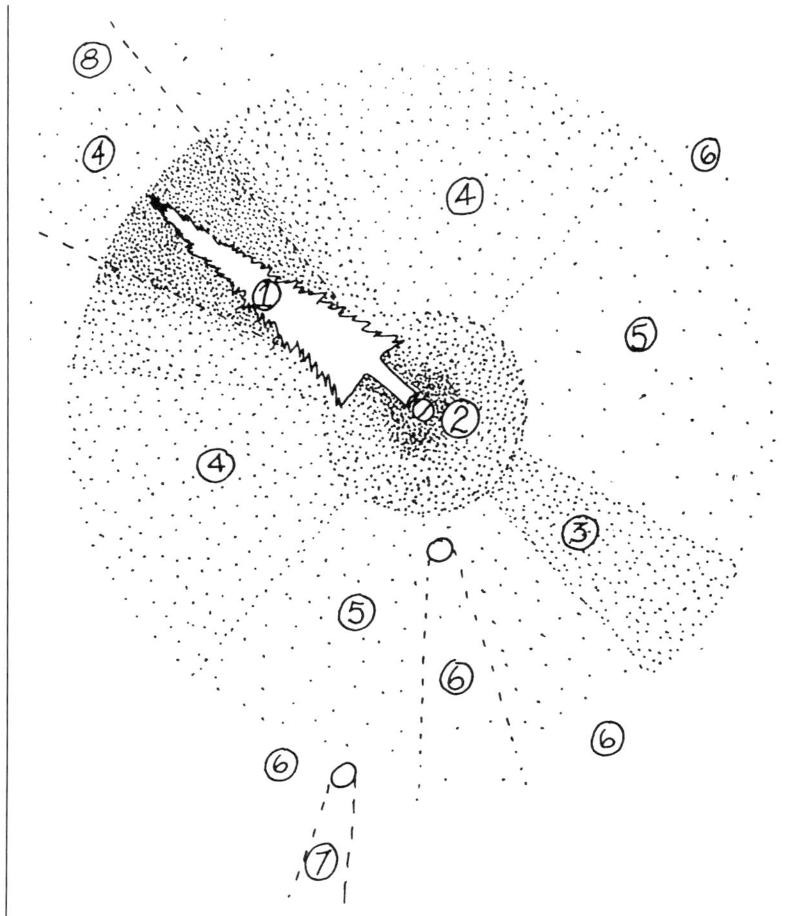

Safe and hazardous areas relative to a falling tree.
1. Most hazardous where the tree actually falls.
2. Next most hazardous in the general area of the stump.
3. A tree often falls opposite to the intended direction.
4. Some hazard.
5. Relatively safe.
6. The safest area within the reach of the tree is behind a protective tree in the safe sector, or outside the reach in the opposite direction from the tree's fall.
7. The safest of all is behind a protective tree, outside the falling tree's reach and opposite to its direction of fall, but on one side.
8. Being beyond the reach of the tree is relatively safe except for the domino effect. The falling tree may knock down other trees.

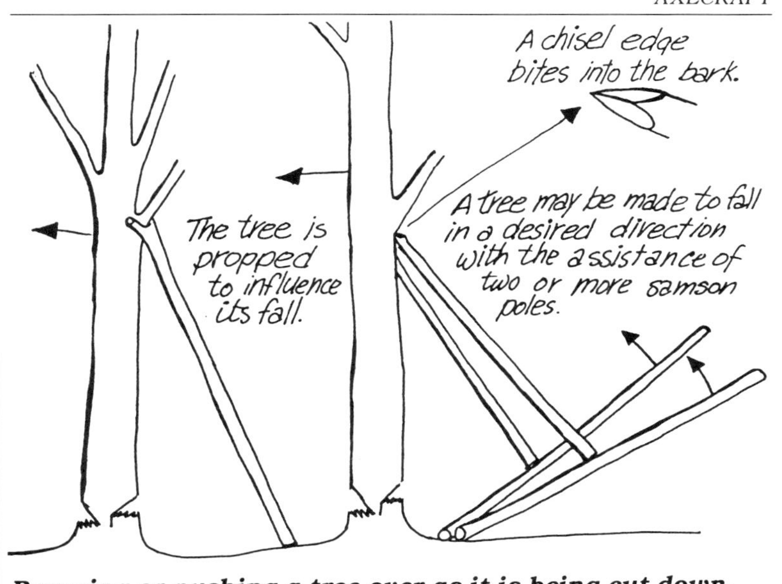

Propping or pushing a tree over as it is being cut down.

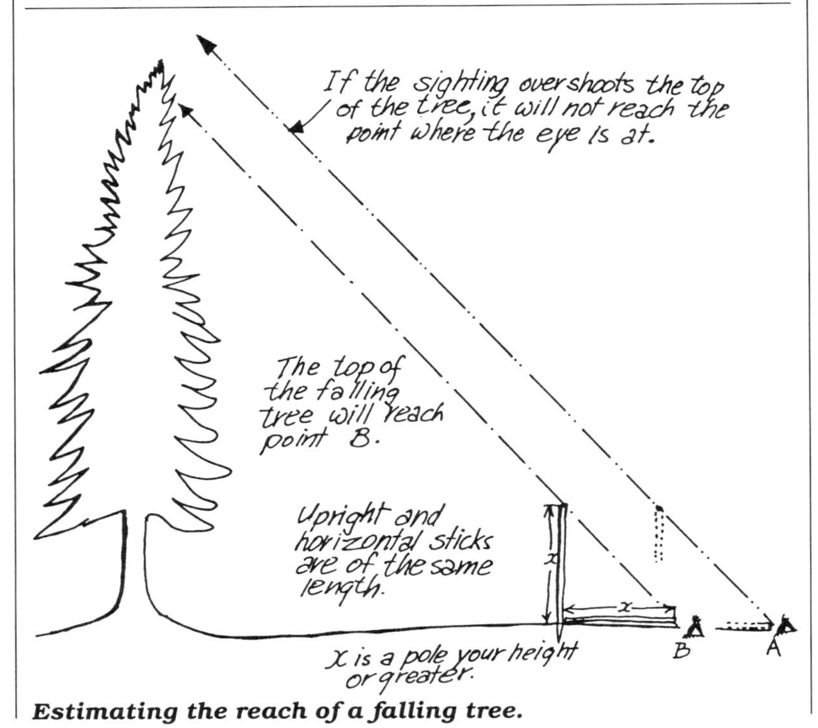

Estimating the reach of a falling tree.

Limbing and Sectioning

It is easier to limb a tree by cutting towards its top, if the limbs point upward. Black spruce is the exception, as the branches tend to point downward. Limbing is best done on the far side of the tree, using the tree itself as a barrier between the axe and your legs. If you limb on the same side, chop so that the axe is swung away from you or the cut is made behind you.

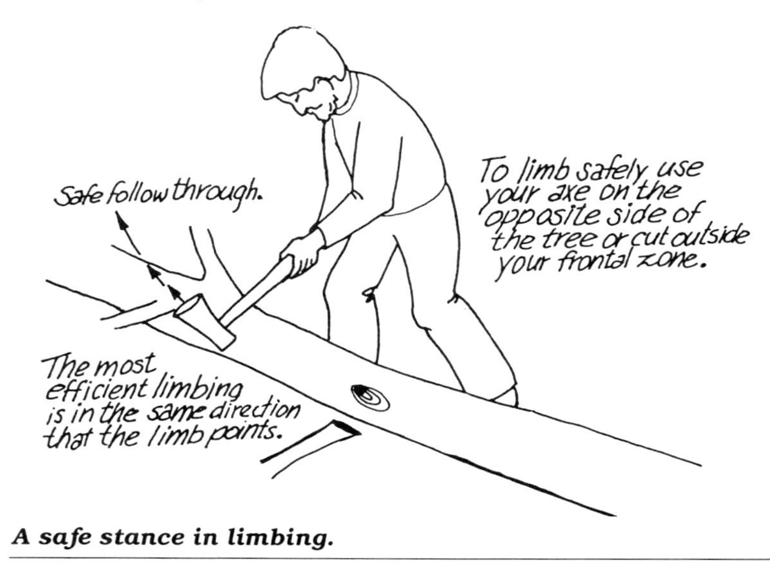

A safe stance in limbing.

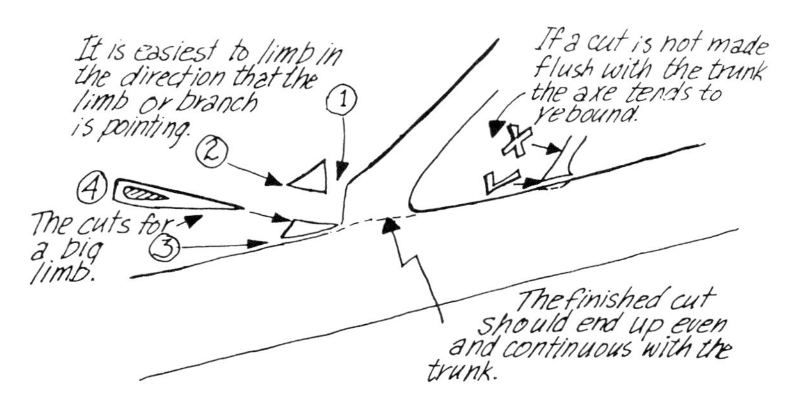

Techniques in limbing.

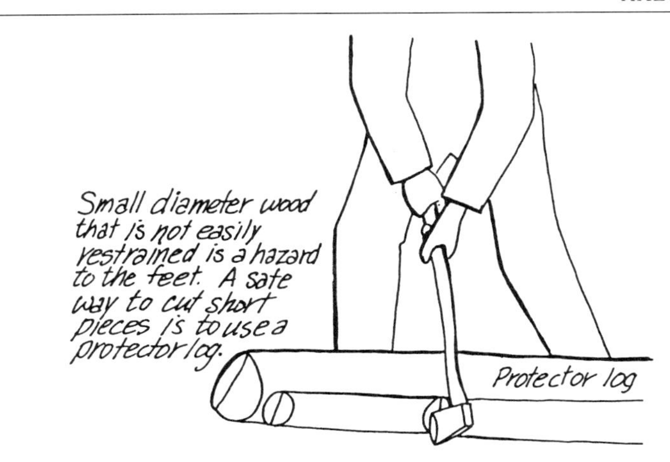

Using a protector log.

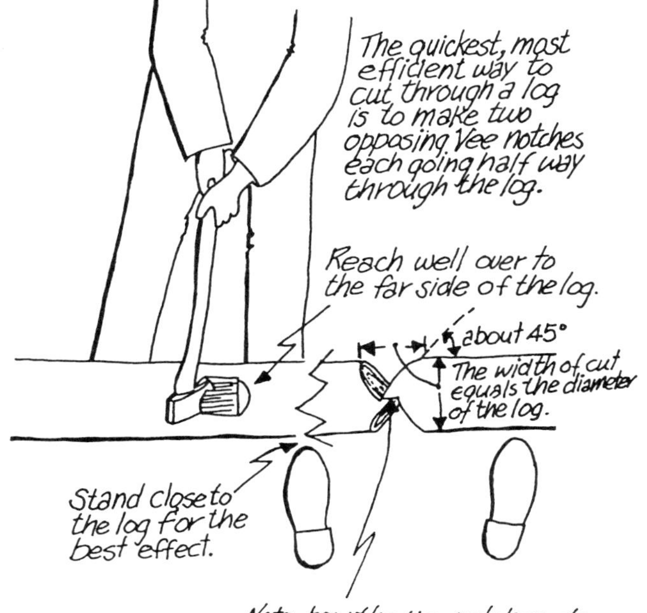

Using a safe stance in cutting through a log.

Standing on a log to chop through it.

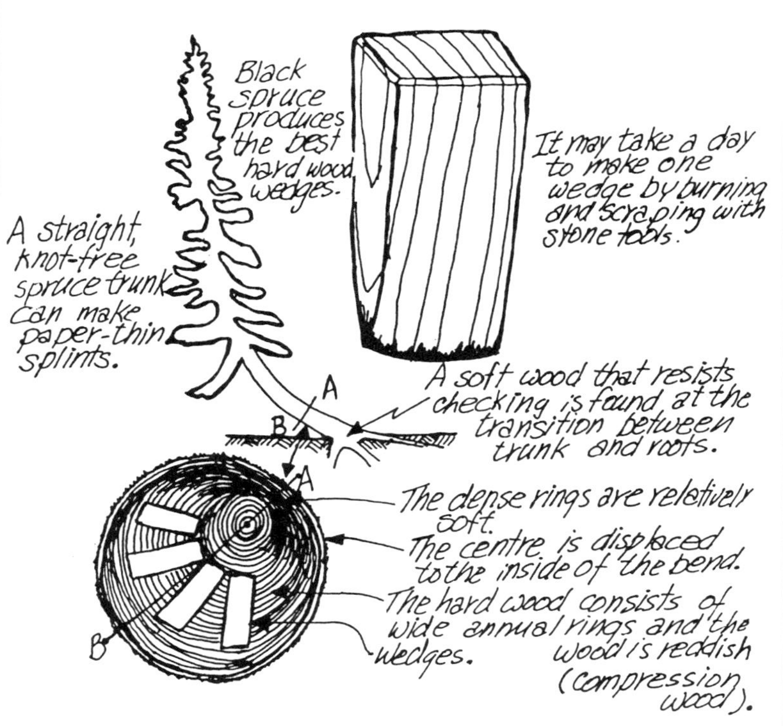

The source of black spruce compression wood wedges.

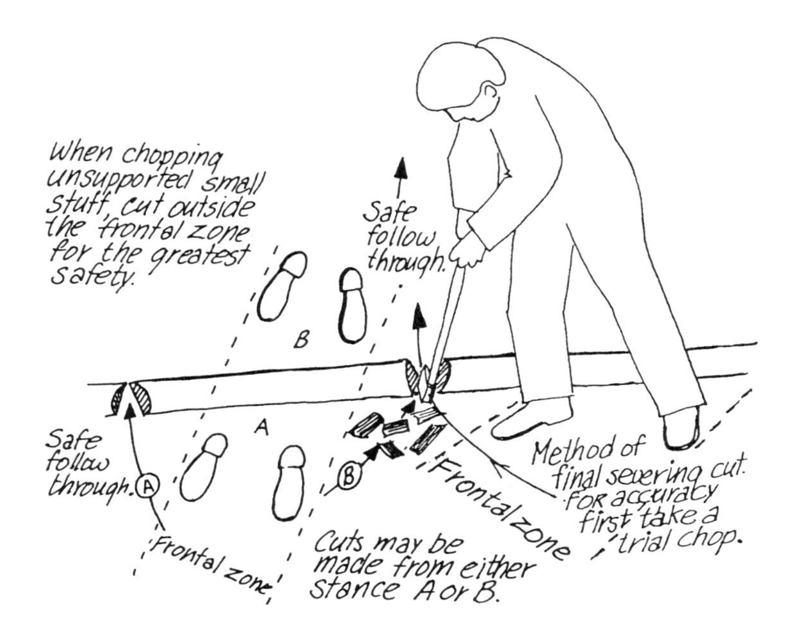

Safe cuts outside the frontal zone.

To section a log, it is easier to cut it half-way through from opposite sides rather than cut it all the way through from the top. A stance with legs well apart is taken as close to the log as the length of the axe handle will permit, being careful not to have the toes protrude under the log. Standing too far back may cause you to over-shoot the log, especially with a smaller axe. Standing on top of a log or steadying it with the foot, may result in a cut to the instep unless the point of impact of the axe is kept well below the boot sole. When sectioning smaller logs into firewood use a barrier log between your feet and the log being cut.

The width of the cut should be equal to the diameter of the log. The cuts are made at an angle of 45 degrees to the log's centre line. If the log is of a large diameter, a smaller notch is made and then enlarged, or the chips will not dislodge easily.

The simplest way to split a log is to use wooden wedges. Three or more wedges used at the same time last longer. A large log may be easily split by using a small hatchet to make and tap in wedges.

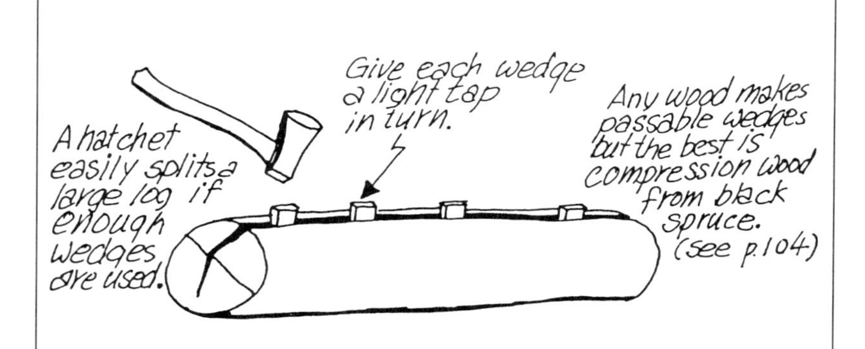

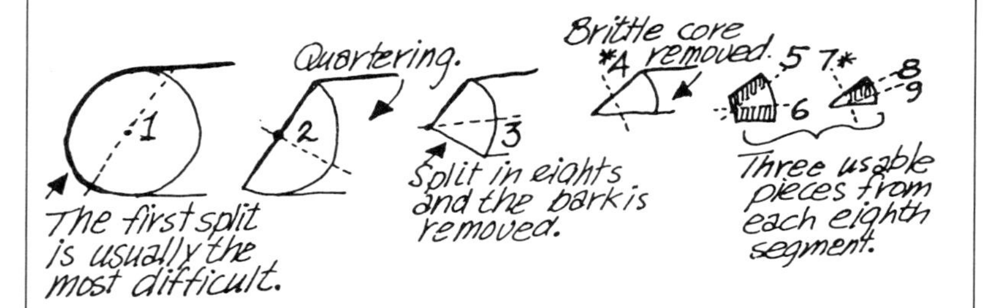

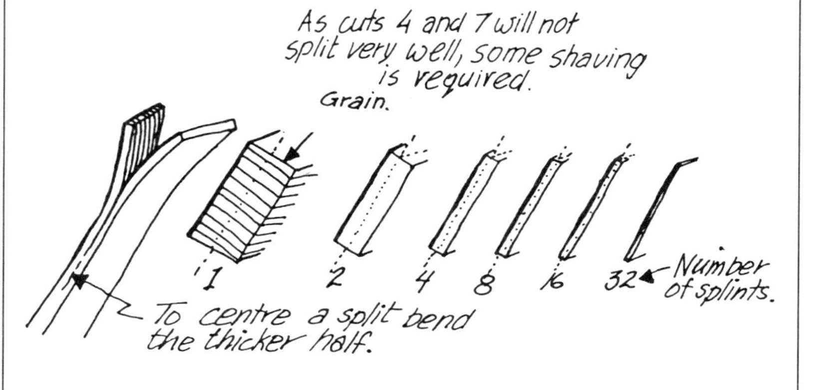

Making splints from black spruce wood.

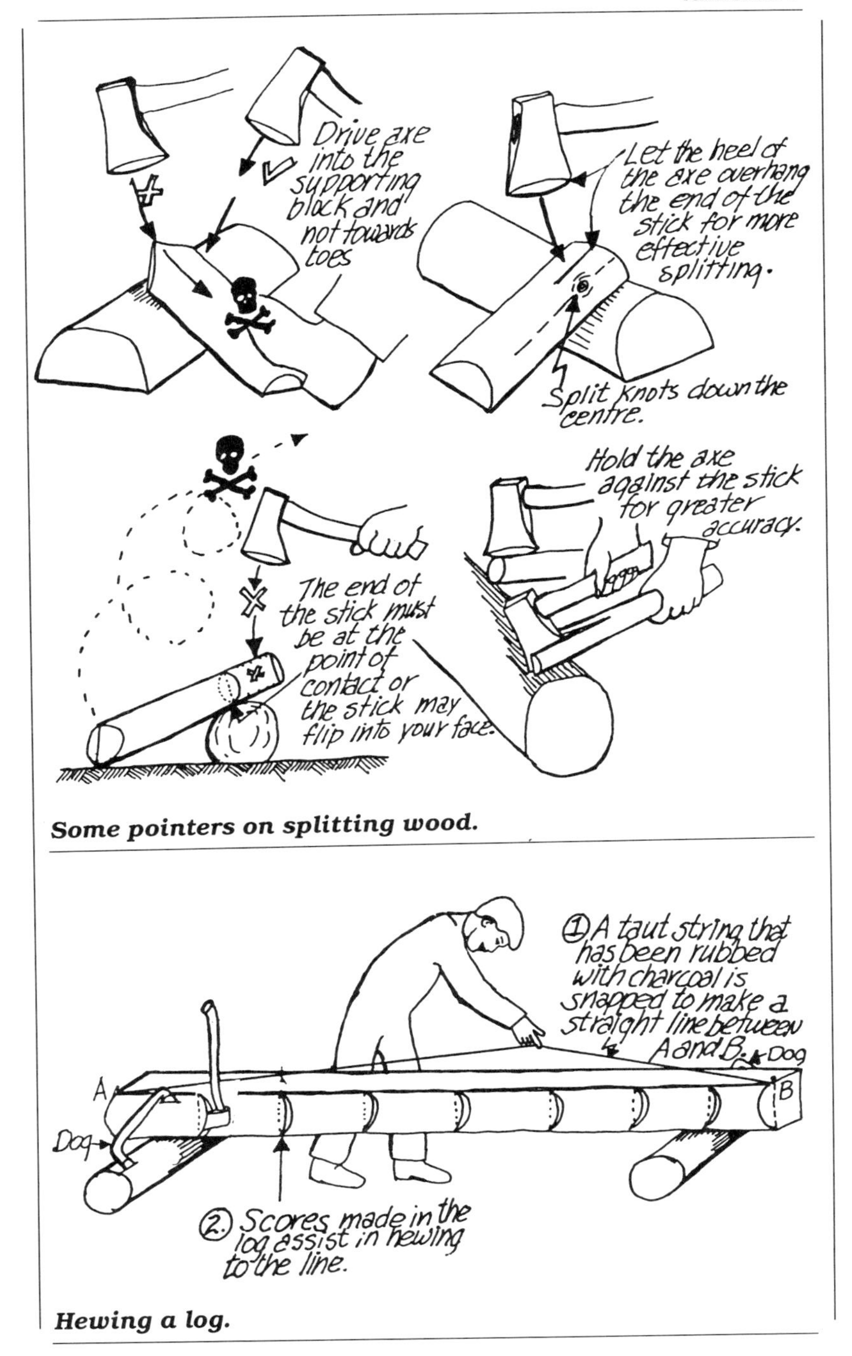

Some pointers on splitting wood.

Hewing a log.

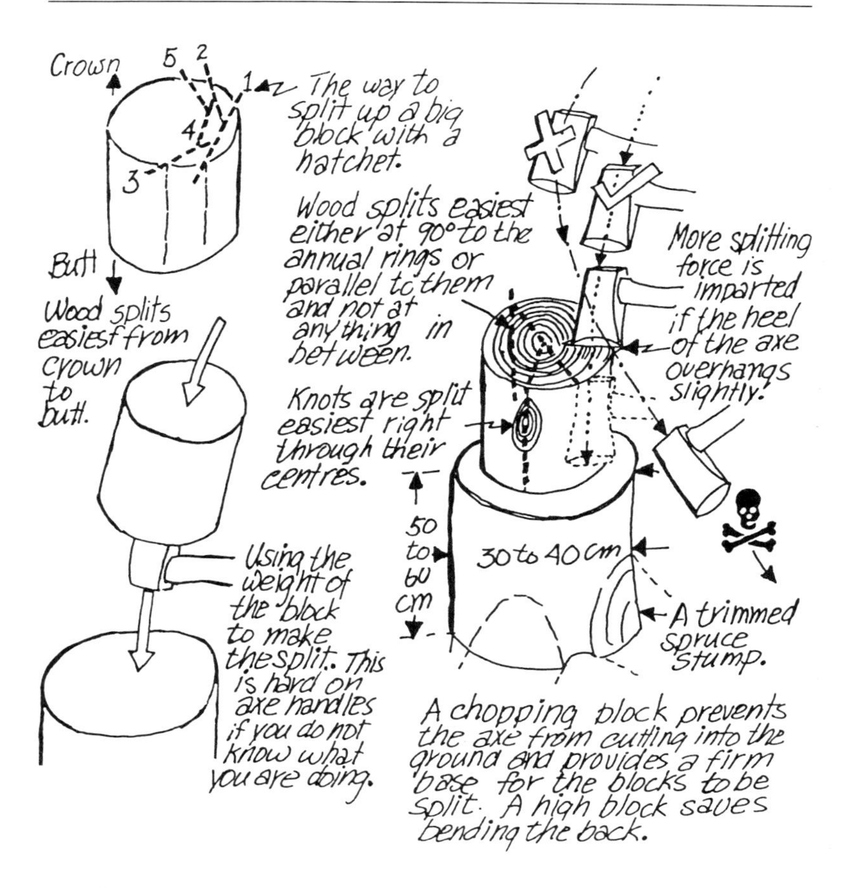

Making difficult splits in wood blocks.

3

KNIFECRAFT

The knife is the smallest and most portable of all the cutting tools. Light and unobtrusive, the knife is readily available for hundreds of everyday tasks in bush living.

THE BUSH KNIFE

The general-purpose bush knife should have a blade as long as the width of the palm, although blades half or twice this length are within acceptable limits. A blade five centimetres long would be an excellent survival knife except for being too small to fall and limb trees of wrist-thickness. A blade 10 to 15 centimetres long will do intricate work like carving a netting needle, yet be large enough to present a good target for a baton when cutting down small trees. A blade 20 centimetres long is a superior tool for heavy work, but awkward to use for fine work.

All general-use knives should have the blade tip close to the profile center line of the handle. The back of the handle and the back of the blade should be on the same line. The back of the blade should not be thinned down or sharpened so that a baton can be used more effectively without being cut up. There is absolutely no advantage to a two-edged blade in bush living.

The blade should be of a good quality carbon steel, from two and a half to three millimetres thick and about two to two and a half centimetres wide. This size of blade is light in weight, yet difficult to break. The steel should be soft enough to be maintained at a shaving edge with common sharpening tools, without frequent sharpening. Such steel is found in Mora (Sweden), Solingen (Germany) or Sheffield (England) knives. Carbon, unlike stainless steel, can be used as the striker in the flint and steel method of fire-lighting. Inexpensive stainless steels have had a bad reputation with respect to producing a keen edge let alone holding it. The Mora stainless steels however, are every bit as good as their carbon steels.

The metal of the knife blade should extend for the full-length of the handle (a full tang) for strength. The handle should be a durable, water-resistant material that can be shaped to the user's hand if necessary. The knife should

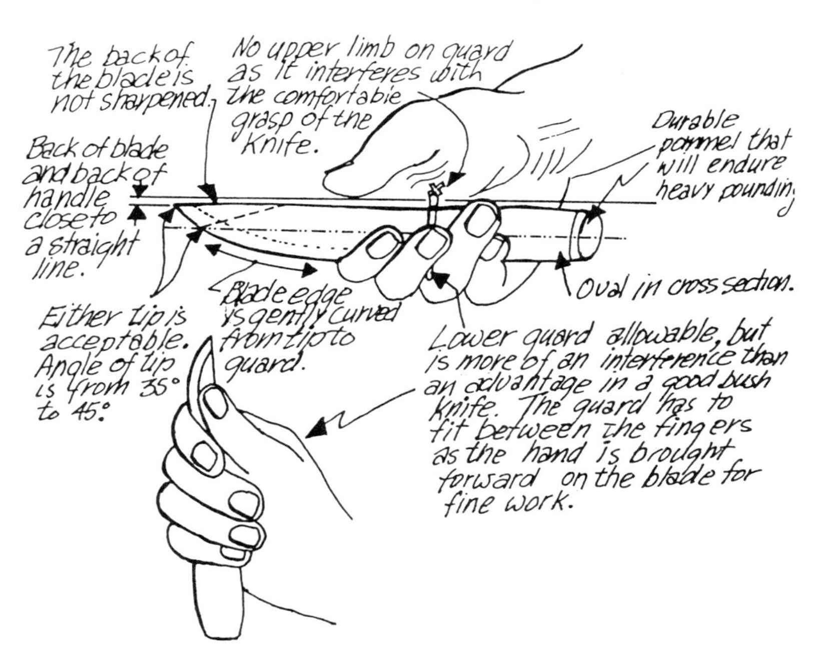

Some desirable features of a general purpose bush knife. *For fine work and incising, the knife blade is held firmly to prevent any movement of the hand relative to the blade.*

have a strong pommel that will protect the handle if the knife is driven tip first deep into wood.

The curvature of the cutting edge should extend for the full-length of the blade. This cuts well and is one of the best shapes that quickly sharpens to a razor's edge. The knife blade should have a sharp enough point to penetrate deep into wood with a minimum of effort.

The knife handle should be about as long as the width of your palm. A handle that is too thick or too thin fatigues the hand and causes blisters. The cross-section of the handle should be oval instead of round or rectangular. An oval handle provides an adequate indication of the direction of the cutting edge and raises fewer blisters than handles with angular or rounded corners.

A guard on a bush knife is in the way and detracts from many operations. It prevents the use of a simple, secure, deep sheath. Some people prefer a guard for fear of slipping forward onto the knife edge, but unless the knife is used for stabbing, the hand should never slip in this way. In all my years of instructing I do not recall an injury due to the lack of a guard.

As a test of strength, a good knife should not break when driven four centimetres into a standing tree at right angles to the grain, and the handle bears your weight as you stand on it.

First Aid for Knife Cuts

The more you learn about using a knife, the less likely you are to cut yourself.

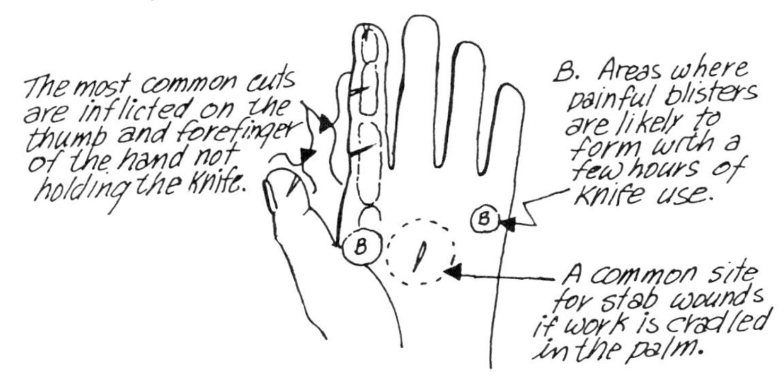

Common knife cuts to the hands.

Keep your hands and knife clean. Always have a first aid kit handy that contains some means for wound closure, non-sticking dressing and an antibiotic (opthalmic) ointment. The faster you close a wound or cover it and exclude the oxygen, the less pain and the quicker it should heal.

There are two common knife cuts. The first is straight in creating a gaping wound. For faster healing, this type of wound should be closed. Modern adhesives are so effective that sewing may not be necessary. A gaping wound can heal from the bottom up, but takes longer. This is the preferred

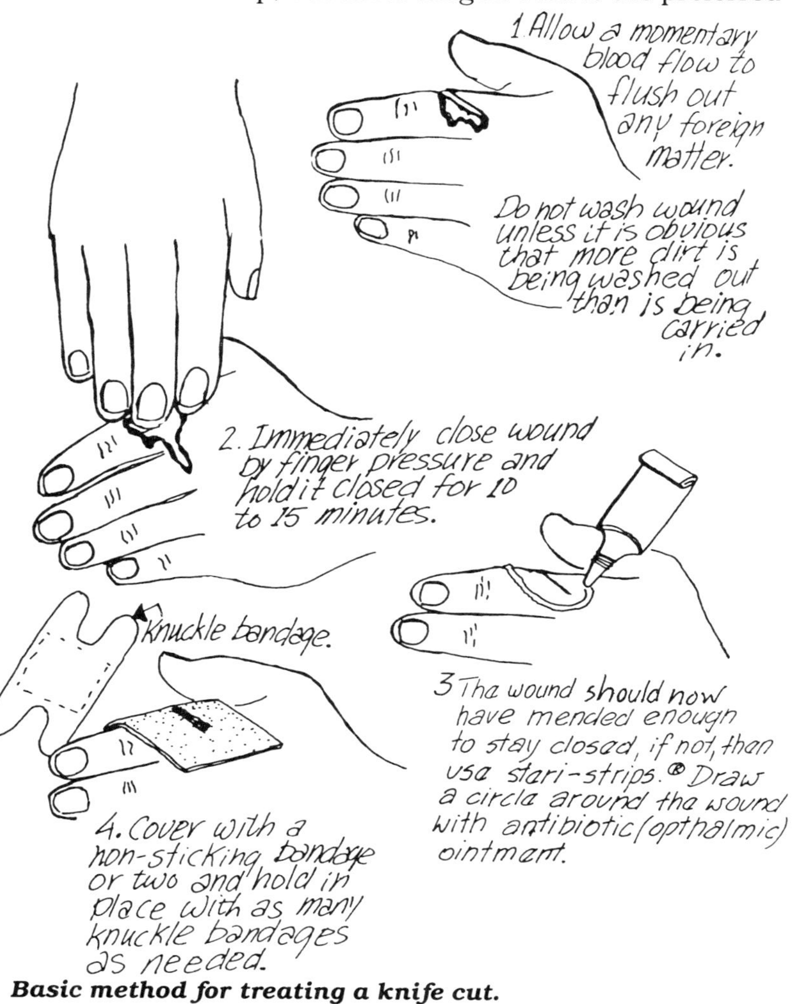

1. Allow a momentary blood flow to flush out any foreign matter.
Do not wash wound unless it is obvious that more dirt is being washed out than is being carried in.
2. Immediately close wound by finger pressure and hold it closed for 10 to 15 minutes.
Knuckle bandage.
3 The wound should now have mended enough to stay closed, if not, than use stari-strips.® Draw a circle around the wound with antibiotic (opthalmic) ointment.
4. Cover with a non-sticking bandage or two and hold in place with as many knuckle bandages as needed.

Basic method for treating a knife cut.

method if the wound is contaminated with dirt or the cut is made under water. The second type of wound is a flap made by an oblique cut, which is easy to close with simple pressure. Should any foreign matter get under the flap, pus formation will prevent healing.

For any cut, the prime concern is to stop bleeding immediately by applying pressure and elevating the wound. Simple direct pressure should be sufficient to arrest any bleeding from a knife cut without having to apply pressure against a blood vessel some distance from the wound.

When a cut occurs, it should be allowed to bleed for a moment. This action flushes out any foreign matter that may have entered on the cutting edge. Some people react by sucking on their cut—a bad practice considering the undesirable germs found in the mouth that may contaminate the wound. Next, without a moment's delay the edges of the wound should be brought together and pressed closed. If a non-sticking pad is quickly applied to exclude oxygen, the pain of the cut will be reduced. Should excessive seepage occur through any pads, leave them in place, add more and apply more pressure. In a severe cut, pressure may have to be maintained for at least a half-hour. Once the pressure is released and there is no further blood flow, leave the pads in place for a few hours. Non-sticking pads should come off without reopening the wound.

If the area of the wound is reasonably clean, do not wash it, especially to remove dried blood,as you will only cause a greater contamination of the wound. Wash a wound only if there will be more infectious material removed than might be carried in. Instead, draw a circle around the wound with an antibiotic ointment and cover with a non-sticking pad. On retiring, replace the more durable daytime dressing with a loose airy one that is less restricting and allows more air circulation. Whenever possible remove everything and expose the wound to the sun. An increased intake of vitamin C (rose hips) also promotes healing.

With conventional bandages keep in mind the ease of removal when they have to be replaced. It is counterproductive to rip the wound open when putting on a fresh dressing.

When nothing else is available, cover the wound immediately with a clean cloth well-smeared with the resin found in the bark blisters of balsam fir or Porsild's white spruce. This dressing is left on until the wound has healed as it is unlikely that pus will form under it.

Cutting Down Trees with a Knife

Any green tree can be cut down with a knife if it can be bent. A wrist-thick tree can be bent with one hand while the other is occupied in cutting it. Larger trees are softened by flexing them back and forth a few times using the weight of your body. Two people can tackle larger trees if one does the bending while the other carries out the cutting.

After the tree is bent, the cut is made at a fairly steep angle at the point of the greatest bend. The bending action puts tension on the wood fibers and opens the cut to allow the blade to slice through the wood more easily. As the cut nears completion, the tree must be restrained from falling too soon and breaking, or extra effort is required to finish the cut.

Dry or frozen trees are difficult to cut down with a knife. A frozen tree will break easier if the fracture is started with a cut while the tree is bent.

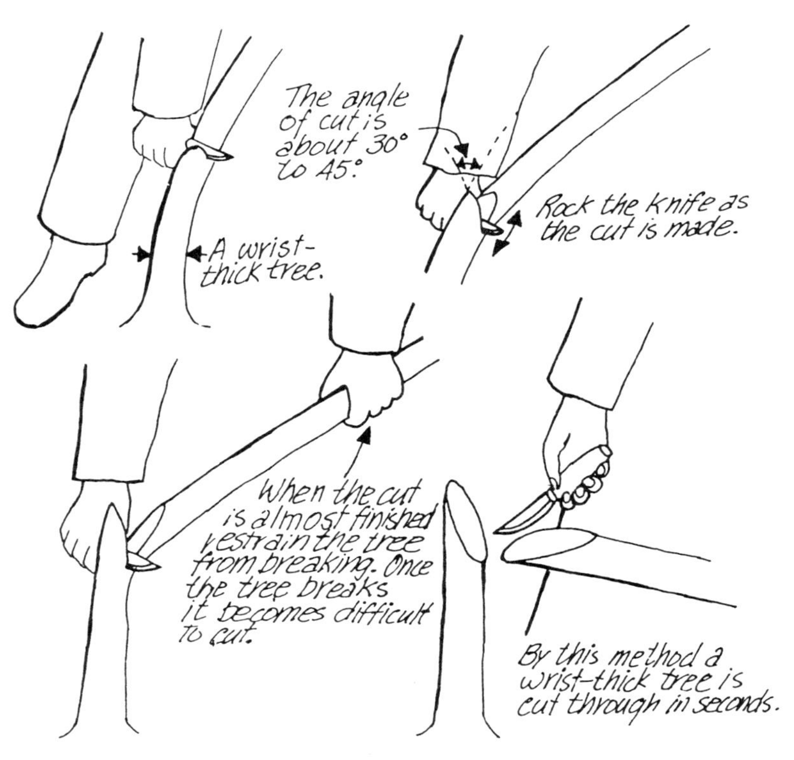

Cutting down a tree with a knife.

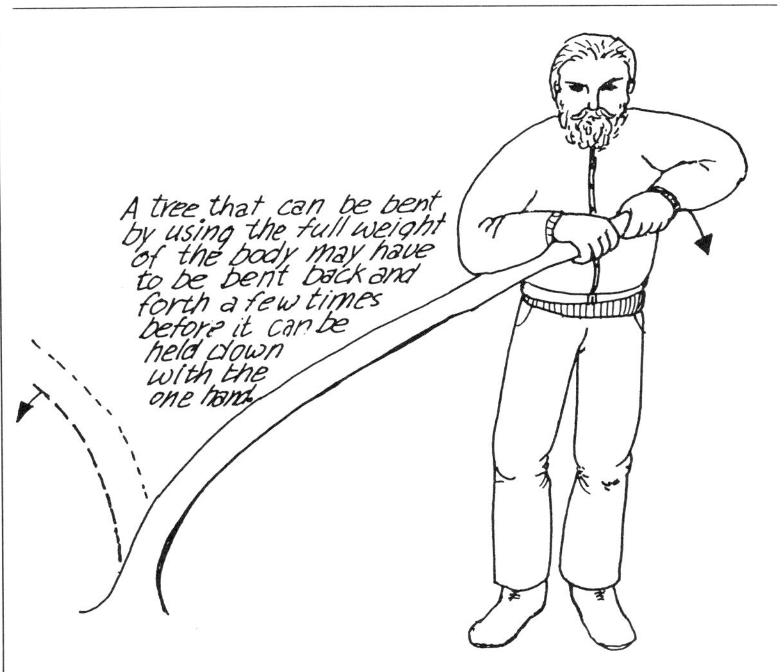

Bending a tree.

Limbing with a baton.

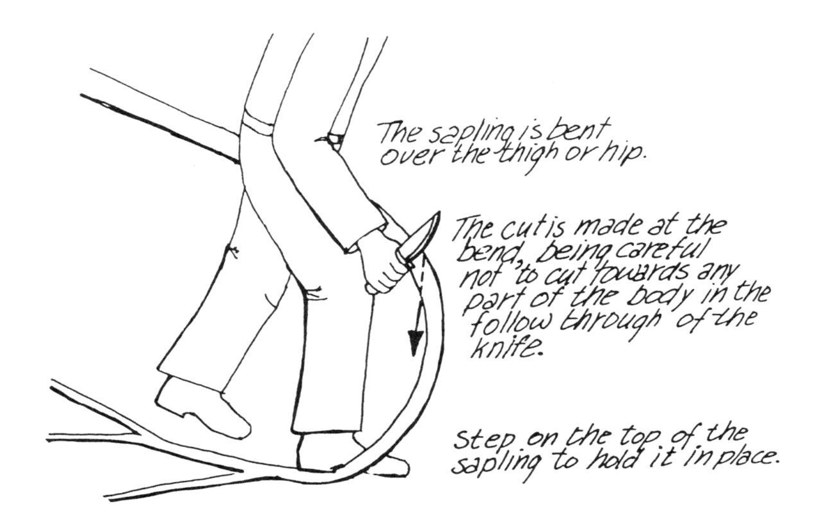

Cutting the top off a sapling.

A knife makes a poor chopping tool as it has no weight behind it. However, if the knife back is struck with something heavy, it can make respectable cuts. Any sound, heavy stick (baton) that is comfortable to hold, will assist a knife in cutting down and limbing small trees, splitting wood and making many cutting operations easier and faster. Trees about ten centimetres in diameter and too thick to bend can be cut down in a few minutes with a baton.

The knife used with a baton must be sturdy enough to withstand the abuse or it will bend or break. Using a folding knife puts a severe strain on the blade pin.

Various Safe Knife Operations

One method for cutting through a stick is to make a series of nicks around it. A thick stick requires this procedure to be repeated a few times, each time cutting deeper. When the cut is half or two-thirds through the stick, it can be broken off and the end trimmed.

Peeling a stick is a basic technique that leads to skillful wood shaving. Peeled sticks dry out quickly and become lighter and tougher than unpeeled ones. Heavy knots and branches should be trimmed off beforehand, perhaps with

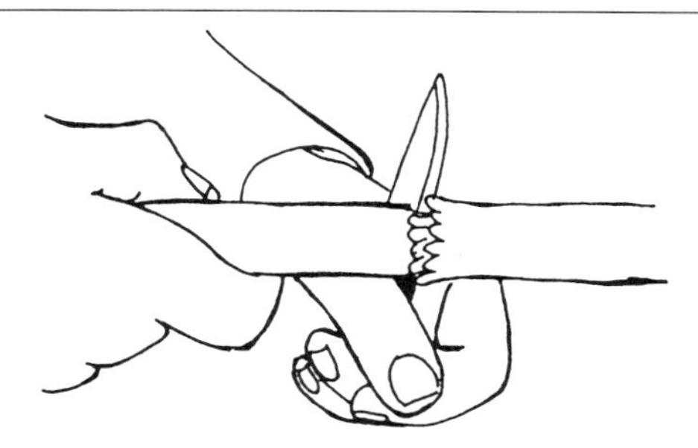

***Cutting through a stick.** Make a series of small cuts all around it. (For a large stick, this may be repeated a number of times.) Each time around, the blade can cut a little deeper. Once the cut is deep enough the stick may be broken. The fractured wood is trimmed off to complete the cut.*

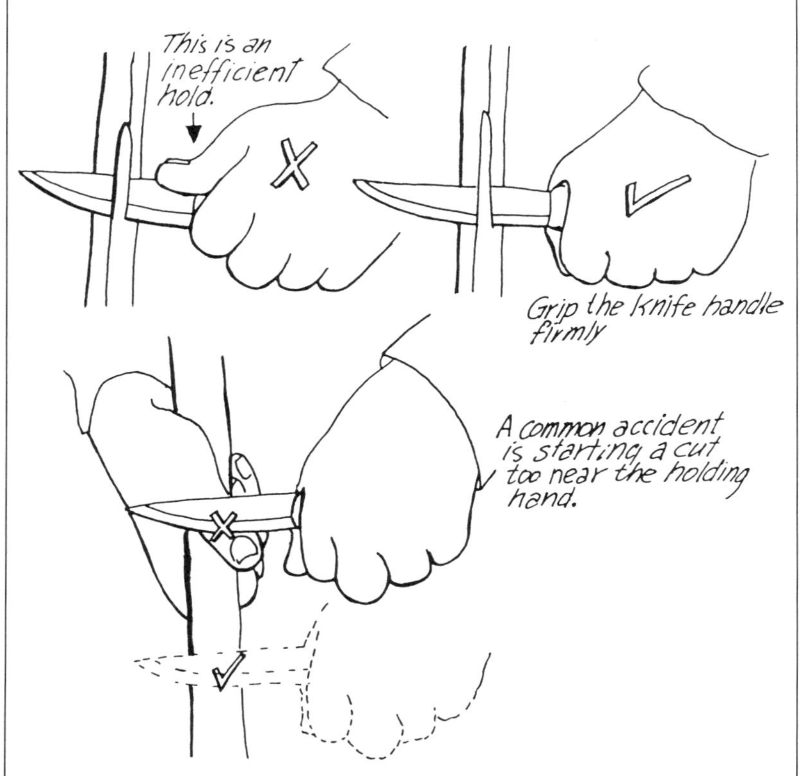

This is an inefficient hold.
Grip the knife handle firmly
A common accident is starting a cut too near the holding hand.

Peeling a stick with a knife.
Wrap fingers firmly around the handle and make strokes away from your body.

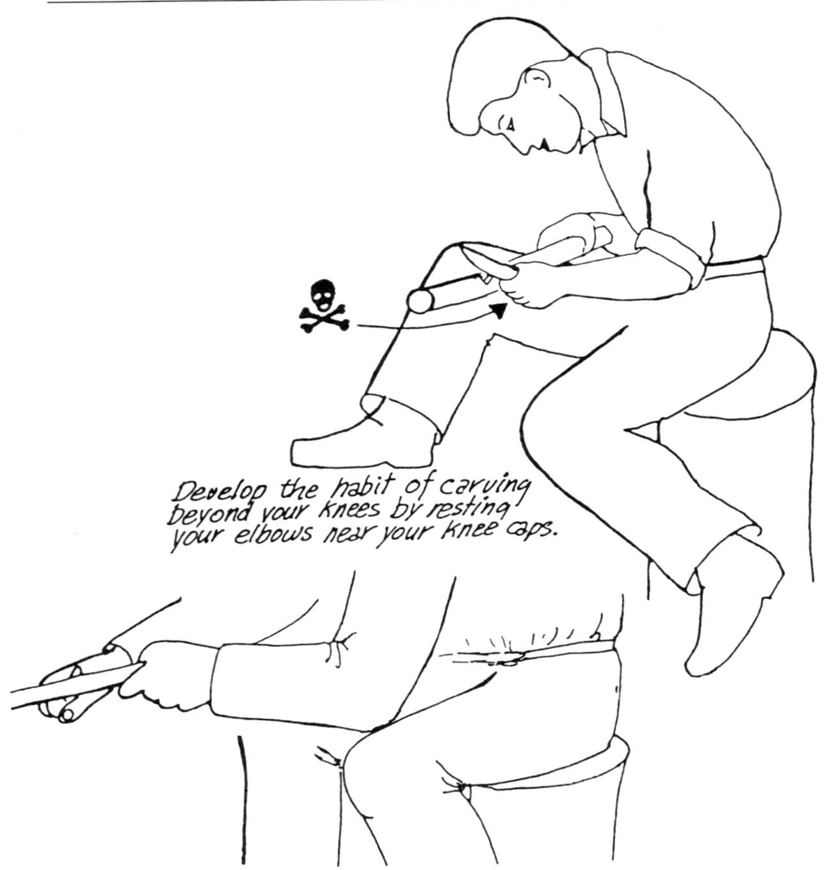

Proper carving technique.
Keep all cutting edges well away from the femoral artery.

the assistance of a baton. Small spruce saplings are a challenge to peel because of the many small knots. Use a short, forceful stroke, progressing down the stick in increments of a comfortable knife stroke of 30 to 50 centimetres. A tree your own height and pencil-thin at the small end can be peeled in a minute.

Holes cut through a stick with a knife have to be square or rectangular, as round ones drilled with a knife tip are poor and fuzzy. The diameter of a pole or stick is reduced by making parallel faces on opposite sides. If the stick is made too thin, it is weakened, if too thick, the hole is more difficult to make. Deep holes may be made by working from both

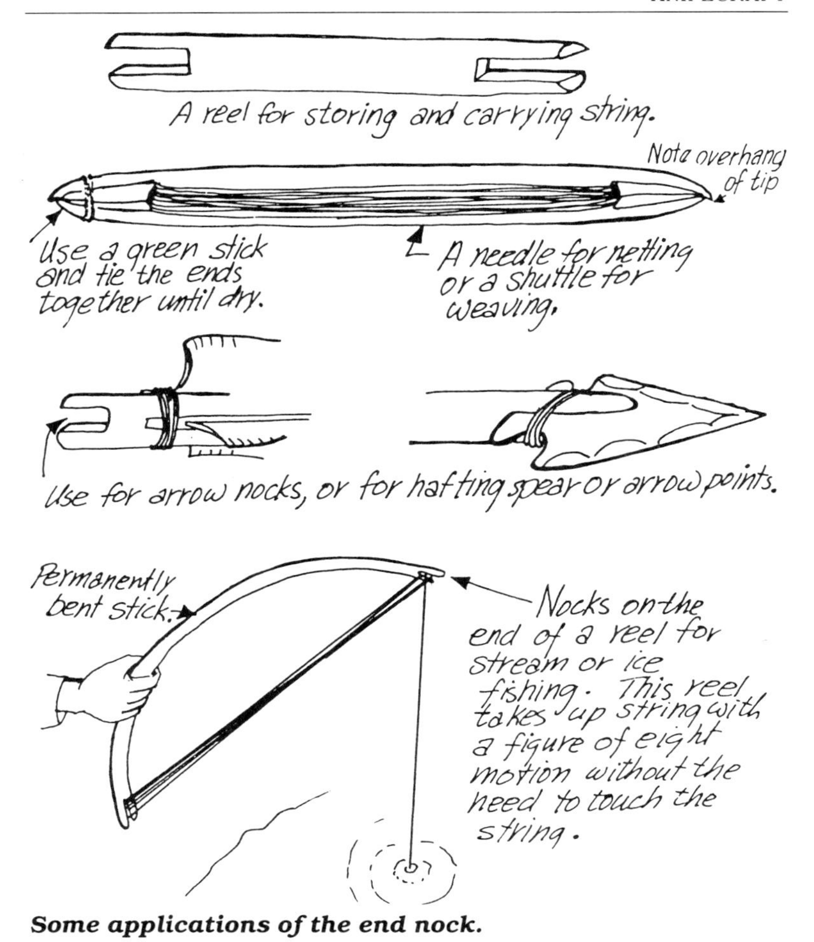

Some applications of the end nock.

sides. This is useful in fashioning the bow in the bow drill, when building choke bars in snaring, and in the construction of folk toys.

The end nock is a notch made on the end of a stick. It is used for hafting arrowheads or spear points on their shafts, for making netting needles or fishing reels.

A knife can provide the cutting edge for a form of shear to cut short pieces of sticks for a variety of applications or for trimming wands and spokes in basketry. The knife is driven into a wrist-thick limb just below a knot to prevent the limb from splitting. A V-notch is made to hold in place whatever needs cutting. If heavy cuts are made with a shear,

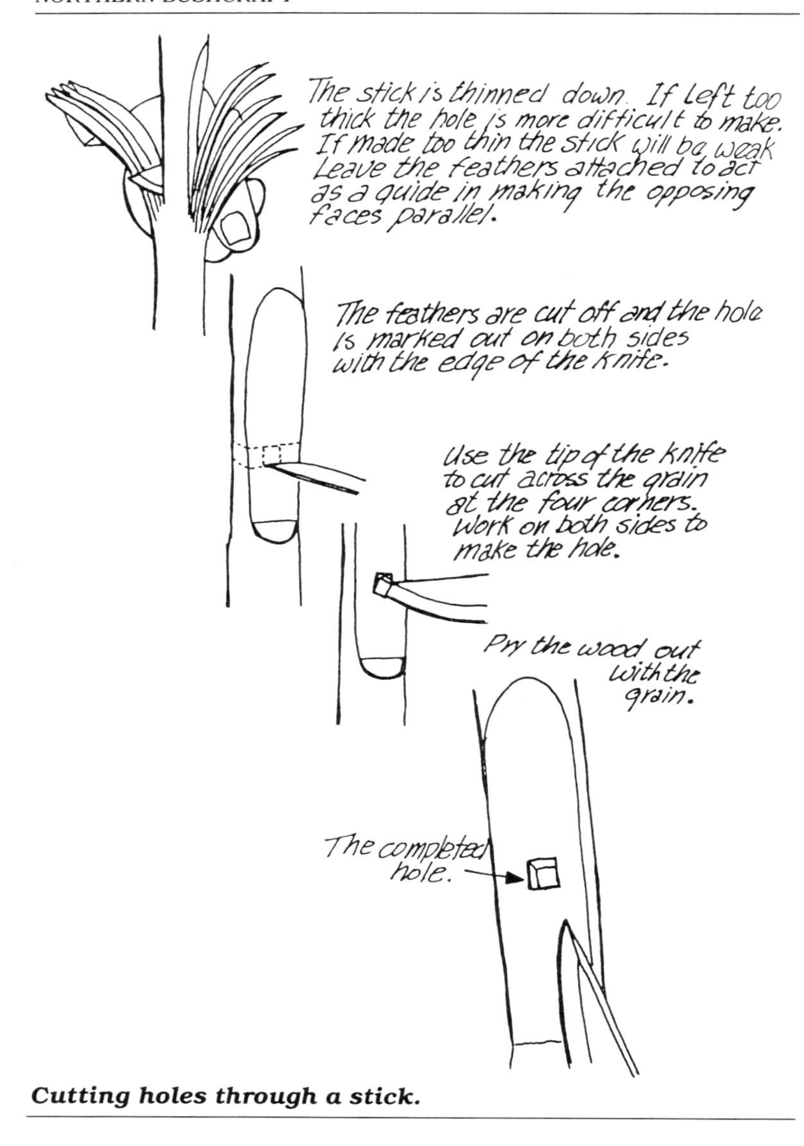

Cutting holes through a stick.

an insufficiently sturdy knife may bend at the handle.

To smooth down shafts, a form of sliding plane utilizes the knife blade as the plane iron.

A knife can be made into a strip cutter when combined with a guide. With the blade parallel to the guiding face, regular basket weaving splints, birch bark strips and leather

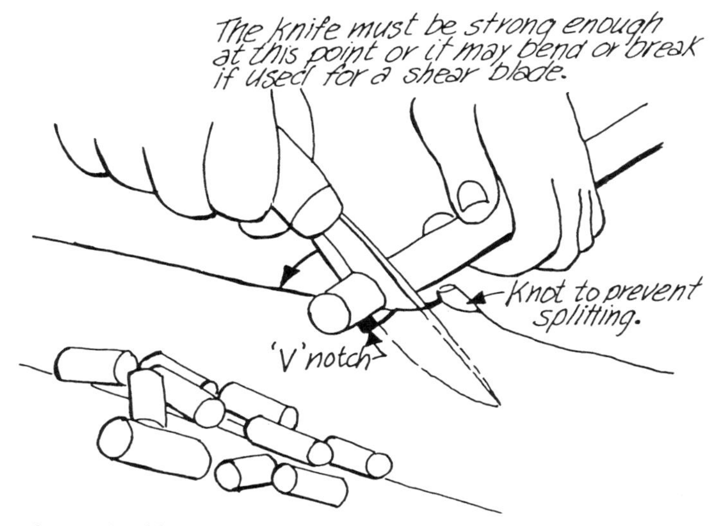

Using a knife as a shear.

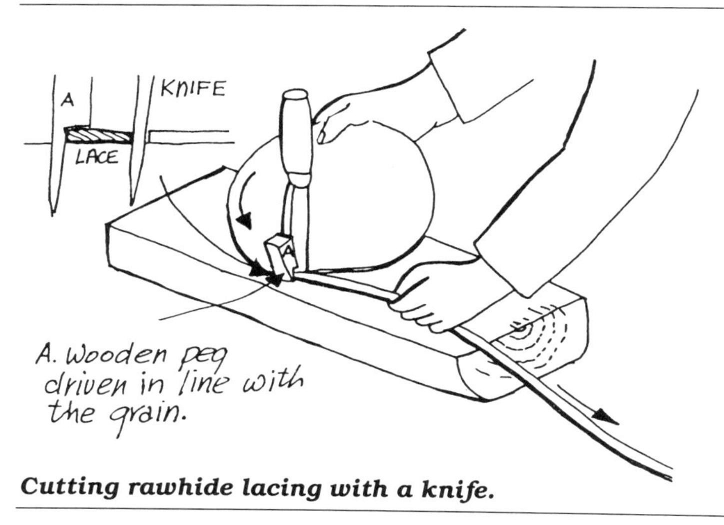

Cutting rawhide lacing with a knife.

or rawhide tongs can be made. If the knife is driven in at 90 degrees to the face of the guide, the knife tip can be used as a groover or router.

A sharp knife and a small baton can be used to cut or trim hair. To cut hair, tap strands of it against the sharp edge of the knife with the baton.

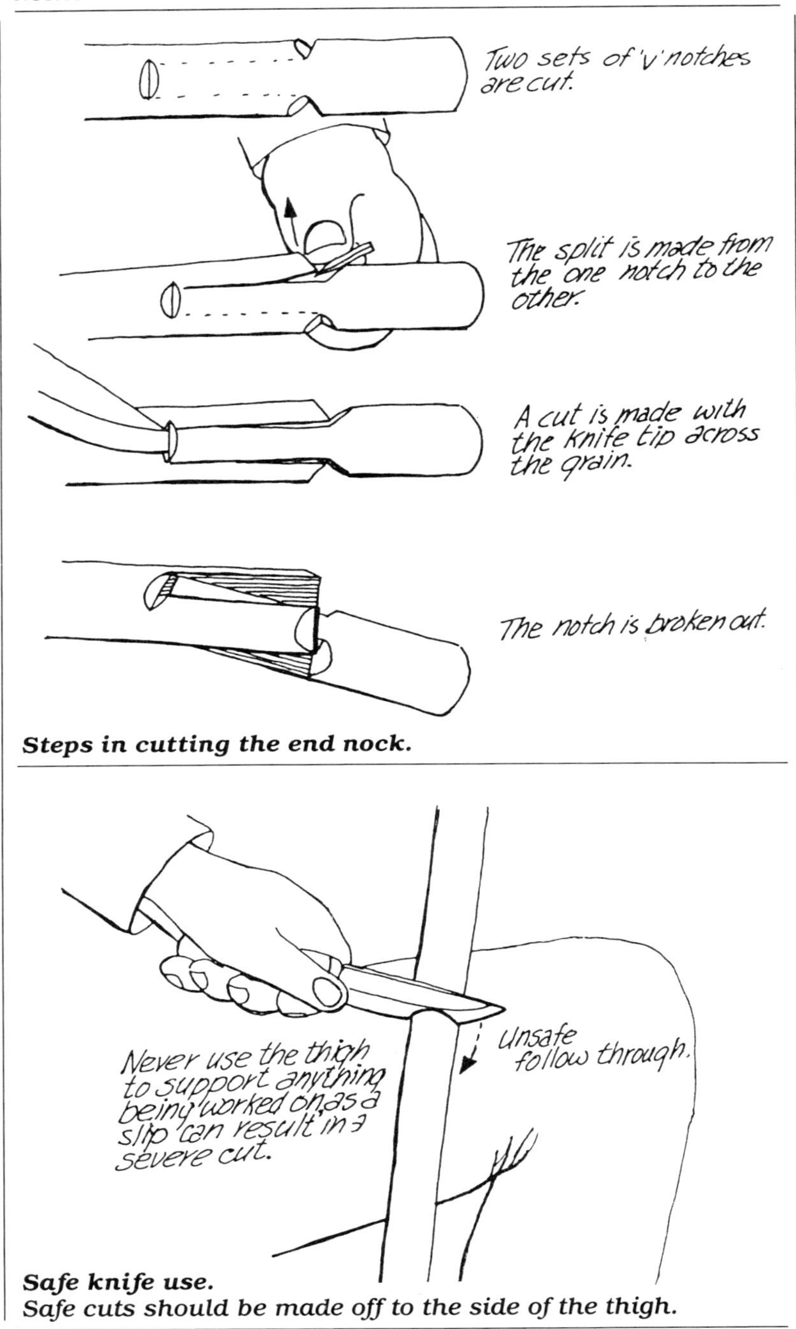

Steps in cutting the end nock.

Safe knife use.
Safe cuts should be made off to the side of the thigh.

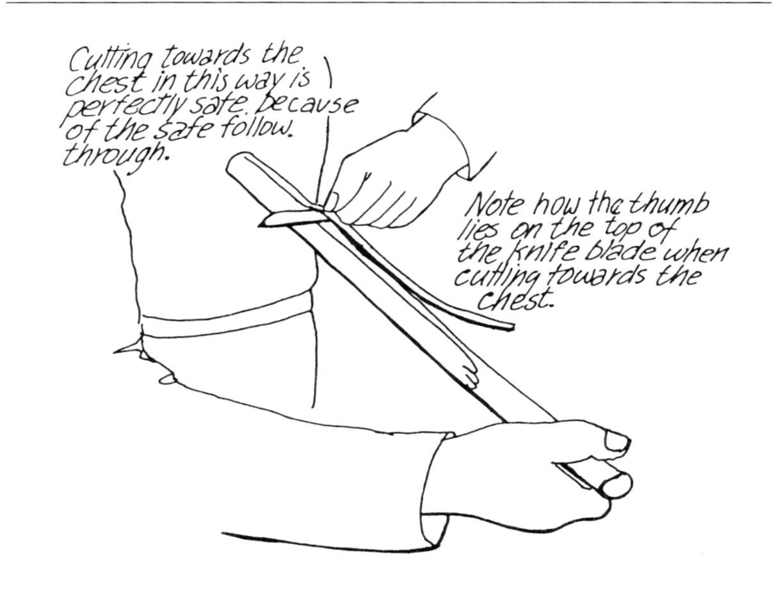

Safe knife operation—cutting toward the chest.

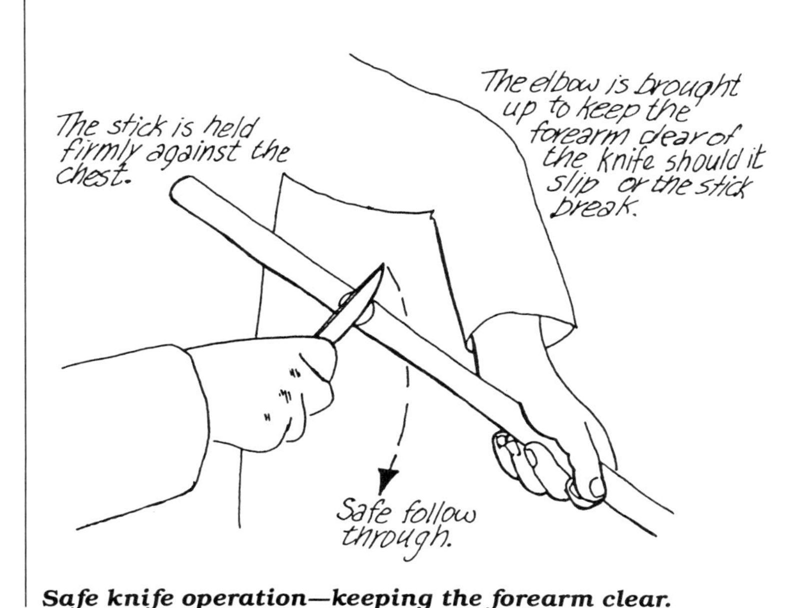

Safe knife operation—keeping the forearm clear.

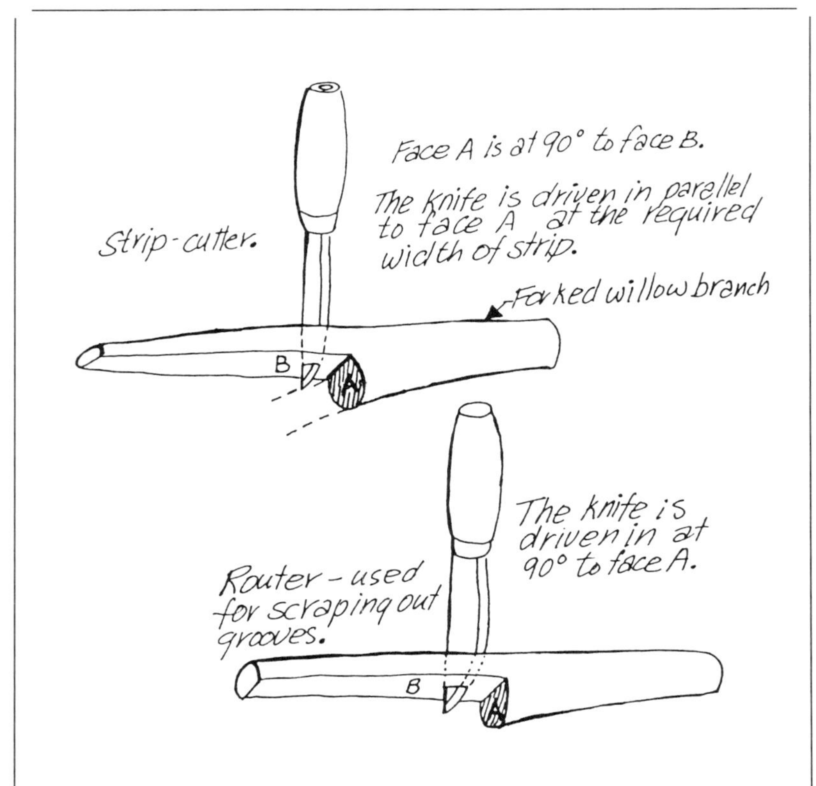

The strip cutter and router.

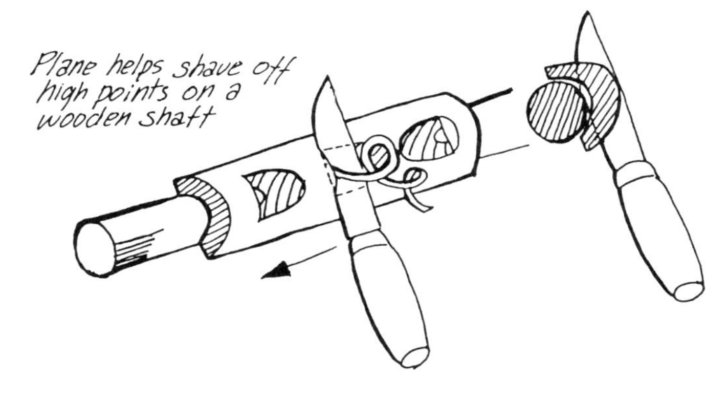

The knife plane.

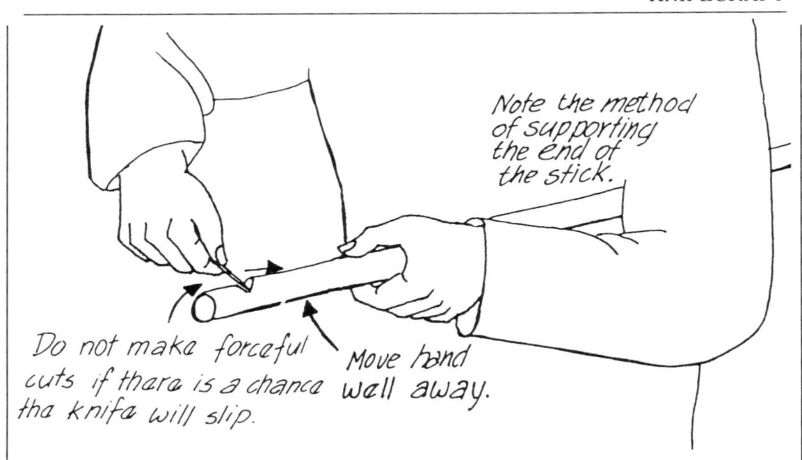

Safe knife operation—supporting the end of a stick.

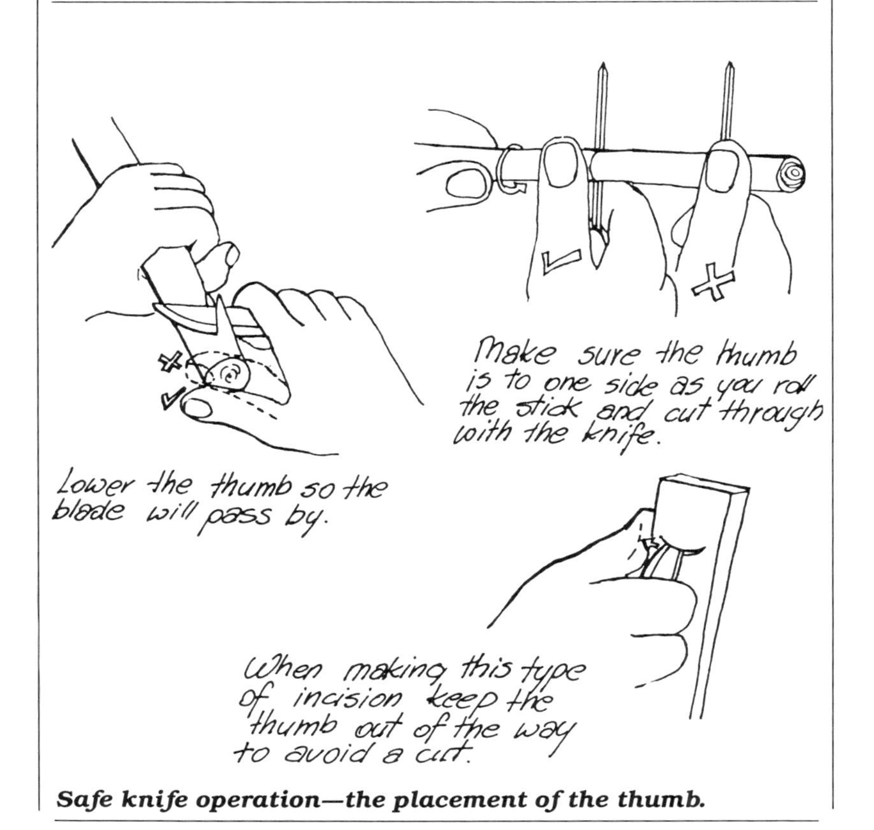

Safe knife operation—the placement of the thumb.

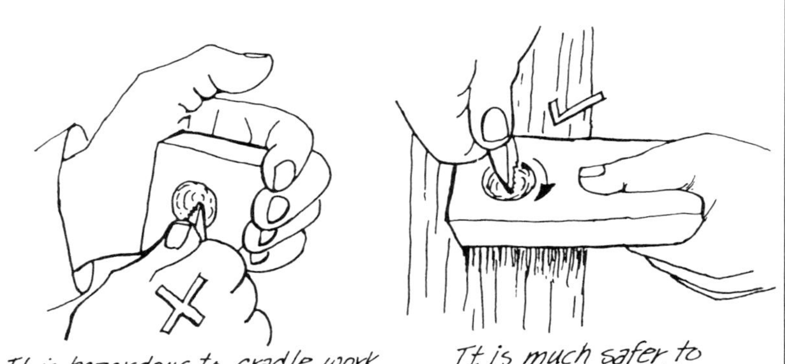

It is hazardous to cradle work in the palm of the hand when carving.
It is much safer to support your work on a log or the ground.

Safe knife operation—using a log support.

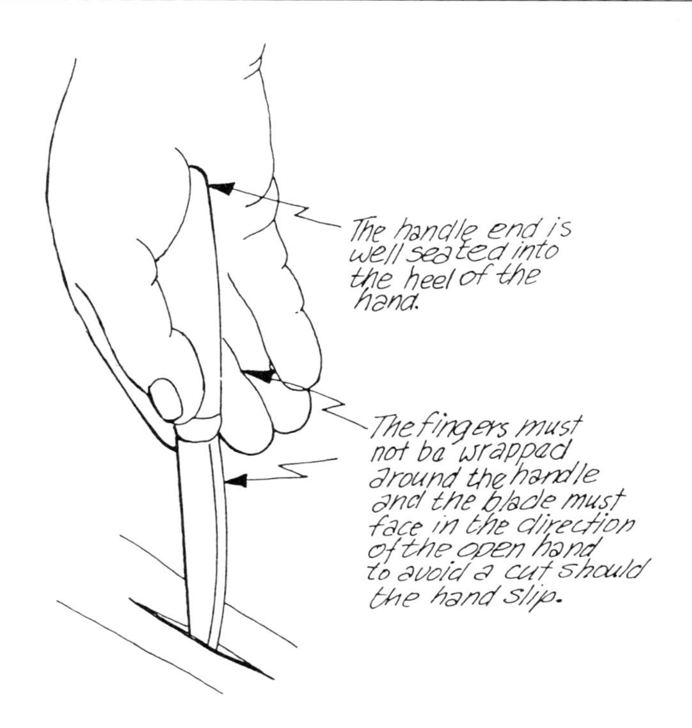

The handle end is well seated into the heel of the hand.
The fingers must not be wrapped around the handle and the blade must face in the direction of the open hand to avoid a cut should the hand slip.

Safe knife operation—making cuts across the grain in splitting with either a straight or folding knife.

Using the knife as a shear.

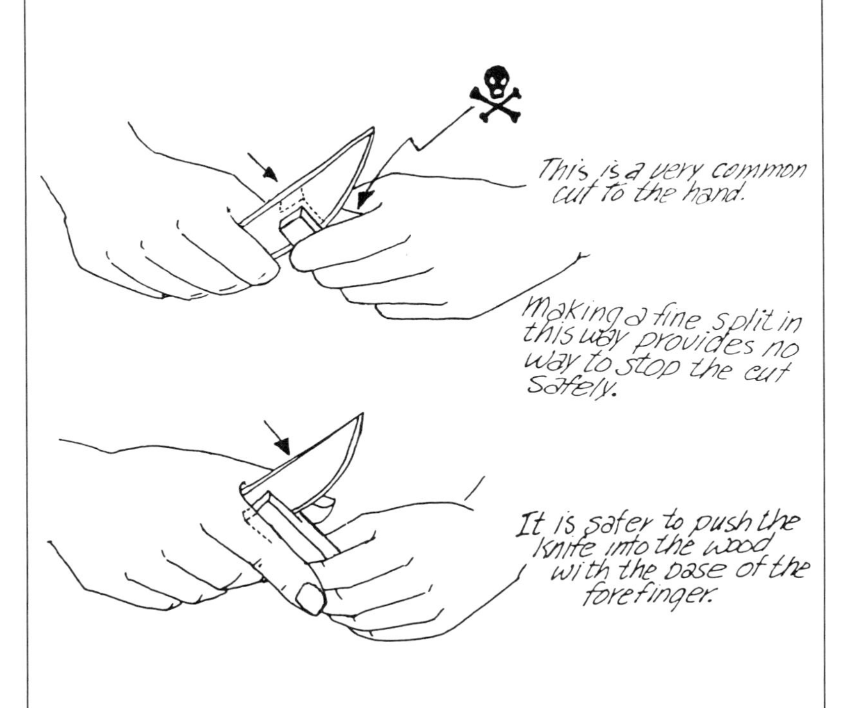

How to make fine splits safely.

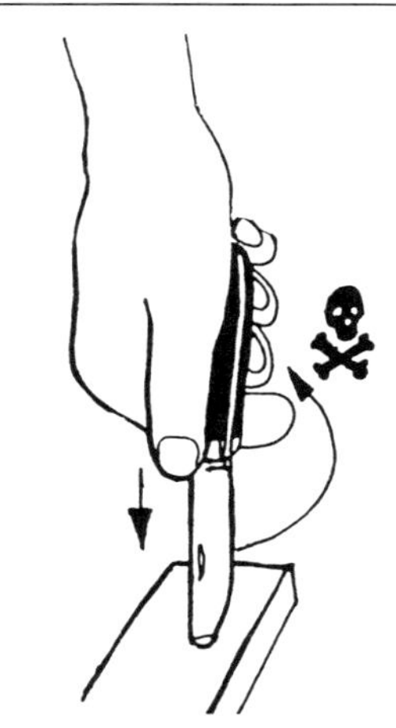

The hazard of bearing down with a folding knife tip.

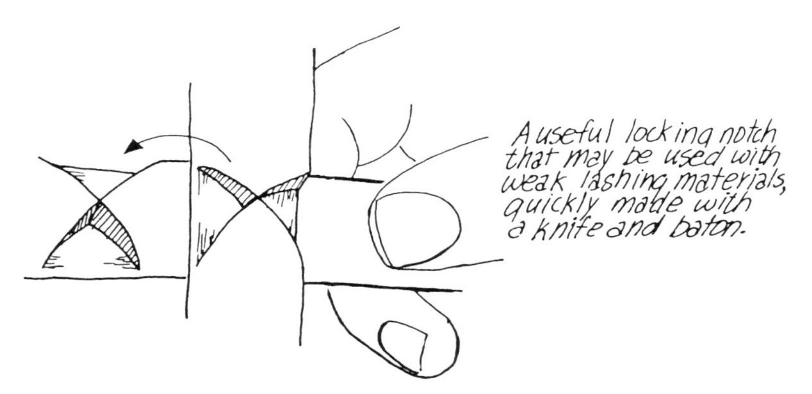

Interlocking notches used with weak lashing materials.

Knife Sharpening

A passable substitute for sharpening stones are abrasive surfaces of carborundum paper, emery cloth, wet-and-dry sand paper and crocus cloth fixed to boards with carpet tape or glue. Sharpening boards will help you master the basics of sharpening inexpensively without the chance of damaging costly stones through ineptness. You may discover you do not need anything more elaborate or you will be better able to decide what you need in the way of regular sharpening stones.

You may use a full sheet of abrasive or any convenient fraction. Full-size sheets are useful when sharpening large or long bladed knives, while a board 5 by 15 centimetres is handier to carry for touching up your knife.

The thin abrasive surface on a sharpening board can be gouged if too much pressure is applied. Use lighter and more frequent strokes instead.

Boards with fine surfaces become more valuable with use. The worn, fine surface approaches a hone's surface texture that is useful in the second last stage of sharpening. Hones are also made of crocus cloth.

A magnified dull edge will appear flat or rounded where the sharp edge should be. Sharpening removes the metal on one or both sides of the blade and re-establishes a new edge. This is accomplished with abrasive surfaces that grind away the unwanted metal in five stages: coarse, medium, fine, hone and strop.

A coarse abrasive will remove metal rapidly, but leaves a rough bevel face and a saw-like edge where the serrations from one side of the blade meet those of the other. This saw-like edge seems to cut well momentarily and must be wiped clean frequently to regain its sharpness when skinning or cutting meat where fat and fibers are caught between the teeth. Such an edge also dulls quickly when cutting wood as the teeth readily break off.

Employing too fine an abrasive too soon prolongs sharpening. Using a coarser surface too long imposes needless wear on the blade and the sharpening surface.

Once the coarse surface establishes an edge, the medium surface replaces the coarse serrations with its own. Then the fine surface erases the medium serrations. The saw edge is now fine enough to be shaped into a toothless edge by the smooth, hard surface of the hone. The honed metal should shine like a mirror.

Sharpening board.

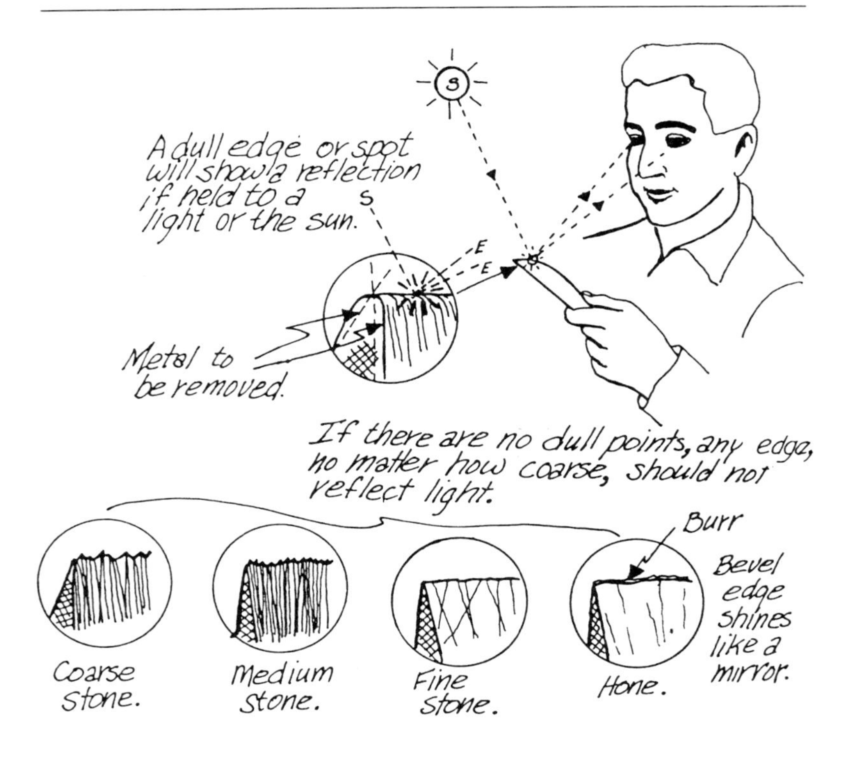

Magnified representations of an edge at various stages of sharpness.

Honing, more so than the previous sharpening stages, produces a fine hinge of metal or burr that resists removal by a hard, smooth abrasive surface. It is produced when the steel in the blade reaches a thickness that is so flexible it keeps flopping over to the side opposite the honing surface until it is long enough to tear off.

The burr is difficult to see with the unaided eye and is therefore often ignored. During the first few cuts, it tears off taking some of the good edge with it, or it leaves the edge in a disturbed state that dulls more rapidly. The burr formed when leading with the edge is finer than the one produced when the edge is dragged. The more substantial burr removes a greater amount of the good edge as it tears off. Thus when the burr is properly removed with a strop, the edge remains sharp longer.

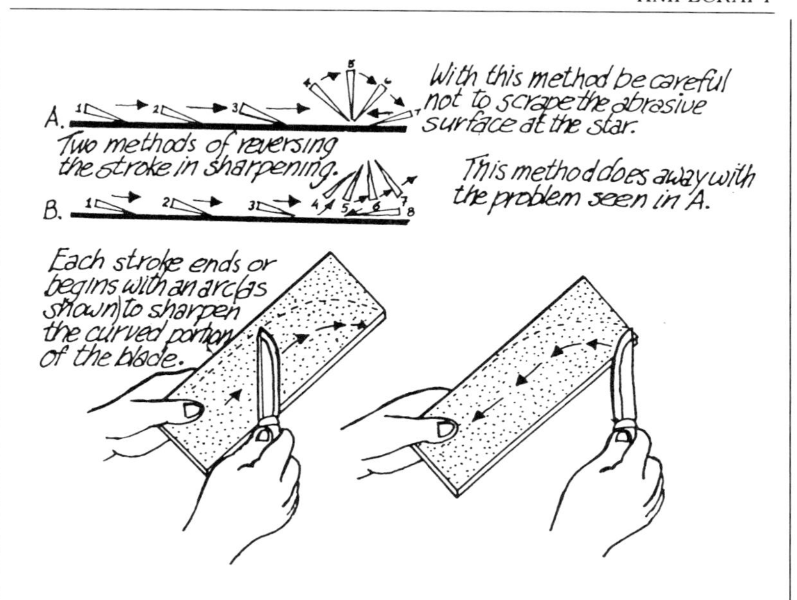

Using a sharpening board.

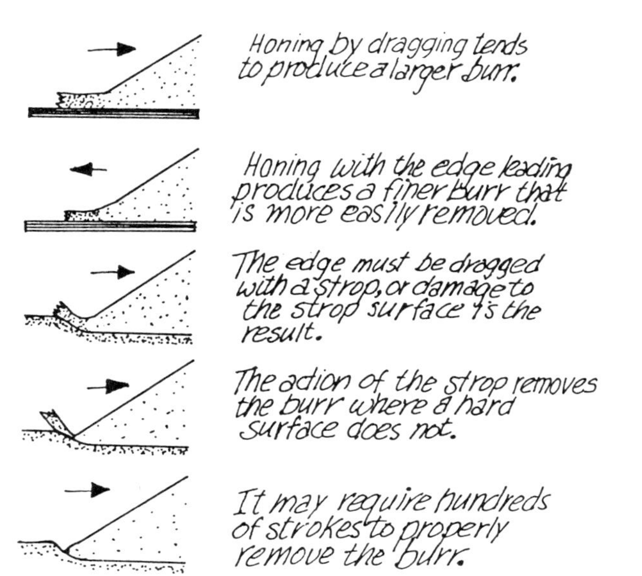

How a hone and a strop work.

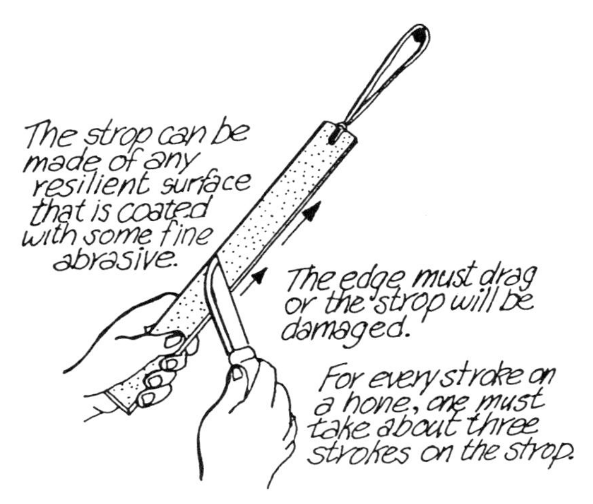

Using a strop.

The strop's fine, abrasive, resilient surface removes the burr as it bulges up behind the edge of the blade. The edge must be dragged or the strop will be damaged. The hand can serve as a strop, but it is slow. An old leather belt makes an excellent strop. A fast-working strop is belting, webbing or a few folds of cloth tacked to a board, saturated with cooking oil and dusted with domestic cleansing or abrasive powder.

The angle at which the blade is held as its edge is drawn across an abrasive surface has a bearing on how well the edge will cut and hold up. For the general-purpose bush knife, that angle is about 8 to 12 degrees. This angle may be more precisely determined if related to the thickness of a dime. The measurement is made to the middle of the back edge of the different widths of blade. A blade one centimetre wide uses one dime; one and a half centimetres, two dimes; two centimetres, three dimes; two and a half centimetres, four dimes; three centimetres, five dimes and finally a three and a half centimetre width requires six dimes.

The dime test should prove that knives displaying a distinct bevel next to the cutting edge need only have the bevel face flat against the abrasive surface to achieve the proper angle for the cutting edge which is about 20 degrees (twice the angle at which the blade is held to the abrasive surface). This type of knife is easy to sharpen correctly. When the whole bevel face shines like a mirror, the edge should be sharp.

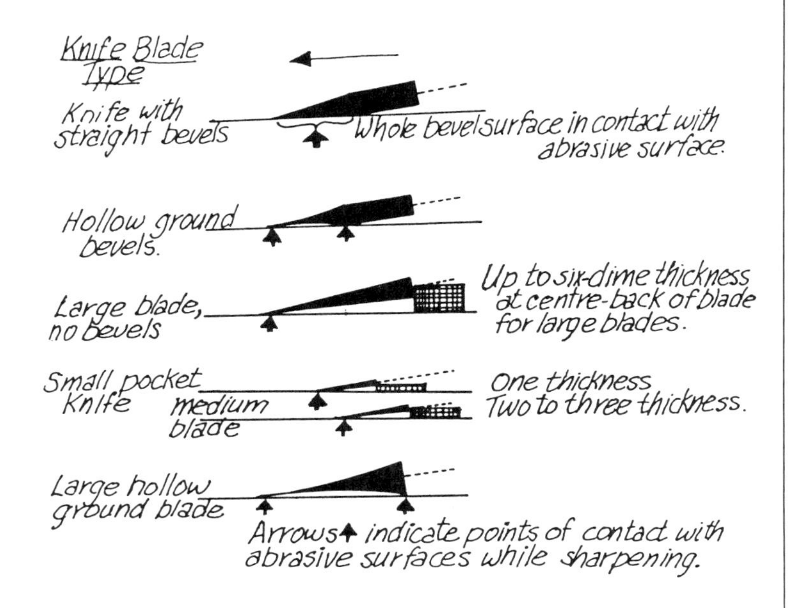

The angles used in different blade configurations.

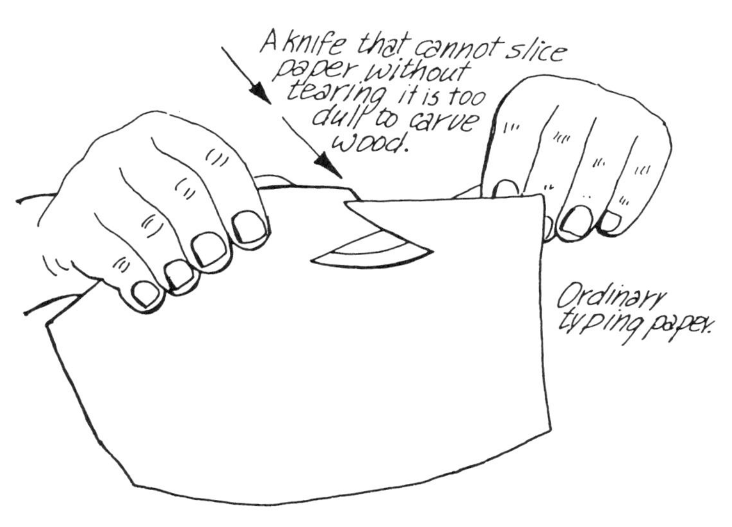

The test for knife sharpness.

Maintain a constant angle when making your sharpening strokes. With a curved cutting edge, the stroke must also be curved or the entire edge will not come in contact with the abrasive surface. At the end of the stroke the blade is raised sufficiently to avoid scraping its edge against the abrasive surface. Holding the blade at a precise angle is more important than speed. With experience the motions will speed up.

Once the edge is established by a coarse abrasive surface, the number of strokes taken on the medium surface multiplied by three will be a rough estimate of the minimum strokes required by the fine surface. If the medium surface required 30 strokes, the fine will require 100, the hone 300 and the strop 900.

The test for minimal sharpness for woodworking is cleanly slicing thin paper. For skinning, meat cutting and surgery, the test is painlessly shaving wet hair on the forearm with one clean stroke.

A knife's edge can be maintained with sand and smooth, natural stones. Trial and error will determine what surfaces and materials will work best during the coarser levels of grinding. For fine work, sand may be mixed with grease and used on a board. The sand may have to be crushed for fine sharpening.

4

SAWCRAFT

Knowledgeable selection, use and maintenance of a Swede saw is an important bush skill.

THE SAW AND AXE

The saw and the axe are complementary in function. The axe is the more hazardous tool, requiring experience and constant attentiveness to use safely. The axe is especially dangerous to use after dark. A saw, on the other hand, may be used by a blind person under most circumstances. The axe takes weeks of constant use to master whereas the saw requires a few hours.

A big saw and a small axe are a good combination employing the best functions of both tools when there is no time to master the axe. Most of the work is accomplished by the saw and the axe serves as a back-up. Limbing is more conveniently done with the axe. Wedges are easily made and pounded in with an axe.

The axe is more versatile and must be the first choice if limited to one tool. An axe may fall, limb and section any size of tree. Splitting and shaving wood, making and pounding in pegs or chopping holes in ice are impossible with a saw.

The depth of a Swede saw's bow limits the size of tree it can cut through. Outside of this restriction, it can fall and section a tree with a fraction of the exertion and with greater convenience in confined or awkward situations, such as cutting in dense growth or above the head. With the assistance of wedges, a saw can fall a tree in directions impossible with an axe alone, but the saw can not make or pound in the wedges. The saw can make squared ends and thin sections of log or boards with a minimum of waste. To saw out boards, a different tooth arrangement (similar to that of a bandsaw) must be used. The saw is the handier tool to use when cutting stove-length wood.

The axe is more versatile and durable, but more dangerous than the saw. The replacement for a broken handle can be fashioned with the head itself if necessary. The cutting edge can be maintained with locally-found natural stones. In comparison, a saw blade is quite fragile. Unless a blade breaks near the end, it can not be salvaged. A twisted or bent blade is impossible to use and difficult to straighten. If the set or tooth arrangement is disturbed, the saw cut becomes progressively more dished, causing such severe drag that it becomes impossible to pull the saw back and forth. Without the appropriate tools to maintain its edge a saw will have a limited period of use.

A saw is easily trapped in its cut, a situation the experienced person knows how to avoid. A small axe can release the sawblade by chopping it free.

Saw Use

A saw frame should be heavy enough to keep its blade under considerable tension. A collapsible saw that can meet this criterion is rare. Compactness and portability should not be sacrificed for unrestricted function and durability. An inferior but portable tool is useless in serious wilderness living. A big bow saw may be awkward to carry, but it recoups the extra energy used in lugging it around in the first half-hour of sawing. On a winter's day when you are tired, cold and hungry the last thing you need is a tool that is the shadow of the real thing.

All saw blades should have guards to prevent cuts to the hands, clothing, packs, tents and pots. You can be severely injured by falling on an unprotected blade.

Using a saw above the head puts sawdust in the eyes, the

worst being the sharp, dry, brittle branches of spruce or pine that one often trims to make head room when making camp near a big tree. Tamarack sawdust can cause a severe physiological reaction as well. Keep the eyes closed enough to help the eyelashes exclude the saw dust.

Back strain is reduced by the use of a sawhorse when a considerable amount of firewood is being cut

With a good-working saw, the teeth are properly arranged and the blade perfectly straight. Any technique that adversely affects the tooth arrangement should be avoided, such as twisting, kinking, bending, heavy pushing, pulling or downward force. A gently used saw will stay in working order for a long time.

Cutting close to the ground so that dirt is pulled into the cut or sawing sand-encrusted driftwood will quickly dull a blade.

Use the weight of the saw at first, without any downward force. As you become more skillful, you may apply downward force with the wrist of the hand holding the saw. When you can use the saw smoothly and unconsciously after having developed a sensitivity to its cutting action, you will know how much force to use to make it cut even faster.

Fast cutting is a judicious combination of the speed with which the saw moves back and forth and the downward force on the blade. If too much force is used you will tire quickly. A full-length stroke is worth three short ones that take twice the effort.

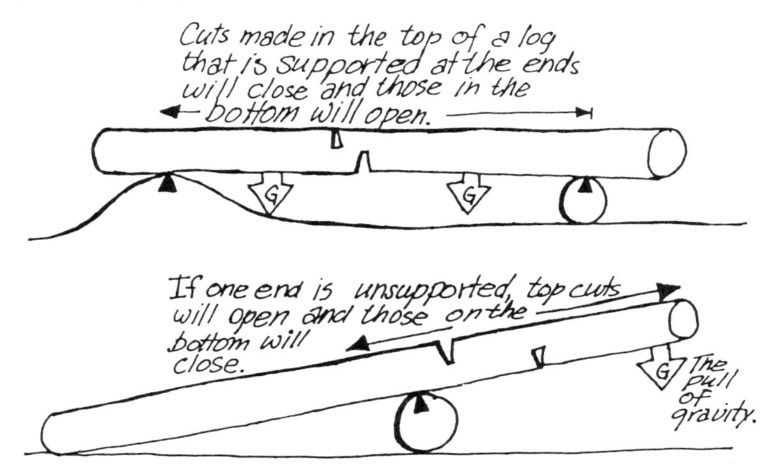

The opening and closing of saw cuts.

The function of the set in a saw blade is to cut a kerf wider than the thickness of the saw blade so it can move freely in its cut. If the log is supported at its ends the kerf closes behind the blade without interfering with its movement. In a hung up, small diameter green black poplar or aspen, the closing forces are strong enough to pinch the blade sufficiently that the only way to free it is to chop it out.

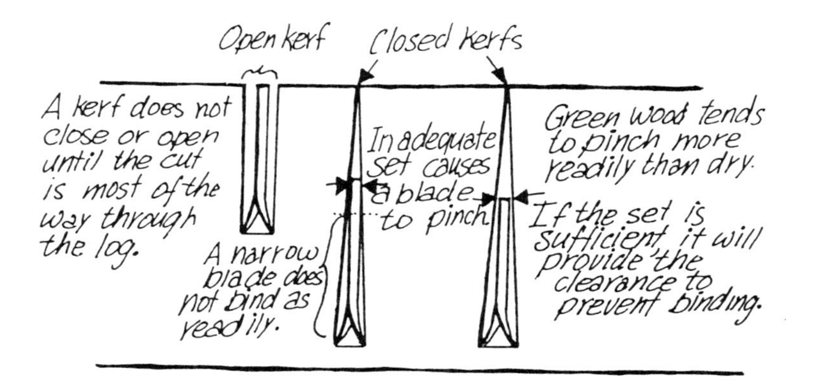

How a saw blade is pinched.

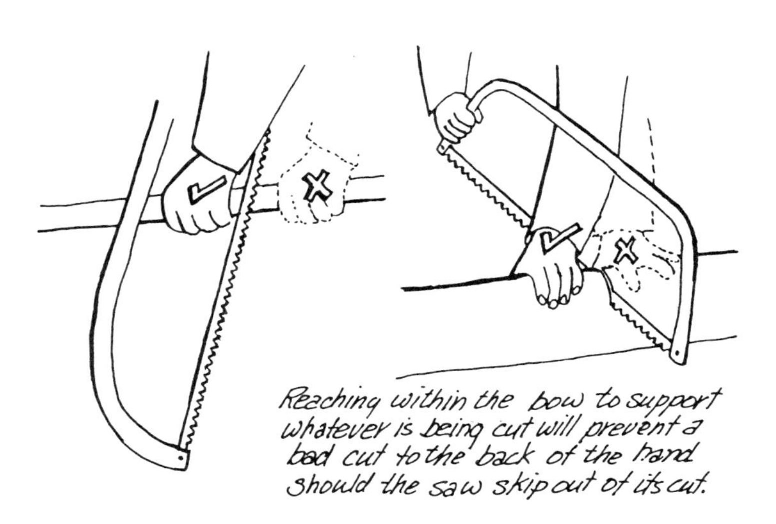

Avoiding saw cuts to the back of the hand.

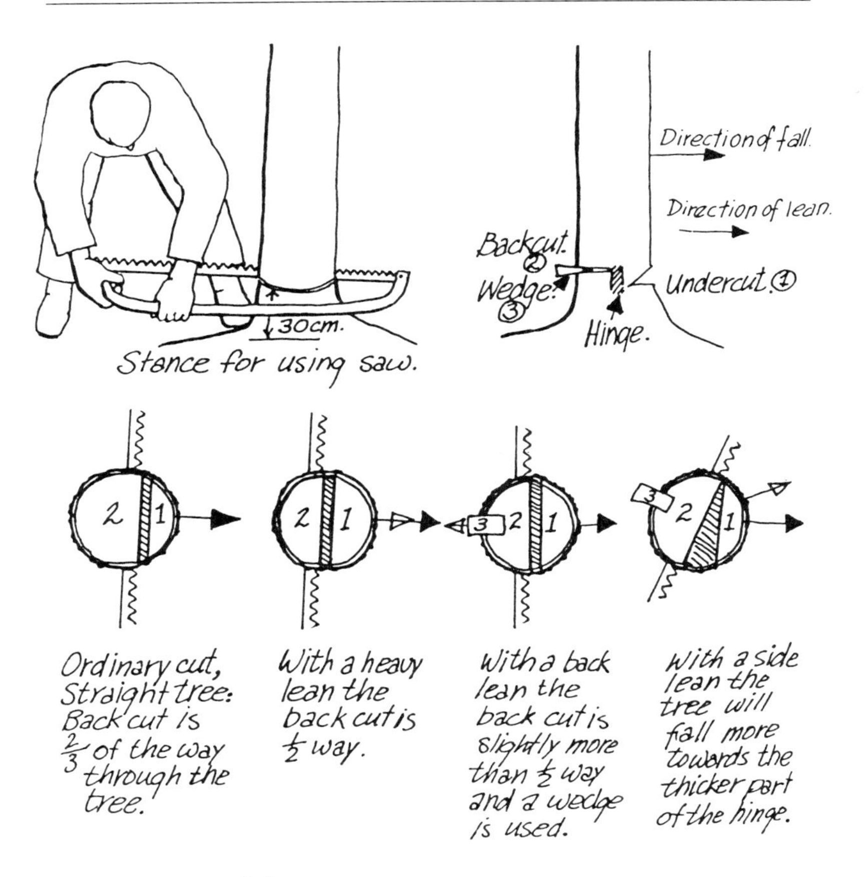

Falling trees with a saw.

Usually the kerf closes behind the blade without restricting the saw, but if the diameter of the log is greater than its throat, the saw is trapped. The saw may be released by either unlatching the blade or notching down the top of the log with an axe to a depth where the saw can complete the cut. A top cut can be opened by prying beneath it with a pole.

A log suspended off the ground and supported at the ends is cut from the top down as far as possible, short of the kerf closing. If there is enough space the cut is continued from underneath where the kerf will tend to open as the cut nears completion. Where an unsupported end is being cut off the opposite is true.

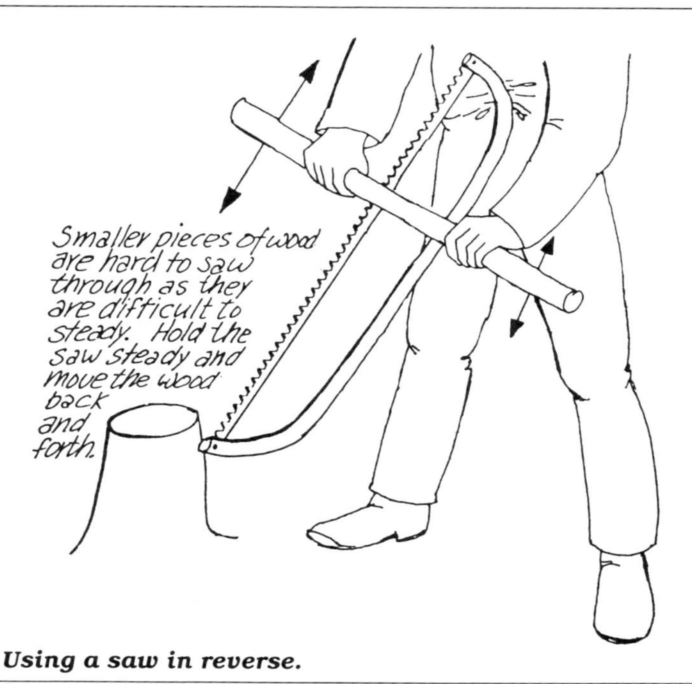

Using a saw in reverse.

Saw Sharpening

A dull saw is usually sharpened with a small triangular or diamond file. Work in good light to see clearly the filed surfaces on the teeth. File one bevel in turn on all the single-pointed teeth. Repeat this procedure for all the bevels. The number of strokes needed on each bevel depends on how dull the saw and how fresh the file. During your initial strokes, watch closely to ensure the entire face of the bevel is filed and count the strokes needed to establish the point on the first tooth. If six strokes are taken, then use half that number, as the other half of the sharpening will be done when the companion bevel is filed. By allowing each bevel the same number of strokes the basic relationship of the teeth is maintained for at least a few sharpenings. If very dull you may have to go over the blade a number of times. The double-pointed teeth known as rakers are filed about the same number of strokes, and they must be slightly shorter than the other teeth. Devote considerable attention to making each file stroke as even as possible.

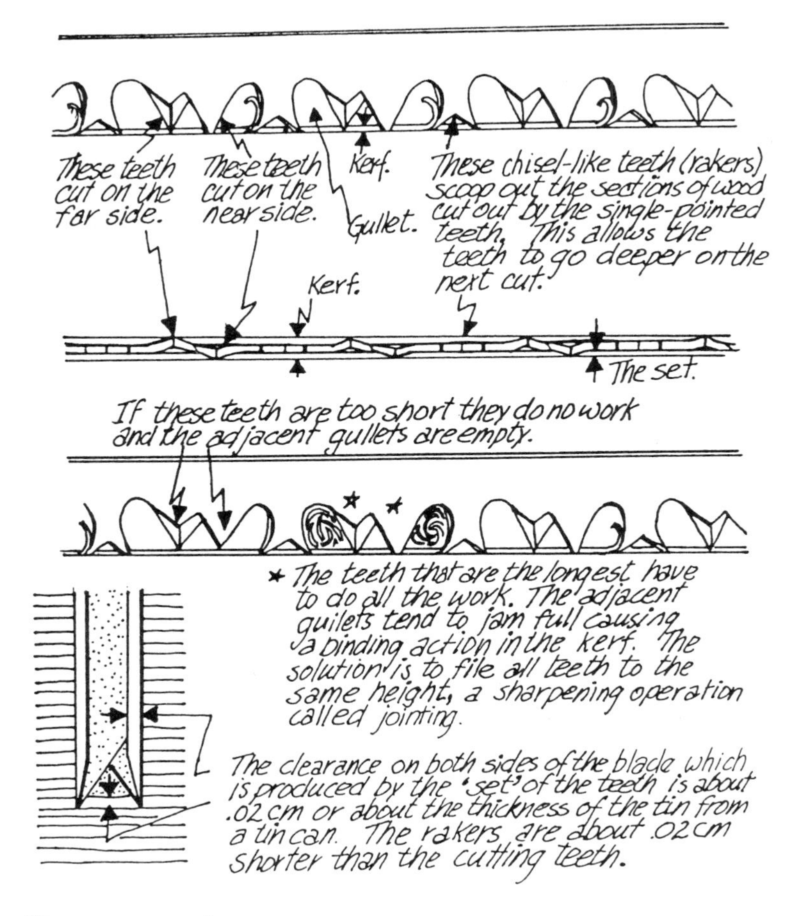

How a saw cuts.

A major reworking of the teeth is more complex, usually involving seven steps.

1. Jointing the Teeth. Saw teeth are of even height so that all will do the same amount of work, otherwise only the longer teeth do all the cutting, which results in slow work and rapid dulling. Jointing involves running a file on the points of the teeth for the length of the blade to make all of the teeth even with each other. Every tooth should show a "jointing flat" as a guide for sharpening to the proper height. The file must be kept at right angles to the blade so that the teeth are filed to an even height on both sides.

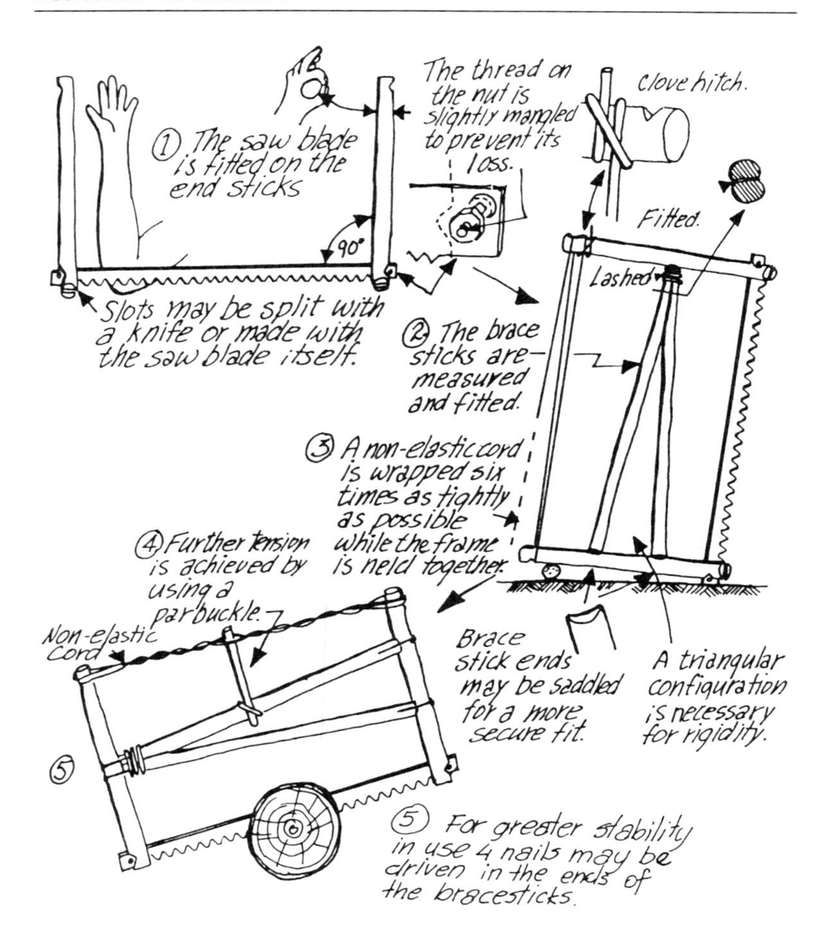

The improvised frame saw.

2. Jointing the Rakers. Rakers must be filed about a half-millimetre shorter than the other teeth. Check by touching down on the jointed teeth with a straight edge and insert a thin metal shim. Take a book with thin pages and measure how many will be a centimetre thick. The number of pages divided into a centimetre is the thickness of one page. Put together the number of pages closest to the desired thickness. Find a piece of tin, razor blade, etc., that is close to this thickness to use as a shim.

3. Reshaping the Gullets. As the saw cuts, sawdust collects in the spaces between the rakers and the other teeth. Every

A simple saw horse.

second or third time the blade is reworked, these spaces or gullets must be restored or the sawdust will jam in them and cause the saw to drag. The round bottoms of the gullets need a round file and the valleys between the pointed teeth need a diamond file.

4. Setting the Teeth. The even-numbered teeth are bent to one side and the odd teeth are bent in the opposite direction so that the spread will make a kerf wider than the thickness of the blade. Specialized tools are required to set teeth. For maximum efficiency, the set should only be enough to allow the saw to move freely in its kerf. This is an angle of about two degrees or an offset of about a quarter-millimetre. Sight along the blade to check if the teeth are set in an even manner. Regardless of the length of the tooth, the amount that is bent for the set is from half to three-quarters of a centimetre from the tip of the tooth.

5. Sharpening the Teeth. File a smooth bevel to the mid-point of all jointing flats for all the teeth for that one particular bevel, then remove the burr by dressing as described below. The adjoining bevels are now filed so the jointing flats are completely removed. The bevel angle for the teeth is about 40 degrees.

6. Dressing. Dressing removes most of the burr from the cutting edges of the teeth. This is achieved by lightly running a fine abrasive surface back and forth on the sides of the teeth

7. Sharpening the Rakers. The rakers are sharpened until all the jointing flats are removed and shortened as already described under sharpening. The rakers are sharpened like a chisel to a 35 degree bevel.

5

BINDCRAFT

Cordage-making is an important skill in many aspects of wilderness living. The applications may range from sewing thread to a tow cable. Cordage and other means of binding may be improvised from materials readily found at hand for shelter-making, fishing, snaring, making weapons, packing and fire-lighting.

CORDAGE TECHNIQUES

The simplest cord or rope made by hand is two stranded. A number of fibers make up a strand. The thicker the strand, the thicker and stronger the cord. If the strands are twisted in a clockwise direction at both ends, a kink will form a short piece of cord. Fiber twisted clockwise is termed Z-twist and counterclockwise is S-twist.

The harder the strands are twisted the steeper the twist angle, the more strength is derived from the fibers, and the stiffer the cord. The number of twists per unit length is directly related to the diameter of the strands used. For a hard cord of four millimetres thickness, two twists per centimetre are required as compared to 12 twists for a half-millimetre thickness.

To avoid weak spots in the cord, the fiber added to the strands as the rope lengthens must be staggered, and the twist in both strands be equal. The fingers rolling the strands will have a better feel of any thickness changes than can be seen by eye. For the smoothest cord the fibers added should be tapered at both ends. New fibers may be added by laying them along the old fibers and the ends either trimed off with a knife or singed off by passing the finished cord through a hot fire. The latter is done only slowly enough to singe off the fibers, but not to burn the cord.

Adding a third strand almost doubles the strength and durability of the cord. A two-stranded cord is first made and then the third strand incorporated, or all three strands are made to keep up simultaneously with each other.

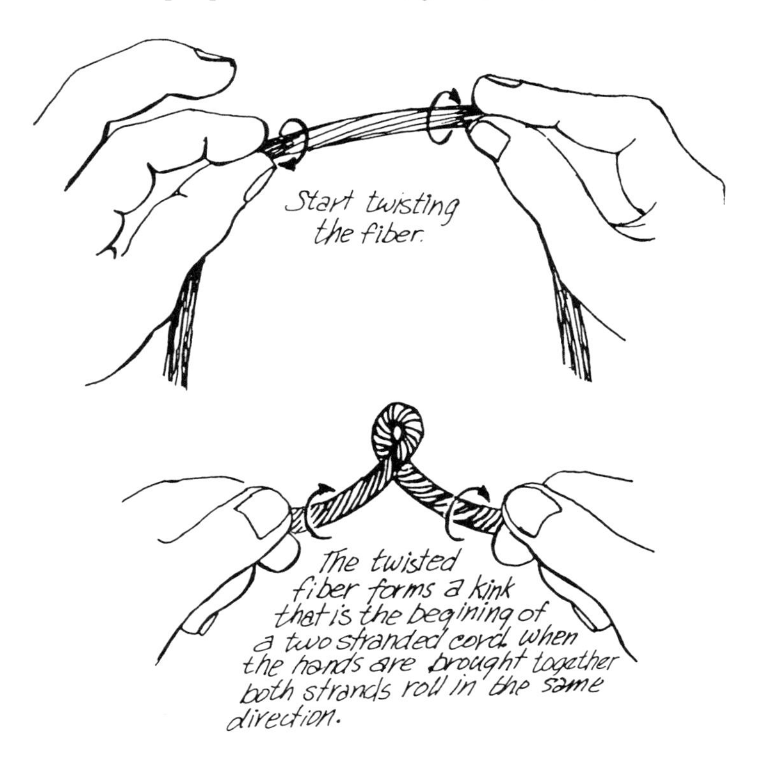

The initial step in making a simple cord.

The completed cord is rolled between two flat surfaces such as a rock and boot sole or two boards. This smooths the cord and evens out minor inconsistencies in the twist. The cord is rubbed back and forth to raise the surface fibers that are to be singed off.

The time and effort in making a cord should be matched to its intended use. A quickly and crudely twisted grass rope will do as a lashing in shelter building. A carefully and precisely twisted bow string may take hours to make.

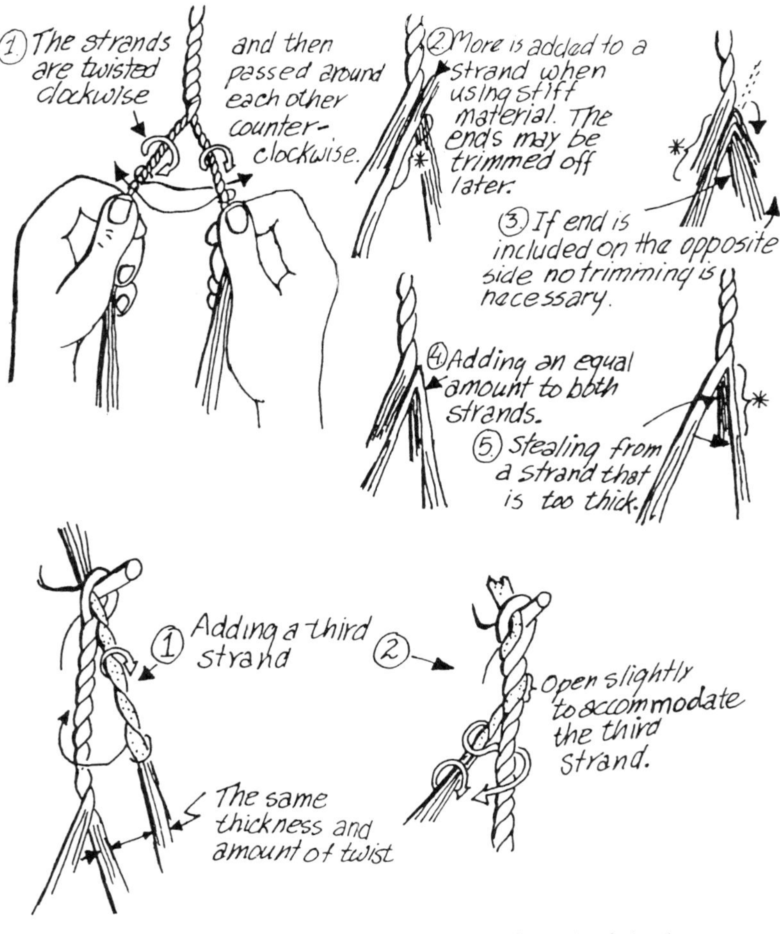

A simple two stranded cord can be twisted with the fingers.

When making fine cordage such as sewing thread, fish line or netting string, the hand twisting method is slow and tedious. The process is speeded up by rolling the separated strands by hand on the thigh. The fibers to be added to the strands are prepared by rolling them singly on the thigh, or between the palms.

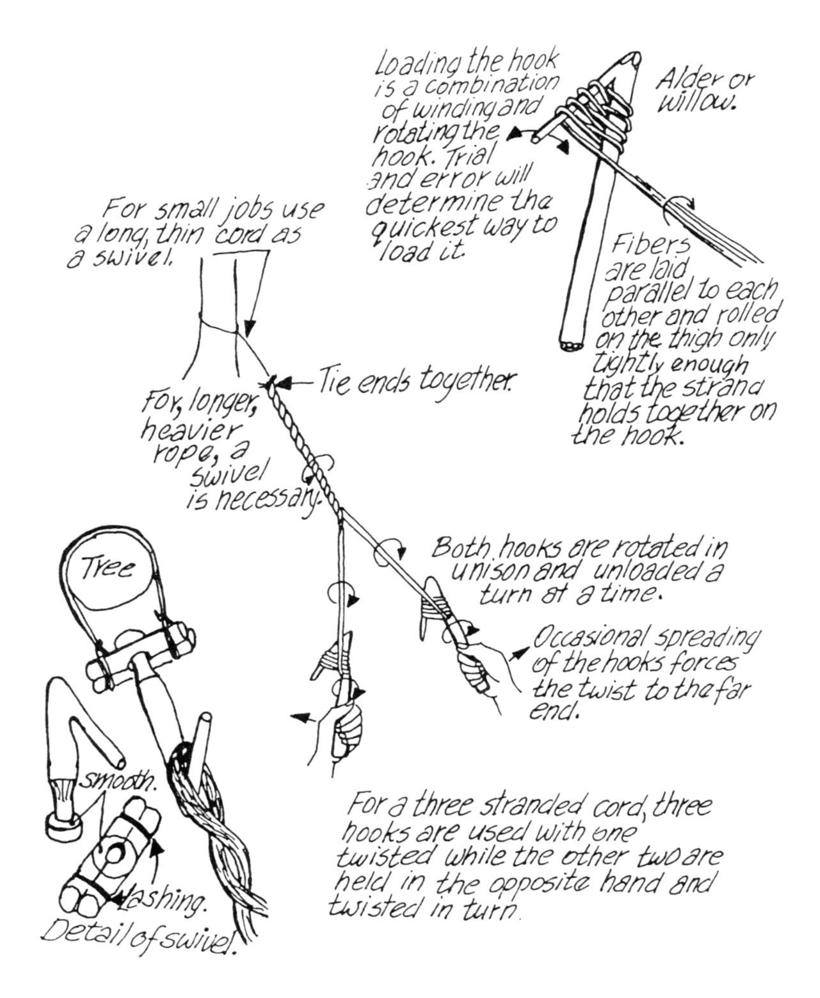

Using roping hooks.

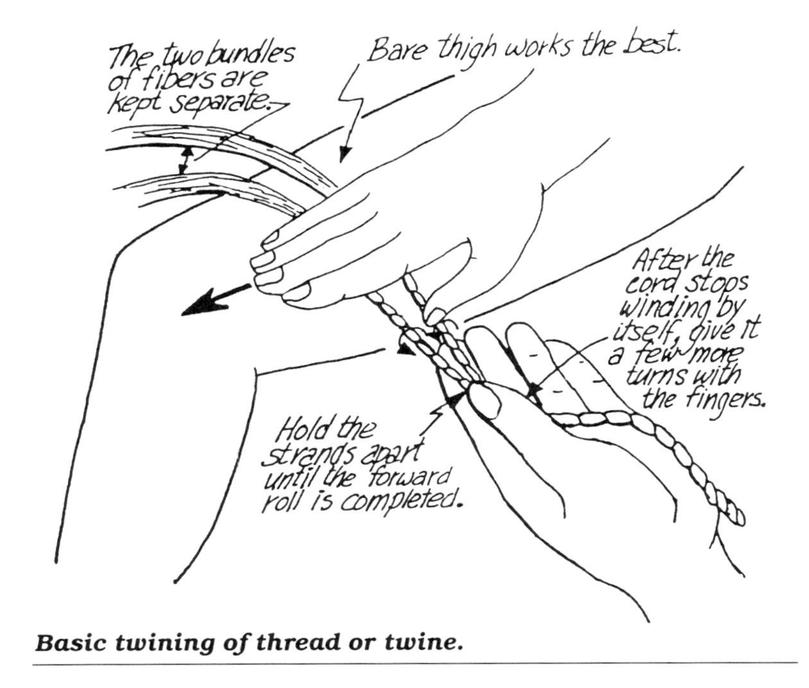

Basic twining of thread or twine.

Different Cordage Materials and their Uses

Cattail. Fall and early winter leaves will make a good looking but weak rope for lashing and weaving. Cord made from cured leaves gathered in late June and early July is very durable as plant development is arrested at a stage when the leaves remain supple on drying. The cured stalk of the flowering plant can be split and the halves twisted into a stiff cord with a high tensile strength.

Dogbane. This plant is processed and used like nettle which it resembles in strength and texture.

Fireweed. Like thistle, the outer bark of the mature, but green stem, yields a fiber of sufficient strength for snare cord.

Grasses. Some grasses are available during the fall and winter for snare cord, pole lashing, crude climbing rope, and tow cables. Any grass that resists crumbling can be made into cord or rope. Hairy wild rye grass found under spruce trees where the snow is shallow will make an adequate cord for snaring or lashing. The sedges, having a high tensile strength, will make a cable strong enough to pull out a stuck vehicle. If grass is dampened before twisting it is more manageable. Green grass shrinks as it dries, making a loose, weak rope. Grasses are at their best as soon as they have died in the fall before weathering begins. Unprotected, most grass-like cordage materials gradually degenerate to the point of being useless by late winter.

Roses. The bark is collected in the spring and summer and the prickles and outer bark scraped off with a sharp edged stick. The remaining bark can be twisted into cord or twine that is about as strong as that of wolf willow.

Saskatoon. Similar to the rose, the bark is stripped from the mature shrub and the crumbly outer bark scraped off. What remains is shredded and twisted into a stiff cord that is similar in strength to wolf willow.

Stinging Nettle. The fine, soft-textured, elongated phloem fibers found near the skin of stinging nettle are some of the strongest in the plant kingdom. Stinging nettle is often substituted for sinew, but is likely not as strong. The fibre is useful in making bow strings, fish lines and fish nets. Although the fiber can be extracted from the mature green plant, it is best after the plant has turned brown in the fall. However, the longer the plant is allowed to weather after it dies, the more the fiber deteriorates. Store the plant in a dry place out of the sun until it is ready to be processed. Large-scale processing techniques for nettle fiber are the same as used to extract linen from flax. A small-scale method to remove the fiber is to pound the stalk until most of the stem crumbles out. A simpler method is to split the stalk, starting at the top of the plant, and peel back the fibers to the leaf joint. Break the stalk near this joint and again peel away the crumbly stem. Try to remove most of the fibers in two strands. Each strand is rubbed vigorously between the hands or between a hand and a smooth-barked tree to remove what remains of the flaky outer bark. The lightly rolled strands are now ready for twining into cord, string or thread. If a fine thread is required, the strands may have to be divided accordingly.

Thistles. The outer bark of most green thistles can be used for snare cord.

Willow Bast. The inner bark of willow, particularly the large Beaked or Bebbs willow can be made into cord and netting twine. The stiffer outer bark is separated from the more flexible inner bark with the hands or by slicing with a knife.

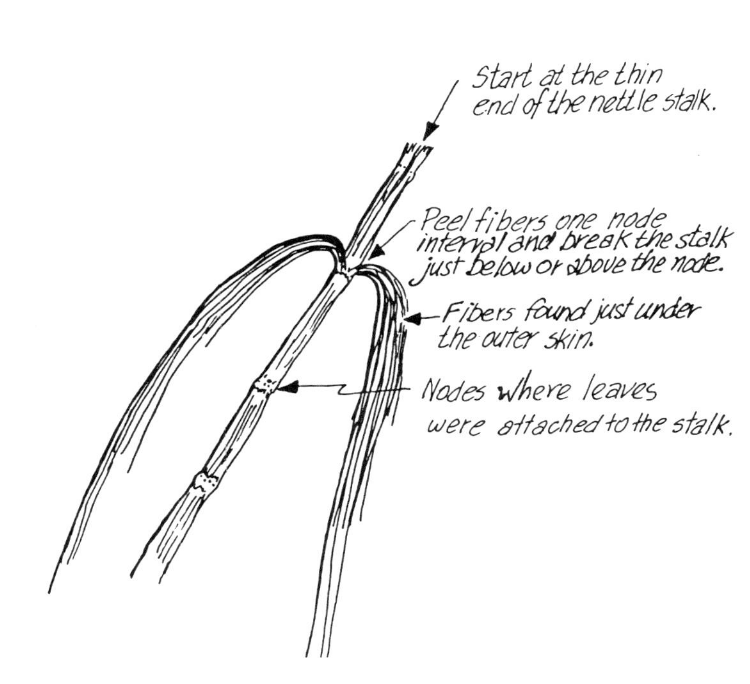

Extracting nettle fiber.

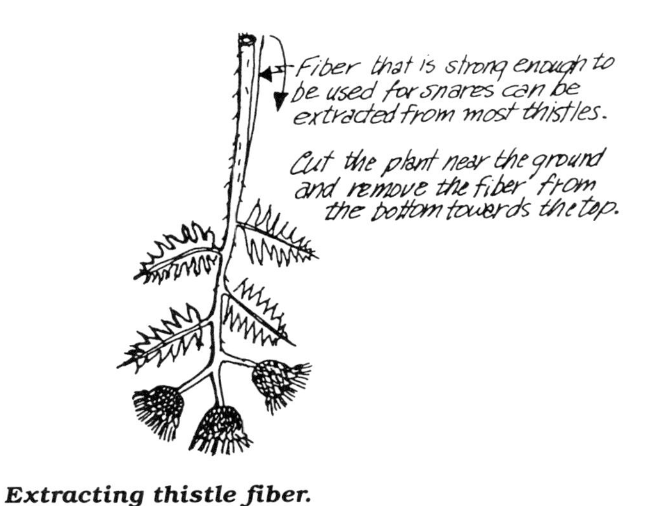

Extracting thistle fiber.

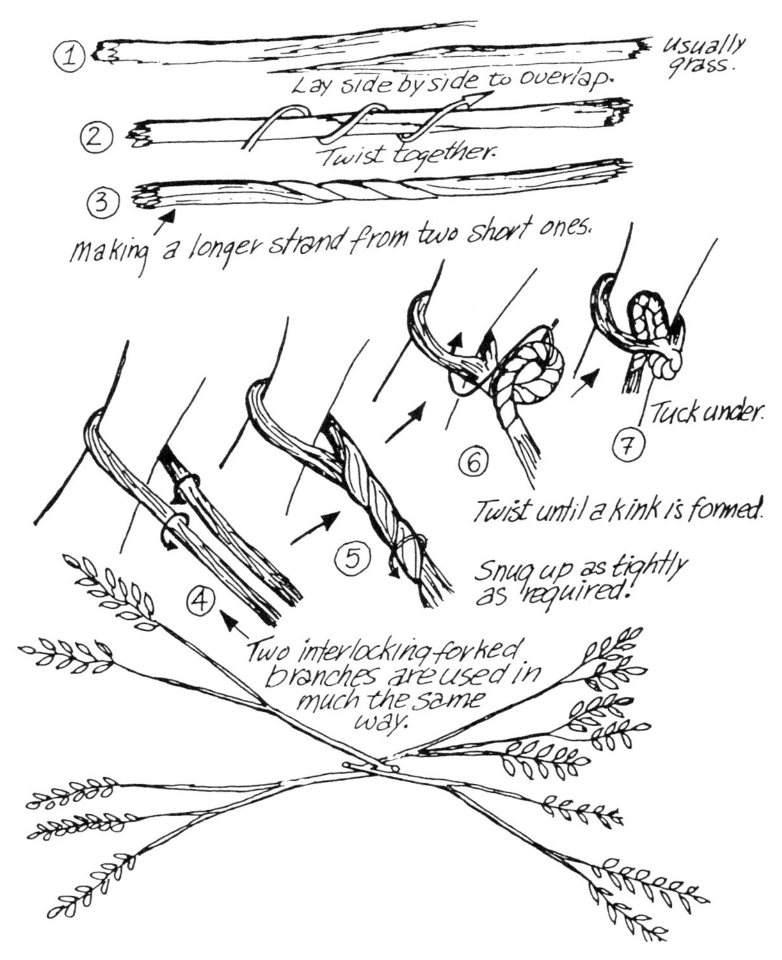

The binding tie.

The inner bark is shredded and twisted or twined in the usual way. If the bark is gathered as soon as it starts to peel in the early spring and for a few weeks thereafter, it remains flexible. At this stage the cord will turn reddish brown. If the bark is used at other times, it will become brittle on drying, and remain white or greenish in color. It is still useful for netting, but the net must be folded immediately after it is taken from the water and handled gently when dry. The net must be thoroughly soaked before being unfolded.

Wolf Willow. The inner bark from the trunk and roots of this shrub will produce a moderately strong cord for general binding. The plant is used all year except for a short period in the spring when the bark layers are thick and porous. The bark peels in strips and may be used directly for binding, or it may be twisted into a cord that remains flexible when dry. As the outer skin has no tensile strength, and the bright green layer next to it is weak, both are discarded. The inner layers, up to eight in number, are used for making cordage. For a fine-textured cord, the layers are separated and shredded into fine fibers for the strands. Wolf willow cordage is useful for snares, fish line, and the cord for the bow drill. The wood is quite tough but the forks are easily split or torn apart, so that the bark can be removed without tools.

Other Materials and Methods Used in Binding

Conifer Roots. The roots of black and white spruce, tamarack and the pines may be used for many binding purposes. The straightest and longest roots are from black spruce and tamarack growing in *Sphagnum* bogs.

Pick a mossy area with little growth other than spruce or tamarack to minimize interference with the gathering of the roots. Roots must be completely free from the moss to be extracted in one piece. The best time to debark a root is immediately before it dries. To remove the bark, pull the root through a split in a stick, between two sticks squeezed together, or pressed between a stick and a log. Roots can be kept under water indefinitely and peeled as needed. From mid-August onward, the roots become progressively more resistant to peeling and the bark must be scraped off with a knife. The roots become too weak to be of any use just before the forest freezes over for winter. Conifer roots can be peeled, dried and stored for future use. The roots are softened by boiling or soaking. Drying and boiling the roots once will increase their strength over the fresh roots, but repeated drying and soaking weakens them. Conifer root can be used for lashing, but becomes brittle on drying, so that its best application is where no flexing occurs, such as in static lashings. Once in place the root dries rigid making it superior for sewing birch bark canoes and making baskets.

Roots thicker than the little finger are too large to work before splitting. A root may be split into many strands in a variety of ways. A split is started at either end and must

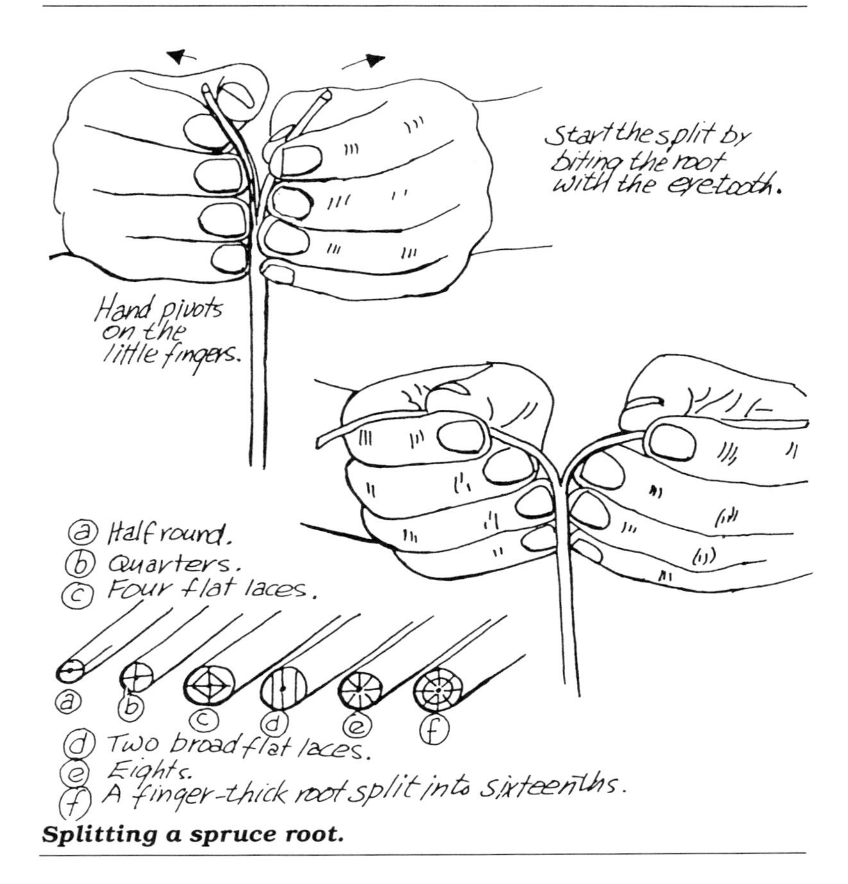

Splitting a spruce root.

be maintained precisely down the middle of the root. If the split runs off to one side, the thicker side can be bent a little to center it again. The split will always run off on the side that bends the most.

The best knots to use with conifer roots are fishing line knots. More information on working with spruce roots is covered in Chapter 8.

Pincherry Bark. Pincherry bark can be removed as a spiral to produce a long narrow strip. It has the unique property of being both slightly elastic and unaffected by moisture so that it can be used for tightly binding spear points and fish spears.

Rawhide Lacing. Rawhide cut into strips is first soaked and stretched slightly to make it pliable. Rawhide shrinks on drying, to produce a very tight bind. Its disadvantage is

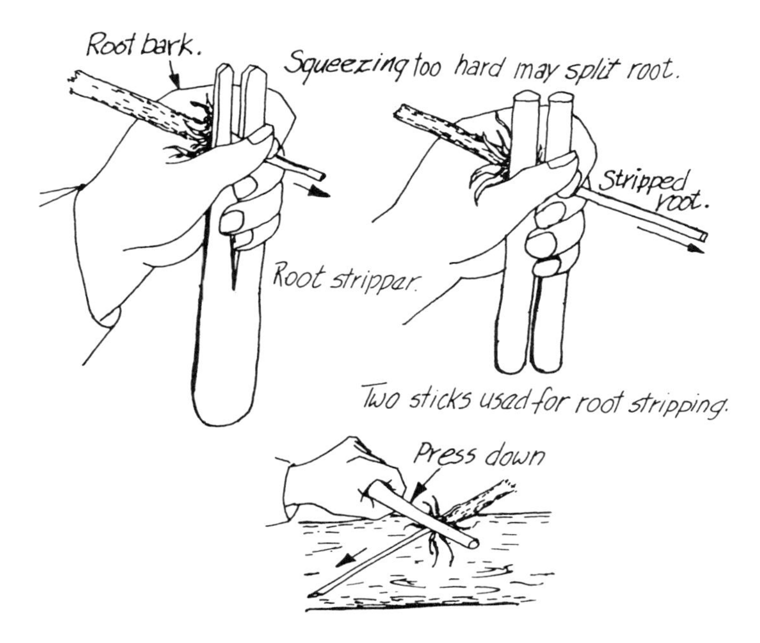

Techniques for removing the bark from spruce roots.

that it stretches when wet. Rawhide is used for snowshoe lacing and sled and toboggan construction.

Sinew. Sinew is one of the strongest animal fibers known. The more useful lengths come from the larger animals such as moose, although a varying hare will produce enough to make one snare. The ligaments from the back and occasionally from the legs are removed, cleaned of fat and flesh and attached to a board or stick to dry in the sun. Once dry, these can be stored indefinitely. The thoroughly dry and hard tendons are supported on a smooth surface and carefully pounded with a hammer until the fibers separate enough to be plyed apart to any desired thickness. Take care not to cut the fibers in the pounding process. Sinew is useful for stringing beads, sewing, binding and for bow strings. Sinew, like rawhide, stretches when wet and shrinks on drying.

Willow Wythes. A method of binding with willows is to interlock two forks, leaving the fine ends free to complete the tie by twisting it into a kink which in turn is forced between what is being tied and the lashing material. When longer lashings are made from willow wythes, they are braided together to the required length.

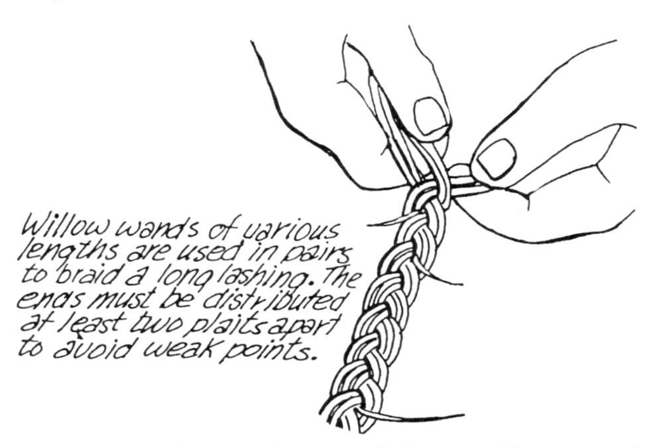

Making a long lashing braid out of short willow wands.

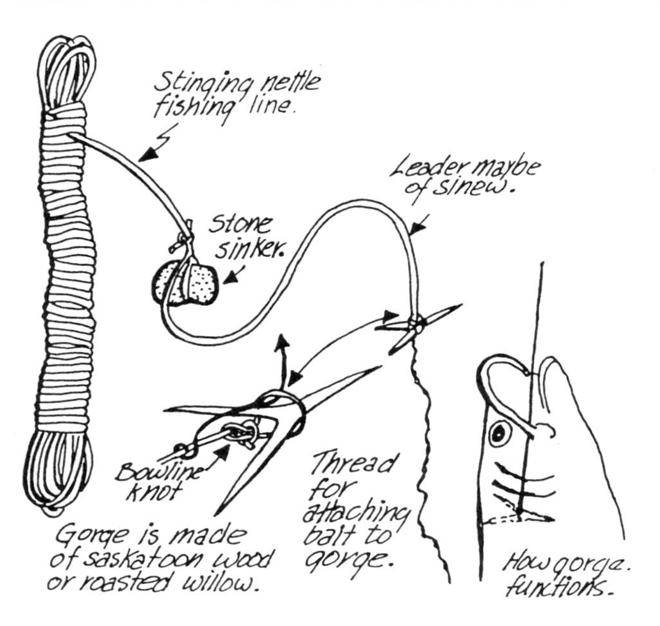

Detail of a fishing line made from natural materials.

6

SHELTERCRAFT

Our clothing protects us from the cold, wind and rain while we are active or travelling outdoors. Shelter can be defined as clothing for the family, or an extension of our clothing.

SHELTER CONCEPTS

Shelter provides a micro-environment that supplements inadequate clothing or allows you to shed cumbersome layers, especially when you stop moving and when you want to sleep in cold weather. Shelter also enhances the effect of a warming fire.

Various shelters will ward off cold, rain, snow, wind and insects. Some may fulfill only one specific role, while others withstand all environmental impositions comparatively well. The specific shelter required is determined by many factors, such as intended application, the raw materials and tools available and the expertise of the builder.

The simplest shelter uses insulative material to keep the occupant warm. This is particularly useful when it is too cold to sleep in one's clothing, but too warm to maintain a fire. With the right kind of dry insulative material you can build a suitable shelter for the coldest of conditions. A framework, such as a simple arch shelter or small teepee will keep the materials from shifting as you toss and turn while asleep. Crude grass coverings or quilts can be woven to provide a better cover. Mosses, especially those without a strong mouldy smell, such as *Sphagnum*, may be used, after being dried on a framework near a fire. A disadvantage of the insulative shelter is the lack of a work space.

Where insulative materials are scarce or when there is no time to gather or dry them, or camp is changed daily, a fire and shelter combination may be more appropriate. There are over 20 fire-shelter variants to choose from and each one is suited to a particular situation.

Fire by itself provides quick relief from cold. A shelter helps provide more warmth for less fuel by keeping the elements at bay. Most cold weather shelters in the Northern Forests depend on fire to improve their effectiveness.

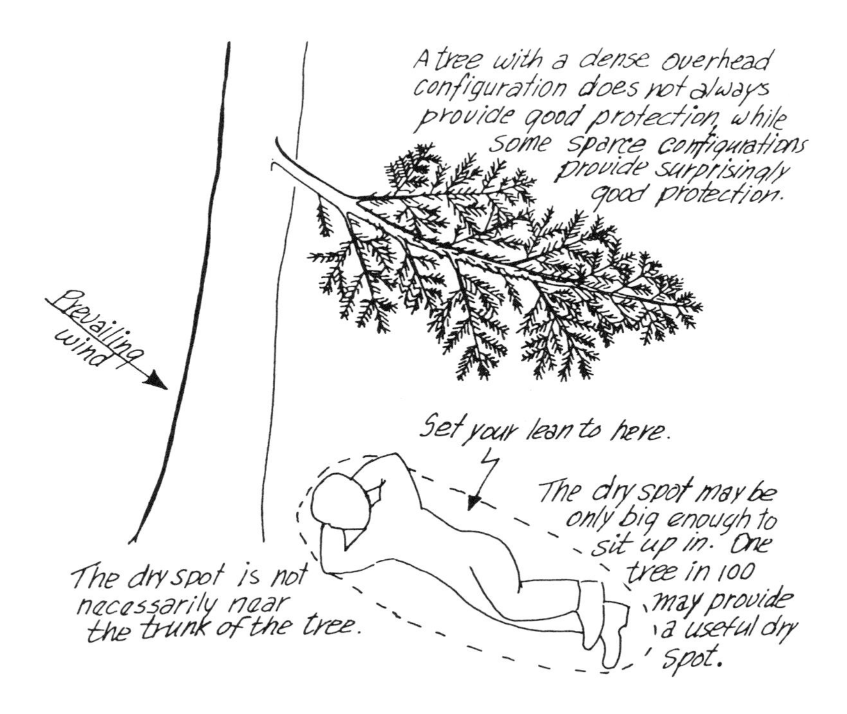

The dry spot under a tree.

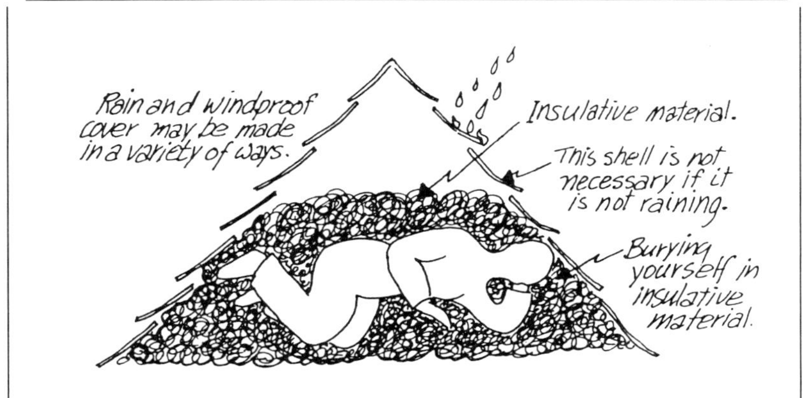

Using insultative material in a rain proof shelter without a fire.

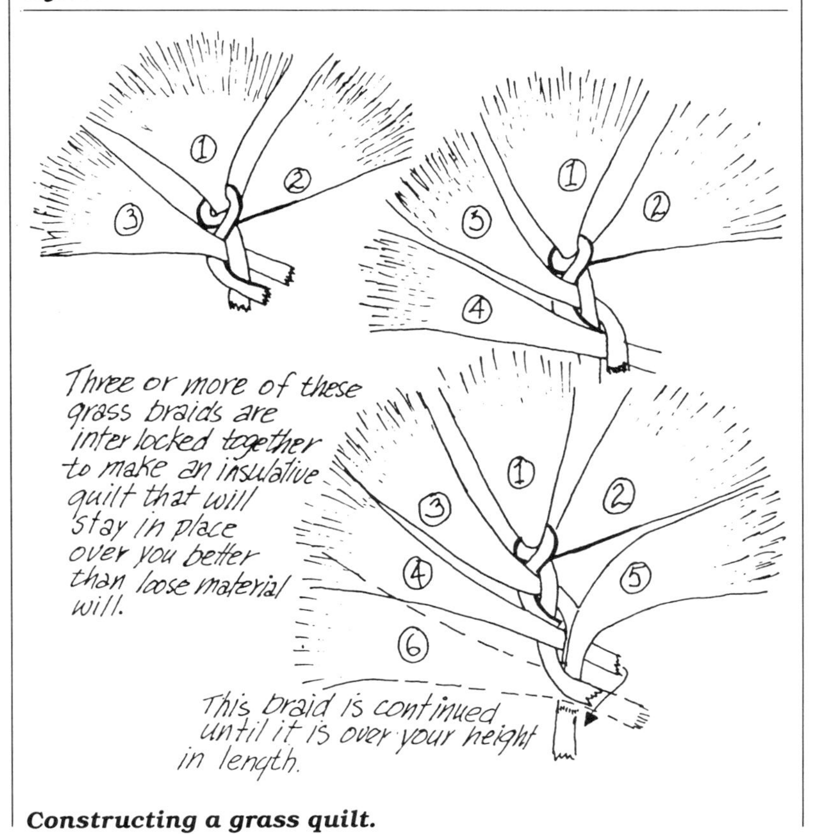

Constructing a grass quilt.

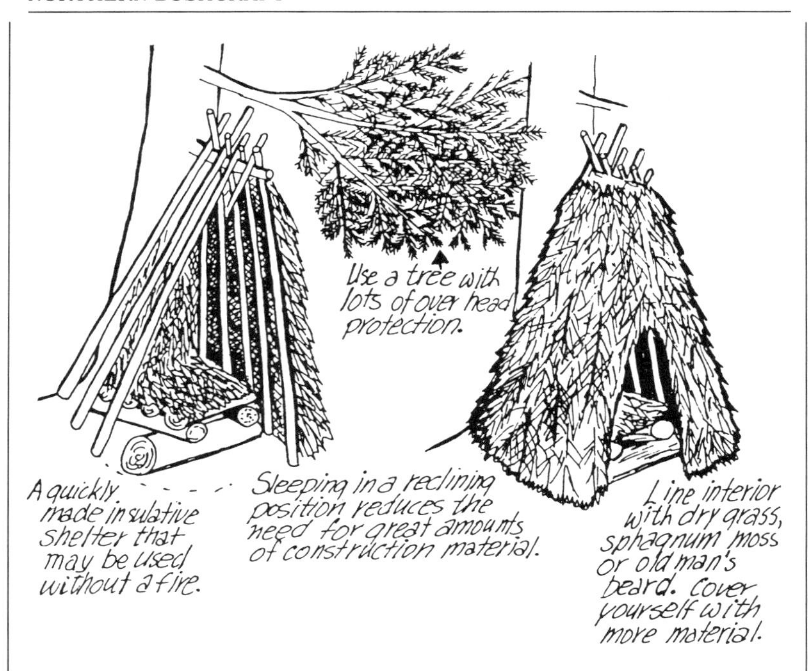

The sitting-up insulative shelter.

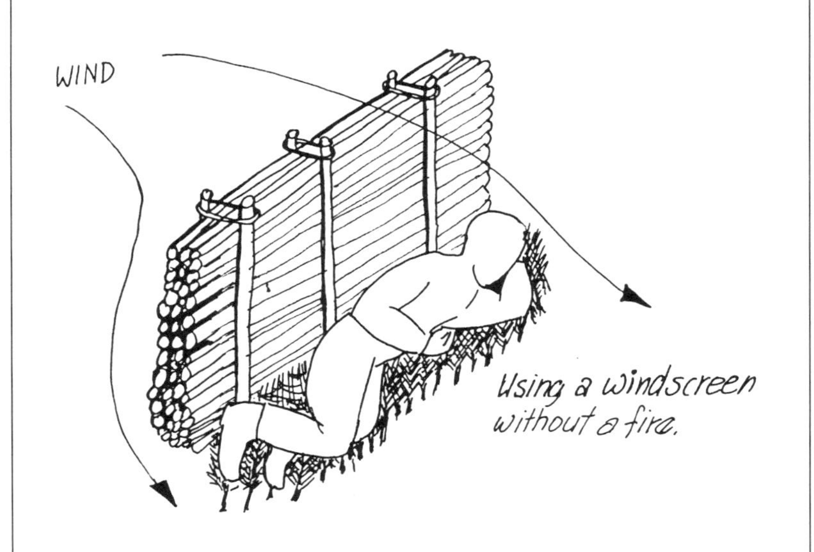

A simple wind screen.

The Open-Fronted Shelters

Open-fronted shelters use the most readily available local materials and are often the simplest to construct without tools. The open-fronted shelter creates a space that can be warmed to a comfortable level by a fire in front of it, regardless of the outside temperature. Some common types are the arch, the ridge-pole or a half-teepee.

An open-fronted shelter warmed by a fire has certain requirements to be effective. The occupant must sleep parallel to a fire that is as long as he is tall. The back of the shelter must be near enough to the fire to be warmed by it. There must be no cold air movement into the shelter. The bed, the fire and the wind must be parallel to each other or problems will result from smoke movement through the shelter.

The open-fronted shelter can be broken down into at least five elements. Any one shelter may use a given element or be composed of any combination of elements, depending on weather conditions.

1. The heat source is usually a parallel or wall-backed fire *that is as long as you are tall*. The fire should be built one good step away from the front of the shelter. The proper management of a fire in front of an open shelter demands constant attention resulting in relatively short periods of rest. The radiant aspect of the fire warms the user and the immediate surroundings, much like the effect of the sun.

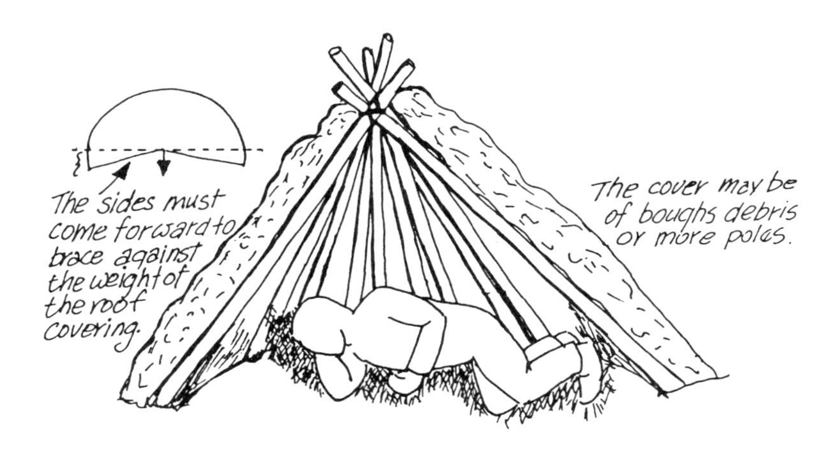

An example of an open-fronted shelter—the half-teepee.

Whatever needs to be warmed must be positioned close to the fire and exposed directly to its radiance. Any warmed air rises providing little warmth, beyond that flowing around or past you. Objects intercepting the fire's radiance will warm up and in turn emit some radiance, but in a much longer or cooler wavelength.

2. Back protection *blocks the infiltration of cold air on the side away from the fire.* By absorbing the radiance from the fire, the back protection provides warmth on the far side of your body. Split white wood will reflect some of the radiance back toward your far side. The back protection should be as close to the fire as possible without any space between the back protection and your far shoulder.

3. The base or bed should be an insulative and resilient surface, comfortable enough to sit or sleep on, *that protects you from the cold or wet ground.*

4. Overhead protection is back protection extended upward to offer *protection from rain or snow.* It also helps direct the radiance of the fire downward onto the bed.

5. Side protection *blocks the wind on the windward side.* When a fire is used with an open shelter, the wind must blow

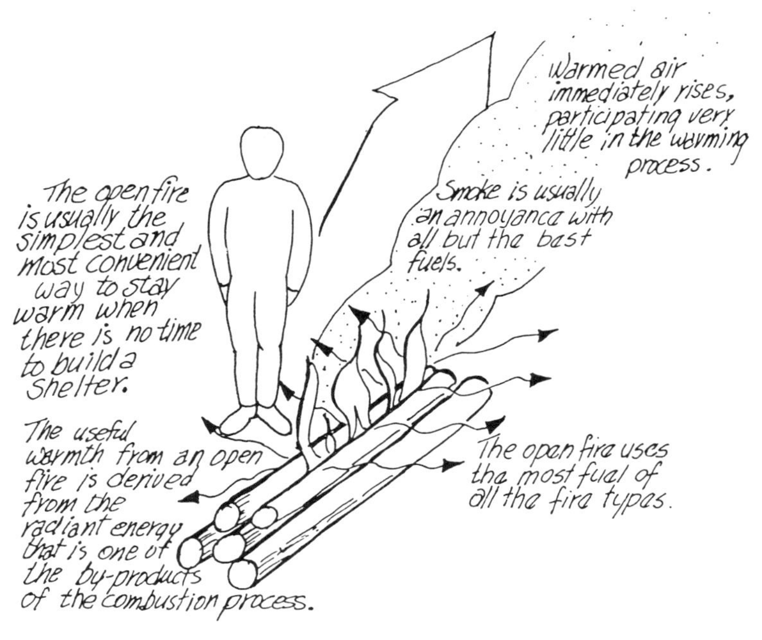

The use of an open fire.

parallel to its front so the end of the shelter, and not the back, blocks any wind. By itself, this is considered a wind screen.

The number of elements incorporated in a shelter depends on the needs of the moment. Under warm and dry conditions locate a protected place for a resilient bed. If air movement is a problem use a suitable screen. In rainy situations provide overhead protection. If it is cold, first make a good fire (your height in length) then collect an adequate fuel supply. If there is no precipitation the fuel pile can act as your back protection with your bed positioned between it and the fire.

A satisfactory shelter site can often be found at the base of a large white spruce with long overhanging boughs. The ground near the base is usually soft enough to lie on and may even be dry after a prolonged rain or free of snow in the winter, thus making overhead protection and a bed unnecessary. Side or back protection may be all that is required so that the amount of building materials is reduced.

One should be cautioned that ticks also find shelter at the base of spruce, particularly in the foothills region, and should therefore not be feared elsewhere.

Overhead Protection

There are many ways a rain or wind-deflective roof can be made for a bush shelter. Green spruce boughs make poor roofing, but are often the only available material. Compressed handfuls of dead, lichen-covered branches are best. Balsam fir is an improvement over spruce because the flat configuration of the boughs allow dense packing and the flat needles shed rain. All boughs are placed on the roof with the stem up and the underside facing out to an uncompressed thickness of about 30 to 40 centimetres. The boughs are most effective if compressed with logs.

The pitch of a bough roof is critical if it is to shed rain effectively—a roof that leaks is likely not steep enough. The heavier the downpour, the steeper the roof, and the higher it must be extended, to protect the bed adequately.

In the wintertime, cold air is prevented from seeping through the boughs by banking with snow. A 15- to 30-centimetre thickness of boughs adequately insulates the snow from the heat of a fire.

Thatching with grasses, swamp birch branches and compacted dry spruce branches produces the most effective

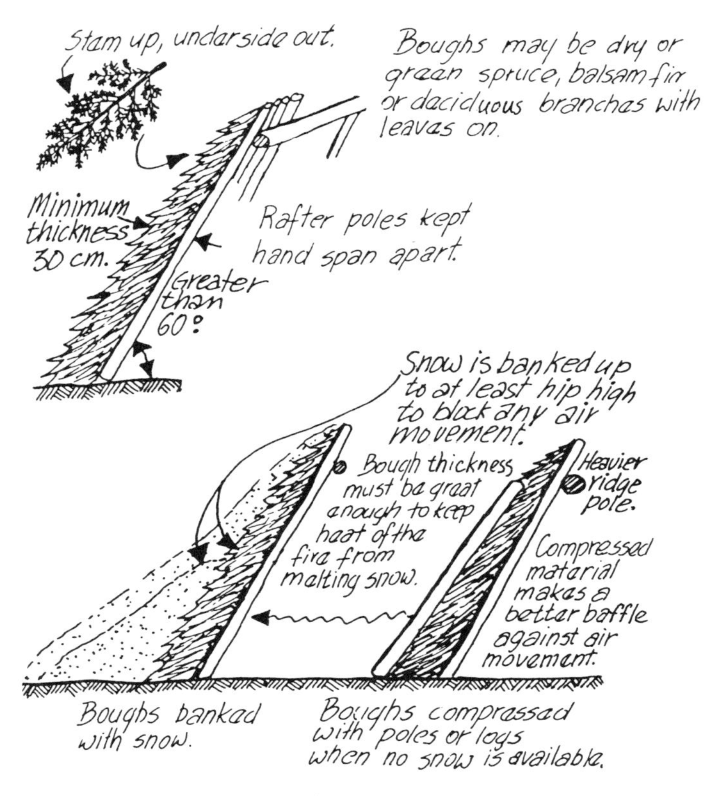

The use of boughs as roofing.

wind and rain-proof configuration.

One of the more effective backs to an open-fronted shelter are straight poles touching side by side. The arrangement is wind-proof, as well as a good absorber and re-emiter of warmth because of its thermal mass. The first layer is chinked with moss which in turn is compressed with a second layer of poles. This is sufficient for winter use, but for rainy conditions, a third layer may have to be added.

When -40°C or colder, it is easiest and quickest to build a lean-to from split aspen logs (green, frozen aspen splits in half remarkably easily at this temperature).

Whenever trees peel easily, the bark can be incorporated into a roof. Most barks tend to curl on drying, therefore, place the bark between two layers of poles to prevent this.

A single person, open-fronted shelter may be expanded

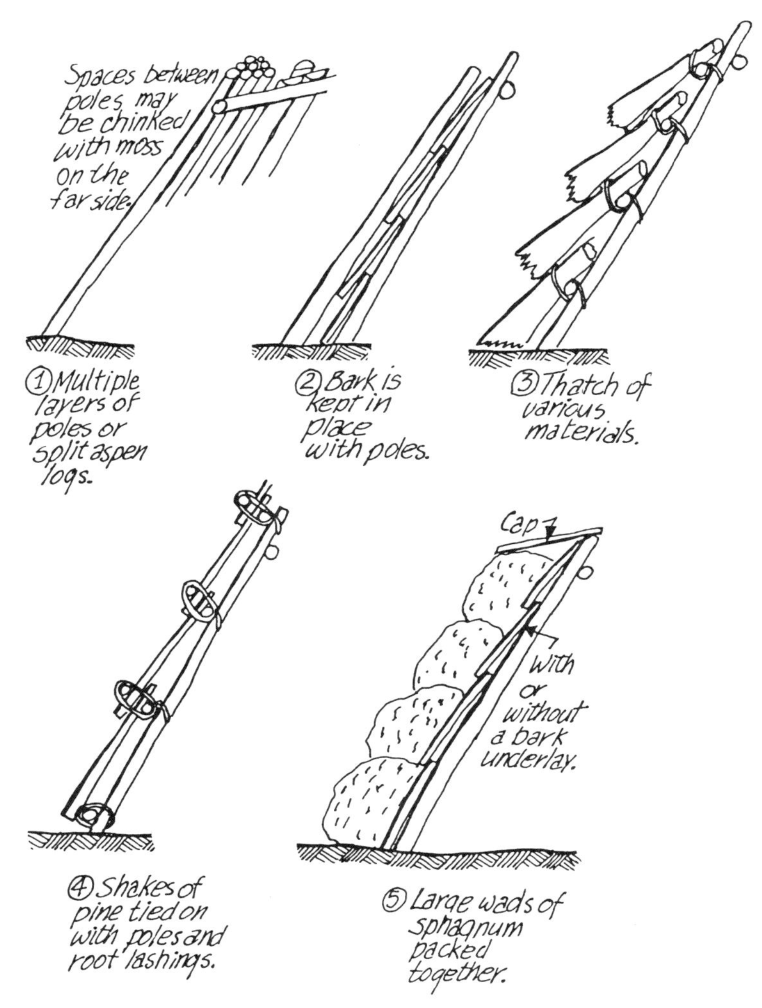

Some available roofing materials.

to accommodate two people by extending the length of the bed and shelter by one-third. Each person sleeps opposite the other with bodies overlapping from heels to hips. Three or four people use two shelters facing each other. For more than four people, or during a long stay involving one person, a brush or wooden teepee may be more appropriate. The time spent in constructing the more elaborate shelter is offset by a greatly reduced fuel requirement.

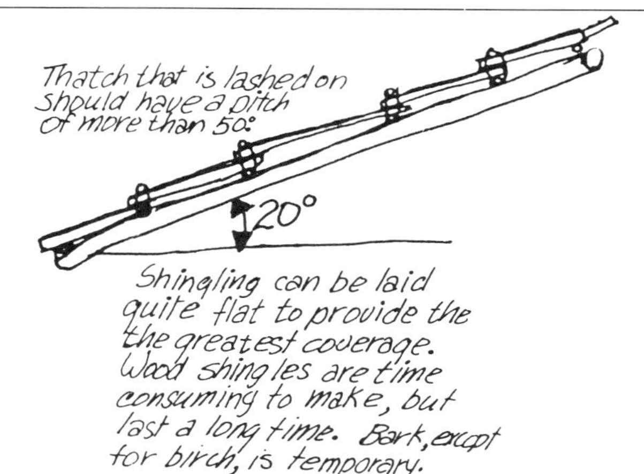

Thatch that is lashed on should have a pitch of more than 50°
20°
Shingling can be laid quite flat to provide the the greatest coverage. Wood shingles are time consuming to make, but last a long time. Bark, except for birch, is temporary.

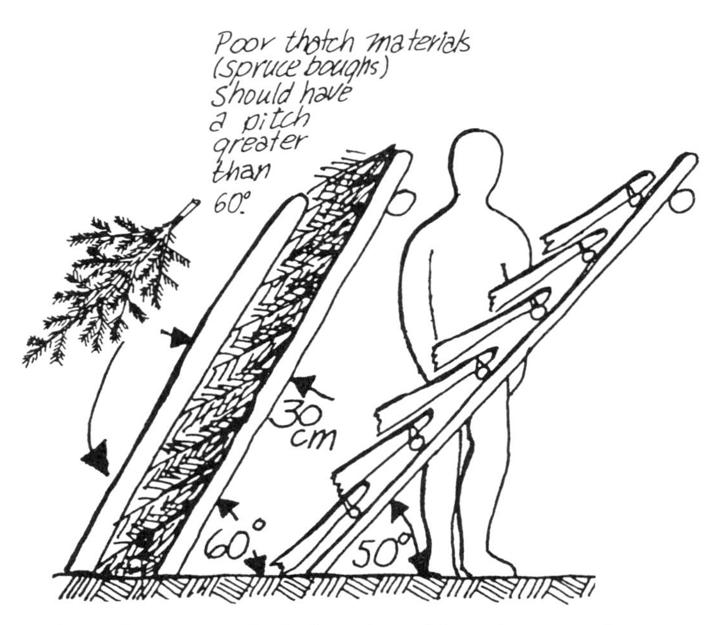

Spruce boughs are an inferior thatching, but used properly this abundant material can serve passably well.

— The angle of the roof has to be over 60 degrees. The stronger the rainfall the steeper the roof must be.

— The boughs are more effective if compressed.

— The best effect is achieved by using the boughs with the stem up and the underside out to the weather.

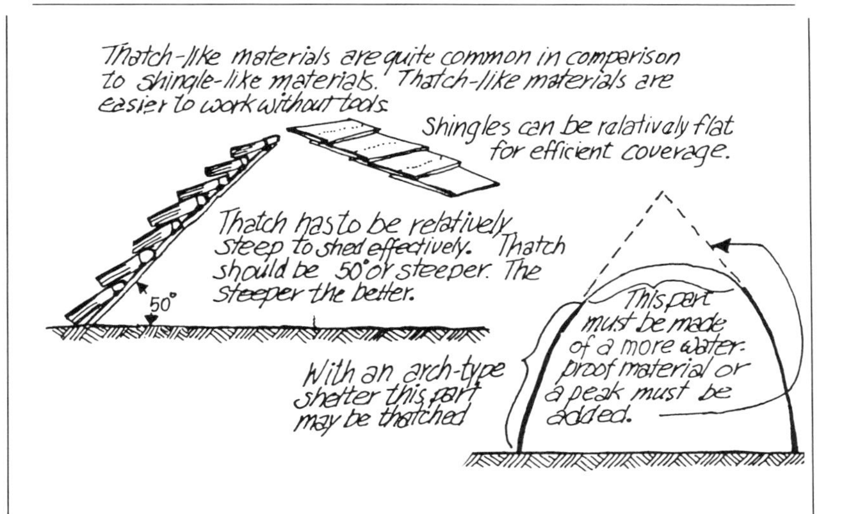

Pitch and roofing material.

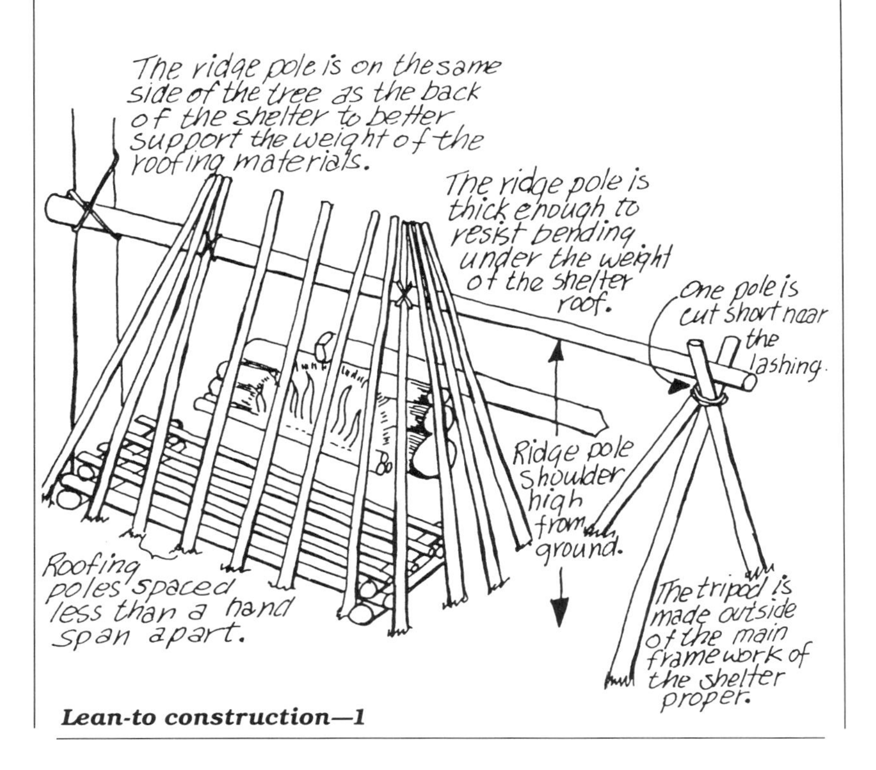

Lean-to construction—1

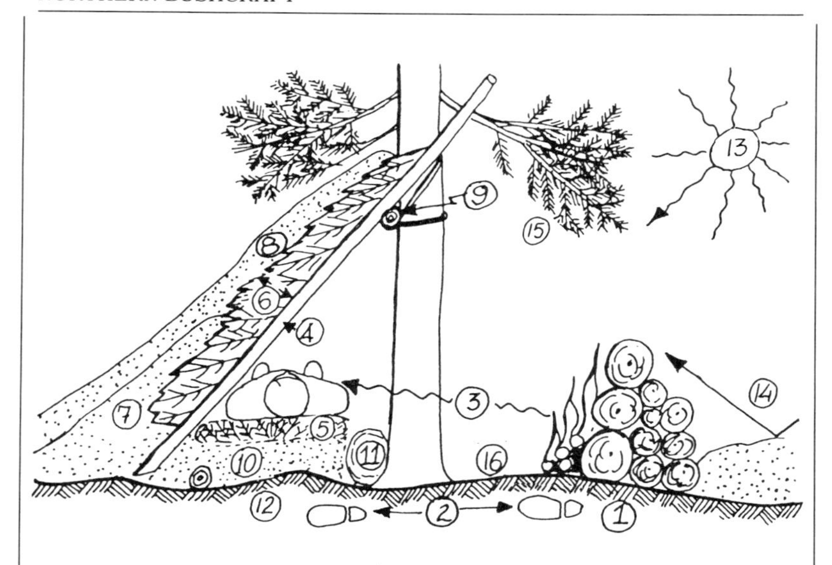

A cross section of a winter lean-to.

1. Wall backed fire is waist high.
2. Fire one good step away from the edge of the bed.
3. Fire made hot enough to force you to stay one step away.
4. The back of the shelter is as close to the fire as possible.
5. The bough bed is at least four fingers thick when compressed.
6. Boughs are thick enough to prevent heat penetration from melting the banked up snow.
7. Snow is banked up to prevent infiltration of cold air.
8. If possible, bank up the whole roof with snow.
9. The ridgepole is substantial enough to hold up the weight of the bough and snow cover. The ridgepole is parallel to the wind. It is about shoulder high off the ground providing room to sit and work under the shelter roof.
10. The core of the bed is made of snow. It is about chair seat high.
11. Snow retaining log prevents the snow from melting out from under the bed.
12. With an elevated bed the ground can be uneven.
13. Face the shelter towards the sun.
14. A clear expanse of snow in front of the shelter provides more warming effect from the sun.
15. Make the shelter under a tree that provides some overhead protection.
16. The snow is cleared away between the fire and edge of the bed.

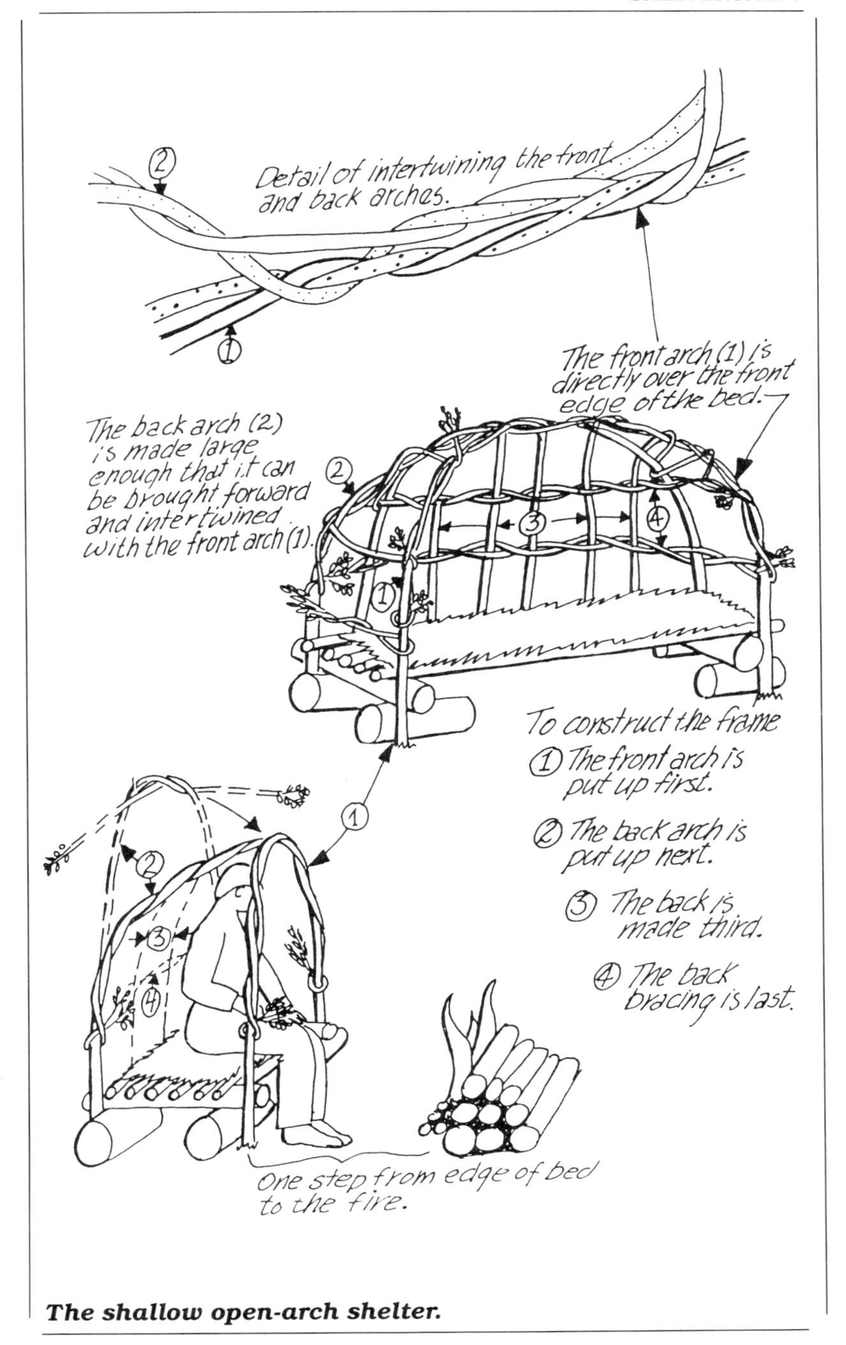

The shallow open-arch shelter.

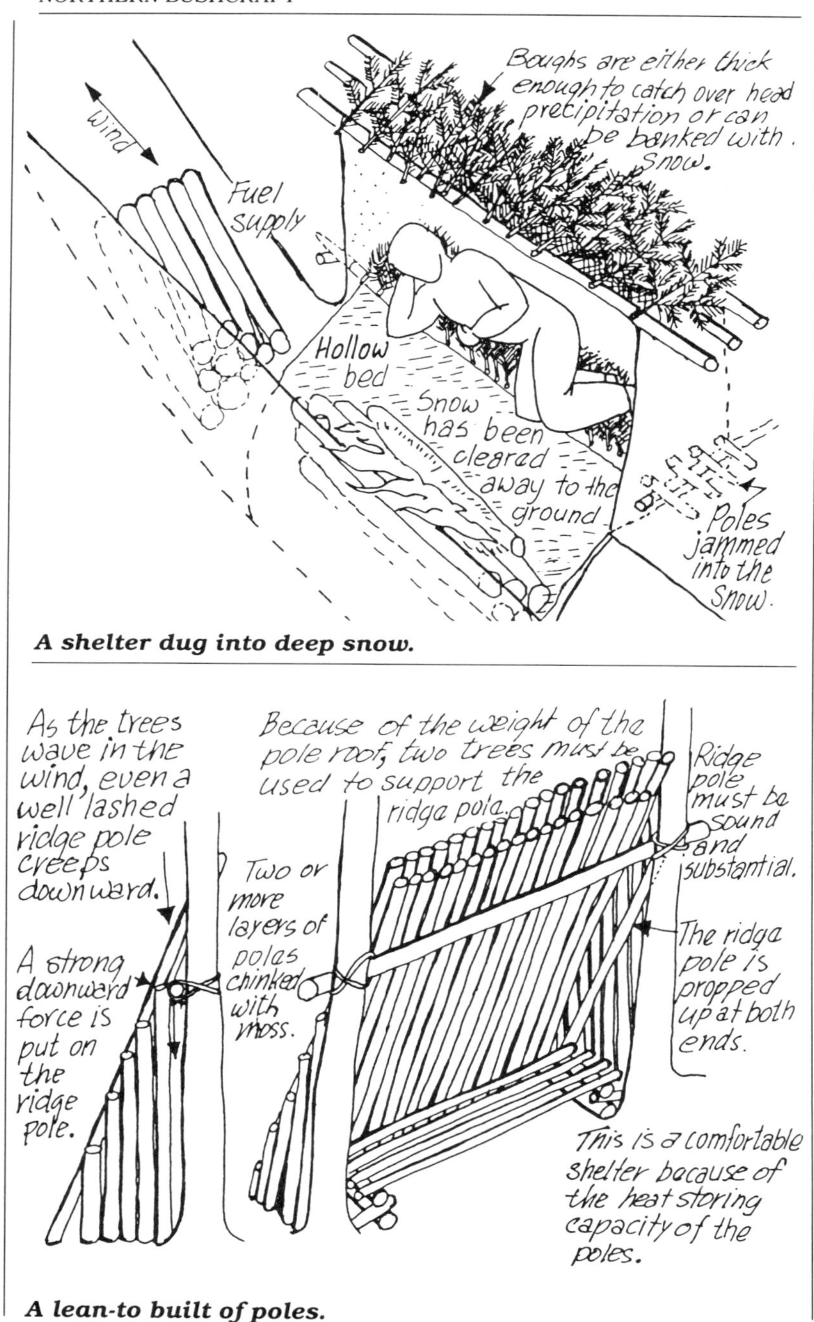

A shelter dug into deep snow.

A lean-to built of poles.

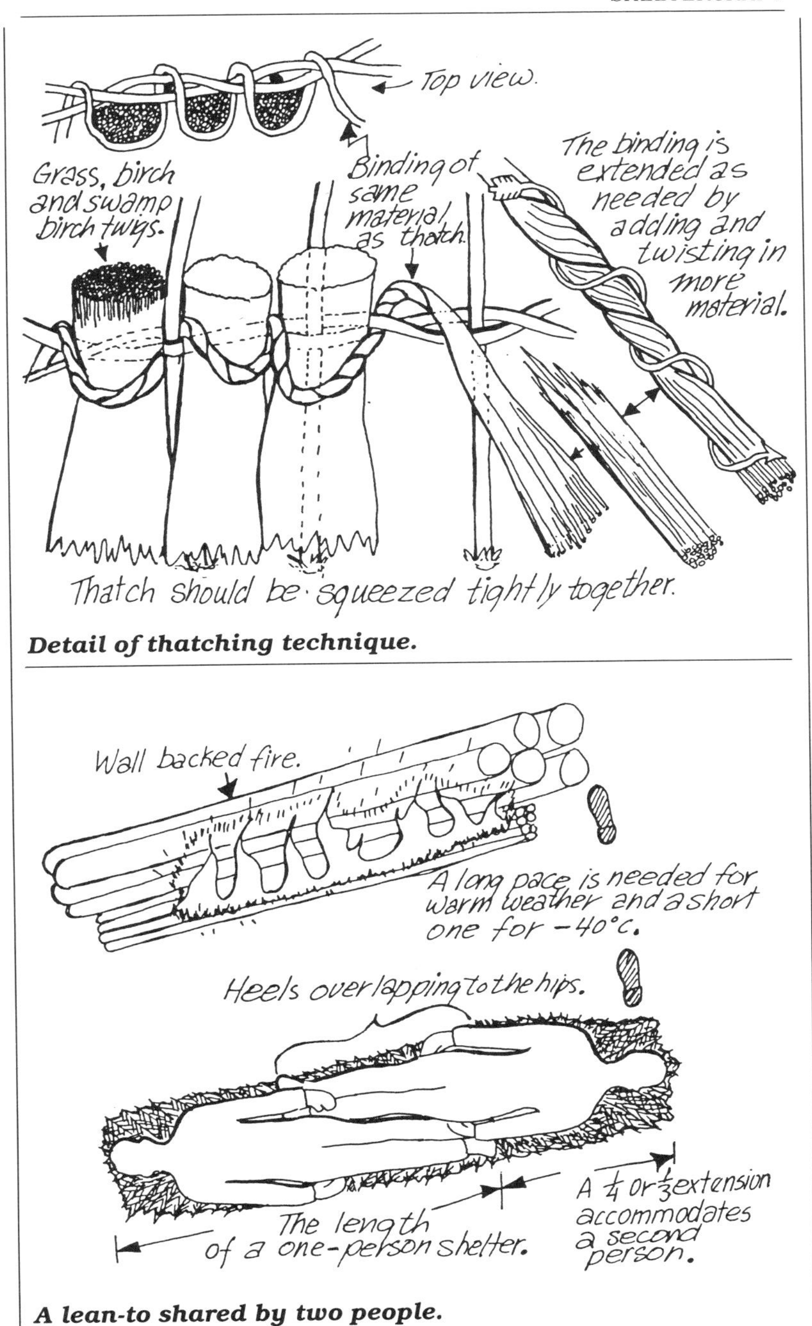

Detail of thatching technique.

A lean-to shared by two people.

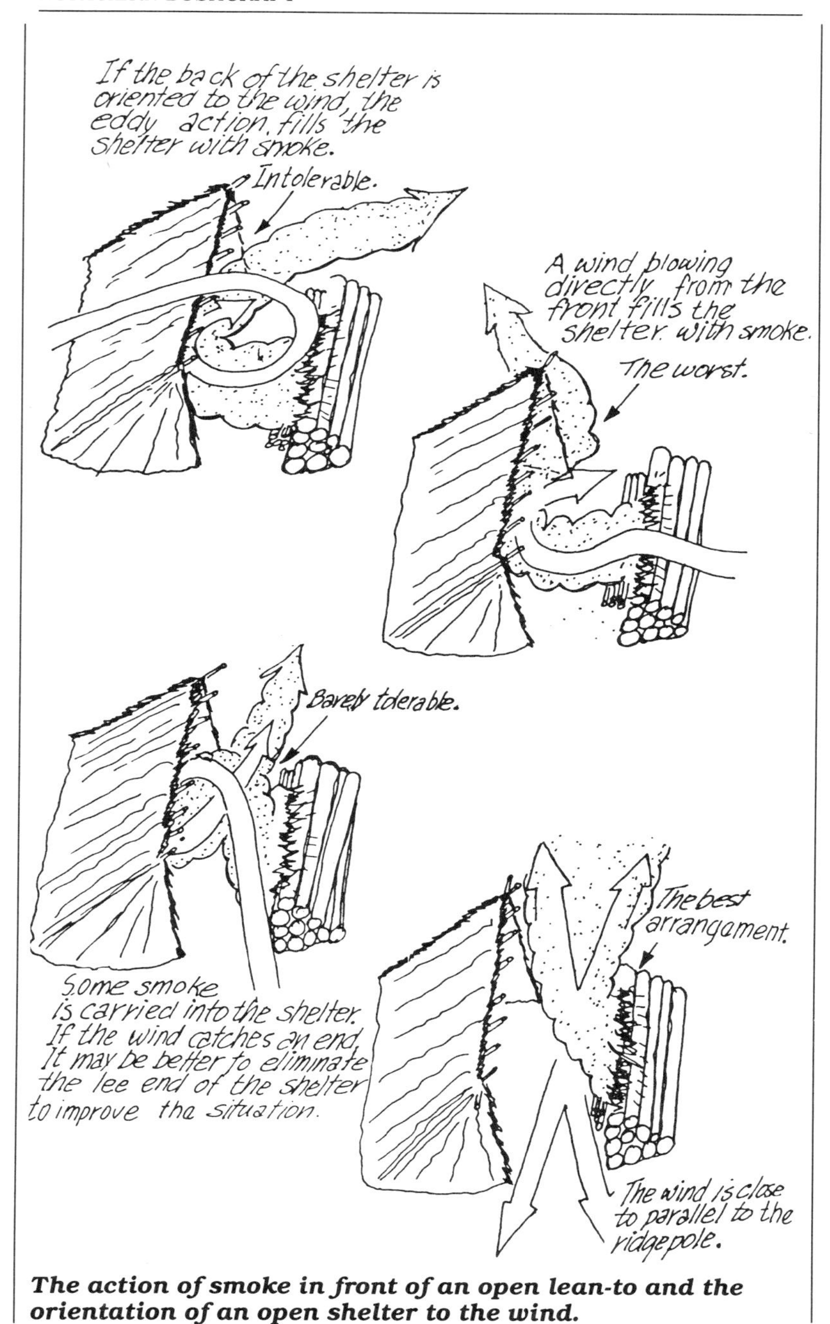

The action of smoke in front of an open lean-to and the orientation of an open shelter to the wind.

① This lashing takes the weight of the ridge pole.
② This lashing prevents the ridge pole from shifting sideways.
③ This lashing keeps the leaning roof poles from shifting any further inwards.
④ The edge of the bed is directly under the ridge pole at shoulder height.
⑤ The stronger the rain, the steeper the roof.
The better the overhead protection, the less effort needed in making the roof waterproof.
For cold weather the wall backed fire is waist high.
Wall is about a step from the edge of the bed.
The bed is chair seat high.

Lean-to construction—2

Bush Beds

Although spruce boughs are popular for making bush beds, they are not the only suitable materials, and not necessarily the best. Anything will make do providing it is fine at the tips and no thicker than the thumb at the stem. Any shrub such as willow, alder, red osier dogwood or swamp birch, and any branches such as aspen, black poplar, birch or pine (with or without needles or leaves) are suitable. Forbs, such as clover, green or dry grass, sedge, cattail or bulrush are adequate. (Wherever the word "bough" is used, one may substitute any of these materials.) All can be arranged in a similar fashion to provide resilient insulation from the snow or cold ground. A ground sheet is unnecessary if the compressed bed is four or more fingers thick.

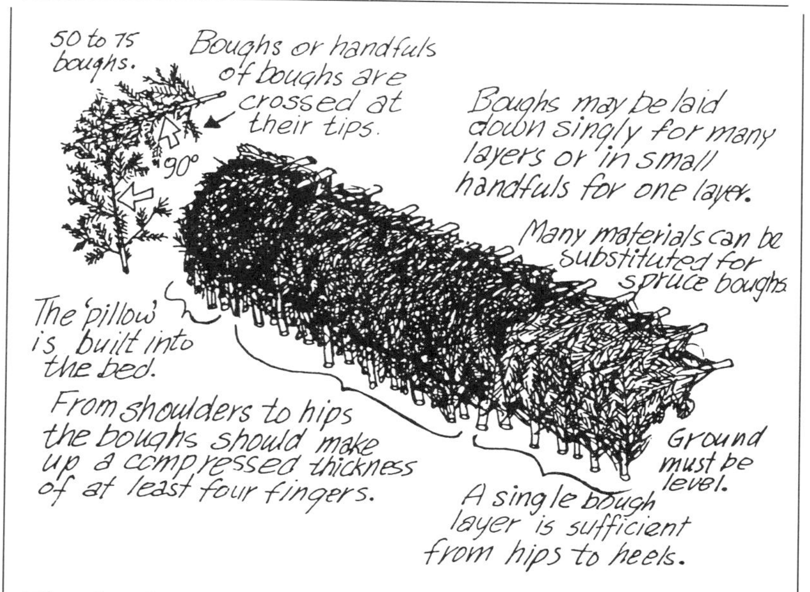

The simple bed.

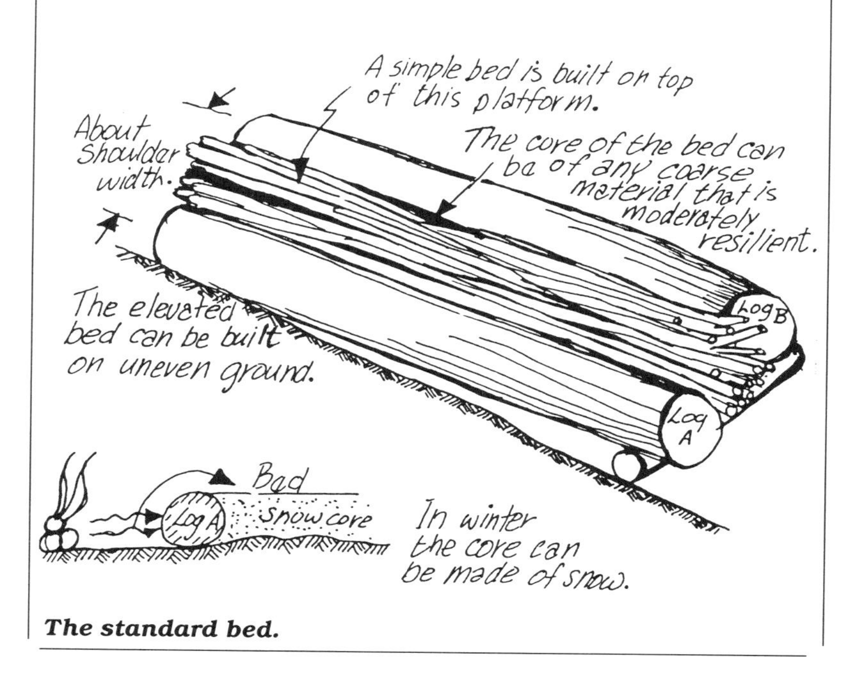

The standard bed.

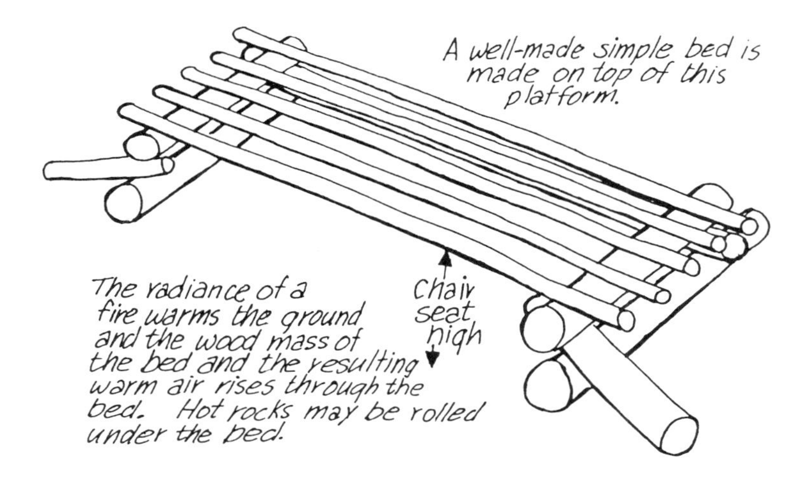

A well-made simple bed is made on top of this platform.
The radiance of a fire warms the ground and the wood mass of the bed and the resulting warm air rises through the bed. Hot rocks may be rolled under the bed.
Chair seat high

The hollow core or elevated bed.

Frozen boughs may crumble under your weight unless they are warmed to make them supple. Wet boughs should have excess moisture shaken off before use. Dry, dead, needle-free boughs make a more insulative but less resilient bed than one made of green boughs. As a bough bed will flatten with use, a fresh layer should be added every three or four days.

The simplest bed is the uppermost layer or mattress component of the more complex beds described in this section. The simple bed is adequate in the summer or to supplement a mat and sleeping bag in the winter. The bed can be built on level ground or packed snow. Fifty to 75 boughs that are about elbow to finger tip long are laid down singly or in small handfuls in a chevron-like pattern, with the tips crossing slightly. For the greatest resiliency, lay the boughs down the same way they grew on the tree. A layer or two of boughs (made from small handfuls) with a compressed thickness of four fingers is an excellent mattress. One layer should extend for the full-length of the body. Additional layers extend only from the head to the hips, as the legs do not need any more resiliency or insulation beyond the first layer. For multi-layered beds, use the thick stemmed and coarser boughs first. Long, bare stems should be broken off and used directly on the ground for the best effect. Boughs thicker than the thumb should be used to cover the ground layer.

Handfuls of smaller, shorter branches of pencil-thickness may be jammed stem first into any holes in the bed. A source of short boughs is usually the top two metres of a spruce tree. It is better to leave the top in one piece and unlimbed in the base of a bed. A log at the edge of the bed nearest to the fire helps to keep you from rolling off while you sleep. For a pillow, tuck a small armload of branches or sticks under the boughs at the head of the bed.

The standard bed incorporates a base to raise the simple bed about 15 to 20 centimetres. This proves to be more resilient than the simple bed and is useful on uneven ground. Two logs, about your height in length, are laid down shoulder-width apart and leveled. The space between the logs is filled with big boughs, shrubbery, spruce tops, or small trees, and the simple bed is then made on top of this.

The deluxe bed provides as much comfort as nature can provide when it is bitterly cold and you have to sleep in your clothes without a sleeping bag or mat. An injured or ill person may require such a bed. A platform for the simple bed is made about chair-seat high leaving a clear space between it and the ground. The front is left open and the back of the space is lined with logs. The radiance of the fire warms everything beneath the bed and the resulting warmed air rises through it. Hot rocks can also be rolled under the bed.

In cold weather, an elevated bed is always more comfortable than one made directly on the ground where the air is coldest. Snow makes a good platform and is a good insulator from the cold sink of the ground. The front edge is lined with logs so that the bed will not melt out from under you. The packed snow is leveled and the simple bed built on top. A hollow bed can be made with long poles supported at the ends by heaped up snow.

Deep Open-Fronted Shelters

The deep open-fronted shelter is inadequate in cold weather. It is difficult to maintain uniform warmth within the structure. Your feet may be comfortable, but your head will be cold unless you are able to stretch out beside a fire that is as long as you are tall. Deep shelters are useful in warm and cool weather where insulative materials and body heat prove adequate. The easily constructed frameworks are useful for supporting waterproof covers or for making the hollow core when constructing snow shelters.

Partly-Enclosed Open-Fire Shelters

The conical shelter is very efficient. It provides a large floor space in relation to the amount of cover required. The shape allows for standing room in the middle, and an easily heated low overhead volume. The design is stable in wind and is useful in heavier forms of construction.

The coverings for conical shelters are made in much the same way as for open-fronted ones. Use boughs, compressed with logs and various types of thatch or barks, from both coniferous and deciduous trees. Because the cone is stable,

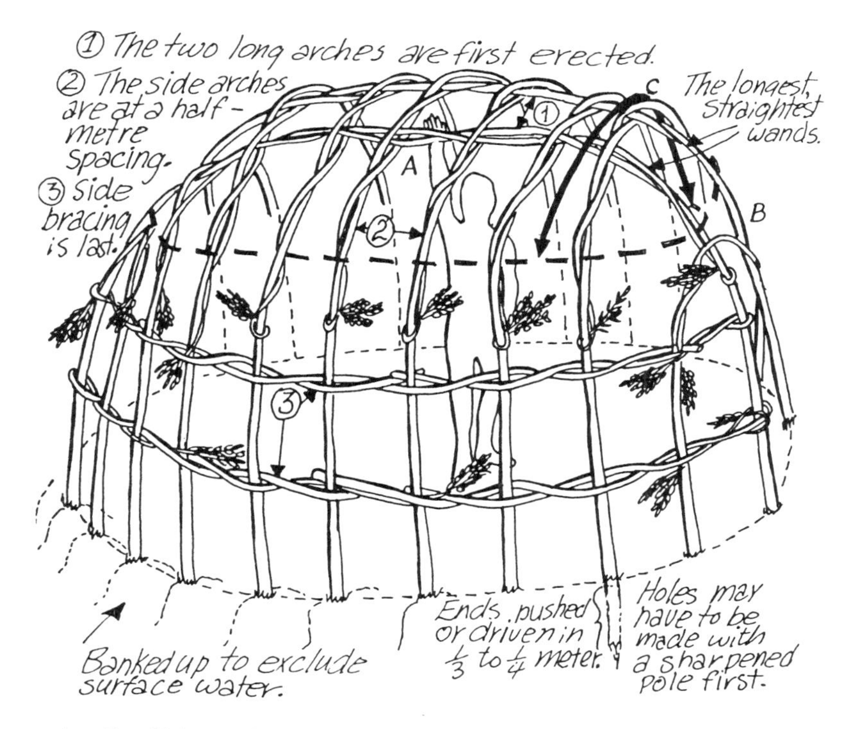

The flexible arch-dome structure.
A. For 4 people, the structure is a full reach high and wide, and two full reaches long. This amount of headroom is necessary when an open fire is used.
B. The framework can be made from any flexible wands such as willow, alder, thin pine and spruce. If less flexible or thicker wands are used they are lashed instead of woven.
C. The point at which the pitch of the roof is less than 60 degrees must be shingled to properly deflect rain.

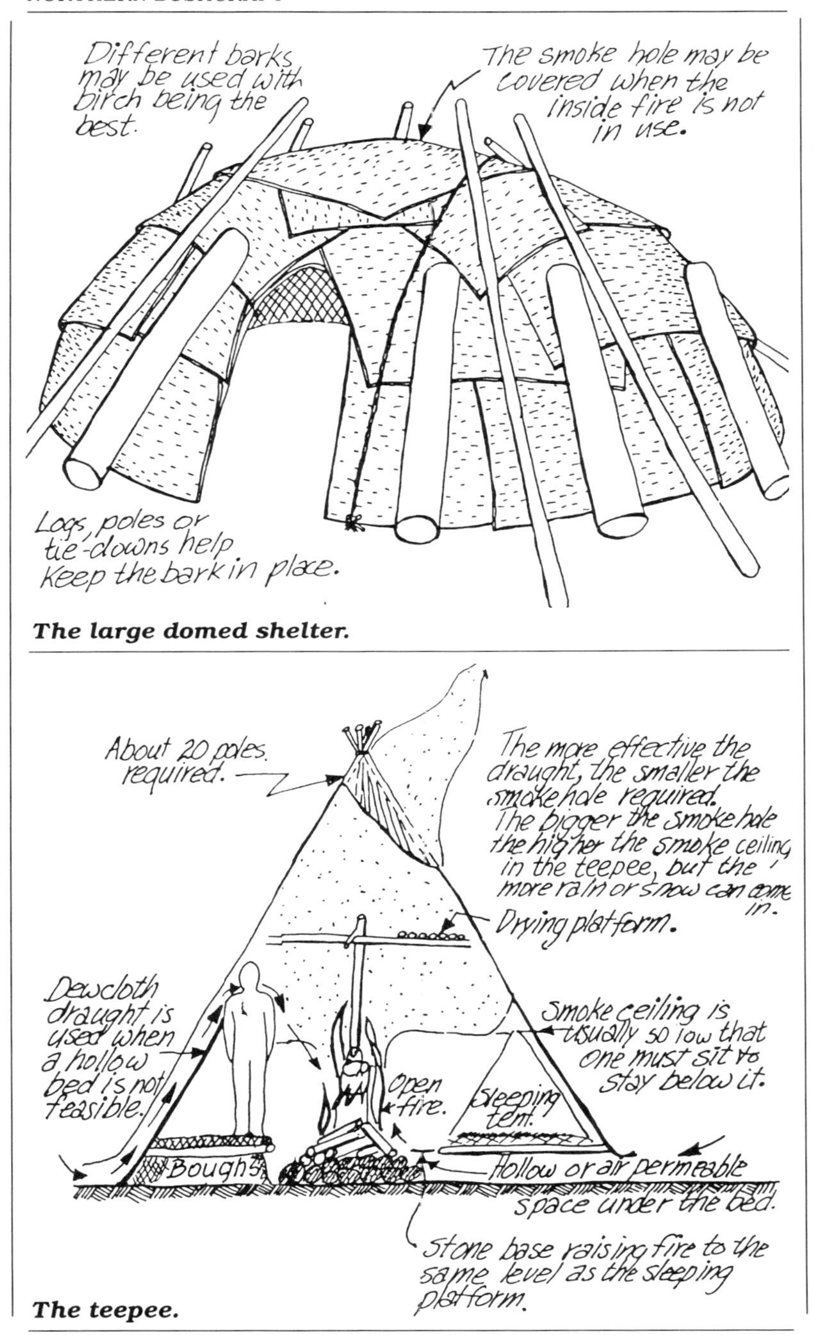

The large domed shelter.

The teepee.

it can be banked with earth. Some conical forms are dug into the ground for cover, ground warmth and thermal mass. The earth-covered shelters are usually unpleasant to live in during the rainy season because of dripping and dampness.

Birch bark makes an excellent cover that is reasonably portable. It can be peeled almost all year around, whereas the bark of other trees is only available from midspring to midsummer. Birch bark is boiled to make it more flexible then sewn into long strips for more manageable and efficient coverage.

In Lapland, natural cover materials were replaced with canvas in the summer and horse blankets in the winter. Now, such covers are made of durable woven polyethylene. Most of the nomadic peoples of the Northern Forest regions used tanned hides as shelter covers at one time or another. Felt mats were also popular in some parts of the world. Hair or wool covers have a good reputation for being rot resistant, insulative, rain deflective, light and durable. Other common cover materials are mats woven from various reeds.

Another shelter found in the Northern Forests is the domed framework of bent trees or saplings. This type provides more headroom compared to the conical configuration and functions much the same way in all other aspects.

Partially-Enclosed Shelters

The partially-enclosed shelters that use an open fire may be looked upon as open-fronted shelters built in a circle. They are less sensitive to wind effects and use less fuel, but continue to lose any warmed air through the smoke hole. They may be compared to a stove large enough for one to live inside. The shelter configuration strongly influences the quality of the fire used in it through the size of its smoke hole (damper) and fresh air inlet (draught). The smaller the shelter, the lower the smoke level.

To be comfortable in a small shelter where the smoke level is within a metre of the ground, you must recline and not use an elevated bed. Dry, good quality, smokeless fuel is more important here than in open-fronted shelters.

A shelter with a long cone acts more like a chimney drawing out the smoke, but more cover material is needed. A good air inlet at floor level also helps, but this may create uncomfortable draughts in parts of the shelter. This may be overcome by the use of channels in the floor or under the elevated beds. The Plains teepee employs a structure known as a dew cloth that allows the draught for the fire to pass overhead.

With a low smoke ceiling the sleeping benches should be raised just above the discomfort of the moist or cold ground. Elevating the fire on a pile of stones also raises the smoke ceiling. The larger the smoke hole, the higher the smoke level. A compromise must be struck between the smoke level and the amount of precipitation the opening allows into the shelter. If you can stay below it by stooping, the smoke

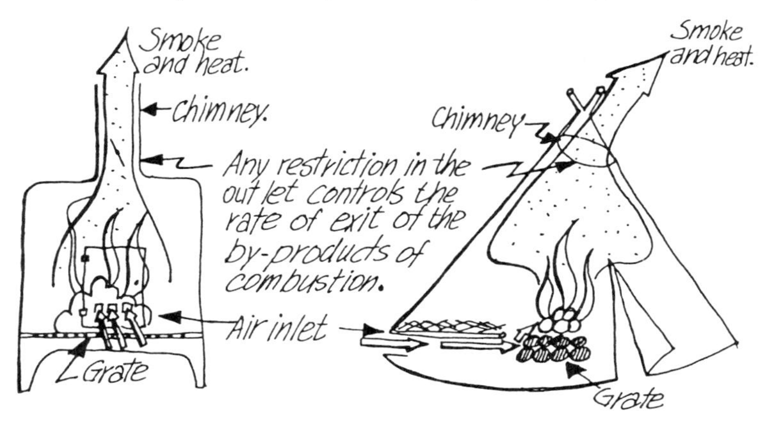

An enclosed shelter with an open fire functions much like a large stove with a small fire in its centre.

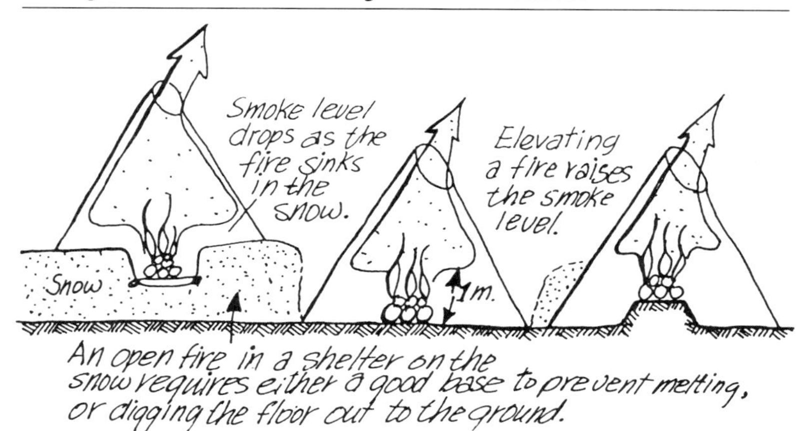

Smoke levels inside a shelter with an open fire.

level is high enough.

In some earth covered and underground shelters the smoke hole may be the only fresh air inlet for both fire and occupants. It also serves as the skylight or window and the only entrance into the shelter.

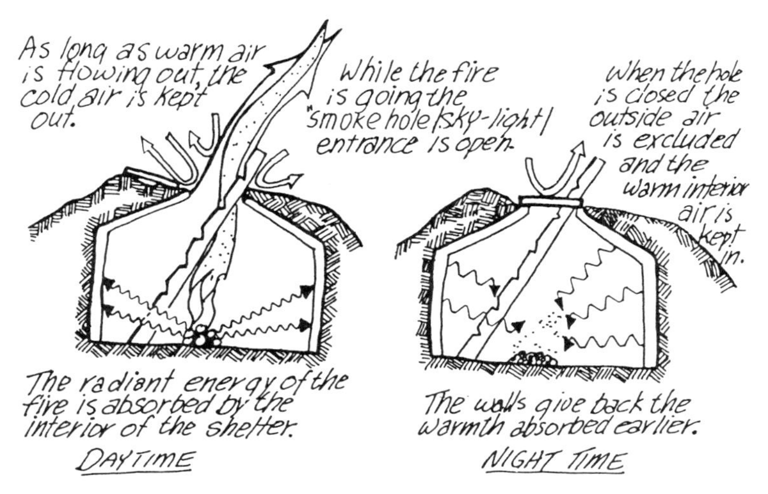

The multi-functional smoke hole.

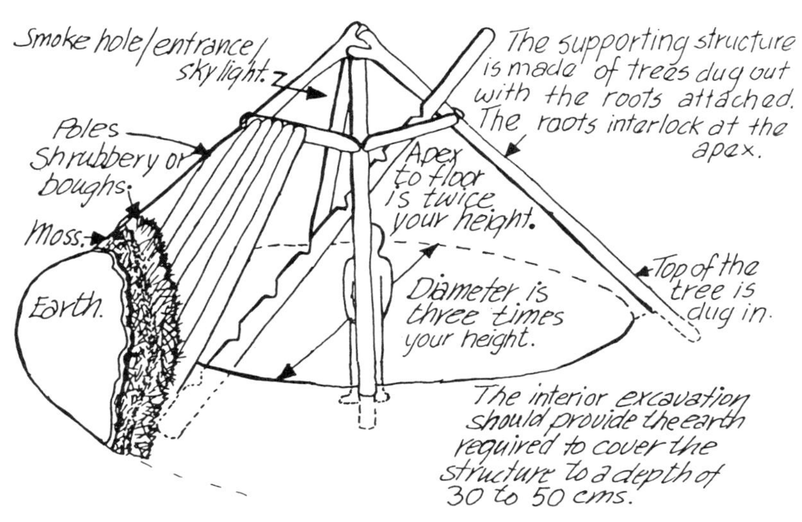

One method of constructing the semi-subterranean shelter.

A thin-shelled shelter cools quickly when its fire is out. A shelter with enough thermal mass, such as a subterranean one, absorbs heat from the fire during the day. When the fire is out, the smoke hole is closed to retain the warmed air, doing away with the need to stoke a fire at night.

The partially-enclosed, open-fire shelters are more portable than other structures as no stove or stove-pipe is required and the shelter covering is often light. The fire provides illumination so a lamp is not required.

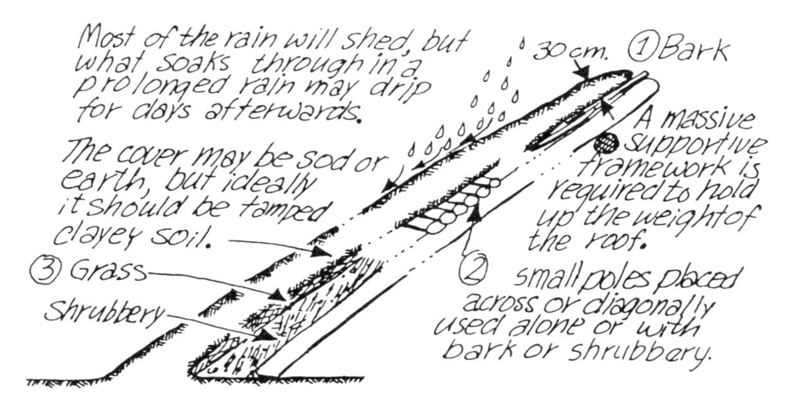

Three methods of making a sod roof.

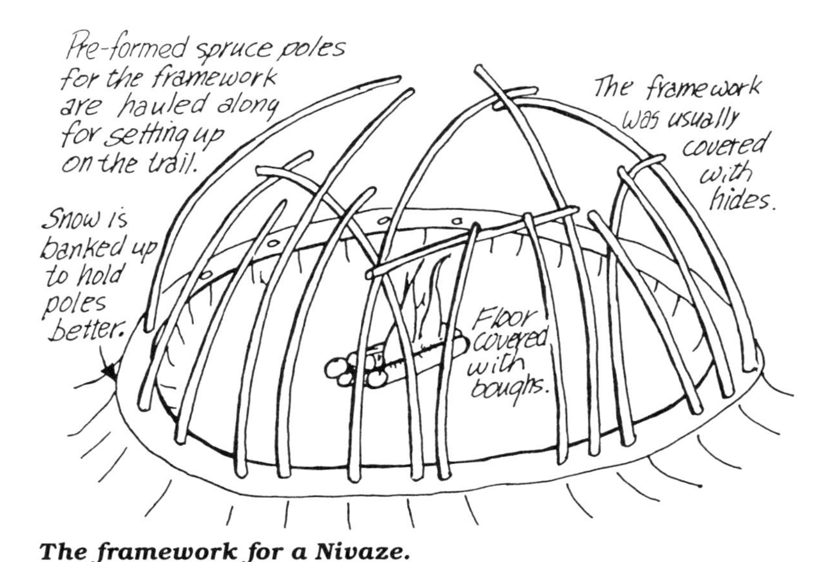

The framework for a Nivaze.

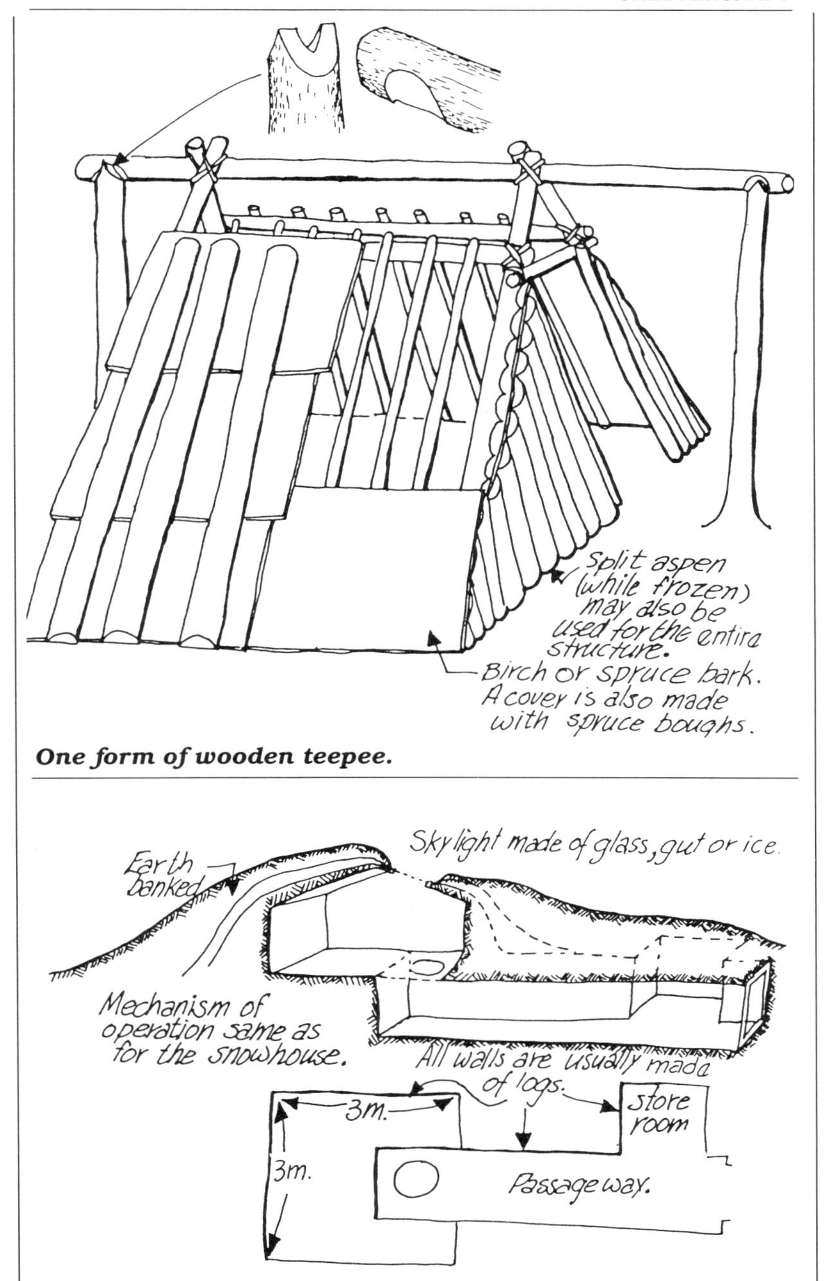

One form of wooden teepee.

The Kugeri—an Inuit semi-subterranean dwelling.

Enclosed Shelters

Enclosed shelters are the most efficient and fuel conservative. They capture a bubble of warmed air produced by a stove, fireplace and/or the human body. Ideally, this type of shelter should have sufficient thermal mass and external insulation to retain enough warmth during the waking hours to last through the night.

A problem with enclosed shelters, built with natural materials, is a source of light. It is difficult to find natural substitutes for glass. Windows that let in light, but exclude cold, have been made of parchment, gut and ice slabs. A fireplace provides light, but a stove is usually so well-enclosed that it is a poor light source.

The enclosed shelters that use body warmth as their main heat source require a highly insulative shell of a low thermal mass. The better-known of these shelters are made of snow, such as snow houses (igloos), quinzies and snow caves. The Inuit also used a semi-subterranean structure called the kugeri or qasgiq, constructed on similar principles as the traditional snow house, that functioned like the conical earth covered shelters. Some also used an insulated tent that trapped body heat.

Snow shelters are at their best when the temperature is less than -15°C; when there are no problems from moisture and dripping; and, when clothing does not become overly wet in building or hollowing out the structure.

When there are no tools for gathering firewood, or fuel is scarce, the enclosed snow shelter may make life easier. Instead of transporting a shelter, the building tools are carried or made on the spot from local materials. It may take longer to make a snow structure than to erect a tent, but this is offset when breaking camp as there is nothing to take down.

The properly built snow shelter has many ideal features. The shelter is well-insulated with a low thermal mass that is easily warmed. It is as dry as any shelter can be under the circumstances and is sound and windproof. The shelter can be constructed to provide more or less room, depending on immediate needs. The interior of the shelter is bright and psychologically uplifting.

There are many ways a snow shelter can be built. If there are large drifts, you can tunnel into them in a variety of ways. Make a large opening for easy excavation then close it off with snow blocks.

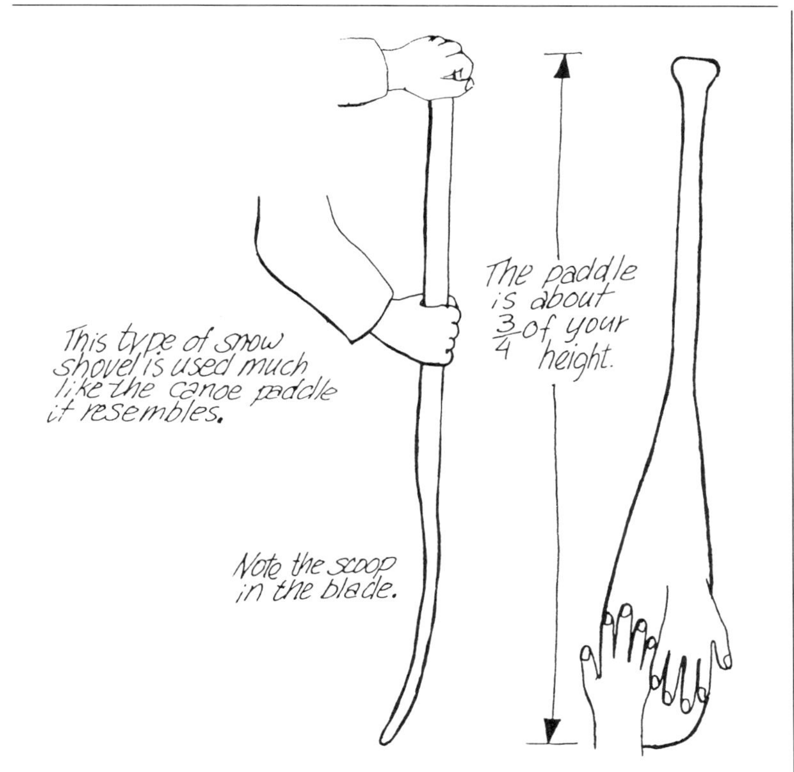

The wooden snow shovel.

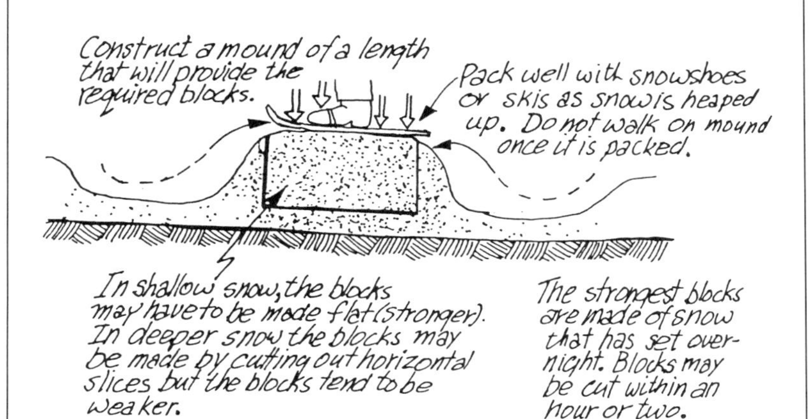

Making artificial blocks.

If consolidated snow or drifts deep enough for shelter construction are unavailable, then powdery snow is heaped up, allowed to set for a few hours then hollowed out. Snow may also be heaped up and packed. Blocks are then cut for use in building a hollow structure.

Snow that is disturbed, compacted or mixed, tends to consolidate and can be handled in blocks or slabs. Mixing the snow pushes the crystals together so they weld to one another. The moister, warmer layers of snow near the ground fuse with the colder crystals near the top of the snow. Consolidation takes as little time as half an hour and as much as two hours. If excavated too soon, the mound may collapse. If allowed to set too long, the snow becomes so firm it is difficult to work.

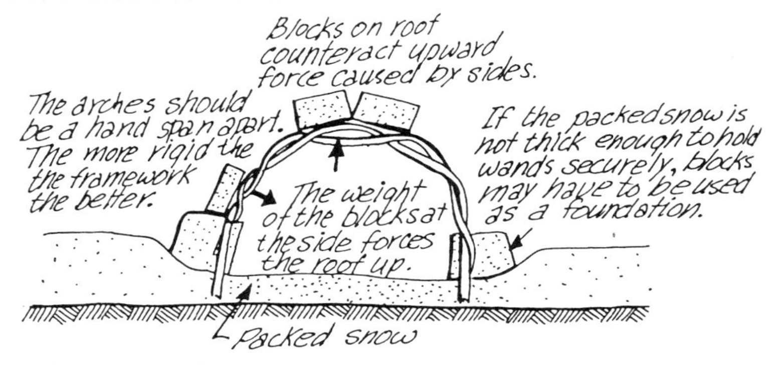

Arch method of producing a hollow core for a snow shelter.

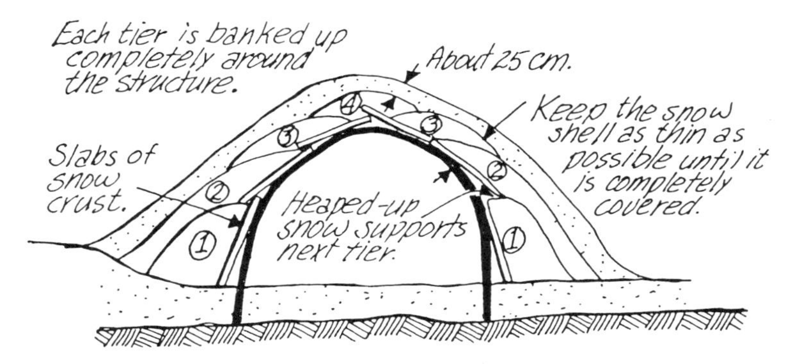

Using a "skin" to exclude loose snow in building a Quinze.

Loose snow less than 30 centimetres deep is a poor construction material for snow shelters. It can be packed in small lots, allowed to set for at least four hours then transported in block form. Once packed, it should not be walked on or the blocks made from it will crumble.

The most useful tools in snowwork are shovels and carpenter-like saws. A snowshoe can substitute for a shovel, especially if the tip is rounded. A wooden shovel, similar to a canoe paddle in outline (with a slightly scooped blade), can be used in much the same way as a canoe paddle to move snow.

A thin-bladed knife for cutting blocks can be carved from wood. Both the blade and handle should be about elbow to finger tip long. The long handle allows for more leverage when making cuts. Skis can be used for both packing snow and cutting blocks. Cutting blocks in dense drifts with a proper saw is hard work to begin with, so these makeshift tools may be slow and tiresome to use.

When the snow is poorly consolidated and you have only sticks to cut with, then a supporting framework of alder or willow wands will simplify construction. If the framework material is frozen it may be too brittle to wrap and weave in the usual manner. The solution is to tie together the wands making the arches and to tie the arches to each other wherever they cross. The irregular blocks may be leaned against the framework to build a solid shell, which will become a stable domed structure the instant it is completed.

The floor of the shelter is packed and, if necessary, more snow is added to a thickness of about 30 centimetres. The butts of the wands are now inserted deep enough to stay anchored in place. In shallow snow, a block foundation may have to be laid down and the wands inserted into it. The framework must be rigid enough to support the weight of the snow blocks. The construction should proceed in an even fashion up the sides of the structure. When the sides are partially built, the roof blocks may be placed to counteract the upward thrust of the framework. After the structure has been completed and the snow has set for a short while, a door may be cut out and the framework removed if necessary.

The framework can be covered with fabric or boughs then heaped with loose snow. Snow crusts leaned against the framework can be banked up to their upper edge, at which point another tier is leaned against the framework and the process repeated.

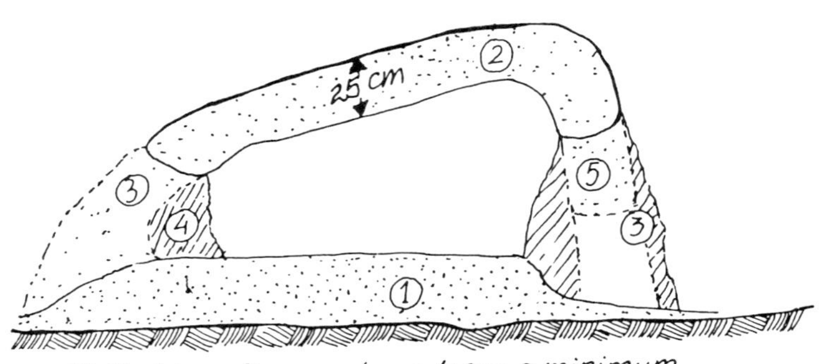

(1) Build up floor and pack for a minimum thickness of 15cm.

(2) Heap up snow and let it settle for at least two hours.

(3) Tunnel through the mound from both ends.

(4) Fill in non-entrance end and clean up from the inside.

(5) Fill in entrance end, re-cut door and clean up.

Sequence in constructing a Quinze.

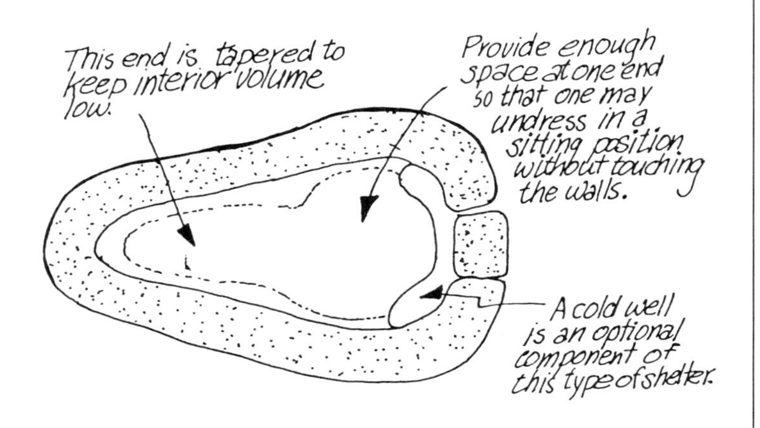

This end is tapered to keep interior volume low.
Provide enough space at one end so that one may undress in a sitting position without touching the walls.
A cold well is an optional component of this type of shelter.

Floor plan of a Quinze.

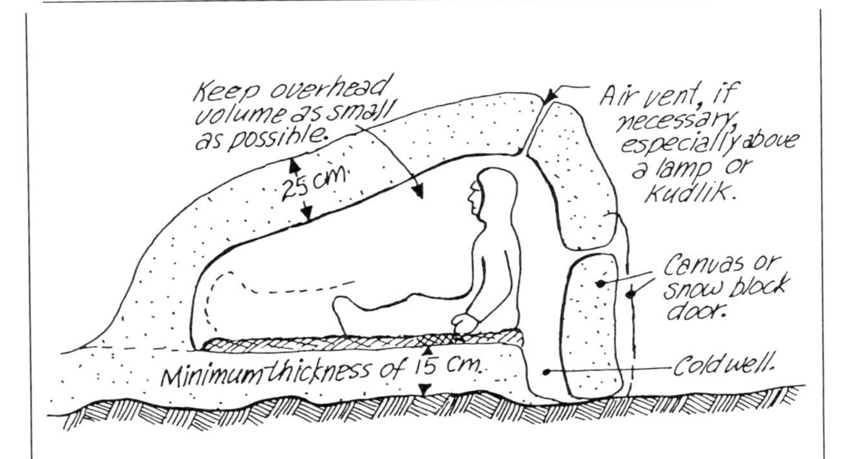

Cross section of a Quinze.

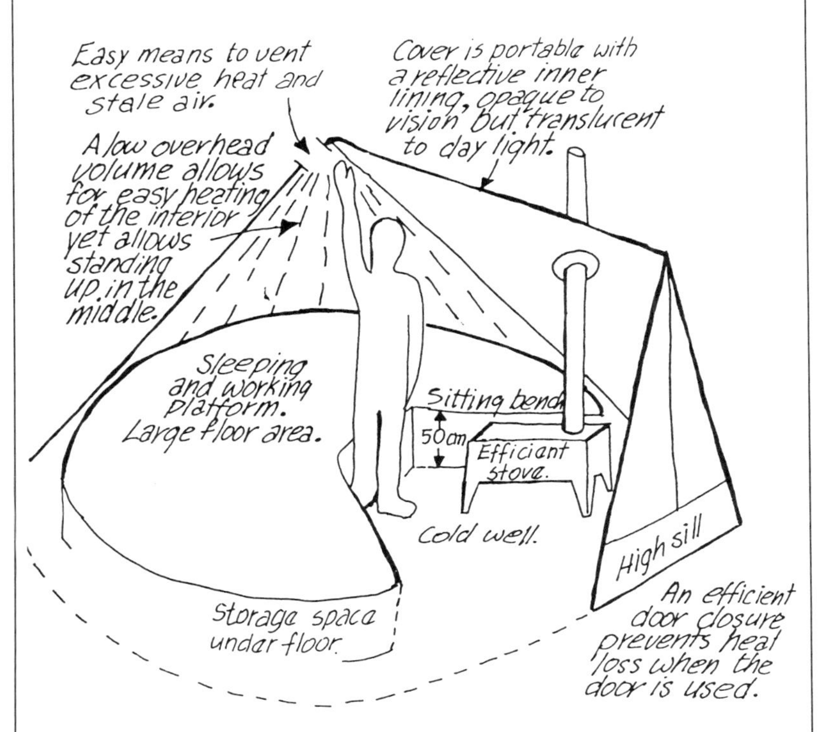

The ideal shelter is difficult to achieve with wilderness materials.

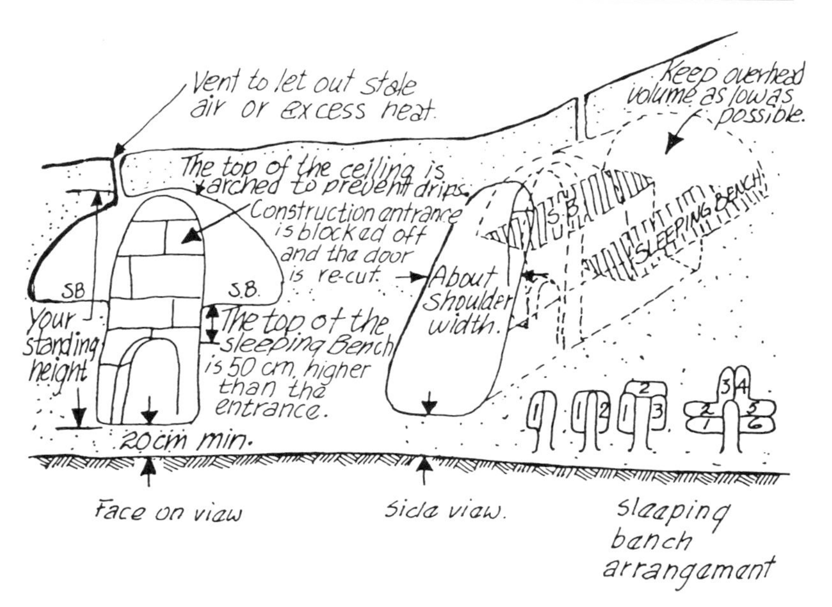

Excavating a snow shelter in a deep drift.

The shelter floor can be covered with anything insulative such as boughs or grass. A well allows the heavier cold air near the top of the floor to drain off. Do not scrape away the snow to the bare ground inside the snow structure. Normally, under good snow cover, a temperature of about -3°C to -5°C will be found at ground level regardless of how cold it is above the snow. Ground at this temperature still acts like a heat sink when it is near a body at 37°C. Although snow cannot be warmer than zero, it is still more insulative and reflective than cold ground at -5°C. To counteract this, about 15 centimetres of packed snow should cover the ground.

7

THE BIRCHES

Birch is one of the more beautiful and useful trees of the Northern Forests.

THE PAPER BIRCH

There are at least 30-40 species of birch often recognized by their smooth, white bark. The whiteness or silvery color results from air trapped between the cells. The air acts as insulation and keeps both the tree trunk and sap cool. This prevents the sap from rising prematurely in the spring when freezing may damage the tree's cells. Birch—one of the most northerly of trees—is capable of withstanding the merciless arctic summer sun striking at a low angle for 24 hours a day with an intensity never found in the tropics. The tree's ability to tolerate the sun shining on all sides of its trunk is not a common trait in the plant kingdom.

The paper birch may be found growing in the Arctic tundra as a severely beset dwarf whose roots are never more than a few centimetres from permanently frozen soil. It is also found growing in more southerly latitudes as a stately tree at least 25 metres tall and up to 45 centimetres in diameter.

The birch is a vigorous colonizer of abandoned clearings. Birches were among the first trees to move North in the wake of the receding glaciers during the last ice age, and probably for all the other ice ages since the mid-Cretaceous.

Pure stands of birch generally indicate a well-drained sandy or silty loam that is not ideally suited for agriculture. The birch can tolerate poor soil, but not shade. Birch stands are never dark. The trees grow widely spaced with open crowns that throw a light shadow, allowing shade-loving plants to thrive beneath them.

In the fall, each of the tree's cones produce hundreds of tiny, winged nutlets that are carried away on the slightest breeze. When the tree is cut down, the stump normally sends up numerous shoots that perpetuate the original tree. The tree trunk is easily killed by fire, but can quickly reproduce itself by developing shoots. As a result, it does well in burnt and cut-over areas.

The birch is relatively short-lived, maturing in about 80 years although it may occasionally attain an age of 140 years. Trees over 100-years-old make poor lumber due to degeneration.

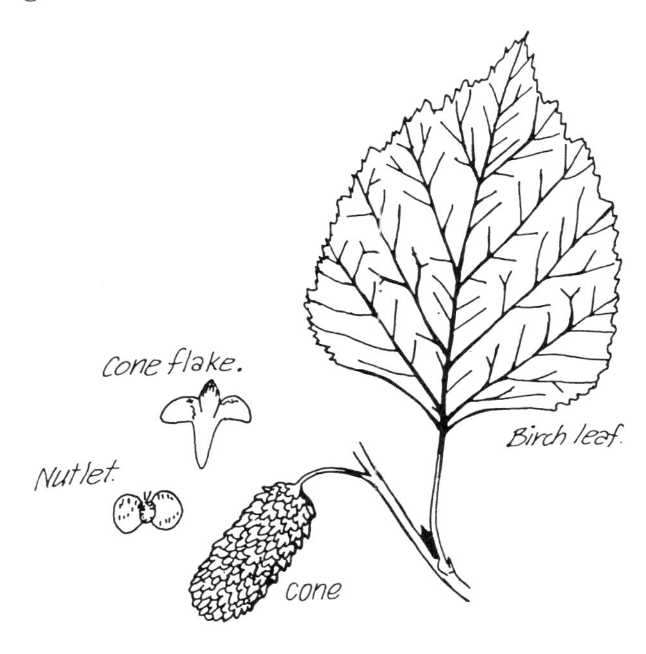

Birch leaf, cone and seed.

Split and dried birch is one of the best firewoods in the Northern Forests. Tamarack is the only northern wood approaching birch in heat value.

The following table gives the approximate heat value per cord (80 cubic feet of solid wood or 32 cubic metres) of dry wood in millions of B.T.U.'s.

Most Oaks	29.0
Ash	23.5
Birch	23.5
Tamarack	22.5
Jack Pine	18.5
Most Spruces	17.0
Aspen	16.5
Balsam Fir	15.5

As a firewood in northern or mountainous regions, birch is superior to aspen, balsam fir and pine. It burns with a brilliant flame and produces a lasting, intense heat. Highly esteemed for its pleasant aroma, it is also the principal firewood in Scandinavia and other northern or alpine lands. Birch is never found naturally seasoned in the forest as it begins to rot as soon as it dies. The green wood burns passably well, especially if split into many pieces. Birch also makes a high-quality charcoal for gunpowder and steel making.

Carving Birch

Birch was the only dense and heavy hardwood available for everyday applications for the Northern peoples. It carves well and machines on a lathe to a smooth finish—a property for which it is renowned. Compared to other hardwoods, the birch's rings, grain and pores are all obscure. Although the grain is obscure, it is definitely noticeable when working the wood. The fine pores or veins throughout its substance results in a dull, lusterless texture that takes a satin finish. The color is an even cream to pale yellow-brown. There is little difference in appearance between the heartwood and sapwood. If the tree is injured, the heartwood may turn a more contrasting light brown.

As long as birch is kept dry and used indoors it is a good furniture wood. The wood rots very quickly if kept damp and in contact with the ground. Birch does not bend as well as other woods used in furniture-making, but will nonetheless meet the needs of the Northern bushcrafter.

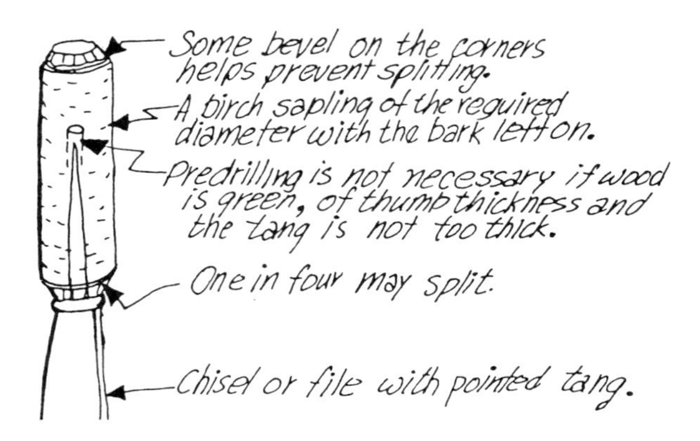

Handles made of small diameter birch.

Small diameter trees with the bark intact make good handles for tanged tools, such as files and wood chisels. The tang may be driven into the green wood without pre-drilling. A few handles may split but those that do not last for a long time. The handles are impact resistant and rarely work loose.

Hewing Toboggan Planks. Although other woods, such as dry tamarack may be used, green birch is preferred when building the traditional toboggan. The boards used may be from three to four metres long, three-quarters of a centimetre to one centimetre thick and from eight to 18 centimetres wide. The last dimension is determined by the diameter of locally available trees. A toboggan 35 centimetres wide, made of two boards, requires a tree at least 30 centimetres in diameter. Ideally, a toboggan is built of two boards, though more commonly with three and if necessary, with four.

The wood at the lowest part of the trunk bends the best and is therefore reserved for the upturned portion of the toboggan. The wood closest to the bark is also more flexible.

A birch log 30 to 35 centimetres in diameter should yield two boards 18 to 20 centimetres wide. The log is split by chopping out grooves four centimetres deep on the top and bottom, through which the split is made with an axe or wedges. The central portion of the trunk is hewed near enough to the bark to ensure the making of a 20-centimetre wide board. When dressed down and dried, this board should be about 18 centimetres wide. The hewed boards, if planed with a carpenter's jack plane, should be about one

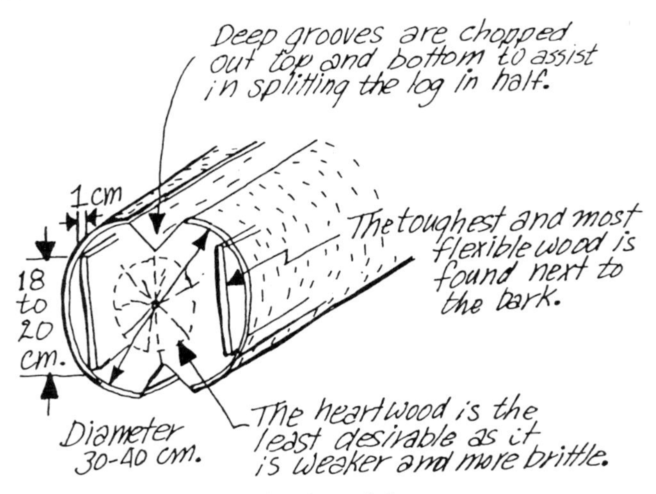

Hewing out toboggan planks with an axe.

centimetre thick for a final finished thickness of three-quarters of a centimetre. The boards must be flat, true and even.

Hew the boards by leaning them against a tree and work on each bottom half in turn, or "dog" the logs horizontally to bed logs to hew them. Strings rubbed with charcoal are strung and snapped down to provide guide lines for straight hewing. To remove wood, the face that is worked on is scored to as regular a depth as possible and the wood is hewed to the bottom of the scores. Someone who is experienced in this work may take up to six hours to make two boards.

Although a passable job can be done with the axe alone, the boards are usually finished with a carpenter's plane or crooked knife.

Birch Sap

Birch sap is best collected before the buds open in the spring. Although the sap has some sugar, it tastes like birch-flavoured distilled water. The root pressure sent up by the tree is quite strong. Pruning birch trees in the spring can cause a considerable loss of sap.

To tap a tree, cut into the wood proper where the sap rises through the vessels in the outer layers of the wood. By using

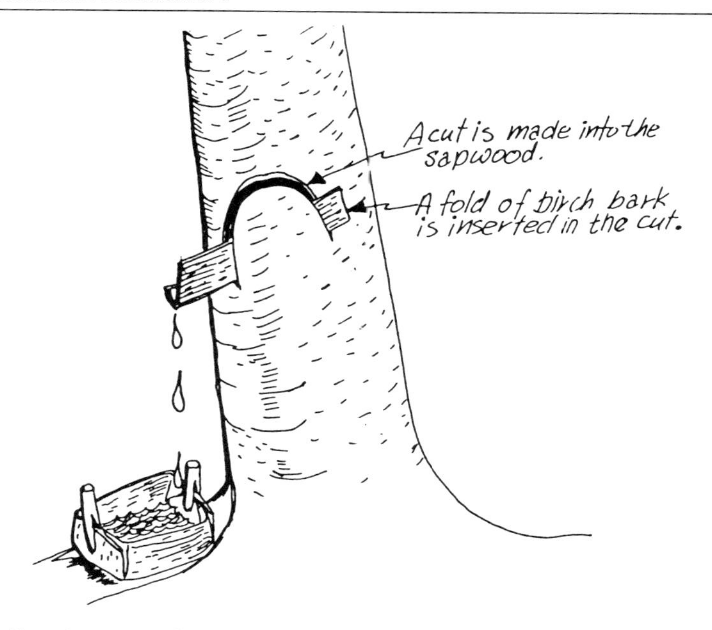

Collecting sap from birch.

a herring-bone pattern, a litre of sap may be collected daily. The sap can be used directly as a drink or shampoo. As a drink, some Russian people hold the sap in high esteem as a useful tonic for anaemia, gout, scurvy and rheumatism in particular. Enormous quantities of sap are evaporated to make a syrup or sugar resembling that of maple. The sap can be made into either a form of mild vinegar or a light alcoholic beverage.

Here is an ancient recipe:

> *To every Gallon of Birch-Water put a Quart of Honey well stilled together, then boil it almost an hour with a few cloves, and a little Lemon-peel, keeping it well scum'd; when it is sufficiently boil'd and become cold, add to it three or four Spoonfuls of good Ale, to make it work, which it will do like new Ale; and when the Yeast begins to settle, bottle it up as you do other Winey Liquors, it will in a competent time become a most brisk and spirituous Drink, which is a very powerful Opener*—Moses Cook (1717), *The Manner of Raising, Ordering and Improving Forest-Trees.*

When the sap is not running, an emergency source of water can be obtained by falling a birch downhill, cutting off the top then collecting the flow which should emerge within half an hour.

Birch Twigs and their Use

Birch twigs are an important accessory in the Finnish sauna. Handfuls of fresh or dried twigs with the leaves on (about elbow to fingertip long) are tightly bound with one of the twigs. The bundle is then used as a fan to circulate

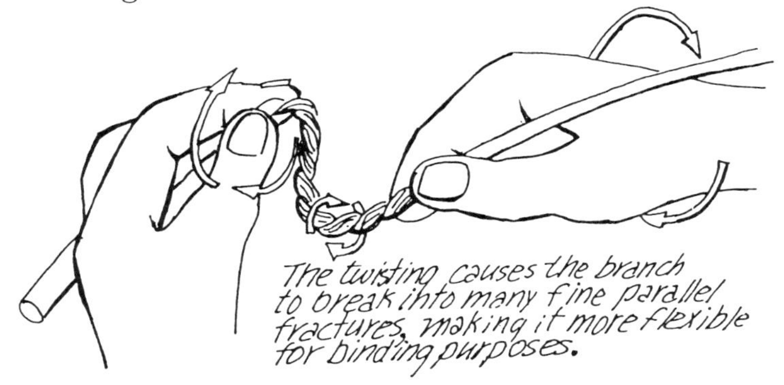

Twisting birch to make it flexible.

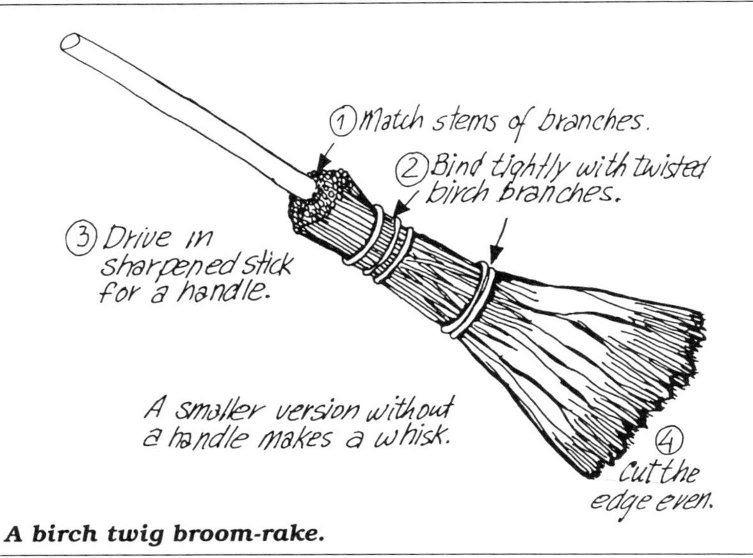

A birch twig broom-rake.

the hot air in a steam bath, to sprinkle water on the rocks and to drive heat deeper into the body by gently slapping the skin and leaving the wet leaves against the skin for a few moments.

A birch twig made flexible by twisting has many applications as a simple binding. It can be used for tying rails on fences, closures on gates, sheaves of grain and so on.

The twigs can be fashioned into a broom that is useful as a spring-toothed rake around barns, gardens and foundry floors. It can also be used for beating out fires in controlled burning of forest and field.

Twigs are cut in the winter, dried and bound into tight bundles. The thick ends are left even and a short stick is forced between them to act as a handle. Smaller bundles are useful as whisks for eggs and sauces or in the manufacture of vinegar. The twigs are also used in bough beds, roof thatching, weaving of rough baskets, wicker fences and as a base in road construction.

The winter twigs provide a bait for snaring ruffed grouse which feed heavily on birch buds. A fence can be fashioned from boughs and sticks with openings in which snares are set. Handfuls of twigs are stood up on each side of the fence. A grouse feeding on one handful may attempt to pass through an opening to another handful and, as a result, become entangled in the snare.

Birch Bark

Birch bark is composed of both papery and corky layers. For situations where the paper or outer bark is desired, it is best harvested in the months of May and June when it requires the least effort to remove. The bark comes off so easily it can be damaged as it falls away from the trunk. To remedy this, spiral a string around the trunk to hold the bark in place. From late fall to early spring, the two barks may adhere so tenaciously that separating them is both time consuming and damaging to the paper bark.

The papery or more precisely, leather-like layer is used for containers and canoe construction. The inner corky bark is much thicker than the papery layer and has entirely different properties. In some forms of canoe construction the two are used together and provide a thicker skin requiring less sheathing and ribs. Removing the outer bark and leaving the corky layer intact will disfigure the tree, but not kill it, though the exposed inner bark will no longer form paper layers. Inner bark allowed to regenerate for a few years can be peeled off, weighed down and dried flat for use as a table top, or a cutting board for filleting fish.

The inner bark contains some starch and can be ground up and used as an emergency food. Native Northerners believed that the tea drink derived from the inner bark could help sustain a flagging libido.

The dry distillation of the bark of various species of birch produces different oils for a variety of applications. The sweet birch *Betula lenta* produces an oil identical to wintergreen oil. A cord of branches and stems will produce approximately two kilograms of oil. The bark is distilled at a high temperature and the oil produced is used for tanning leather, especially the renowned Cuir de Russie or Russian leather that has a birch-like odor. This dark-brown, viscous oil is useful in folk medicine and for repelling insects.

An oil derived from the inner bark is a preservative for tarring sails, nets and cordage in outdoors applications.

The best outer bark is gathered in winter when it is both the firmest and the most difficult to remove. Spring bark is second best. The thin, dark-brown spring bark layer can be moistened and scraped away to produce a contrast with the lighter colored bark underneath. Bark gathered in midsummer to the middle of fall separates into layers more readily. The inside surface of this outer bark is golden or yellowish in color. The best bark comes from sound trees.

Bark from dead trees has limited uses. The older the bark, the more brittle and unsuitable it is for folded baskets (though useful for crudely woven ones). The best effect is achieved by weaving strips of bark torn out along the grain with the fingers rather than cut into regular strips. The same weaving techniques for spruce splint baskets may be used.

Individual trees have certain peculiarities. Ideal basket-making bark may be found in one tree out of 20. Bark that will separate into a paper-like single ply for writing on is rare. Birch bark writing paper is very enduring. A clearly legible mark made with anything sharp-pointed will far outlast ink or pencil. India ink or ball point pen write well on birch bark.

The internal characteristics of the bark can be determined to a certain extent from exterior clues. It is a waste to begin peeling a tree only to discover that the bark is unsuitable. The desirable qualities may be verified by first prying out a small flap about a centimetre wide. The bark is then examined for thickness and tendency to separate into layers.

The diameter of the tree is not a reliable clue to the thickness of the bark. For canoe building, the bark should be at least three millimetres thick. A careful cut is made to avoid injuring the inner bark and the flap is pressed back if the bark is found to be unsuitable. A tree that appears to pass the test should be subjected to more thorough bending, twisting and folding on a slightly larger flap.

Examine the bark surface closely for fissuring in the lenticels. Long lenticels may have pin holes through the bark, and a bark that tears easily along the grain. Old trees and and those found growing in shady environments tend to have deeply-fissured lenticels. A tree that sheds a lot of bark is likely to be thin-skinned.

Bark below the snow line tends to be inferior to bark found higher up. However, on occasion it will be superior by being thicker, tougher, more resilient and separation-resistant. Before the tree is cut down the lower bark may first be peeled as high as can be reached from the ground. Where there is some concern that the bark may be damaged when the tree falls, or if the tree is to be left standing with only the outer bark removed, a ladder is used to reach the higher bark.

Some bark gatherers purposely hang up the tree above the ground or cut a tall stump with the trunk remaining attached to hold the tree off the ground. Others purposely "barber chair" the tree by cutting it on the side opposite from its direction of fall (in the hope that the tree trunk will be suspended well above the ground).

If the tree falls flat, it may have to be sectioned so that it can be rolled over to remove the bark.

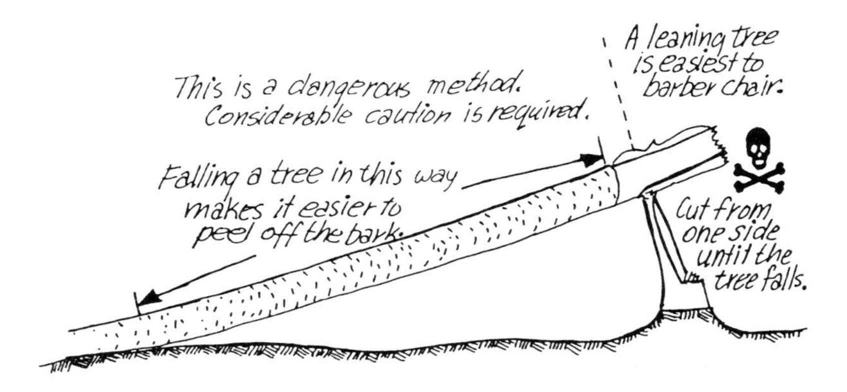

Purposely barber chairing a birch tree.

Examine the trunk to determine where to make the best cut down its side. Cut through a flaw, rather than leave it in the middle of the sheet. If a tree leans, it may peel best on the leaning side. A wooden wedge is used to loosen enough of the bark to provide a good grip for the hands. The more intact the bark is to remain, the greater the care needed in the early stages of loosening. The bark is peeled a little at a time all the way along the trunk. In some cases, hot water is poured over the bark and into the separation to facilitate removal. The areas of bark that have grown over old branch stubs may have to be pounded gently to loosen the bark.

Bark tends to curl in the opposite direction from the natural curve around the tree. To counteract this action roll it with the underside out at 90 degrees to the natural curling tendency. To help flatten the fresh bark or roll it up for transport and storage, warm the inside surface with a torch. This may be either a twig torch or one made on the spot by splitting the end of a stick and inserting folds of thin birch bark. The bark is rolled up with the inside surface to the outside then tied with cord or spruce roots.

The bark is at its best when used as soon as it is removed. It should be kept in the shade and as cool as possible. When stored moist or underwater, the natural oils will not evaporate as readily, but the bark may mildew and become discolored.

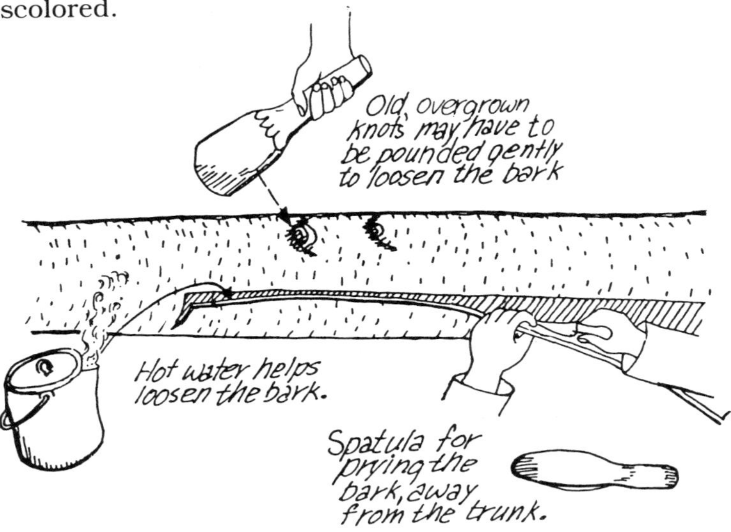

Methods of loosening birch bark.

Birch bark contains natural waxes that make it waterproof, remarkably rot resistant and flammable; properties that make it an excellent wet weather kindling. Rolls of large pieces of bark make good torches and a rope twisted of thin layers makes a form of candle. The bark burns with a sooty flame producing a characteristic odor that readily clings to clothing. Some Natives claim that animals detect this odor and may avoid it thereby adversely affect hunting success.

Birch Bark Articles

Many forms of baskets can be crafted with birch bark. Some are quickly made and as quickly discarded, while others will last 100 years.

Temporary Utility Container. A rectangular bark container can be made in minutes by folding the corners and pinning them in place with clothespin-like clamps, or by using a few spruce root stitches. The corners can be made with the folds to the inside or the outside. Wide containers may need four pins and narrow ones only two. To make sharp folds at the corners without cracking the bark, heat it gently at the point where the fold is to be made. This container is particularly useful for containing hot grease or pitch, and as a result, is usually short-lived.

Simple Stitched Basket. Wherever clamps are used, they may be replaced with a few well-placed root stitches. Greater durability is achieved with split willow stiffeners, combined with pieces of bark, whose grains are oriented at 90 degrees to each other.

The Reinforced Rim. The strongest baskets have a rigid and durable rim. The rim may be attached with the quick spiral stitch or the more involved whip stitch. The whip stitch may also be applied at intervals. With split willow, a long, tapered lap joint makes a smoother looking rim. The joint on the inner rim should be on the opposite side of the basket from the one on the outer rim. If the rims are preformed and dried they are easier to manage and less clamping is required. A section of rim is clamped and stitched and the clamps removed as the work progresses, or the clamps are leap-frogged along.

The Mocock. This is a traditional basket form determined by the character of the particular bark used and how it may best be formed into a sturdy basket. The basket with its rectangular bottom that is larger than the round or oval rim,

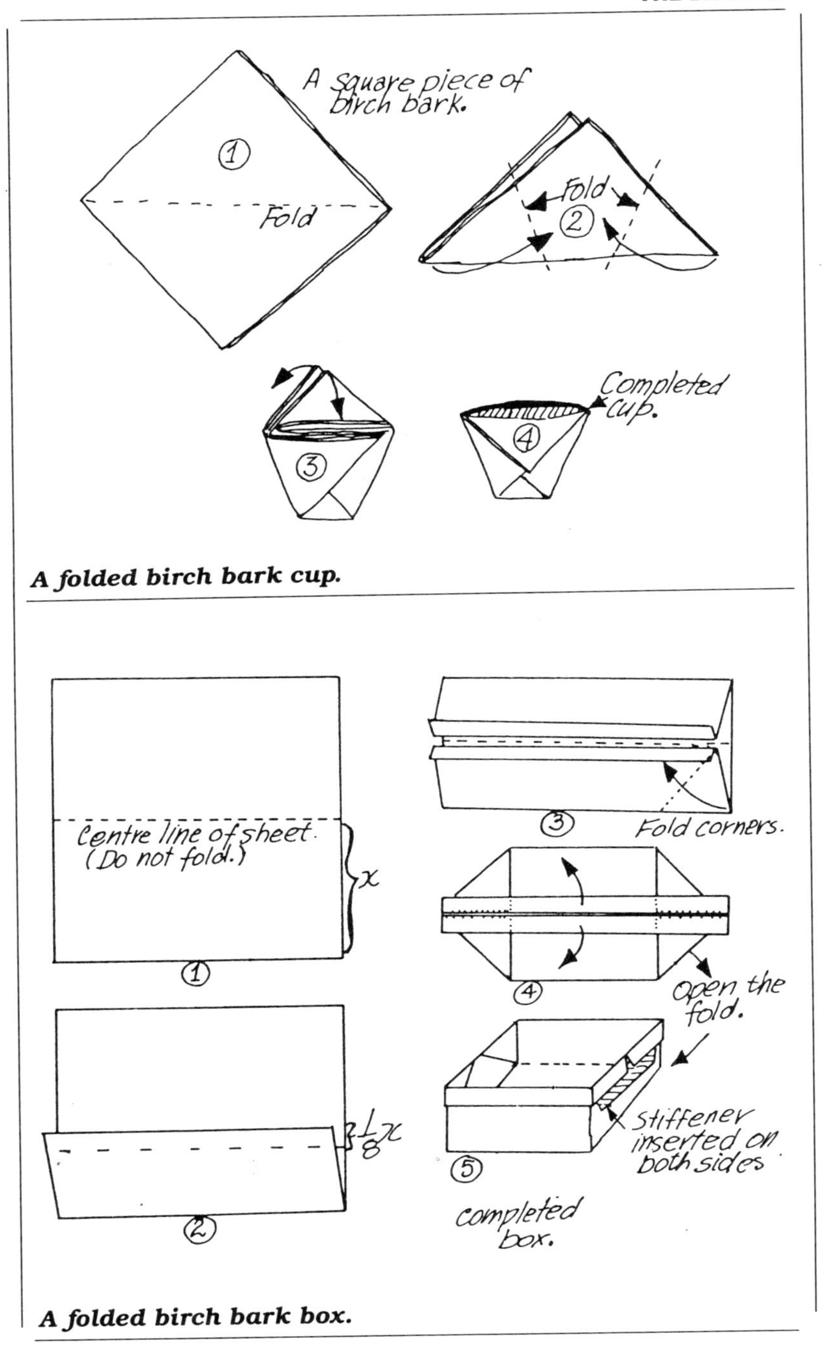

A folded birch bark cup.

A folded birch bark box.

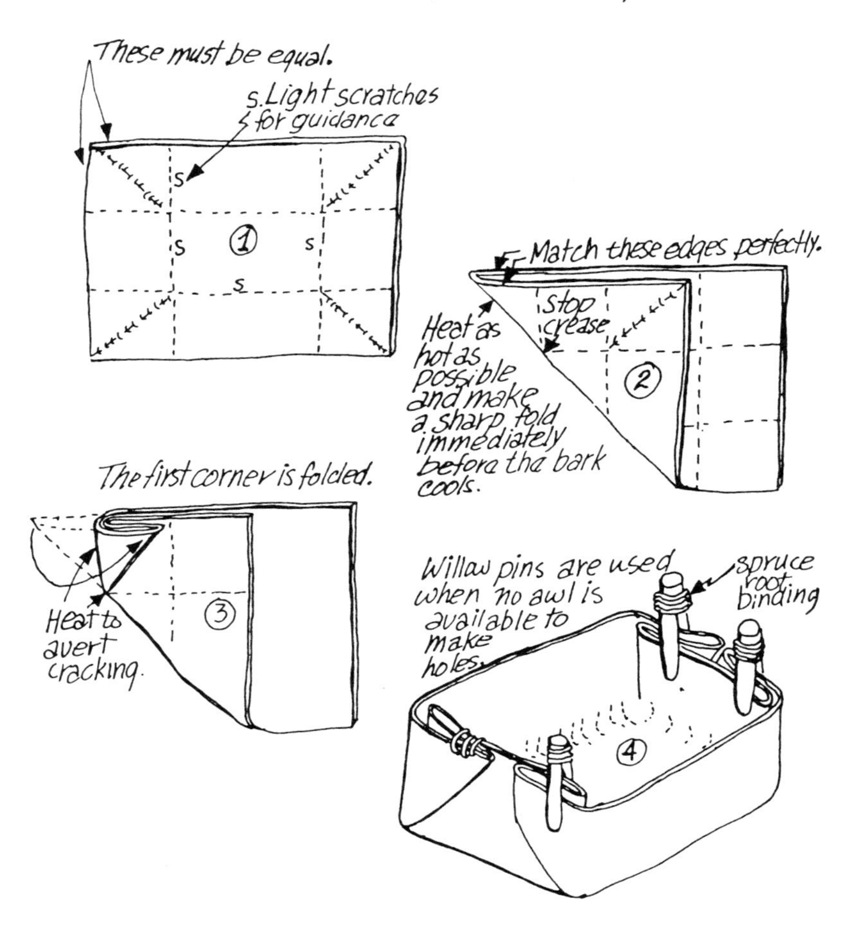

A temporary birch bark container.

is noted to be particularly stable for setting on uneven ground. The pattern can be altered to obtain a variety of shapes. To be assured of proper symmetry during construction, an accurate template of the pattern is made and the basket's shape established with pegs. The bark is warmed to facilitate folding and everything is held in place with

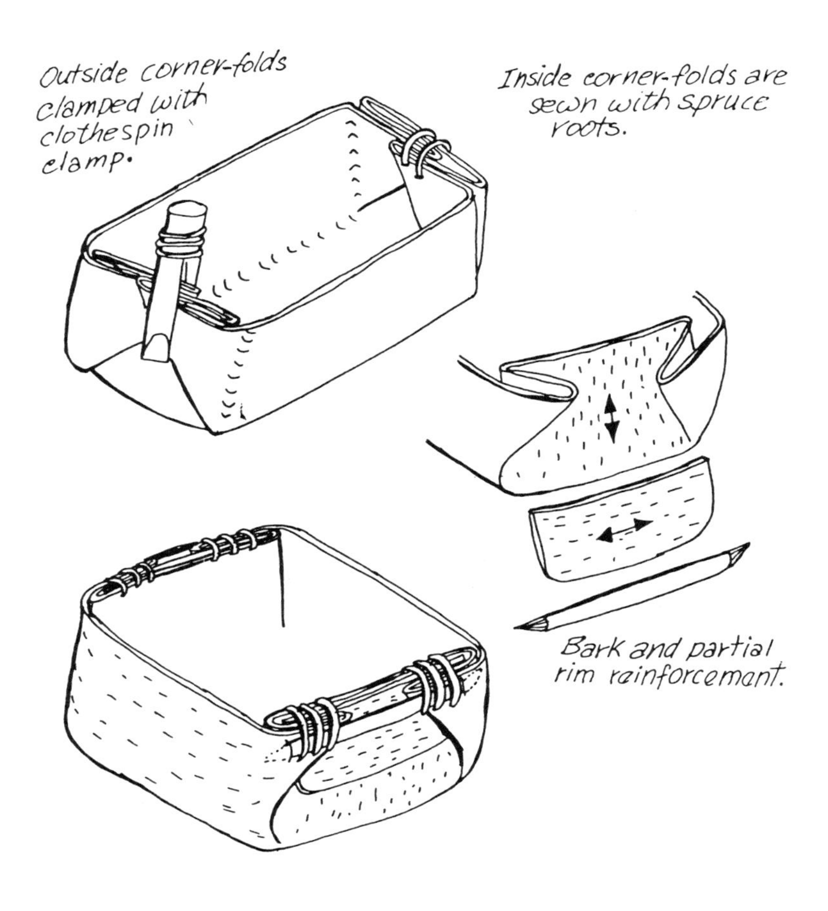

Simple stitched baskets.

wooden pegs, buckthorn spines or nails which are removed as the stitching progresses. All the seams are double stitched. The rim is completed last. When clamps are not available the rim reinforcements are pre-formed. It is possible to make a waterproof mocock without having to pitch the seams if fresh bark is used, the folds are made carefully and sewn with roots of regular thickness.

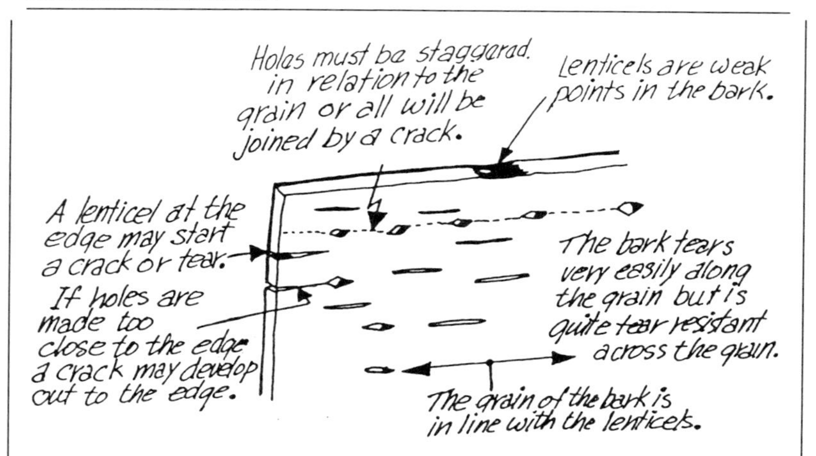

The grain and lenticels in birch bark.

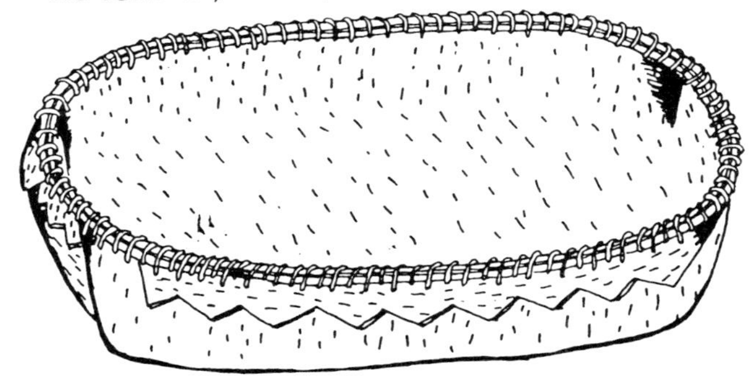

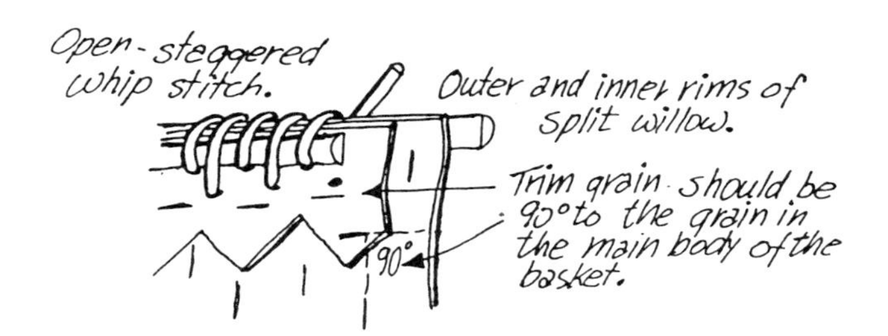

The shallow water-tight birch bark basket.

The Moose Megaphone. A birch bark cone used to amplify the voice when calling moose. The cone can be stitched only part way up the narrow part as the hand will only go so far into it. A decorative stitch may be used on the large end and a turkshead knot made of conifer root can be forced over the small end to hold the cone together where it is not stitched.

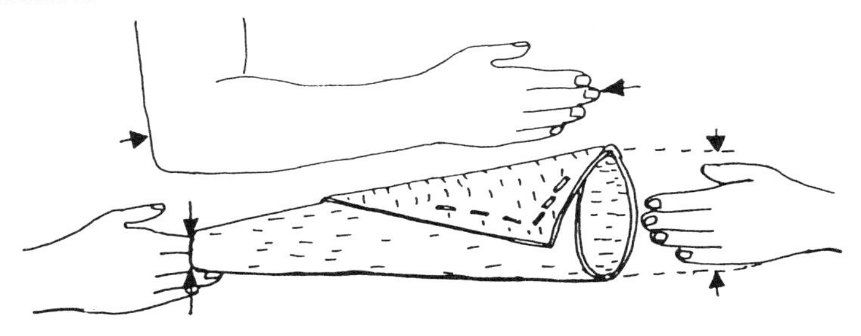

Moose megaphone dimensions.

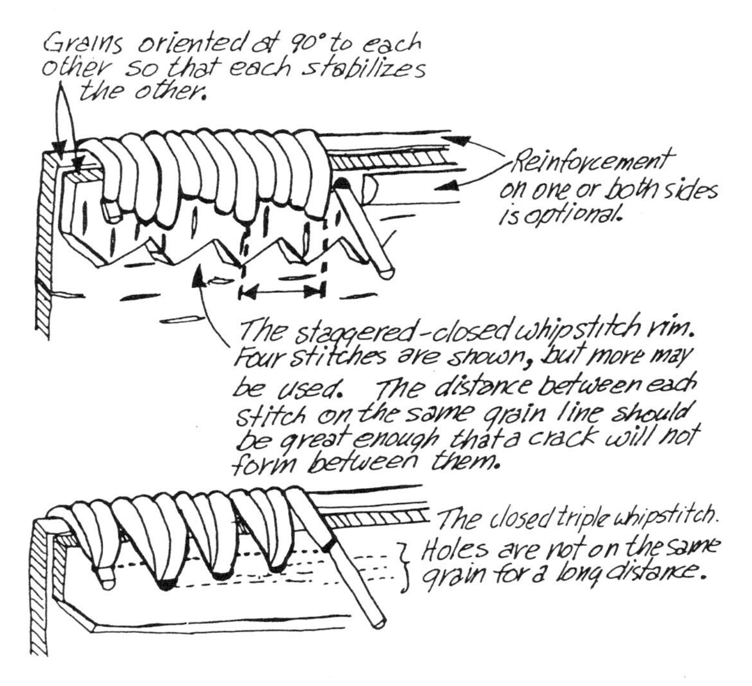

Detail of durable rim construction.

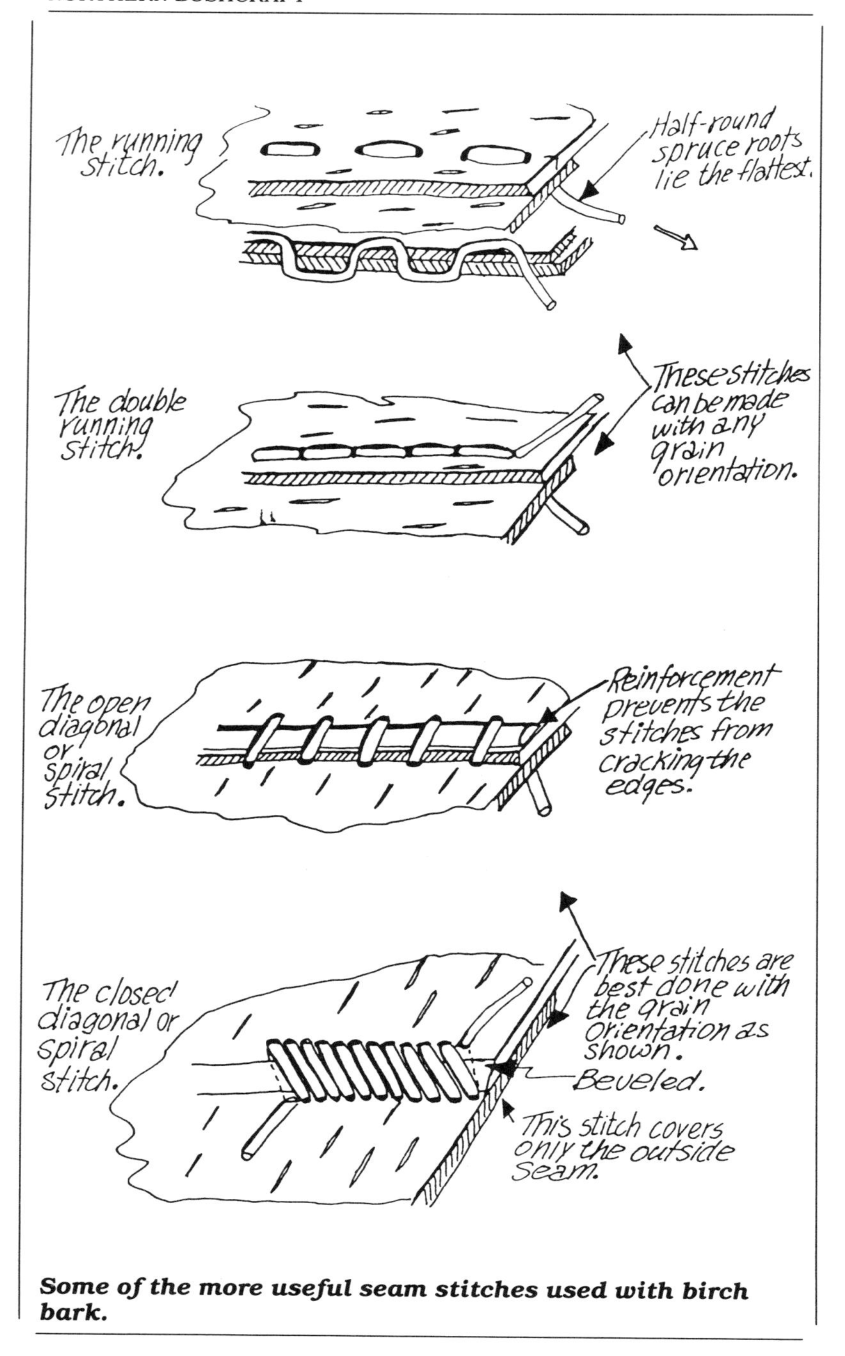

Some of the more useful seam stitches used with birch bark.

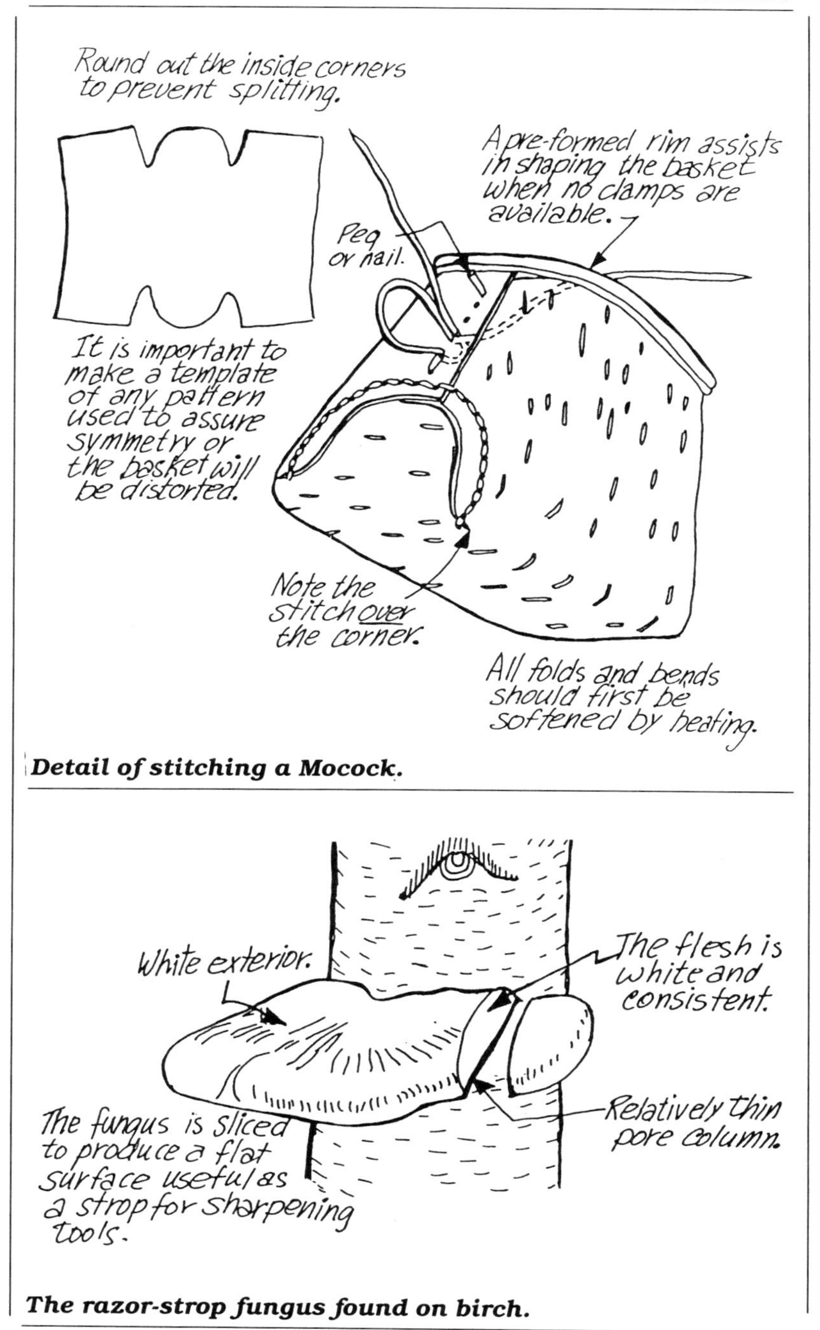

Detail of stitching a Mocock.

The razor-strop fungus found on birch.

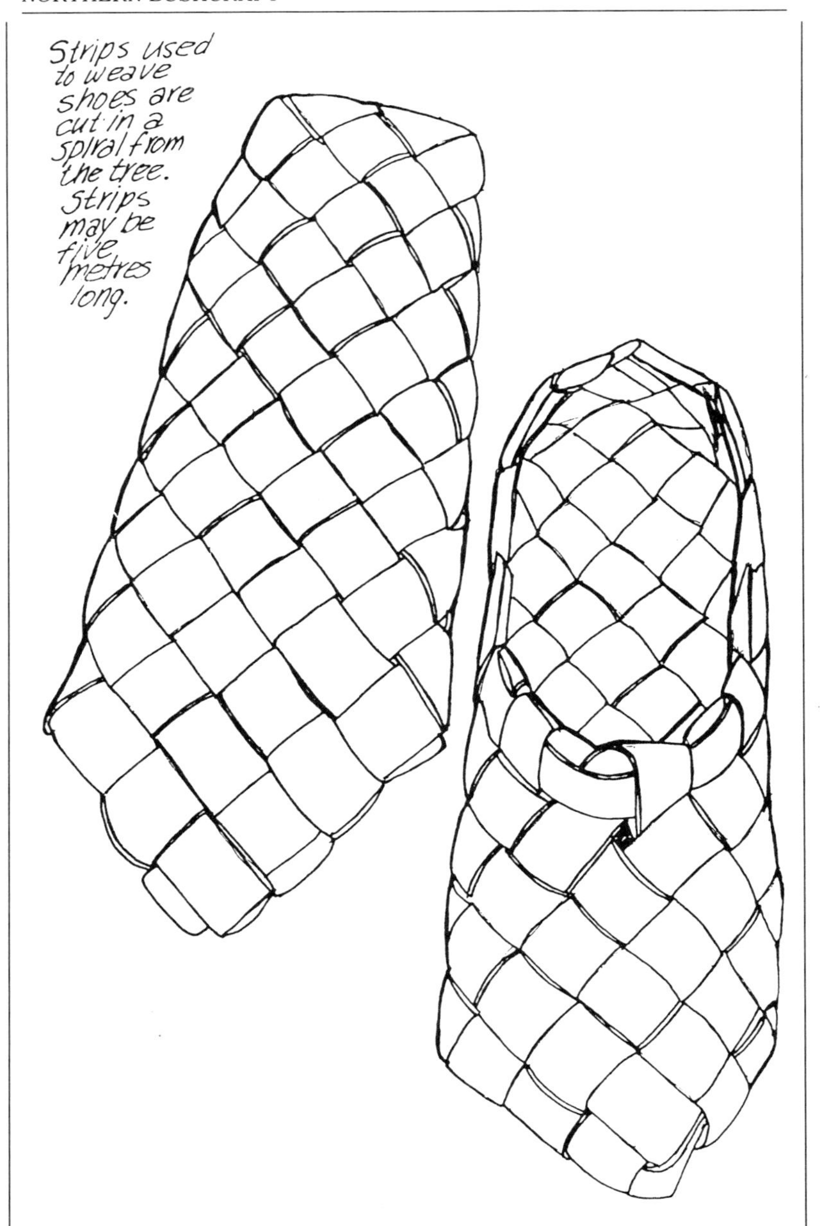

Strips used to weave shoes are cut in a spiral from the tree. Strips may be five metres long.

Birch bark shoes woven from strips of bark that are three or four metres long. *The bark must be cut off the tree in a spiral to obtain such long weaving strips.*

THE ALDERS

The alders are recognized by their broad, oval, double-toothed leaves and by their catkins or hanging flower clusters. The woody cones that remain on the alder after the nutlets have dropped instantly differentiate this tree from the closely related birch or any other northern tree. The male and female flowers are separate. They are formed in the autumn and remain on the tree throughout the winter.

Alders have nodules on the roots which, like the peas and the clovers, harbour micro-organisms that change atmospheric nitrogen into nutritive protein. This allows the tree to thrive in nitrogen-deficient soils.

The common alder has a frustrating tendency to overgrow seismic lines, old trails and other clearings in the forest. An old trail overgrown by alder is worse than thick bush to walk through.

As a firewood, dead alder is easy to gather and break into small pieces without the use of tools. The light, dry wood burns fast and its pleasant smoke eases a headache. Green alder was used for smoke-curing fish and meat—one of its more important applications in the Northern Forest.

The long, flexible wands found in dense stands are useful when constructing various arch-type shelters. Branches are easily torn off by hand.

When a green alder is cut, or the bark injured, the wound turns yellow, then orange and finally a deep red, as though the tree were bleeding. In the past, the popular imagination looked upon this as signifying real blood, and the tree became a symbol of evil. The Ingalik Indians, for example, thought that the handling of cut alder was detrimental to one's hunting success, and analogous to associating with menstruating women before the hunt.

The tips of alder twigs were boiled, dried and pulverized for use with (or without) mint leaves as incense or to cure headaches. First a rock was heated on the fire, rolled out, then sprinkled with alder powder, and the smoke breathed in. The strong odors from cooking wild meat can be cleared from a cabin by sprinkling the incense on a hot stove.

The twigs have a sufficiently high tannin content for use as an astringent. An astringent causes tissue to become more compact, such as in the contraction of a muscle fiber, blood vessels or the coagulation of protoplasm of the surface cells, thus diminishing either discharge or bleeding

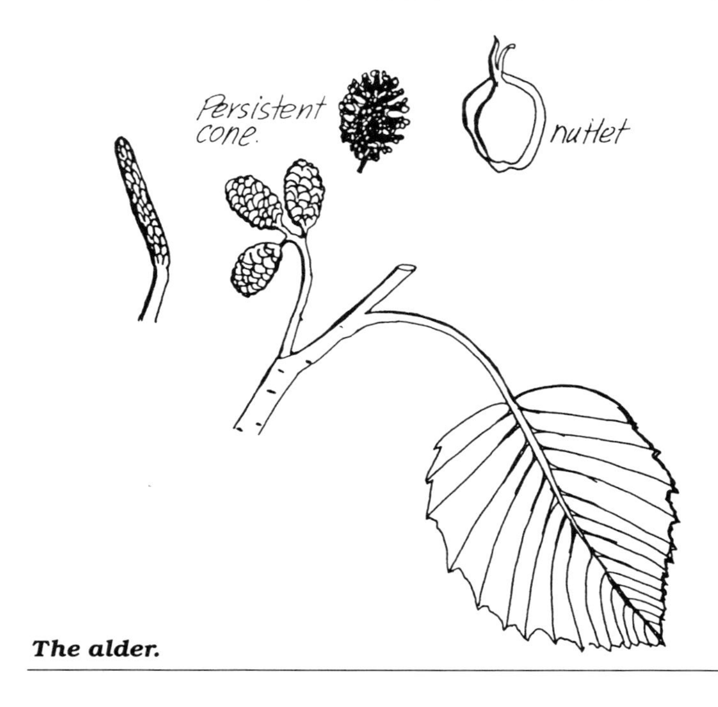

The alder.

from an external or internal body surface. In the case of a wound or sore, discharge is reduced or stopped, tissue tone improved and healing quickened if the water in which alder bark has been boiled is used as a wash. A moist poultice of the inner bark can be applied to wounds that bleed profusely.

With the use of a mordant (a substance which fixes coloring matter to another substance) such as alum, five colors can be obtained from alder. The bark will produce a tawny-red that changes to black with the addition of copperas (hydrated ferrous sulphate). The fresh wood will give a pinkish-fawn dye, the catkins a green, and the young shoots a yellow color.

8

THE CONIFERS

The conifers provide the most readily accessible and abundant raw materials for crafting and survival.

WHITE SPRUCE

The white spruce is one of the more widely distributed trees in Canada.

To identify white spruce look for the following points:

1) The buds and twig tips are hairless between the needles.

2) The branches tend to go straight out from the trunk on the lower part of the tree and upwards on the upper part of the tree.

3) The crushed needles are aromatic, with an odor reminiscent of cat urine. The needles are often covered with a white bloom. The needles will roll between the tightly pressed thumb and forefinger.

4) A silvery-white inner bark is revealed when the outer bark is carefully shaved away.

White spruce wood has no taste or odor which makes it suitable for food containers. It carves easily, takes a high sheen when sanded and its superior resonance makes it a good wood for stringed musical instruments. It is an excellent wood for paddles and oars.

The smoke from white spruce is as irritating to the eyes and lungs as that of black spruce. It is used as a firewood only because it is more common than most other woods.

The preferred resin for making the caulking pitch for birch bark canoes is gathered from white spruce. Collect the resin in early spring. Remove a long, vertical strip of bark two to three centimetres wide from the trunk, chopping out a reservoir at its lower end to collect the resin. The fresh resin is

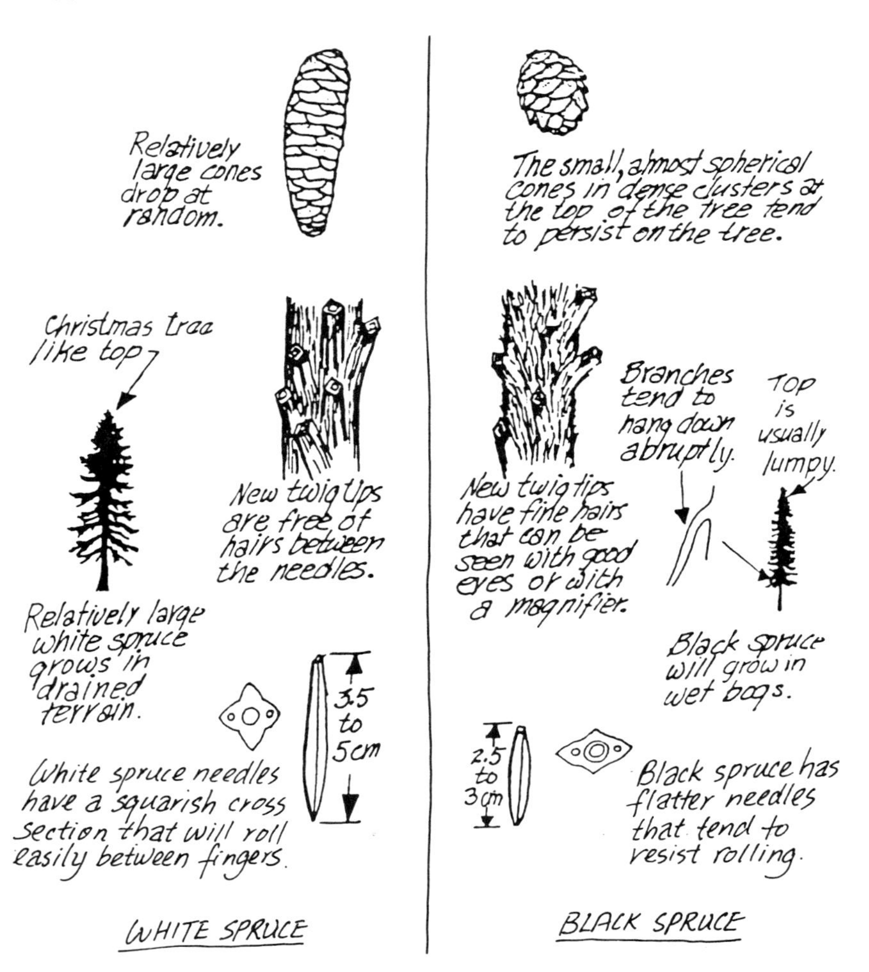

Comparing white and black spruce.

heated and mixed with powdered charcoal and fat to make a pitchy mixture that will not crack if dribbled on a piece of birch bark. If too thin, it will run with the heat of the sun. If too thick, it will crack when flexed.

Many trees may be found within a given area with the bark ripped off in long strips by bears. They expose the cambium layer to obtain the sweet sap. The sap is also used by humans as an emergency food.

Whenever any conifer is injured, an emission seals off the wound. This is an oleoresin which originates in ducts found in the sapwood. When the volatile substance in the oleoresin evaporates, it becomes more and more viscous until the familiar hard and brittle spruce resin forms. This is an excellent fire-starter (*see* Chapter 1). For a heat or light source in a snow shelter, a small fire can be maintained by using this resin as fuel. Build a tiny fire with twigs on a flat

Mosses commonly found in the spruce-moose forest.

rock or a board covered with earth and add a lump of resin whenever needed. A chimney may have to be made directly above the sooty fire or everything in the shelter will become grimy.

If pounded together with charcoal, the resin forms an inferior glue that is sticky when hot. The glue is used for setting arrowheads and spear points on their shafts before they are bound on. The glue fills the voids and prevents any movement of the projectile point in its binding.

If chewed like gum, the hardened resin causes considerable salivation and spitting. It was popular in the era before chicklet chewing gum became commercially available. Ingalik women claimed that chewing spruce gum caused an increase in bust size. The chewed gum was also used in an emergency as an inferior substitute for caulking birch bark canoes.

A variety of spruce known as Porsild white spruce, has a smooth bark displaying small blisters containing a sap-like oleoresin. It is an excellent antiseptic for cuts, wounds, and burns. Applied fresh, the resin thickens as the volatile principle evaporates, becoming as sticky as the resin of balsam fir. The fresh oleoresin is covered with cattail fluff, cloth, thin birch bark or tissue paper. Large wounds may require more resin and protective layers. The wound is bandaged or protected for a few hours until the volatile component of the resin is dissipated by body heat, after which the resin and covering material may stay on of their own accord. The resin provides the antiseptic and the binding and the fluff protects the wound from abrasion. Resin may be removed from clothes or skin with turpentine.

The roots of pines, spruces and tamaracks are useful for lashing, lacing or weaving. The roots of the black spruce are superior to those of the white spruce.

White spruce boughs can be used for making insulative and springy beds, waterproof thatch for shelters, and an intense, white smoke for signal fires.

BLACK SPRUCE

Black and white spruce share much the same geographic range. White spruce requires dryer conditions while black spruce grows in dry or wet soil, often associating with

Sphagnum bogs. The only other tree that fares better in a bog is tamarack. Black spruce has the unique property among the spruce of propagating through layering when its lower branches rest on the ground. The wood from black spruce is white, soft and resilient.

Black spruce differs from white spruce in the following manner:

1) On close examination or with a magnifying glass, the twig tips between the needles are covered with fine, short, brown hairs.

2) The branches tend to point downward at the trunk. A black spruce is easier to limb from the top down, as opposed to other trees. The black spruce is rejected as a Christmas tree because of its unkempt, ragged appearance.

3) The needles are a dark, bluish-green without luster or a whitish bloom.

4) The live inner bark is a deep olive-green.

5) The needle resists rolling between tightly pressed fingers.

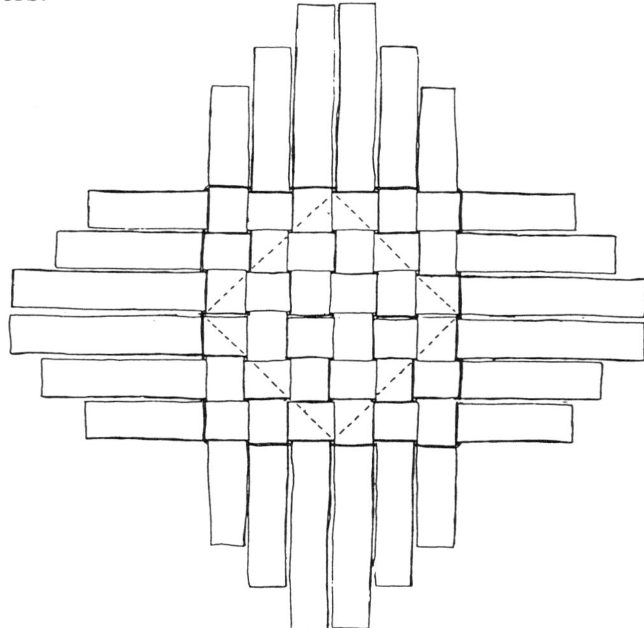

***a) Spruce splints are being woven into a basket.** The bottom has been completed and the splints are held in place with cord or a fine spruce root.*
b) The basket corners are folded up.

Samuel Herne, who observed the Native people's way of life before the advent of European trade goods, found it difficult to believe they did not have iron woodworking tools. The wood and bark implements were marvels of handiwork made with wood or antler splitting wedges, beaver teeth dressing and mortising chisels, stone scrapers and certain abrasive sands and stones. The Natives fully exploited woods like black spruce that could be worked to a uniform thickness with these simple tools. (Knotless, straight-grained, green black spruce can be split 90 degrees to the

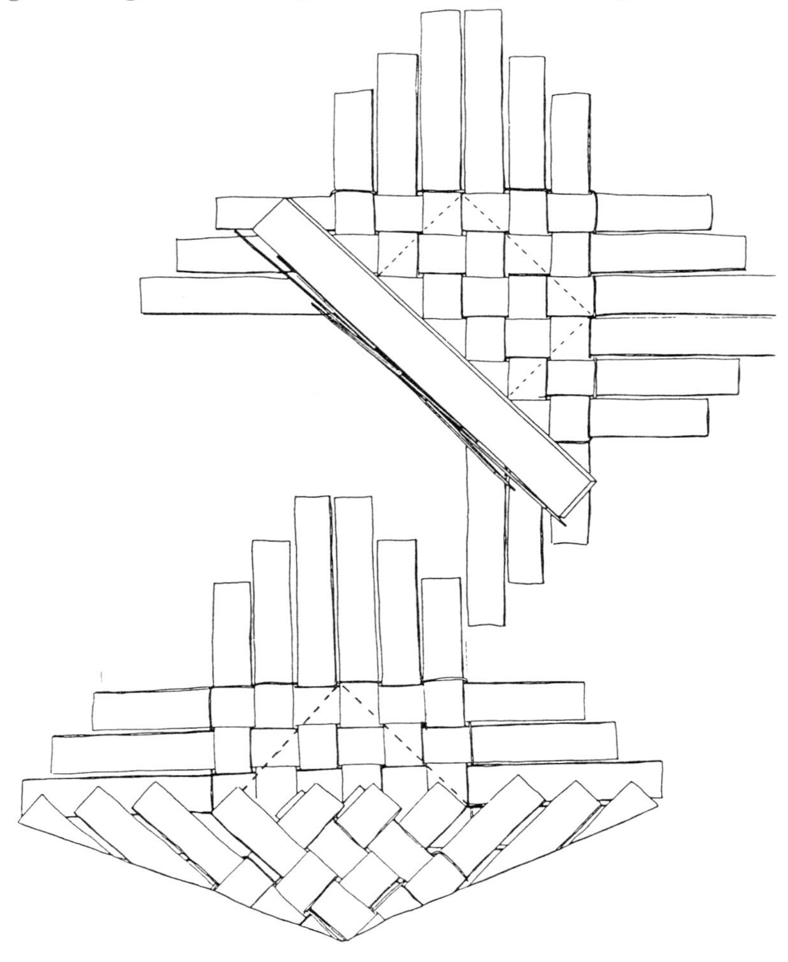

The corners are woven to the end of the splints.

grain into splints of a millimetre thickness. These splints are readily woven into durable baskets.)

Careful examination of the wood surface under the bark will give you an idea of the grain's nature by a faint grain line. The checks in nearby dead trees are also a useful guide to the nature of the grain of the living ones.

Natural knot-free wood is occasionally found on the side of the trunk facing the interior of a clump. Natives would

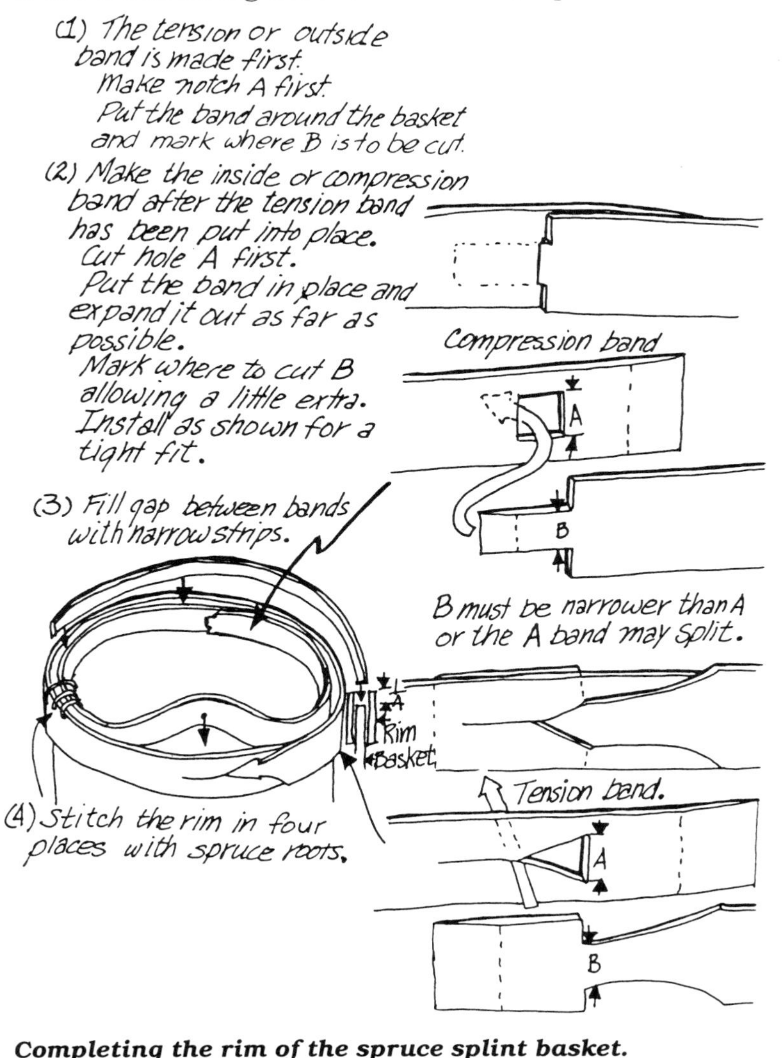

(1) The tension or outside band is made first.
Make notch A first.
Put the band around the basket and mark where B is to be cut.
(2) Make the inside or compression band after the tension band has been put into place.
Cut hole A first.
Put the band in place and expand it out as far as possible.
Mark where to cut B allowing a little extra.
Install as shown for a tight fit.
(3) Fill gap between bands with narrow strips.
Compression band
A
B
B must be narrower than A or the A band may split.
A
Rim
Basket
Tension band.
A
B
(4) Stitch the rim in four places with spruce roots.

Completing the rim of the spruce splint basket.

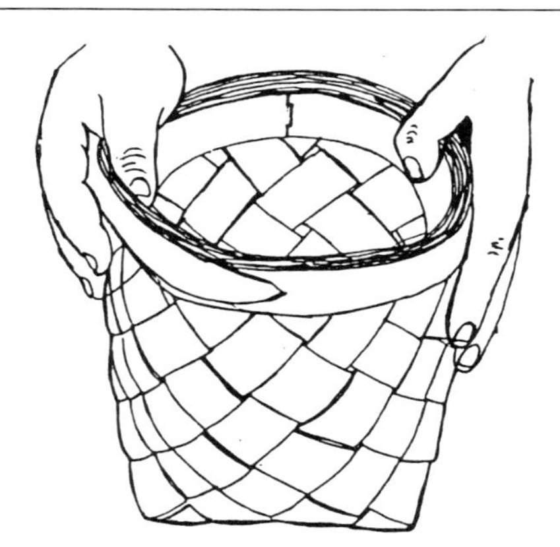

The completed splint basket.

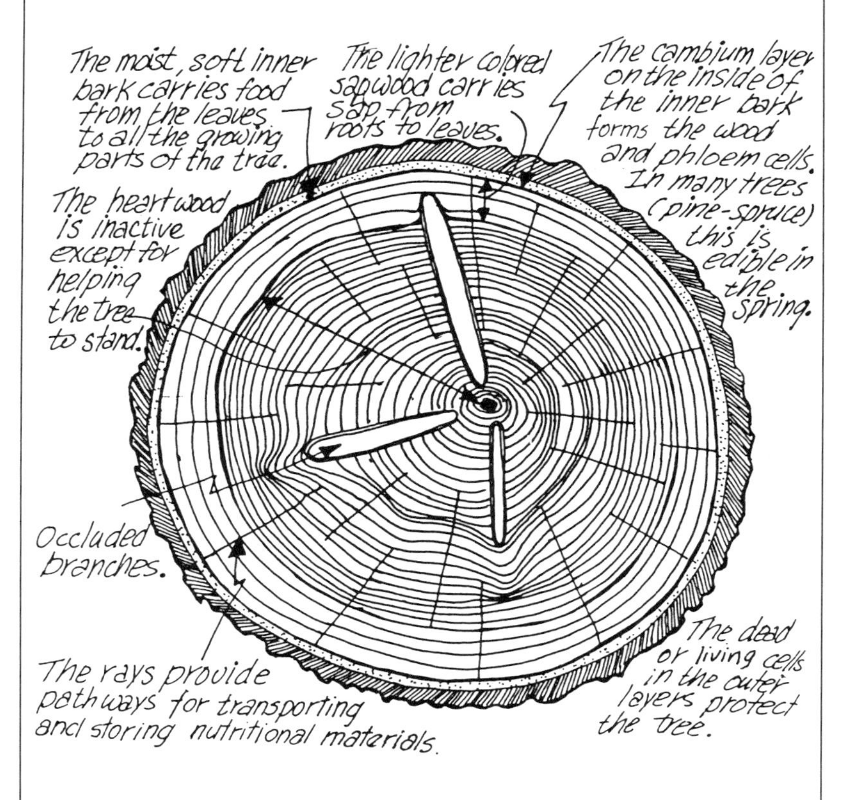

The cross section of a conifer.

limb growing trees so their children and grandchildren would be assured of knot-free wood.

Although black spruce is a soft wood, the tree will also produce a very tough wood. If the tree leans and attempts to right itself, the annual rings will be found to be much wider on the outside of the resulting curve. These wider rings are redder in color than the rest of the wood. This wood is useful for making tough, durable wedges used in splitting.

Another special wood is found where the transition from trunk to root occurs. This wood is more tenacious than the regular wood and makes good bowls and mauls.

Spruce Roots

Spruce roots have many applications as lashings, dead fall trigger mechanisms, lacing and sewing for bark containers and canoes, whipping, basket weaving, nets, and recreational crafts.

The ideal place to gather roots is a deep *Spagnum* bog where the water is close to the surface. In shallow moss, the roots growing into the ground are more irregular and kinked. If possible, avoid patches of Labrador tea or willows, as the roots of these plants interfere with the gathering process. Remove the moss until a large number of roots are exposed before you start gathering them. Each root must

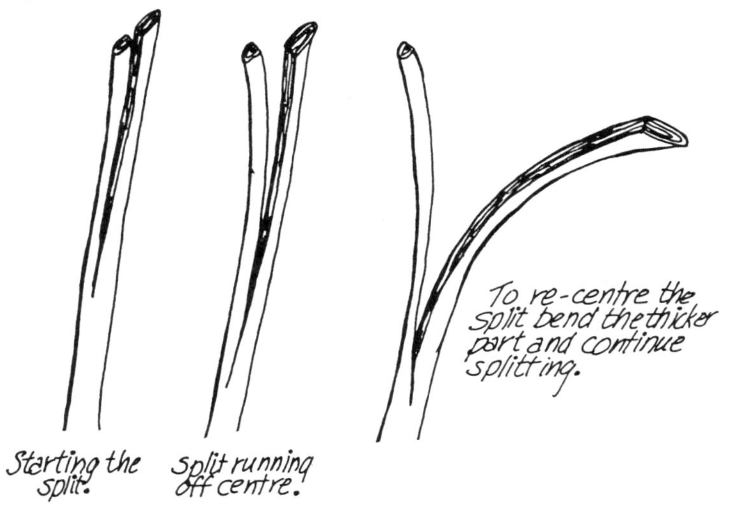

How willow wands or spruce roots are split.

be followed along and released from the moss. Pulling may break it or those roots crossing it.

Remove the bark from the roots immediately or keep them wet, as debarking becomes difficult if the root dries.

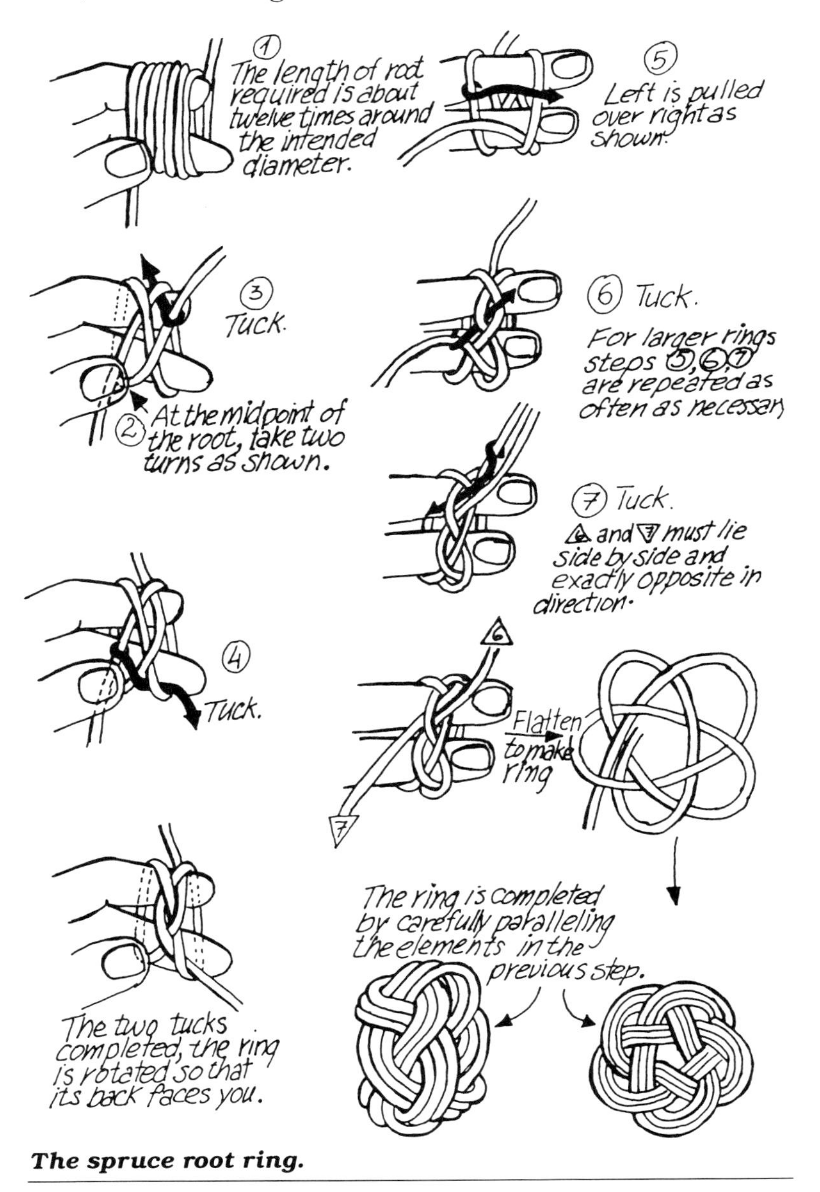

The spruce root ring.

Unpeeled roots may be kept in water for months without affecting their quality, but they may become discolored. From mid-May until about mid-August the bark peels easily. Sometimes peeling can be accomplished with the fingers alone, but usually a root-stripper is required. Each root is trimmed, split, and coiled for later use. If the roots are to be used within the next day or so, they are kept moist. Otherwise, they should be dried. To restore suppleness soak or boil the roots. The roots gain strength by being dried and soaked once, but repeated drying and soaking has a detrimental effect.

Roots thicker than the little finger must be split as they are too large for most applications. The split is started at the thicker end with a thumb nail, awl, knife or by biting with the eye tooth. If the split runs off to the side it is centered by bending the thicker part more than the thinner part. Halves of equal thickness must bend equally for the split to remain centered. If you wish to end the split, severely bend one of the halves. A smaller root may be split in half, a larger one may be split in quarters, and a root the thickness of the little finger may produce eight or more plys of various cross-sections.

The difference between conifer roots and most other sewing materials is that the fresh or soaked root is supple while being used and dries to retain the shape it has been put into. The ends do not have to be anchored, and when dry, they are cut off flush with the surface of the material being sewn without any danger of them pulling out.

Sewing with spruce roots is really a form of lacing as a needle is not used and the sewing hole is produced with an awl. The sewing is done with the thin end of the root, and because the other end is thicker, it fits tightly into the hole when drawn through. This makes the hole watertight and the sewing holds more firmly. Once a few stitches have been made, a consistently strong pull is made on the root with each stitch. Eventually, the pull will break the root indicating the need to change to a new root and discarding whatever remains of the old one. This ensures a consistent, tight and regular stitch.

The most attractive stitching is with split or half-round roots. Occasionally, the root must be given a half-twist in the stitch so that its smooth exterior remains on the outside where it is visible.

The Turkshead Knot. This is a spruce root ring with numerous applications. Depending on its size, it may be a ring for the finger, a choker for a neckerchief, a beret for the hair, or a napkin ring. It may be driven onto the end of the wood handle of a file, chisel or awl to keep it from splitting. Sewn on to a lid of a birch bark basket, or driven on the end of a walking stick, the knot makes a decorative knob.

TAMARACK

Tamarack is a Northern Forest conifer with the unique trait of dropping its needles every fall. It exhibits many suits such as the pale soft-green of summer, the golden-yellow or orange hue of fall, and the desolate, bare tree of winter, which some people mistake to be dead. The lump at the base of the needle tufts, the softness of the needles and the light shadow of the tree all identify tamarack.

Tamarack is associated with muskegs, but on occasion is found flourishing high and dry of its normally sopping-wet habitat. Less aggressive and more shade sensitive than its associates, the tamarack is driven back to the wet conditions which it can tolerate, but others can not. This attractive tree will readily transplant into a dry environment. One can recognize bogs at a distance by looking for this tree, a useful point for avoiding a wet area while travelling through the bush.

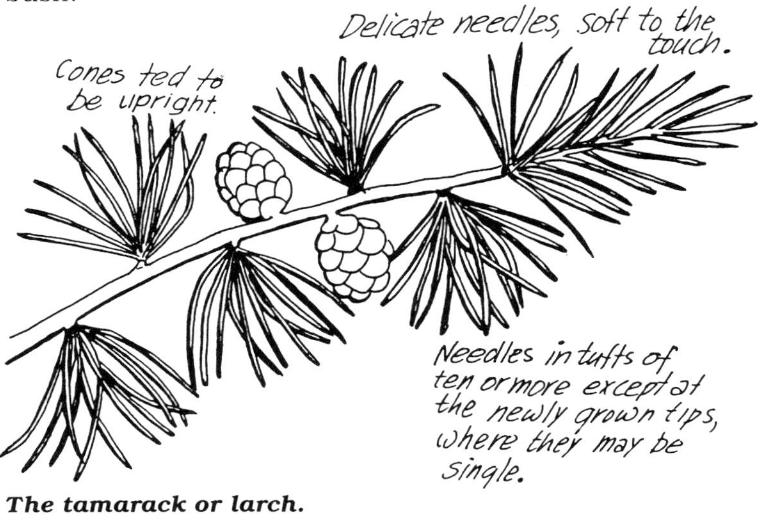

The tamarack or larch.

The fallen needles that cover the moss under the tree in the fall mysteriously disappear by spring. Grouse feed on the fallen needles.

The wood is heavier than that of any other tree found in the Northern Forests. As a firewood, weight for weight, it produces about the same amount of heat as some mine coals. The wood is very durable especially in contact with the ground or submersed in water. The pioneers considered tamarack wood to be poisonous. The slivers fester badly in the skin and the sawdust can cause a severe rash. The most durable fence posts come from trees attacked by a beetle. The healthy tree has a reddish inner bark, while that of the beetle infested one is bluish. The wood was used in boat construction, especially for keels and large elbows made from the root and trunk. Whenever hardness, strength and durability are required, tamarack is apt to fit the bill. The tree is seldom found in any large diameter and as such is used for fence posts, mine pillars or props, railway ties and pilings. It is also a good wood for toboggan construction.

Tamarack roots are not the strongest of the conifers, but they are the straightest, longest and thinnest. The roots are used like those of the black spruce.

The dry roots of the tamarack were used by some Native peoples to carry fire. The root is supposed to burn like a very slow fuse, glowing without flame until it is consumed—a property likely unique to tamarack. A hazard exists if a dead tamarack root leads into a fire site. The fuse-like action of the root may carry the flame far enough away to be missed when the fire is put out.

JACK AND LODGEPOLE PINE

The pines are highly-esteemed by the lumber industry. The wood is of good quality with many applications. The tree thrives on poor agricultural soils.

Jack pine has a strong affinity for sandy soil. Sighting a stand of this pine establishes the presence of sand.

A similar pine with many identical applications is the more majestic Lodgepole pine. It is found from the Rocky Mountain foothills west to the Pacific coast. It prefers glacial till, having as much aversion to sand as Jack pine has to glacial till. The two species readily hybridize whenever they

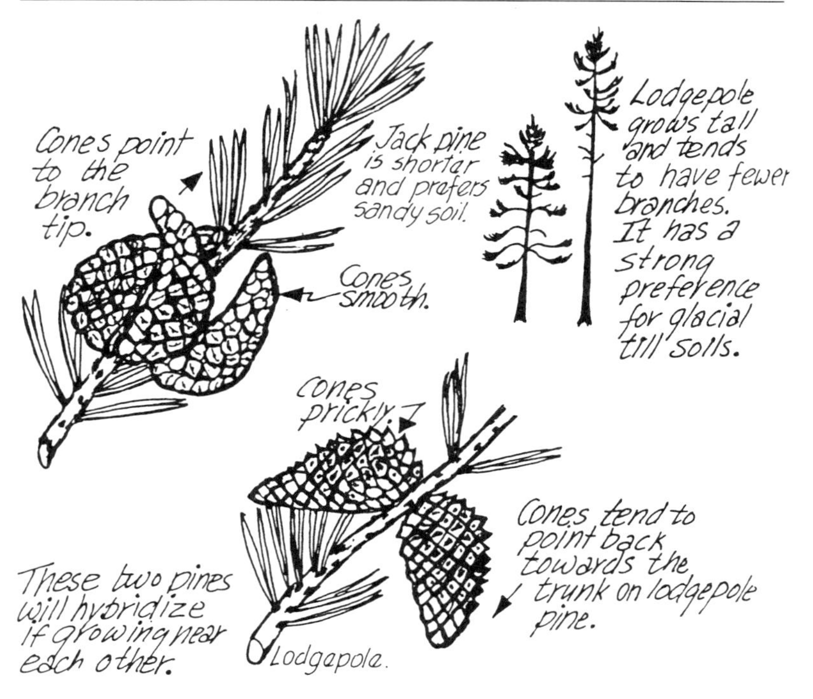

Lodgepole and jackpine compared.

come close to each other. The basic distinction between the two are the cones. Lodgepole cones are armed with recurved points whereas the Jack pine cone is smooth. The Lodgepole cone points back to the trunk of the tree, whereas in Jack pine the cone tip is directed towards the apex of the branch and tends to lay close to it.

The pines grow in dense stands that often exclude other trees. The thick stands and the tree's resinous nature make it quite vulnerable to running fires. In the days before well-developed fire control, thousands of hectares of pine would be destroyed every summer, to be replaced by dense dog-hair stands. The tough and fire-resistant cones harbor seeds that remain viable for a long time. The cones drop from the burned trees and open to free the seeds on fire-burned soil that is very much to their liking.

Scattered throughout most maturing stands of pine are the fire charred trunks of the forest that once flourished before the 1860s. The 1860s and the 1890s must have been dry years, or years with more than the usual thunderstorm activity, as few forests in the North escaped the ravages of fire.

Fire-killed pine seems to contain more resin than those dying of other causes. The sawdust or wood chips from these trees have a very pleasant resinous, turpentine scent. The wood displays a sheen and a glossy smoothness on the cut of a sharp knife or axe. It is an easy and enjoyable wood to carve, suitable for a variety of carving projects. Because the resin makes the wood taste of turpentine, it is unsuitable for eating utensils.

Because of the weather resistant properties of the resin content, straight-grained and knot-free fire-killed pine may be split into shingles or shakes that may last four times longer than cedar. The resin can be extracted to produce a sticky tar. Fill a pail with split pieces of resinous wood and invert it on to a piece of sheet metal, under which a fire is built. A crease in the metal will collect the tar. The tar is useful for dressing wounds on trees and animals and for coating wooden cross-country skis.

Fire-killed pine was not always available, so green pine was used to make shingles. As green pine splits poorly, shingles were shaved off blocks of pine wood by a horsedrawn broad axe pulled in a circle about a pivot. These shingles were of a low resin content and had to be nailed on a roof so air could circulate under them to allow quick drying after a rain, otherwise they would soon rot.

Both the resin content and the carving quality of pine wood make it a good kindling. In open fires this resinous wood is irritating to the eyes and lungs. In a stove it is fast-burning and produces an intense heat although the B.T.U.s per cord are rather low when compared to birch or tamarack. Pine soot, notorious for accumulating in stove pipes, creates a fire hazard if not cleaned out regularly. The soot, which is mostly carbon, can ignite under the right circumstances to produce a white-hot glowing stove pipe that may ignite a wall or roof some distance from it.

Pine is esteemed in log construction because it grows straight and tall with the trees tending to be of similar size in any given area. The log nearest to the ground in a log cabin (the sill log) is the key to the longevity of the building. If the bark is removed on one side of a living pine, the debarked portion will become saturated with resin to produce a rot resistant sill log.

Pine was often used in the production of charcoal for blacksmithing. To make small quantities of charcoal, build

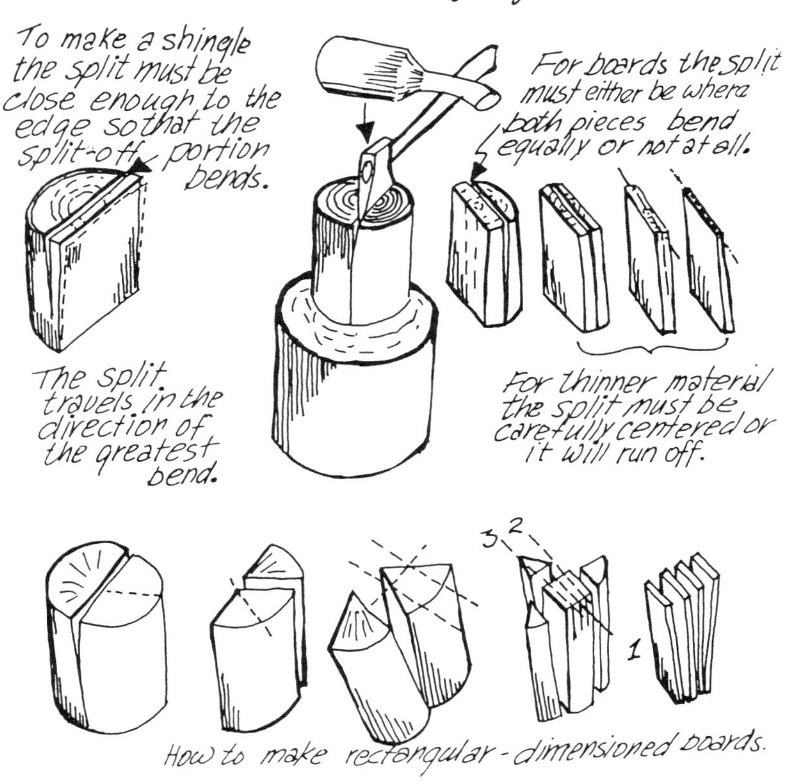

Some splitting techniques.

a fire that will quickly burn down to a bed of coals. Suffocate these with dirt and the charcoal is ready to use when cool. Larger quantities can be made by a scaled-down version of the traditional method used by professional charcoal-makers. Charcoal glows with an intensity that is about three times hotter than normal burning wood. Charred wood will ignite more readily than plain wood.

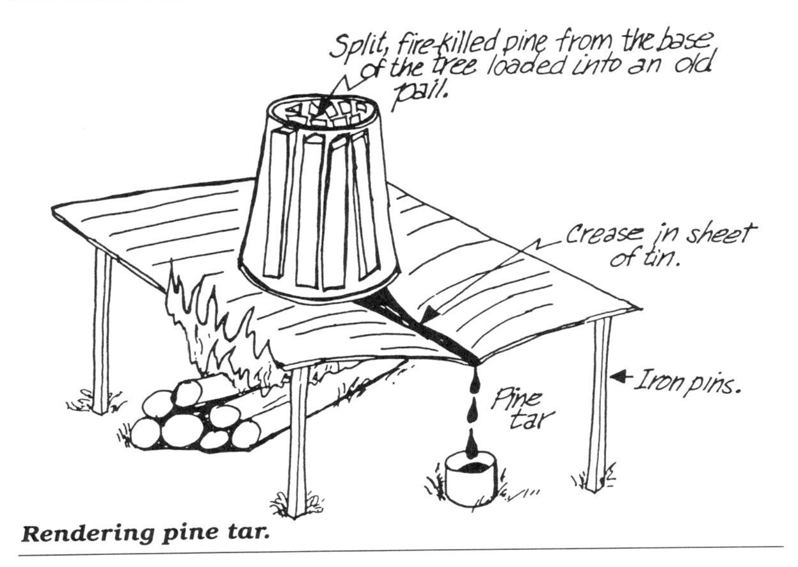

Rendering pine tar.

Like spruce, the roots of the pine are used for sewing birch bark baskets and canoes. They are usually boiled to remove the bark and to make them more supple.

The stumps and other waste products of cut-over pine forests may be processed for their high resin content. The fresh resin may be broken down into turpentine and rosin.

Jack pine was tapped for pitch for caulking baskets and canoes to make them waterproof. Water bottles woven out of spruce roots were waterproofed by coating the interior with crushed resin dust and the bottle gently heated to melt the resin to complete the sealing process.

BALSAM AND SUBALPINE FIR

The firs are a common tree in the more southerly parts of the Northern Forests. The flat needles, smooth, blistered bark, and upright cones make it an easy tree to identify.

A useful aspect of the tree is the contents of the blisters on the bark. Like the resin found on the Porsild white spruce, it is an excellent antiseptic for cuts, burns and scalds. The balsam resin, which is officially called Canada Balsam, is also used for mounting cover slips on slides.

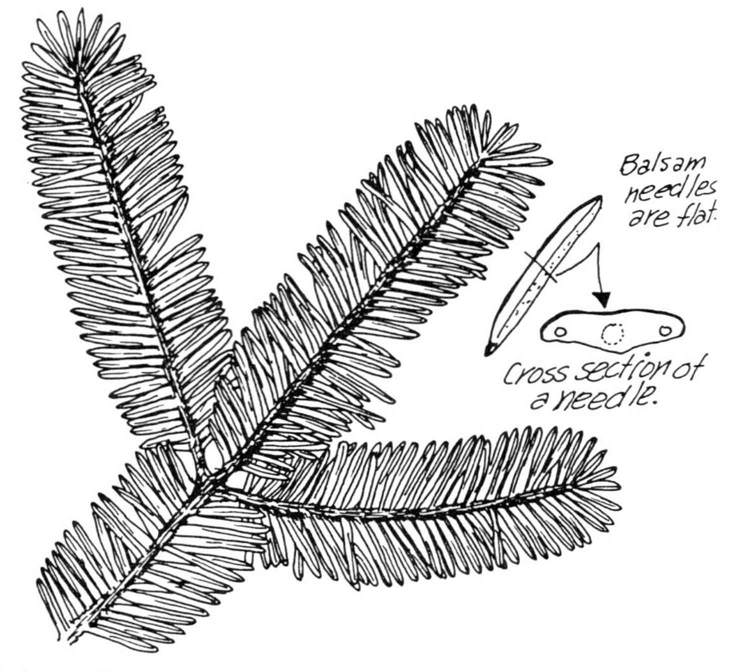

Balsam fir.

Balsam fir boughs, being of a flat configuration, readily pack into a dense layer to make a more rain deflective shelter roof than spruce. The boughs make poorer beds for the same reason. The tender young tips of the boughs can be used as pillow stuffing. The fragrance helps to relieve certain distresses connected with breathing. When the tips are laid over hot rocks in a sweat lodge or sauna, a medicinal atmosphere is created. The rocks should be cool enough that the branches do not burst into flame or excessive smoke will result.

The dry wood of the firs seems to throw about as much heat as black poplar, making it a poor firewood.

9

THE WILLOWS

This large genus of shrubs and trees provides a major portion of the raw materials and fuel for bush living. The willows generally have long, smooth branches which are slender and pliant.

THE POPLARS

The poplars are members of the willow family. They are noted for being hardy, vigorous-growing and short-lived colonizers of spaces cleared by fire, beaver or man. If there are no clearings to fill, the poplar cannot expand because of its intolerance of shade. In fact, it cannot stand the shade of its own species, which accounts for the lack of small trees among adult ones. Trees such as spruce, which are shade tolerant, use fast-growing poplars for protection until they are sufficiently mature to take care of themselves, by which time their "nurse trees" have matured and disappeared.

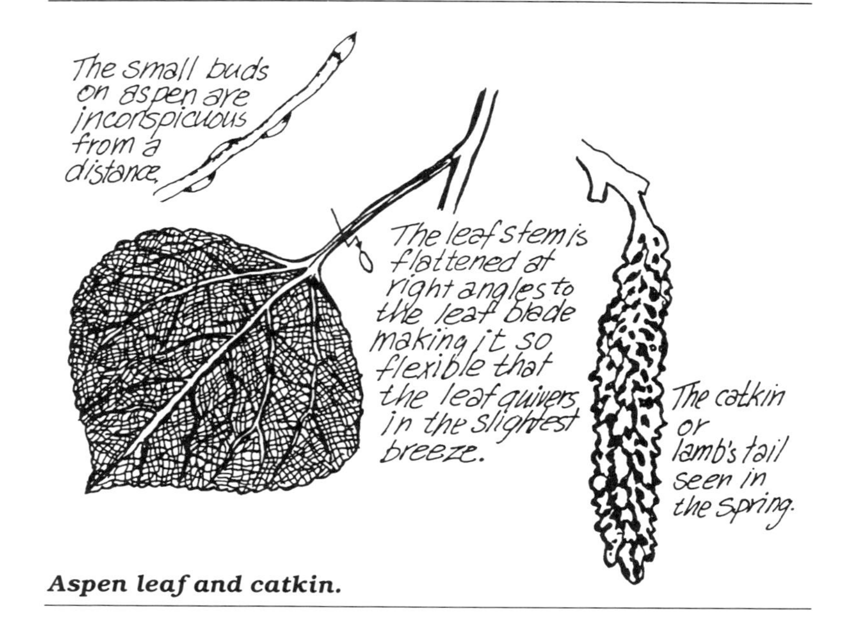

Aspen leaf and catkin.

QUAKING ASPEN

The quaking aspen is also known as the white poplar, popple and trembling aspen. Because of their flattened, slender, very flexible stems, the leaves will quiver with the slightest air movement. Aspen is the most widely distributed tree in North America, ranging from the subarctic to the subtropical regions and from sea level to mountain timberline. Quaking aspen is commonly found on south facing slopes, well-drained benches and creek bottoms. Ideal growing conditions are rich, moist clay or sandy loams with good drainage and a water table within two metres. The trees may reach a height of 24 metres and may live up to 100 years.

Aspen is a host to numerous fungi, all of which, save one, are harmful to it. One of the most common, known as a conk, enters the tree through the dead branch stumps and causes the heartwood to deteriorate. Such a tree can be a hazard in strong winds because of the reduced strength of the trunk. By the time the tree is 70-years-old, a quarter of its wood may be affected by this fungus. The wood becomes either soft and punky or light and firm like balsa. This material will glow slowly and can be used to carry fire. The firm, punky wood makes an excellent board in the bow drill method of fire-lighting. The dry conk makes a good fire board as well. The soft, punky heartwood can be used as towelling for wet or greasy hands.

The sketch pad fungus is also found on poplar. Gathered alive, it may, as its name suggests, be used for drawings or writing. Any mark or drawing made on the live, white spore surface will turn into a clearly contrasting dark brown.

Parasitic mushrooms found on the living tree are *Armellaria mellia*, *Pholiota squarrosoides* and *P. squarrosa*. The delectable oyster mushroom, *Pleurotus* is often found on dead aspen. A symbiotic associate of aspen is the interesting and poisonous hallucinogenic *Amanita muscaria*. The sweetened broth of this fungus is a potent fly-killer. The root-like structure of *A. muscaria* and the terminal rootlets of aspen together form a joint structure called a mychorrhiza. The fungus derives some of its nutrition from the structure, but what the tree derives from it is not clearly understood. Young aspen will die in the absence of this fungus.

Properly cured aspen wood is quite hard, almost white in color with a fine uniform texture. It is almost odorless and tasteless. The wood is suitable for furniture, kitchen utensils and carving. Aspen is durable like birch only if kept dry and not allowed ground contact. In pioneer days, it proved a passable substitute for hickory or ash for the wooden components of horsedrawn equipment. Aspen doubletrees were buried in sodden horse manure which improved the strength and durability of the wood, making it comparable to that of the eastern hardwoods.

Straight, sound, knot-free trees are selected for woodcarving. The bark is peeled off in May or June and the tree allowed to stand or is cut up and stored in a dry place for a few years to cure.

Frozen aspen splits remarkably easily. A wooden teepee or lean-to can be quickly made with the halves.

In the Northern Forests, aspen is second to willow as a favourite open-firewood because of its good blazing properties and pleasant smoke. The coals are short-lived and the ash is whitish-grey, smooth and fluffy. Sometimes the ash is employed as a crude baking powder. Canadian aspen was renowned the world over as a matchwood with an ember that extinguishes quickly, thereby reducing the chances of it blazing up after the flame is extinguished. When water is scarce for putting out a campfire, aspen may be the appropriate fuel to use. When required, aspen may be burned green providing it is split and the starting fire is hot.

Aspen bark is an important food for beaver, moose, elk and varying hare. Horses can subsist on it when all other feed is scarce. In winter, it has to be chopped off for the horses, but in the spring, when the bark comes off easily, felling the tree is sufficient as the horses can peel the bark off for themselves.

Like all other Northern Forest trees, aspen will peel easily from late May to mid-August. The bark can be used to make first aid splints of all sizes or folded into temporary containers and cooking vessels for use with hot rocks. As a

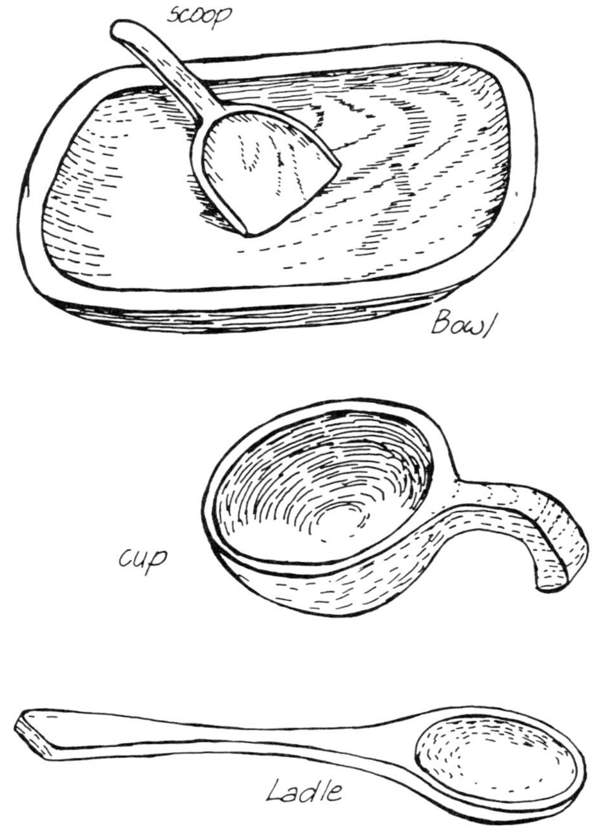

Some utensils made of aspen.

shingle it must be tied or weighed down to prevent curling. It can be used under sod or moss, but is not as durable as conifer bark and is somewhat inferior to birch bark. The bark makes a handy flume when collecting water from small hillside springs.

Like spruce, pine and hemlock, aspen has a substantial and good-tasting cambium layer that can be scraped off the surface of the wood in late spring and early summer. This edible cambium can be dried for future use.

Quaking aspen is commonly known as white poplar, so named for the chalky white powder that forms on the trunk of the tree at certain times of the year. Most of the powder is produced on the side facing the direct rays of the sun. The white patches that may be found on any side of the tree are a white lichen. The chalky material is a reflective sun screen that prevents the premature rising of sap from the warmth of the late winter sun. Should the sap rise and freeze, the tree will be damaged. The powder can be dusted on exposed skin to help prevent sunburn. Some Native people mixed the powder with the vitreous humor of the eye balls of large animals to make a paint for the body or for their artifacts. The powder can be used as a passable talcum. Stockings may be turned inside out and gently rubbed in the powder to reduce chafing.

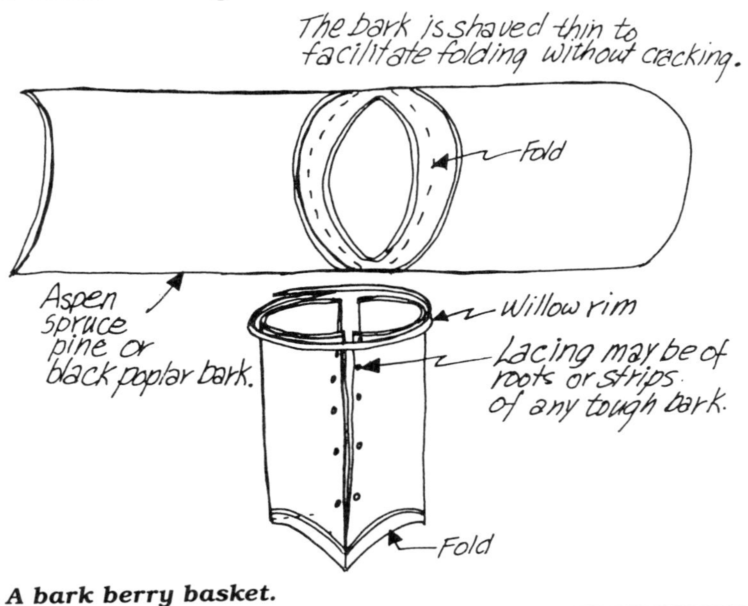

A bark berry basket.

If you examine an aspen stand from a distance (even on an overcast day), the whitish and brighter hue indicates you are looking north; if the hue is greenish and darker, you are looking south.

Aspen roots are relatively weak, difficult to gather, and only suitable for weak bindings.

BLACK POPLAR

Black poplar is faster-growing with a stronger preference for moisture than aspen. The tree is commonly found in river valleys, growing the largest on river banks and sandy islands. The biggest trees are usually associated with large rivers and lakes. Some trees can attain a height of 30 metres and a diameter of well over a metre. Like willow, most of the tree may die save for a narrow strip with a few branches alive at the top.

The wood has many properties and applications similar to aspen, such as the tendency to warp when curing. Slices of the trunk cure without checking, making this large diameter tree popular for constructing rustic tables. The sapwood is white and the heartwood is brown. The cured wood is light-weight, fine-textured and soft. The wood has an attractive grain that can be stained and finished to resemble walnut or mahogany. The wood will rot quickly if in contact with the ground unless it is saturated with moisture, in which case it makes durable flooring in barns. Dugout canoes were made from black poplar by the Native peoples living near large lakes.

Green black poplar wood is higher in moisture content than any other northern wood. For this reason the tree is often struck by lightning and should be avoided during electrical storms.

Black poplar is the poorest of firewoods, producing the least heat per given volume of all the trees of the Northern Forests. The green log is the most fire resistant of woods and is useful in the construction of the wall-backed fire for moderately cold conditions. The punky, moist wood of a rotten black poplar produces a particularly acrid smoke. Once glowing (which is easily accomplished with a spark), a punky black poplar log is difficult to extinguish.

The smooth bark of the young tree becomes thicker and more deeply furrowed or fluted as it grows older. In a big, old tree the cork-like bark may reach a thickness of ten centimetres. The bark is not easy to remove, unless the tree has been dead for a few years. The more superior bark from a living tree is of a softer, more resilient texture than the dead and dry bark.

To remove dry bark beyond your reach, use a pole with a chisel point to pry it off, but use caution as dangerously heavy pieces may fall or slide down the pole if you do not let go of the pole fast enough.

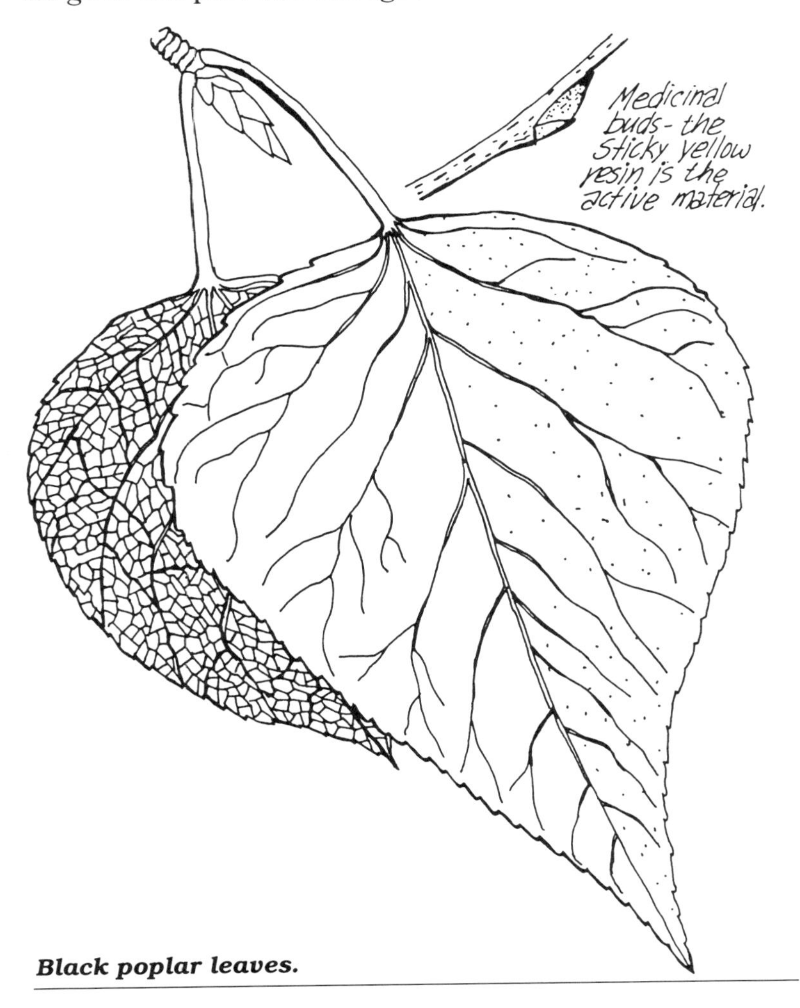

Black poplar leaves.

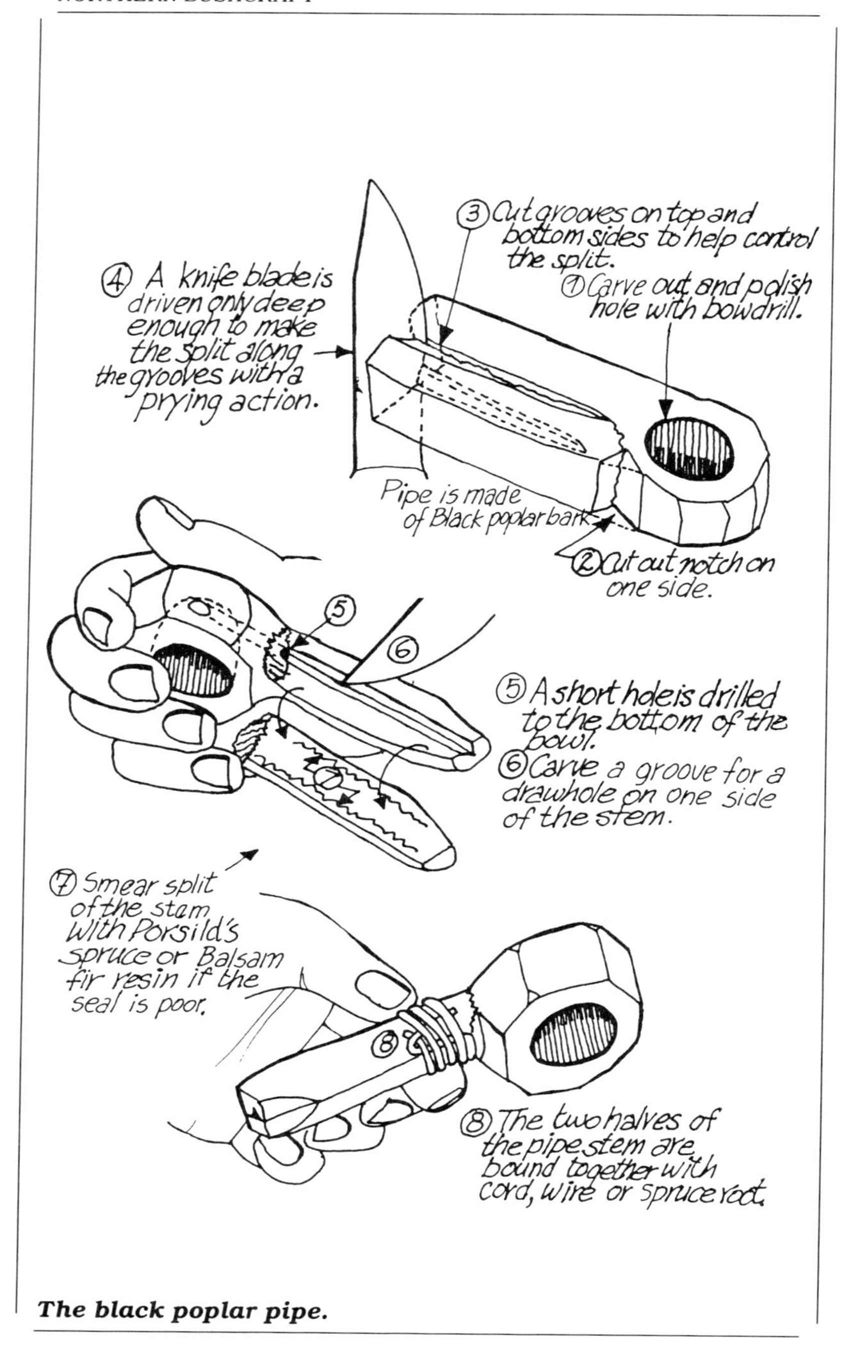

The black poplar pipe.

The bark makes excellent floats for fish nets because of its buoyancy and resistance to waterlogging. It makes a fast burning fuel that produces good baking coals. In a prolonged rain when dry kindling is difficult to find, the wet surface is sliced off and the dry interior of the bark is shaved into kindling. The bark makes a superior socket for the bow drill for drilling holes or making fire by friction. It is quickly fashioned and readily polishes to produce an almost frictionless bearing surface. This same socket hole makes a fine pipe bowl for smoking.

The live inner bark was once used for making casts for broken limbs. A large quantity of the bark is simmered for a day and the resulting liquor strained out. The liquor is then evaporated to a syrup. The hot syrup is spread on a cloth and wrapped around the set broken bone and allowed to harden into a cast. This will last for as long as two months until the bone mends.

Another name for black poplar is cottonwood, because of the cotton-like fluff the tree produces in early June. This may be used with the liquid resin from the blisters in the bark of balsam fir or Porsild's white spruce as a dressing for burns and wounds. This fluff was added to buffalo berries when they were beaten to a froth to make soopolallie or Indian ice cream.

The buds from the black poplar, which are at their largest in the spring just before they open, contain a yellowish-brown, sticky balm. If the bud is chewed, the balm first produces a burning sensation in the mouth then numbs and soothes a sore throat or relieves a cough. A cough medicine is made by simmering the buds in water and then sipping the decoction. Simmering the buds in fat then straining them out produces a wound ointment for both humans and animals.

THE WILLOWS

True willow (Salix species) is one of the most widely distributed tree or shrub genera in the world. There are at least 75 species in North America. This useful plant may vary in size from less than a centimetre to that of a big tree. The features distinguishing willow from all other trees is a winter bud covered with one scale, and the bitter taste of the bark.

Most willow woods are light, soft and tough, and have a multitude of uses. Some are well-known for their peculiar patterns of contrasting white sapwood and reddish-brown heartwood. Willow wood is popular for lampstands, canes, picture frames and coffee tables. Some willows have long shoots that are esteemed for basket weaving. Straight willow shafts are used for arrows or spears. This shrub's preference for moist areas puts it in the right place to control erosion on stream banks and mountain sides. In Europe, willow has long been utilized for willow furniture, wooden shoes, artificial limbs, and carriage bodies. The long flexible wands of many willows can be used for shelter frameworks or for wattle and daub construction.

The twigs, buds and leaves are valuable browse for ruffed and sharp tailed grouse, willow and rock ptarmigan, elk, whitetail deer, moose, beaver, muskrat, varying hare and porcupine. The foliage provides cover and nesting habitat for many birds. Many willows are esteemed for their ornamental horticultural characteristics.

Willows mostly propagate by suckering. Sucker formation is stimulated by cutting or burning down the parent, which also creates openings that allow the sun to shine on the forest floor. In turn, the sun warms the soil to stimulate sucker formation. Suckers that develop from the root system of one parent tree are identical genetically. Taken together as a group, trees that originate from one individual in this way, are called a clone. Clones appear alike, leaf out and turn color at the same time and may have their own unique shade of color when they turn in the fall. Although the willows can grow from seed, conditions for successful germination are so exacting that this is an insignificant means of propagation.

Willow is one of the best open-firewoods easily gathered without tools. When dry, it burns with the least smoke of any wood to produce a hot, steady fire with excellent coals. The smoke is pleasant to eyes and lungs, a desirable quality for a cooking fuel used in an open fire. A drawback is that willow is generally small in diameter. In a pinch, willow may be cut into small pieces for a coal substitute in a forge for working iron. Willow is also a source of a high quality charcoal used in gunpowder. It is the most readily available northern wood for making fire by friction.

The most common northern bow woods are saskatoon, chokecherry, birch and certain willows. Birch and willow in particular, must be broken to determine if they have a long, fine-fiber fracture characteristic of a good bow wood. Conduct this test on a part outside of the main stave. This fracture can be found where moose break down small trees and shrubs to get at the higher twigs.

Bebbs willow, also called diamond or beaked willow, is common in the north. At times it is a large shrub or a small tree, growing over ten metres tall with a diameter of 15 to 25 centimetres. It is one of the sources of "Diamond Willow." The diamond-shaped depressions (as in the diamonds found on playing cards) are caused by a variety of fungi which attack the willow at the junction of the branches and the trunk. The trunk is peeled and carved to reveal a striking pattern of diamond-shaped cavities with the white outer wood contrasting with the reddish-brown heartwood. The wood may be used for canes, lamps, candle holders, coat hangers, gun racks, ashtray stands, stools, tables and staircases, to name a few applications.

The light, durable wood from this particular willow is suitable for making baseball and cricket bats. The withes

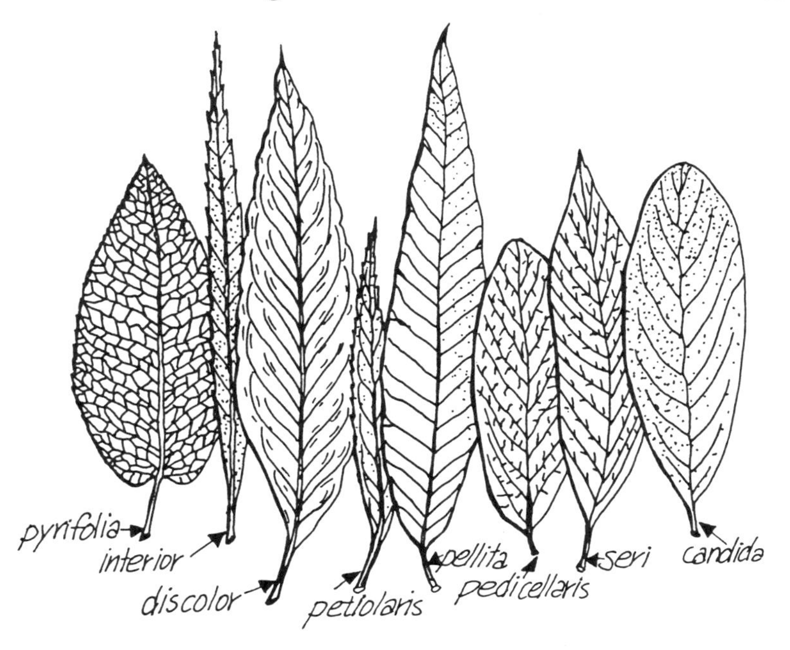

Leaves of various willows (salix) found in the Northern Forests.

have been used for willow furniture and basket weaving.

Bebbs willow provides the bast fiber once employed for making fish nets in the north before European netting twine became available, as stinging nettle is not commonly found in the north (*see* Chapter 5).

10

THE SHRUBS

The shrubs of the Northern Forest are not only a source of food, but provide the raw materials needed to make useful tools or implements for bush living.

SILVER WILLOW

Silver or wolf willow is actually not a willow, but a member of the olive family. Found on river banks and cliffs, sand dunes and other sunny, well-drained locations, the shrub can be recognized from a distance by its distinctive silver foliage. There are times when the whole plant is covered with silvery flakes. The inconspicuous yellow blossoms that appear at the axils of the leaves in May and June have a strong, but pleasant fragrance.

Silver willow bears an edible fruit to which some people are allergic. The fruit which is a drupe, has a stone that makes one of the more attractive natural beads in the Northern Forests. The bead is softened by boiling and a large thorn can be forced through it to make the hole. When the thorn is withdrawn from the dry bead it is ready for stringing. The drupes remain on the shrub well into winter until they drop onto the surface of the snow. Sometimes they are blown along for great distances until they collect in a drift where a new plant colony may start.

The bark from the trunk of the shrub can be made into a cord that remains flexible upon drying (*see* Chapter 5). The outer skin has no tensile strength and is used as a dye for wool.

Silver willow wood is twisted and tough, but splits easily where the shrub forks. This weak point makes it possible to gather the bark from the plant without a cutting tool. The dry, old and weathered wood makes a long-wearing, superior drill for the friction method of fire-lighting.

In sand dunes, silver willow propagates from roots that may grow 20 metres before surfacing as a new plant. They are noteworthy for their even thickness and their strength in the green state, and their contrasting weakness in the dry state. The bark from the root makes a stronger cordage material than the bark from the trunk.

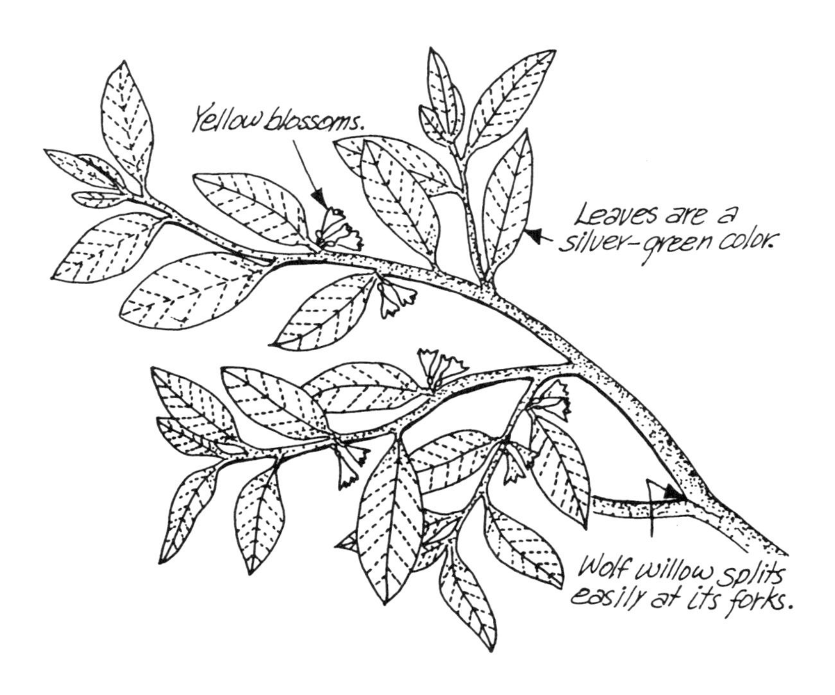

Wolf Willow.

THE SASKATOON

There are a number of different saskatoons that grow in the Northern Forests. The plant may grow as a shrub or a small tree to a diameter of over five centimetres.

The tough wood is difficult to work when dry and is likely the best northern bow wood. It makes tough handles, supple fishing poles, excellent arrow shafts and fulfills any application where resilience and toughness are required.

Saskatoons display a very fibrous fracture when broken, a property found in most good bow woods. The wood can be pounded to produce a coarse brush for cleaning teeth or one fine enough to use as a paint brush in artwork.

The spring and summer bark can be made into cordage similar in strength to that of wolf willow.

Saskatoons are best-known for the berries used in jams, jellies, sauces, pies and wines. The berries may be dried and incorporated into pemmican.

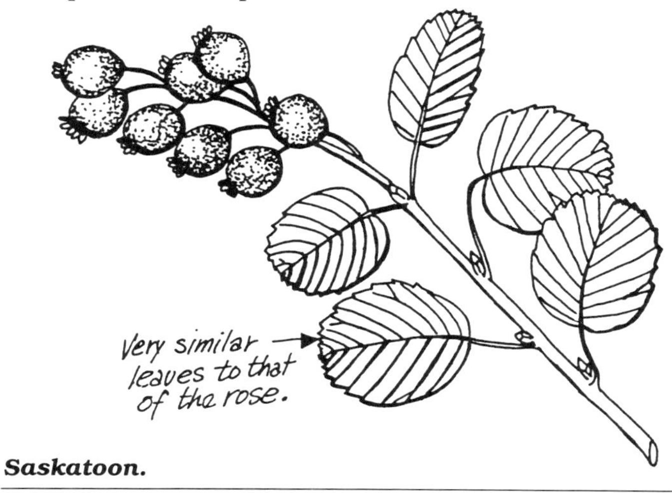
Very similar
leaves to that
of the rose.

Saskatoon.

RED OSIER DOGWOOD

Red osier dogwood is a shrub also known as red willow— a cause for confusion as it belongs to the dogwood family. The color of the bark ranges from a shade of red to a light-yellow. A major point of distinction between red osier dogwood and willows is that dogwood has white berries, whereas the willows never have any berries.

Although the berry is edible, it is thought to be poisonous because of its bitter taste and the fact that many white berries are poisonous. In spite of the taste, many Native peoples used it as food, often mixing it with saskatoon which ripens at the same time.

The inner bark was esteemed as a tobacco additive or kinnickinnick ("that which is mixed"). In spring and early summer the reddish paper-like bark is easily removed with the thumbnail, but in the winter when the wood is frozen, the outer bark must be laboriously scraped off.

The outer bark is discarded because it is too bitter to smoke. The inner bark is scraped so the shavings are left attached in the central portion of the wand. One end of the wand is sharpened so it may be shoved into the ground near a fire to toast the shavings. In five minutes the wand is turned. When the shavings are dry enough to crumble they are ready to use. This kinnickinnick may be mixed with tobacco or smoked alone. Red osier dogwood kinnickinnick may have been the only substance smoked in the pipe of peace or in the steam bath ceremony. It was considered good for any illness relating to the lungs. Mixed with tobacco, it was supposed to cancel out the undesirable effects of nicotine.

The finely-powdered kinnickinnick was also sprinkled on runny wounds and gaping cuts as a styptic (a substance that checks bleeding).

The fresh inner bark was pounded into a poultice for various skin conditions. Indian women who were breast feeding used the poultice when the infant was biting too much. They applied the poultice to the aveola to reduce the pain.

The roots were dug up in the early spring, and boiled, to make a tonic.

The thin, supple wands can be used for basket weaving. The wands have to be gathered in areas inaccessible to moose and elk because of their fondness for this shrub as a browse. The grazed shrub is the strongest proof of their presence.

The thicker rods of red osier dogwood were used to make pipe stems.

THE RIBBED BASKET FORMS

The ribbed baskets are some of the easiest and simplest to weave. This type of basket can be made from a variety of materials and combinations of materials and formed into many shapes. The only tools needed are a knife and an awl.

For a spherical basket of three to four litre capacity, about 200 to 300 wands are required that are as thin and long as possible. Five to seven ribs no thinner than a pencil, and a rim and main rib of a centimetre in thickness are required.

First, fashion a rim with a wand that is thicker than the little finger. If the rim is too thin and flexible it becomes

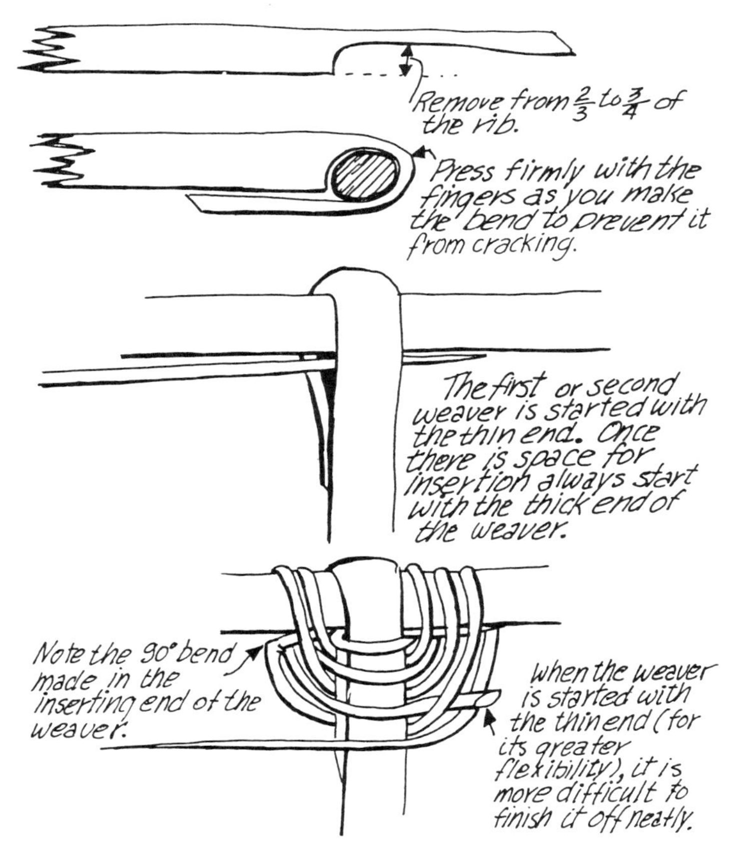

Detail for main rib and its attachment to the rim in the construction of the spherical basket.

distorted during weaving, resulting in an unattractive basket. The ends of the rim are lock-lapped together and are bound so the hoop will not spring apart. The hoop may be dried in this shape or the main rib can be attached directly to it in the green state.

The main rib and carrying handle is formed by making a second hoop the same size as the first, or smaller or larger, depending on the shape desired. The two hoops are placed at 90 degrees to each other and the weaving started. If a handle is not required, the ends of the main rib are thinned down to a one-third thickness and bent around the rim. This may be tied firmly in place with string and then woven in place by starting with thin weavers at both ends. If the rim and main rib are not dried into shape they remain soft and are subject to distortion by the straightening action of the main rib. A cord may be tied across the rim hoop to keep it round. If the basket is to have a flat bottom, a stick is put across the rim and the mid-point of the main rib anchored to it to keep the bottom flat.

After two or three wands have been woven in at both ends of the main rib, two more ribs are inserted. The ribs can be pre-shaped and made of a length that will make the basket more or less spherical or melon-shaped. Both ends of the rib are sharpened for easier insertion beside the rim or other ribs. The ribs are sometimes made from rods of the same thickness as the rim, but split in half.

If the ribs are pre-formed by drying in a form or a pail, the weaving is simplified and the basket takes on a more regular appearance. Weaving without pre-forming is possible, but takes more experience, persistence and finger strength.

Whenever the weaving at the ends of the ribs reaches a spacing of two fingers, additional ribs are inserted. The maximum spacing between ribs at mid-point should be about the width of three to four adult fingers.

The first weaver is thin and started with the thin end because of the need for greater flexibility at the start. However, the thick end is more difficult to anchor as the end of the weaver is reached. When you are finished with this first weaver, hold the end in place and put a new weaver with the thick end next and parallel to it and then continue weaving. When the end of the weaver is reached, the thin tip is tucked into the previous work to keep it from coming undone. All weavers used should be one half or less than the thickness of the ribs. If the ribs bend as you weave, the basket will be distorted.

As soon as there is space to jam in the thicker, sharpened end of a weaver next to a rib, use this method instead of the one just described which is only applied when there is no room to insert the thick end of a weaver. Whenever the weaver reaches the rim, it is usually made to go around it

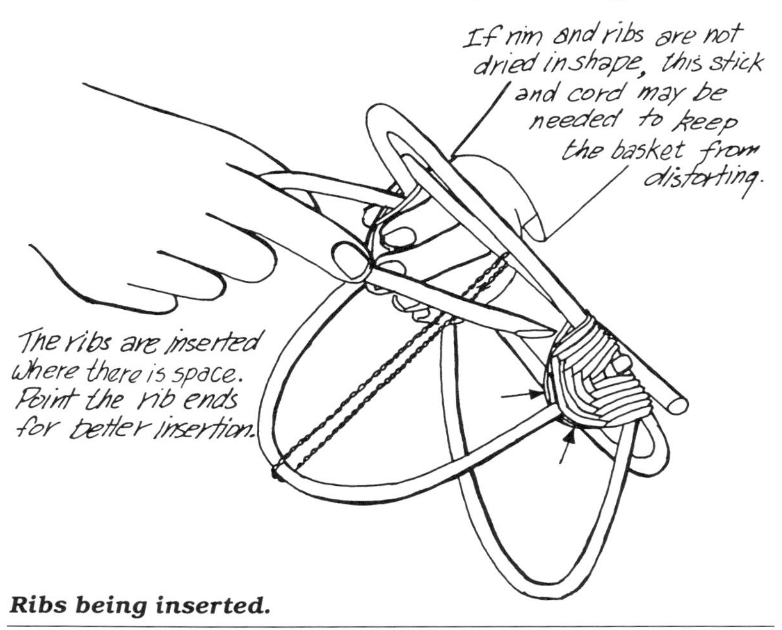

Ribs being inserted.

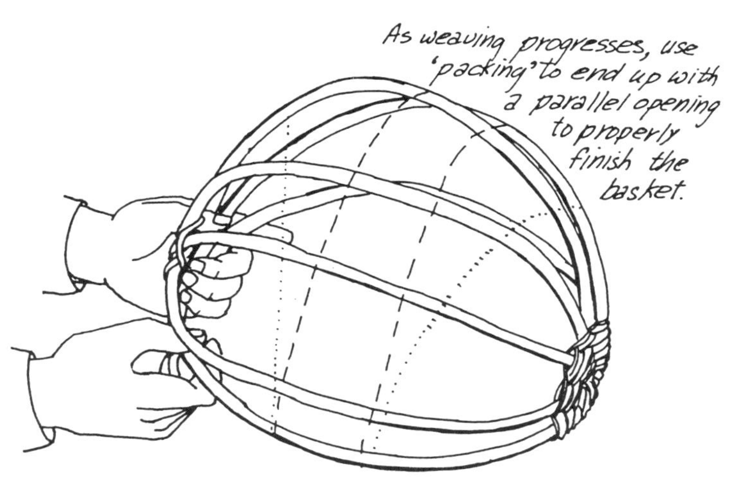

Finishing the weave in a spherical basket.

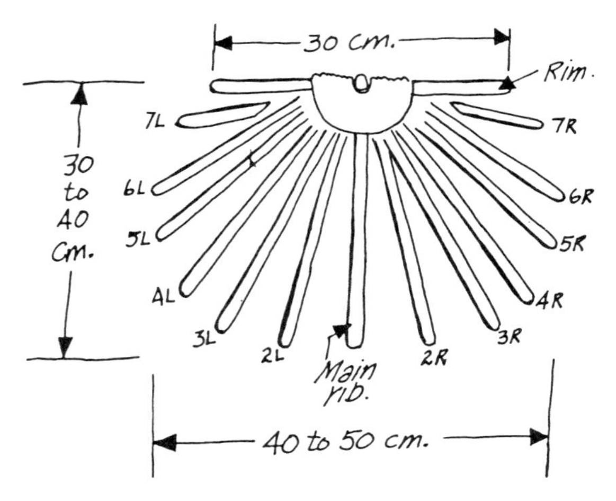

Ribs of the basket shown in detail.

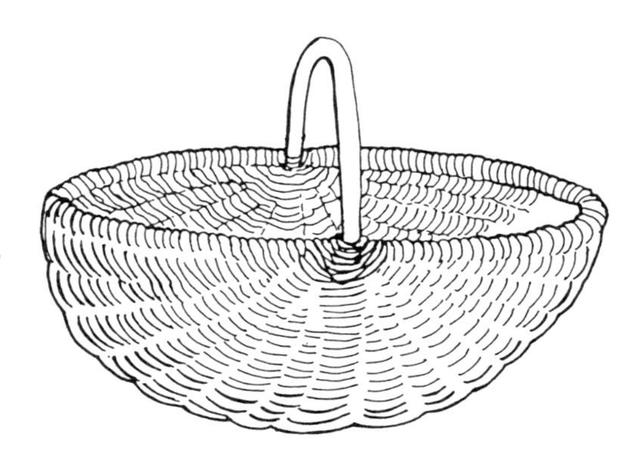

The spherical type of basket with a carrying handle.

twice before continuing in the reverse direction.

As the weaving progresses, both ends should keep up with each other and as the basket nears completion the unfilled gap has to be parallel or there will be large, triangular openings in the weave. Instead of weaving from rim to rim, stop one rib short and then two ribs short and so on until the main rib is reached. The process is then carried out in reverse or started over again. This procedure, known as packing, is repeated until the more-neatly filled parallel gap is achieved.

11

THE MOOSE

With the possible exception of the bison, the moose is the largest and most majestic beast of the Northern Forests and, the largest member of the deer family the world over.

THE MAJESTIC BEAST

The name "moose" is of Algonkian origin and, depending on the authority, translates into "he cuts through" or "he trims" or "wood eater." All of these readily apply to the moose and the way it bites off the twigs and shoots of its favorite browse.

The range of the moose coincides with the range of the Northern Spruce Forests of Canada, Europe and Asia. This is referred to as the Boreal or Spruce-Moose Forest.

Moose Characteristics

Everything about the moose's appearance suggests awkwardness. It has an elongated head with a big nose that extends well beyond its mouth, a large dewlap without an obvious function, a stub of a tail and large, cumbersome antlers. Its weight may range from 400 to 600 kilograms, and occasionally exceed 800 kilograms.

Without a doubt, the moose is unique. The large, broad, palmate antlers found only in the male; the long, slender, big-hoofed legs; the short neck, the large shoulder hump and the small hind quarters all contribute to distinguish it from any other deer. The moose has such long legs and short neck that it has to spread its front legs wide to reach the ground with its muzzle. It often has to kneel on its forelegs to reach water or forage. This same anatomy allows the moose to reach branches up to three metres above the ground and if it stands on its hind legs it easily reaches a height of five metres. The hump over the shoulders is due to high shoulder blades and long backbone spines in the neck and shoulder region.

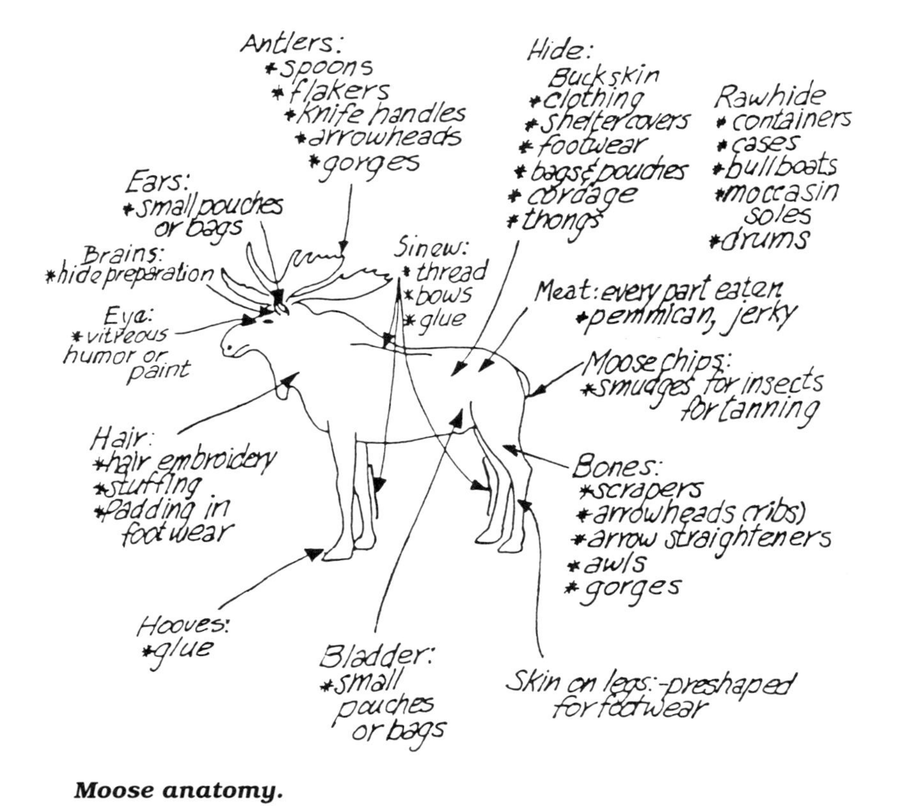

Moose anatomy.

The gestation period for the moose is from 225 to 265 days with the birthing season from May to early June. Single births are the most common, twins occur less often and triplets occasionally. The ungainly calf looks like four spindly legs with a head attached. Unlike the rest of the deer family, the young are born without protective coloration different from the adult. At birth the calf may weigh from 10 to 15 kilograms if born alone and half that if a twin. By November, the weaned animal will weigh an amazing 135 kilograms. In the first month the calf may gain about a kilogram daily and double the amount thereafter. A yearling bull calf may weigh from 180 to 270 kilograms.

The calf does not follow the mother until 10 to 14 days after birth, although it can outrun a man at this age. Many predators exploit the vulnerability of the young calf. The secluded calving-place chosen by the mother is usually surrounded with good feed so that she does not have to go far from her offspring. The mother moose is protective and a formidable defender of her young.

The offspring quickly learn many things from the mother such as using natural camouflage, standing still in thickets, backtracking, swimming and moving with stealth. The offspring accompany the mother for a year or two. The females reach breeding age in two or three years and the males are sexually mature in three, but usually do not have the opportunity to breed until their fifth or sixth year when they reach full adult size.

The male and female do not differ much in appearance. The female lacks antlers, a mane and the dewlap. (The dewlap is a pendant of hair-covered skin hanging from the throat and varies in size from a few centimetres to about a half-metre in length.) The cow is also 10 to 25 percent smaller than the male.

The mature bull is individualistic, independent and unsociable, shunning company except during the rut. Family ties are weak, though on occasion, a bull and a cow with her offspring of two years may form a loose association, more for convenience, than for companionship.

Moose make docile pets or pests depending on how you interpret the situation. The animal has often been domesticated, but is short-lived in captivity. The lifespan of a healthy moose is from 20 to 25 years. Tall fences are required to contain these animals. In Russia, cow moose have been trained to respond to the call of a trumpet to be milked. Moose have been trained to pull sleighs or wagons, and are tireless as any horse. Moose that lose their fear of man (by being fed), may appear regularly for their dole and become downright ornery if not forthcoming. Another problem with the captive moose is its change of character during its rut in the fall breeding season.

The normally timid, retreating, cautious, silent hulk of the woods changes into a short-tempered, belligerent, bellowing, bulldozer during the mating season when it assumes the physical and mental state known as the rut (from early September to early November). The bull becomes preoccupied with seeking out females and challenging competitors, prudently conceding when outclassed by another suitor. A challenge may involve a great deal of bluffing and posturing with a disinclination to make contact while the bulls size each other up. It is a case of intimidating anything smaller or weaker and acknowledging anything superior. Where both are equal in size and determination, a shoving match may result that ends when one concedes defeat and quickly leaves. Occasionally, a serious battle results in injury or death. There have been numerous instances where

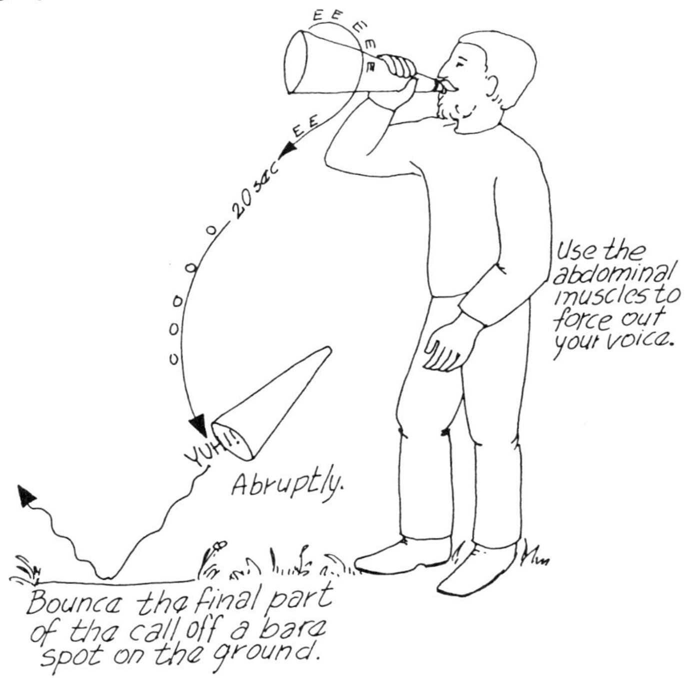

Moose calling with a megaphone.

horns lock permanently and both combatants die of exhaustion and starvation.

Feeding is neglected during the rut, to the point that a bull may loose a quarter of its body weight. Bulls are irritable during the rut and may attack anything that moves.

The cow moose is an active participant during the rut. She will communicate her presence and state of mind with grunts and nasal-entoned love calls that a hunter may advantageously imitate to bring a bull into closer range. The right sounds can also cause a love-sick cow to come bounding in as well. Some people feel moose calling to be unfair, unless used in bow hunting.

A bull will bellow a rising "moo," whereas the call of the cow is softer and much like that of a domestic cow. The newborn calf grunts but later emits a laughing bleat. A bull may answer the call of a cow with a grunt or a bellow, which is usually interpreted by another bull as a challenge to an antler duel.

Once a bull has located a cow, courtship occurs with the bull trying to impress the cow by putting on majestic airs. The bull follows the cow for about a week until they mate then moves on to find another while the cow entertains new suitors. Occasionally, a group of cows will be guarded by one bull. Cows participate in the rut for about a month, while bulls wear themselves to a frazzle in two months or so, mating with about four cows.

Although moose are dangerous during the rut, they are so noisy that one is forewarned of their approach or presence. Approaching a cow and her calf invites an attack. Moose are irritable when the weather is cold, and in particular when food is scarce. They have been known to keep people captive in their cabins for days.

Moose Habitat

Habitat favored by elk and deer will suit a moose providing these animals are not present in great numbers. Moose are found near lakes, ponds, streams, grass-shrub bogs, muskegs, contiguous mixed-wood forests and burned-over areas. Since the 1930s, logging has taken the place of forest fires in extending favorable moose habitat.

Moose prefer the forest edge, as mature forests provide little forage. In mountainous country, moose frequent higher elevations in the summer and the lower valleys in the winter. In winter, the moose may glean the sparse forage of a mature coniferous forest as the understorey has the least snow and also provides protection from wind.

Moose have a home range encompassing a radius of about 15 kilometres. They do not defend any territory. Although they may drift slowly into more optimal habitat, sudden migration is rare. Moose tend to spend a few days in one place then move on, but when snow is deep, they may stay for as long as the browse holds out.

Moose will eat grasses and other forbs and occasionally lichens and mushrooms, but the principal browse is the tips and small branches of willow, aspen, red osier dogwood, saskatoon, birch, swamp birch, alder, hazelnut, and the tender tips of balsam fir. The daily winter consumption of twigs is over 20 kilograms. Moose may straddle large shrubs or small trees, bending them down to bring the finer branches within reach. This results in broken trees that are a common sight in moose habitat. Red osier dogwood, hazel nut and saskatoon exhibit a characteristic clipped, contorted appearance from repeated browsings and regrowths that are a sure sign of the presence of moose.

The willow family responds to wildfire with the sprouting and growth of many vigorous shoots on account of the greater availability of nutrients and the elimination of competition. This results in copious and easy forage for moose. Willow has a great capacity to recover from the effects of browsing. In some cases, a browsed branch produces twice as much new growth in the following year as compared to an uncropped branch.

During the summer, moose prefer subaquatic vegetation such as pond weeds and water lilies. A moose may eat up to 25 kilograms of aquatic vegetation daily. It quickly fills its rumen then chews its cud at leisure, grinding up twigs that are a centimetre in thickness with its heavy molars. Being a ruminant, it has sharp lower incisors and a tough upper gum. Its large, sensitive muzzle is well-adapted for stripping leaves and twigs from trees and shrubbery. The animal feeds most actively at dawn and dusk. Where foraging takes longer it prefers to feed at night and to rest during the day.

Winter's twig forage is low in sodium compared to certain pond weeds that may have 400 times the concentration. Another source of sodium is the bark the moose will strip off the living aspen tree when other sodium-containing forage is scarce. Moose are capable of building up a reserve of sodium for the winter.

A moose is particularly adept in submerging its head for subaquatic forage. Because it has the ability to close off its nostrils as it submerges, the moose may dive as deep as six metres for its favorite food.

Like all ruminants, moose have a strong liking for salt. They favor areas of stagnant mineral-rich water known as salt licks.

Moose have an exceptional sense of smell, very good hearing and eyesight that is poorer than that of humans. As a moose will hear the ticking of a watch at 150 metres, it is difficult to stalk the animal when there is no wind to mask the noise made in walking.

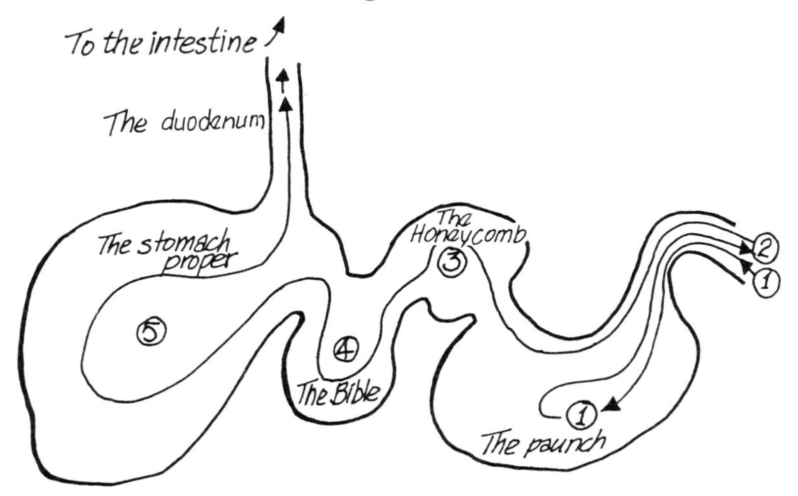

***Stomach of the moose.** The complex stomach allows the moose to subsist on twigs.*

1. Roughly chopped material mixed with saliva is stored in the first compartment (the paunch) then retrieved and chewed more thoroughly.

2. The coarser material is returned to the mouth as cud then chewed into a fine pulp that increases the surface area of the material.

3. The finely chewed food is swallowed again. It now bypasses the paunch to the honeycomb and bible (4) complexes of the stomach where bacteria and ciliates participate in the break down of some of the material. Certain nutrients are absorbed at this stage.

4. The partially processed material with the bacteria and ciliates pass on to the stomach proper where normal digestion takes place.

Except during the rut, moose are cautious and alert. A moose will remain motionless to avoid detection and if unnoticed, steals silently away. When frightened, it may crash noisily through the underbrush, or may do so deliberately during the rut, otherwise it is capable of great stealth. Its brownish-black hide and yellowish-white legs blend well with foliage such as spruce or willow. If you look low to the ground, below the dead branches of the trees that make up a spruce thicket, you may find that its legs give it away before its body will.

If the animal is startled it will maneuver downwind to make a more positive identification by scent and sound—a habit which can be its undoing when hunted by man. When bedding down, it will first travel downwind so the scent of any animal following its tracks will be carried to it.

In spite of its ungainly appearance, large antlers and all, it can move with ease and grace through deadfall, deep snow, muskeg or water. During the reign of Russia's Catherine the Great, the authorities tried to maintain strict control over the domestication of moose because of their use as steeds by rebels and escapees of Siberian prison camps. The horse-mounted authorities were no match for the outlaw riding a moose as it can run from 25 to 35 kilometres an hour through seemingly impassible deadfall.

A clicking sound may be heard when the animal runs across soft ground. The hoof that is spread very wide for the necessary support clicks together when the foot is withdrawn, making a sound that carries some distance.

It is remarkable how little a 650-kilogram moose sinks compared to a 65-kilogram man trying to follow it through a swamp. Moose have a well-developed mode of lifting their feet straight up until the hoof clears the surface when making a foreward step. This facilitates fast movement through deep snow, deadfall and mud with a reduced risk of injury to the foot. Because of its preference for wet and soft environments, moose utilize the dew-claws (located behind and below the fetlock joint) more than any other cloven-hoofed animal. A moose never bounds like a deer.

A wolf can keep up with a moose only in deep snow or on glare ice. A moose is particularly vulnerable on glare ice where it has difficulty in maintaining its footing.

In winter, when snow is a metre or more deep, moose will often trample a system of interconnecting paths to make a "yard." This provides some freedom of movement when defending themselves or travelling to feeding areas.

Another feature associated with moose are wallows. These are small, wet areas where moose may urinate in one place, trample up the urine-saturated soil and roll around in it—a habit related to the rut.

Moose like to submerge in water for respite from bothersome insects. They are powerful swimmers that show no hesitation in crossing large bodies of water on a whim or to escape predators. A mother quickly teaches her offspring to swim. During long swims a calf will support its head on the mother. Moose have been known to swim about 25 kilometres at a stretch. Swimming moose were easy prey to Native people who would approach the animal with a canoe. The animal could then be killed with as simple a tool as a sharpened pole.

Moose Tracks and Antlers

The moose has the largest track in the deer family—as much as 18 centimetres long. In outline, the print resembles that of a very large deer. The moose print is larger and more pointed than that of the wapiti or elk, which more resembles the print of domestic cattle. Cow moose tracks are smaller and more pointed than the male's, which are usually blunter because of the bull's habit of pawing the ground.

Moose have the most massive racks of all the antlered animals. Some may span over two metres and weigh more than 30 kilograms. Antlers are a secondary sexual characteristic renewed annually for the rut. The amount of solid tissue produced is a wonder of the animal kingdom, as a bull weighing 450 kilograms may grow 40 kilograms of antler in five months. The new antlers begin growing in April and are covered with a furry, soft, brown skin resembling velvet. The skin is filled with blood vessels and nerves that participate in the growth of the antlers. There is an increased appetite for salts and minerals during this period of antler development. The antlers are tender, fragile and sensitive to the touch and cause pain if injured. By the time the antlers mature in the summer, the velvet is shed and the animal becomes preoccupied with removing the remaining shreds by rubbing on bushes and small trees, often injuring the bark. When the rut is over, the antlers drop off between December to February. The older the animal, the earlier this occurs. Antler growth imposes as much of an energy cost to a bull as pregnancy does to a cow.

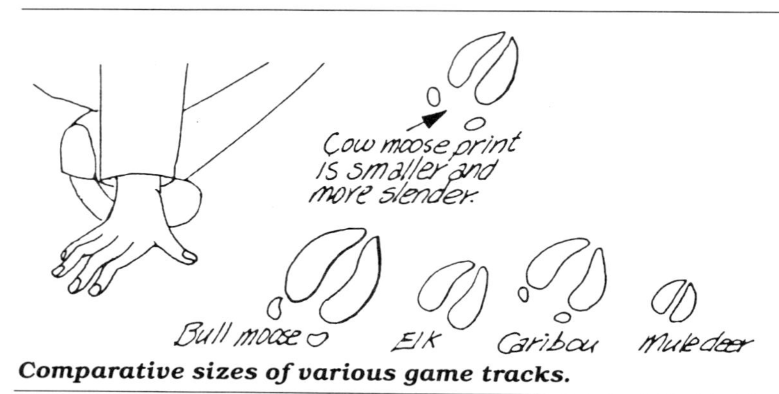

Comparative sizes of various game tracks.

As formidable as the antlers may seem, both the bull and cow can deal out havoc more effectively with their forehooves. A healthy, full-grown moose can be a formidable opponent to a grizzly. It is not unusual for a moose to kill a bear.

The approximate age of the young animal can be determined by its antlers. A male calf will have knobs. A yearling has spikes about 20 to 30 centimetres long. A two-year-old has two prongs and a three-year-old has three. A four-year-old displays the adult pattern. At six or seven years the antlers are at their finest in size and spread coinciding with the full development of the animal. As a moose grows older the points become less pronounced until they are a jagged edge in an elderly bull. With advancing age, the antlers diminish both in size and symmetry, and are dropped earlier.

Hunting Moose

Prime moose meat may not be as esteemed as deer or caribou, but it is nonetheless tasty and an important staple of many of the Northern peoples. A family of four may consume 80 moose a year compared to about three times as many caribou.

The rut has a profound effect on the normally mild, tender and delicious meat when the bulls stop eating and start wandering in September. During the rut the meat acquires a strong, musky odor and looses most of its fat. At the end of the rut the meat loses its gamey flavor but is still dry and tough. By February, the meat is as good as it was before the rut. A quarter of moose can weigh well over a 100 kilograms.

When hunting moose in the Native style, you can expect to travel for several days and cover about 50 kilometres. First, locate a track less than two-days-old. The track's age may be determined from the freshness of the manure, the moisture and nature of the torn soil in the hoof print, and by the freshness of the twig ends eaten off by the animal. An excellent time to hunt is immediately after a fresh snowfall. The tracks will then be recent and silent travel facilitated by the muffling effect of the fresh snow. A moose is easy to hunt in deep snow where it has difficulty in outrunning a man on snowshoes.

Tracking is difficult in dense bush. During the fall breeding season, tracking is unproductive because of the bull's constant and haphazard movement. It is more effective at this time to call up the animal with a megaphone, by rubbing a moose horn or scapula on a tree, or by pouring water from a height to imitate a urinating cow moose.

When tracking, you must be quiet enough to avoid spooking the moose. You should wear soft soled shoes and step carefully. Coughing is a major problem as it may alert moose to your presence from a long distance. Stay downwind from the animal to keep scents and sounds from reaching it. When the trail veers from the wind, you will have to head with the wind then circle into it to intercept the moose trail about a kilometre further down. If the trail is intercepted, and the animal is thought to be more than a kilometre away, the downwind and upwind circle is repeated until the moose is spotted or until you find yourself ahead of it, in which case you have to backtrack to continue a downwind approach or use smaller downwind and upwind circles towards the animal.

When surprised, a moose may momentarily survey the situation before it takes off. This provides you an opportunity for a shot. If the moose bolts, you can follow in hot pursuit and take advantage of its tendency to travel a short distance before stopping to take a momentary survey of what is following before it continues on. Again, this provides you with the opportunity for a shot.

Butchering Moose

The big and majestic moose is relatively easy to butcher. It should be rolled onto a pallet of spruce or willow to keep the carcass off the ground so the body heat can dissipate faster and be butchered immediately. In wet weather, keep the carcass dry, as moisture promotes rapid spoilage. The less hair touching the meat the less gamey the meat will taste. The sooner the meat cools and a dry surface forms on it, the better tasting it should be. Slow cooling may be a prime factor in spoilage, especially when the weather is warm and the animal large.

To gut the moose, insert your knife into the body cavity just below the lowest ribs and cut towards the rear. As soon as the slit allows insert the first and middle fingers of your other hand with the palm facing up. Cut between these fingers to prevent the knife tip from snagging the intestines. Go around the male genitals or udder, over the pubic bone and around the rectum (or female genitals) and tail, cutting about five centimetres deep. Cut through the pubic bone, free the udder, the genitals and the rectum, tying everything off that may contaminate the meat.

Open the throat from the lowest ribs to the lower jaw. Cut around the brisket rather than through its centre. Remove the esophagus and wind pipe intact because of the putrefying bacteria it contains. Reach into the body cavity with your knife and free the diaphram, then pull everything down from the top part of the chest cavity to remove the contents of the whole carcass.

Save the heart, liver, kidneys and the fat encasing the intestines. Remove the tongue by way of the lower jaw. Wipe out any blood in the cavity without using water. Trim away any bullet damaged flesh.

The sooner the animal is skinned, the easier the hide comes off. Because of its weight a moose is usually skinned on the ground. One side is done first, the skin is stretched out and the carcass is rolled on it, then the other side is skinned out. Skinning from head to the rear is the easiest and results in the least flesh remaining on the hide.

Remove the lower legs or shanks by cutting slightly below the joints then breaking them over your knee. Slit the hide along the inside of each front leg to meet the belly cut. Likewise, slit along the inside of the hind legs to meet the belly cut about 20 to 30 centimetres below the tail. Cut completely around the neck close behind the jaws, ears and antlers. Commence skinning from the head towards the rear, peeling the skin away from the flesh and cutting the thin white film that holds the hide to the flesh. In the winter, you must complete the skinning before the hide freezes on.

With the exception of the wolf, the adult moose has few enemies in the wild. When the snow is deep, the moose favors ploughed roads and as a result collisions with vehicles are common. Logging operations may create favorable habitat, but the roads provide easier access for hunters and poachers. Poaching has significantly affected the moose population in recent years.

Encroachment of moose habitat by settlement and agriculture has resulted in the spread of the white-tailed deer that is a host to a meningeal parasitic worm. While it does not affect the deer's health significantly, the worm is devastating to moose.

In some areas, wood tick infestations of moose are a leading cause of its death. In the spring, the deaf and blind female tick climbs to the tip of some foliage and waits in a dozing state for a warm-blooded animal to pass by. Reacting to the odor of butric acid emitted by all mammals, she is roused and tries to grab or drop on to any animal that comes close enough. A tick may survive 18 years while waiting for the opportunity to fill up on the animal blood

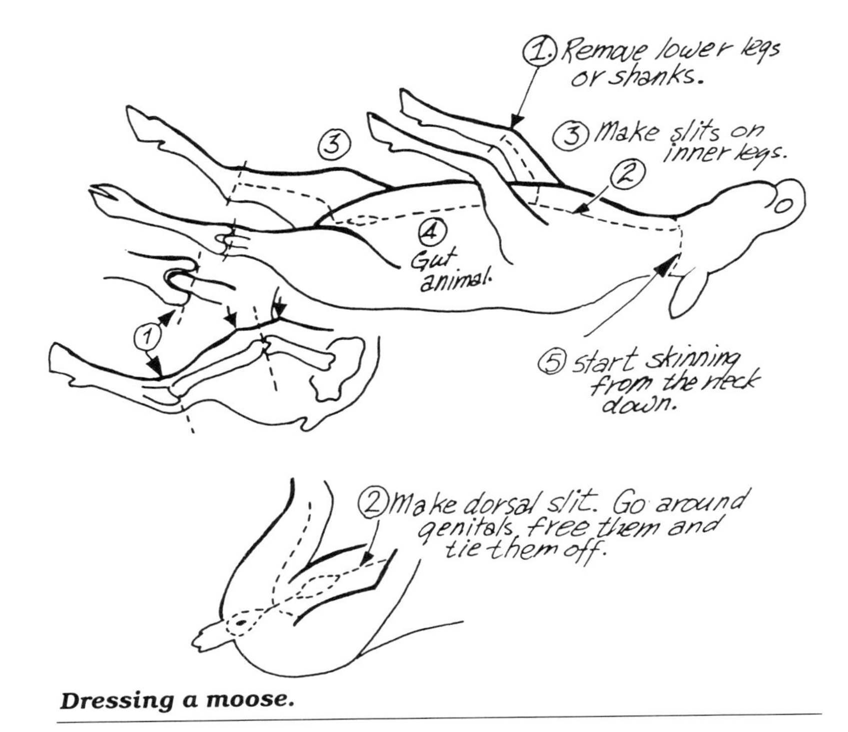

Dressing a moose.

needed to nourish its eggs. The gorged tick drops off its host, lays its eggs and dies.

In the case of humans, the tick prefers the nape of the neck or the back. Should the tick remain attached for a week, a paralysis may develop that can result in death if the offending tick is not removed.

Native Tanning of Moose Hide

Native tanning requires simple tools and ingredients and considerable, tedious, muscular effort. It helps if you have someone to share the work.

The winter hide from an old bull is the thickest and hardest to tan. At the other extreme, the summer hide of a young cow is the easiest to tan.

The first step is a careful skinning, neither nicking the hide nor leaving any flesh on it. Taking the time to do a proper job in skinning will save time in the fleshing step.

The hide should be tanned as soon as possible or else preserved by being salted down. For longer storage it should also be dried. Avoid exposing a hide to the sun by working in the shade or on a cloudy day.

A large moose hide can weigh over 90 kilograms. It will be easier to work cut in half.

To stretch the hide, first cut lacing slots about two centimetres from the hide's edge and about ten centimetres apart. This facilitates lacing the hide to a frame with strong cord. The frame should be large enough to accommodate any stretching while the hide is worked. The cords may have to be tightened frequently to keep the hide taut. You may have to crawl onto a large hide to work it.

All flesh and fat should be thoroughly removed with a serrated scraper made from a deer or moose tibia or piece of iron. The fleshing should result in a slimy looking, but greaseless surface. A drying skin should be dampened as needed. All fat must be removed as its absorption will cause the skin to become hard on drying.

If the hide is tanned with the hair on, the following step is omitted and the tanning carried out on the flesh side only.

The hide is turned over and the hair and scarf layer are shaved away with an adz-like tool. The tool must be sharpened frequently to remove the hair effectively. Once the hair side is shaved clean, the hide can dry on the frame as rawhide.

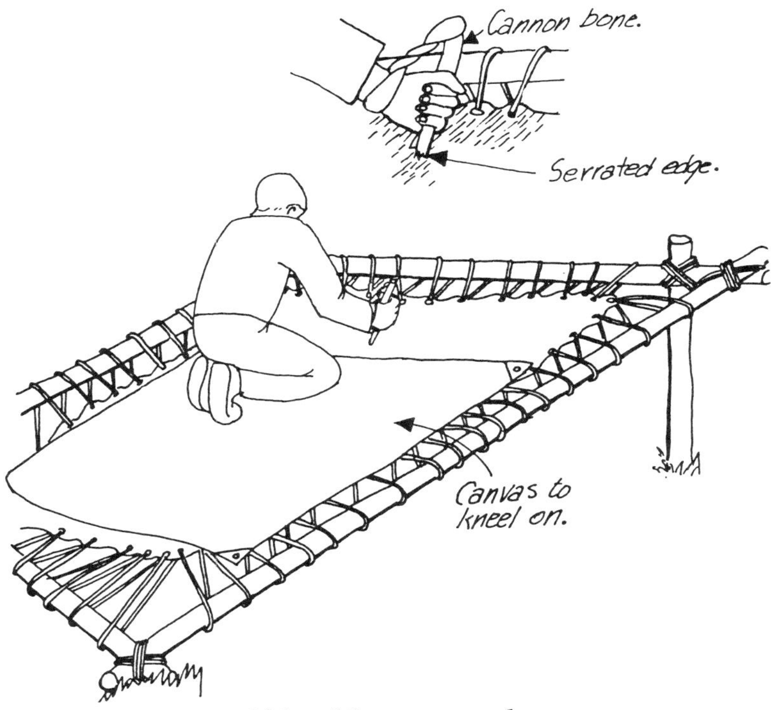

Working a moose hide with a cannon bone.

The slimy texture can be reduced by a preliminary smoking for an hour or two over a small, smoky fire made from punky wood. The hide is draped over a small teepee or arch-type structure and covered with old tarps to retain the smoke. The hide becomes stiff and paper-like at this stage.

The softening process begins by hand-rubbing into the hide a paste made by simmering the animal's dried or fresh brains in a little water. The rubbing is continued until all the paste is absorbed. The brains of the animal should be sufficient to treat the entire hide. However, in the case of a large, thick hide, this may not be so, and the paste must be extended by incorporating finely chopped liver and/or marrow from the larger bones. The dampened hide is rolled up to sit overnight.

The next day, the hide is made into a loop and twisted with a pole and rail to squeeze out any remaining moisture. This completely saturates the hide with the brain paste from the inside out, in preparation for the next step.

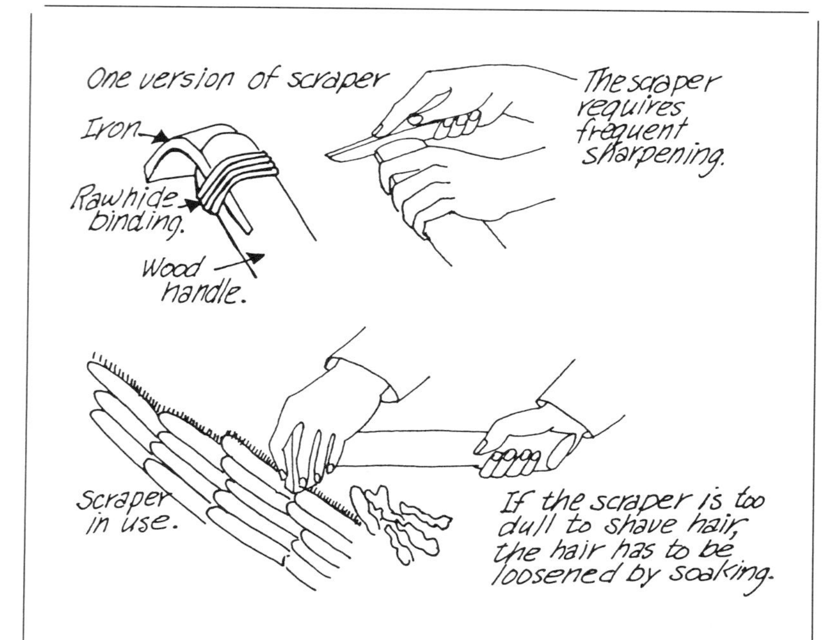

Using the metal hide scraper.

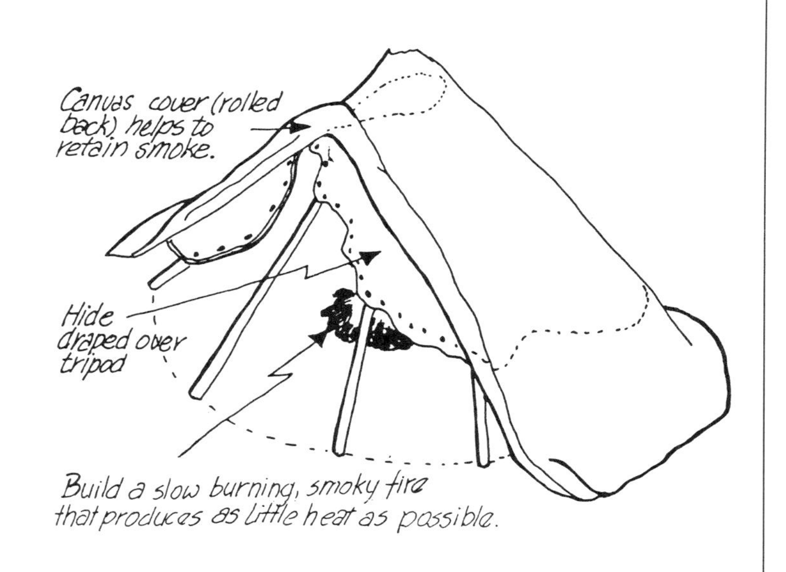

Smoking a moose hide.

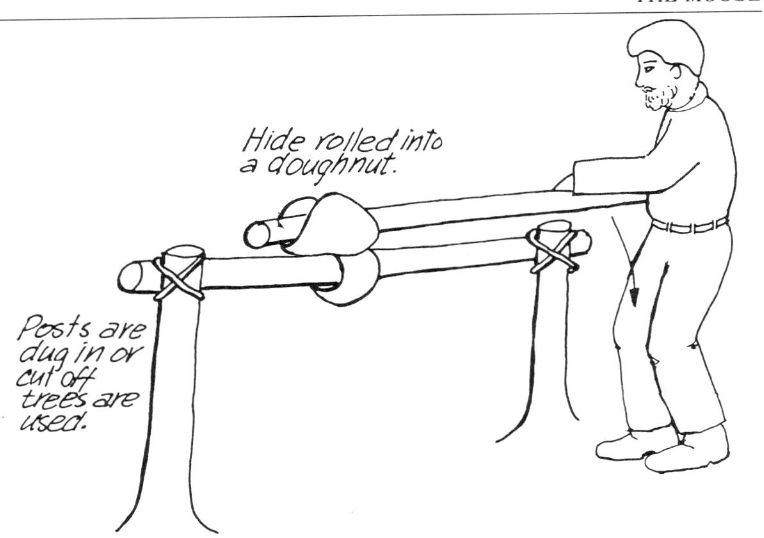

Wringing the moisture out of a hide.

The hide is again stretched on the frame for a final scraping to remove anything remaining from the surface, then allowed to dry out. When dry, it is worked over with a stone scraper and sandstone to smooth the surface to an even texture. The lacing is tightened to keep the hide well-stretched. The hide is softened on the frame with a wooden stretching tool armpit to finger tip long, of a thickness comfortable to hold. The blunt point of the working end of the tool is rubbed into the hide to break and stretch some of the interconnecting fibers. Softening a moose hide will take at least a day. Work in the shade. As the hide dries it should be dampened. If the hide dries hard, it must be reworked with the brain paste. The hide must be worked continuously and consistently but not too forcefully over the whole surface until it is soft, pliant and felt-like in texture.

The final step is a thorough smoking. This preserves the hide's softness and prevents shrinking upon wetting and drying. Too hot a smoke fire will damage the hide. A variety of rotten woods are available, each with its own aroma and shade of color. Rotten spruce, tamarack or birch are commonly used. A dense smoke is made with any punky wood. The smoke fire is first built in a hole and allowed to burn down to coals. The hide is draped over a framework and covered with old tarps wherever necessary to retain the smoke. The hide may have to be moved and adjusted often

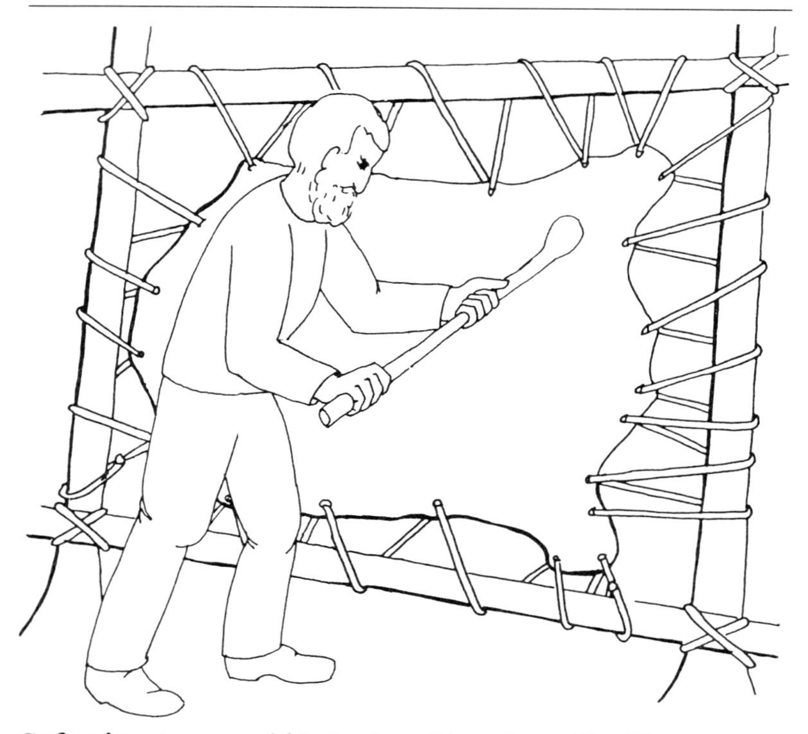

Softening a moose hide by breaking down the fiber.

to ensure an even tan. Smoke-producing materials are added occasionally to maintain the smoke. A draught hole should be provided at the edge of the hide and a small smoke hole is made at the top of the frame. Any other holes in the hide that may allow smoke to escape should be sewn up.

Depending on its thickness and the depth of color desired, the hide may be smoked from one to four hours then turned over and smoked on the opposite side if de-haired. When the smoking is completed, the edge of the hide may be trimmed off at the lacing holes and the trimmings saved for lashing purposes. The skin is rolled up and the tan is allowed to set for a few days.

If the smell of the hide is too strong, it may be aired in the shade or laundered in soapy water. If you have done a proper job of tanning, the hide or any item made from it should remain soft even after many launderings.

12

THE VARYING HARE

The varying hare is one of the key animals in the ecology of the Northern Forest, with the role of converting vegetation into flesh for the benefit of humans and predatory beasts. This role is particularly important in the dead of winter when plant food is scarce.

THE KEY PROVIDER

All parts of the varying hare are edible or useful. The flesh is good tasting, with a low water and high protein content. The hide makes a light and warm sleeping robe comparable to down. Sinews are useful for fish line, leaders and snares. The long, thin bones of the foot make excellent gorges for survival fishing.

The varying hare is at times incorrectly called the snowshoe hare or the snowshoe rabbit. Hares are closely related to the true rodents. They differ by having a second pair of smaller incisors right behind a very conspicuous and large pair of upper incisors. The hares also have the most teeth in the rodent family. As their upper grinding teeth are further apart than their lower ones, hares chew their food with a characteristic side to side movement of the lower jaw.

Twice a year, a hare's coat undergoes a color change. This accounts for the term "varying"—a strategy that helps to camouflage it from predators. In the fall, the brown coat turns white then back to brown in the spring. The change-over takes about ten weeks, during which time the hare is a mottled brown and white. Eventually the animal becomes as white as the snow except for its greyish underbelly and the black rims of its ears and eyes. The shadow is more conspicuous than the hare itself. For rabbit-skin robes, the winter skin is about a quarter more insulative than that of summer. In some parts of the world the hair of this animal is esteemed for making felt, especially for fine hats.

Although hares like young, dense conifer stands, this is not an exclusive preference. Heavy brush consisting of various combinations of trees and shrubs such as young aspen, willow, alder, birch, rose, saskatoon, red osier dogwood, hazelnut and snowberry are acceptable so long as food, shelter and protection from predators is found. Hares frequent the edges of muskegs, heavy spruce thickets and moss-carpeted spruce stands bordered by poplars and pine.

The varying hare.

Hare Predators

The varying hare has a large host of predators. Hawk, owl, coyote, fox, wolf, lynx, bobcat and weasel, to name a few, are dependent on it. When hare populations are low the meat eaters experience trying times. The larger predators are driven to attack bigger animals that they would otherwise leave alone. When hares are scarce the snowy owl ventures further south than usual in search of food.

The hare copes with this incessant predation with a high reproductive rate. The doe may produce two to three litters a year with an average of four to six leverets per litter in good times, and two or three if food is scarce or the health of the population is low. A pair of hares, in optimal habitat, will increase to a population of about 1500 in five years in spite of predation.

Hares and rabbits have been noted the world over for their prolific nature, their sheer numbers at certain times and, their occasional outright scarcity. Densities of 13,000 hares per square kilometre have been known to eventually reduce to two or less. When populations peak, winter food resources may be depleted leading to lower survival and reproduction rates. Overbrowsing reduces regular winter food resources as new shoots and bark are consumed. This accounts for the first two or three years of decline.

There is a corresponding increase in predators with the peaking of hare populations. Predation has little influence on hare numbers at this stage. As food shortages take their toll, predation may account for maintaining low populations after bottoming out, and food resources have returned to adequate levels. When predator numbers themselves eventually decline due to the scarcity of hares, the hare population will increase again.

The depletion of winter food sets the stage for their initial decline and the later interaction with their predators. The hares become scarce, the vegetation recovers, the predators reduce in numbers, and the cycle continues. Generally, the cycles throughout the continent are in phase with each other by a matter of a year or so. Dr. Lloyd Keith, an authority on animal cycles, feels this synchronization is initiated by two successive mild winters occuring during the increase phase of a ten-year cycle. This allows low populations in some areas to peak rapidly, while helping near-peak populations to remain steady under more marginal conditions.

A hare's home or form is best described as a place, rather

than a particular structure. It does not burrow or make nests. A simple hollow in a dense thicket is sufficient.

Polygamous by nature, hares mate mostly in March or April but may start in January and quit in July. Depending on the authority consulted, gestation is anywhere from 30 to 43 days. The young are born between early February and late July, well-furred and with eyes open. They are about seven to ten centimetres long and weigh 50 to 85 grams. The leverets move about on the first day, sometimes remaining together with their litter mates, but more usually scattering about the immediate area. The mother seeks out the leverets individually to nurse them after dark. The leverets

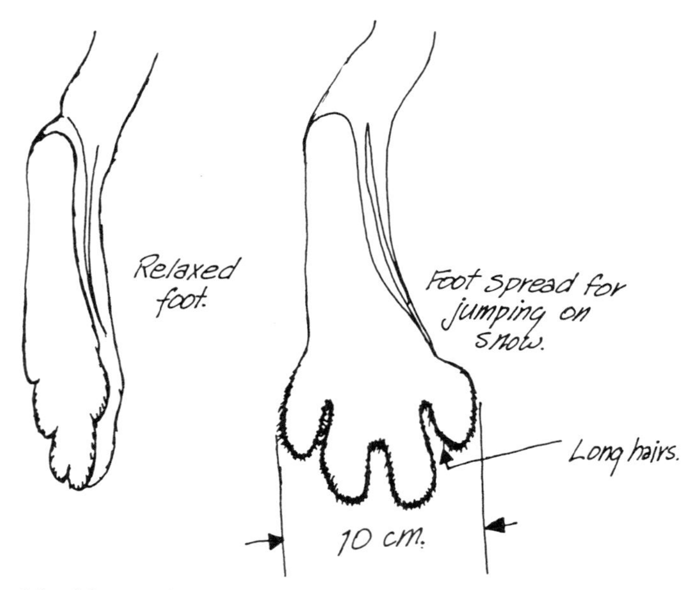

The hind legs of the varying hare are highly-suited for travel over soft snow.

How a hare runs.

can find food for themselves shortly after birth, feeding on greens the first day. They are weaned by the time they are a month old. The hare reaches sexual maturity in about a year. It will then weigh from one kilogram to more than two, depending on the variety of hare and other factors. In the wild, the adult may survive from three to five years.

Hares eat the soft parts of all plants, including the roots and fruit. They eat leaves, twigs, bark and buds of trees and shrubs, as well as various grasses. Their main winter forage is tender young spruce and pine. When hare populations are high they can seriously compete with deer, moose and elk for forage. Normally vegetarian, the hare is occasionally cannibalistic and will eat flesh (attested to by trappers who use meat as bait).

The varying hare depends on its fleetness of foot to outrun many predators. The hare's thickly-furred broad feet allow it to move with ease in deep, soft snow. Where other animals have a bare sole on their paws, the hare has pads that are covered with a tight, springy layer of strong, stiff forward-directed hairs. With the winter coat change these hairs grow longer to provide more support on the snow. The animal also spreads its toes to provide the largest possible treading surface. So equipped, the hare can attain bursts of speed up to 50 kilometres an hour over snow, and outrun any predator it sees in time.

Regardless of how far a hare is chased it will remain within a few 100 metres of its home base. Eventually, lanes are beaten down in snow or summer moss, especially through thick undergrowth which offers few alternate routes. Hares groom their trails of anything that may impede their movement. Although the hare prefers lanes, it is not strictly confined to them. In open country the hare may not make lanes at all. Its tendency to use well-traveled lanes and to go under objects across its path rather than jumping over them, is used to advantage by the trapper.

Hares are most active after dark. At dusk they move to their feeding areas and forage the heaviest in the last few hours of darkness, moving about the most between eleven o'clock in the evening and one o'clock in the morning.

A doe may occupy a territory for a long time, shifting about in relation to available food. A buck may occupy the ranges of two or three females, but does not guard any territory except at the height of the mating season. When fighting, hares tend to bite one another. Hares are not social animals, but they are tolerant of one another.

Snares

The varying hare can be caught with string lifting-pole snares. Because the hare might bite through a string snare it is necessary to raise its forepaws off the ground so that it cannot reach the snare holding it.

To set up the lifting-pole snare, obtain a pole of wrist thickness at the butt end and about an arm span and a half long.

Find a tree within a metre of the hare run to act as the pivot, or drive in a suitable stake near the run.

Hold the thin or snare end of the pole about 30 centimetres above the run and between shoulder and elbow high at the other end then bring it in contact with the pivot tree. You now know how high the pivot has to be.

Erect a cross bar (of broomhandle thickness) over the run, usually, but not necessarily, at right angles to it and underneath the snare end of the liftingpole (about 25 centimetres above the run). This may be done at any angle to the lifting-pole and in many ways other than the one just mentioned.

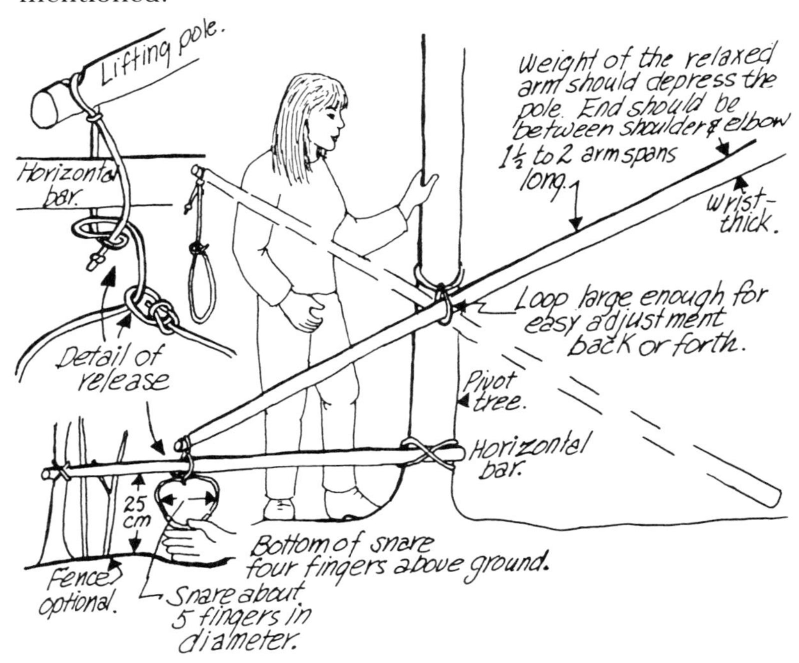

The lifting pole hare snare.

Use a snare cord about as long as nose to finger tip of the outstretched arm. A knot is tied in one end of the string and left dangling to a length of three fingers after the cord is securely tied to the lifting-pole. Cut a notch to keep the string from slipping off the end of the pole.

Holding the short string by the knot, bring the lifting-pole down to the cross bar on one side and using the long end of the string on the other side tie a slippery half-hitch. A noose is made with the end of the long string by tying a running bowline. The bowline eye should be small enough to barely admit a pencil. The diameter of the noose should be about 12 centimetres or the width of the adult palm including the thumb. There should be a space of four fingers between the bottom of the snare and the ground. If the noose is made too large, the hare will be caught by the waist and will likely bite off or break the snare. If the noose is too small it will be pushed aside.

An area may have most of the runs going back and forth in a predominant direction according to the terrain. Snares should be set across this area for the greatest effect. Choose the best used runs and trample or block off the rest. Runs in the snow should not be disturbed or the hares may make alternate paths. Take a round about route to an end of the run area and try to drive some of the hares into the snares by making noise. You may have to set as many as 30 snares in times of low populations to catch a hare a day.

The snares should be checked early each morning. Snares should never be abandoned as the animal will be wasted and endures needless suffering.

Skinning a Hare

A hare can be skinned without tools as the hide tears easily. Start by freeing the skin around the genitals and anus so these parts are left intact until the hare is gutted. The skin is freed from the hind legs and pulled off like a tube down to the wrists of the forepaws. With the skin pulled taut over the head a little cut with a knife or sharp stone at the back of the head releases the skin from the head. The skin is detached at the forepaws. In this form, a skin can be used as an emergency mitt or a storage bag for a fire board and drill or be incorporated into a robe.

The head is detached and the feet cut off. A sharp rock will cut through the tendons of the legs. The head should

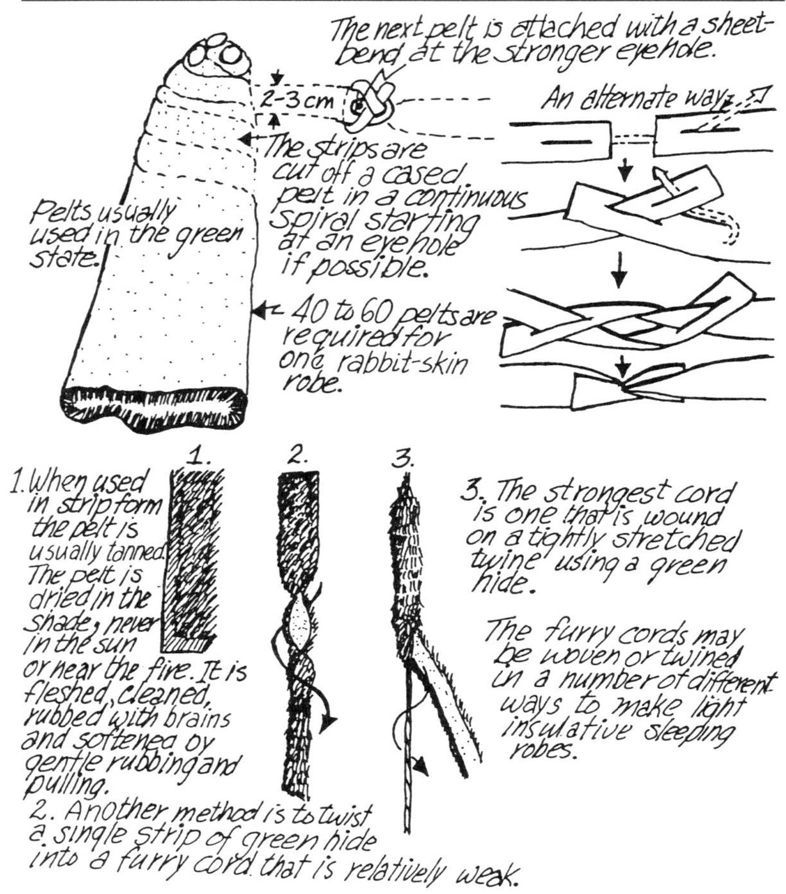

Making weaving strips out of hare skins.

be skinned out and boiled for the brains and the meat remaining on it. The long fingers in the toes of the rabbit may be used to make a gorge for catching fish, an awl or a primitive sewing needle. The tendons and sinews may be twisted into cord for more snares.

Tear through the abdominal cavity and the diaphragm with the fingers. The lungs, circulatory system and esophagus are easily torn out with the fingers. The pelvic bone is broken by bending the thighs back. The genitalia and large intestine are pulled out and downward without contaminating the meat. If there is hair on the carcass do not wash it off until just before the meat is cooked.

Hare Disease

If a hare looks unhealthy, it may have dry land tularemia, a rare condition in the winter. This is primarily a disease of rabbits and hares. One of the symptoms is fever and is sometimes known as rabbit fever. When humans contract the disease, nine times out of ten, it is from an infected rabbit or hare.

Tularemia is a dreadful disease that should be thoroughly understood by animal handlers, hunters, trappers and anyone interested in wilderness survival techniques—particularly when it concerns the use of wild game.

The disease is also known to infect dogs, cats, sheep, pigs, ground and tree squirrels, field mice, prairie dogs, chipmunks, muskrats, beaver, coyotes, fox, deer, various grouse including ruffled grouse, snakes and nearly 100 other animals.

The most common way to contract tuleremia is to handle an infected animal when there are breaks in the skin of the hands, although infections are known to occur through unbroken skin. The disease can be caught from animal or insect bites (such as ticks, fleas and deer flies), drinking contaminated water, breathing in the organism or eating infected meat.

Tularemia is caused by an oxygen dependent bacillus. It is easily destroyed by 10 minutes of heat at over 58°C.

Infected meat can be made safe by proper cooking, with boiling as the preferred method. Roasting may not allow the required heat to penetrate the interior of a larger piece of meat.

Any game showing spots on the liver, spleen, lungs or kidneys is suspect and should be handled accordingly. About one person in 20 contracting the disease may die from it or complications resulting from it. The average course of the disease is about two weeks

Symptoms in humans usually appear in two to four days and occasionally in one to ten days. In many ways the symptoms resemble that of plague. There is a sudden onset of headache, recurring chills and sweats with a body temperature of 39.5° to 40°C. There is usually nausea, vomiting and extreme physical weakness and exhaustion. The lymph nodes swell and may pustulate.

In the most common form of the disease, a small boil-like eruption appears at the site of the infection such as on the hand, eye or mouth shortly after the onset of symptoms. A large ulcer may also appear at the site.

The disease can take on at least three different forms, depending on its point of entry and what organs are affected. If the airborne organisms released when the animal is being skinned and dressed are inhaled, a form of bronchitis, or worse, pneumonia can be contracted. Another type of infection can be typhoidial in nature.

Early diagnosis of the disease is not always easy. However, a variety of antibiotics, streptomycin in particular, are effective in combating it.

If you live in an area where the disease is prevalent and you handle animals extensively, wear protective gloves and clothing. Be aware the infective organism can become airborne in the form of tick feces or while game is gutted and insect bites can pass on the disease. Make it a point to cook wild meat adequately.

If a hare looks unhealthy it may be best to discard it altogether. Sometimes hares have such afflictions as scabby ears and spotted, ulcerated livers, usually in association with population peaks. Some are infected with a lumpy sore on the back. This is the parasitic larval stage of a warble or bot fly. In any case, cooking the meat well should prevent any health problem that could arise from the above conditions.

The most efficient way to cook hare is by boiling and using the broth. To improve the taste when salt is unavailable, the boiled hare may be browned over coals. If a pot is unavailable, the hare may be roasted. It is cut up into convenient pieces and propped up in front of glowing coals on sharpened sticks. A grill may also be used on which the whole or half of the animal is spread out to be cooked. As it is not the smoke or flame that does the cooking, but the radiance of the coals, the meat is not placed over the coals as much as it is placed to the side.

A kilogram of hare meat will provide about 1000 Calories. Hare meat has a much lower water content than most other meats so a smaller quantity is used for a serving.

There is some question as to the value of eating hare unsupplemented by fat. Eating such lean meat will bring on a kidney condition known as "protein poisoning" or nephritis. If you eat hare exclusively, by the end of a week you may be eating three or four times as much food by weight as you did at the beginning of the week. Regardless of the quantity of food consumed you may start showing signs of starvation and an inflamed condition of the kidneys.

Regardless of how much and how often you eat, hunger

persists. The stomach distends and you may feel a vague restlessness. Diarrhea eventually occurs and persists until fat is eaten. Death results after a few weeks.

To prevent this, some Native people would singe off the animal's hair and cook the entire animal. In this way, fat found in the skin, brains and intestines would make up the necessary fat requirements. The intestines and their contents would provide the benefit of the partially digested vegetable matter. The uninitiated may find that hare prepared in this way is difficult to stomach.

Hare Robe

Robes from the skins of the hare are made when the fur is white (the best condition). The hare is case skinned (pulled off like a tube) and the fresh hide is cut into a continuous spiral strip with a sharp knife. The strip may be two to three centimetres wide and three to four metres long. This strip is twisted and gently stretched to transform it into a furry cord. In some cases, for added strength, the strip is wrapped around a cord in a spiral. Some Native people would start their cut at the stronger eye holes, leaving them intact

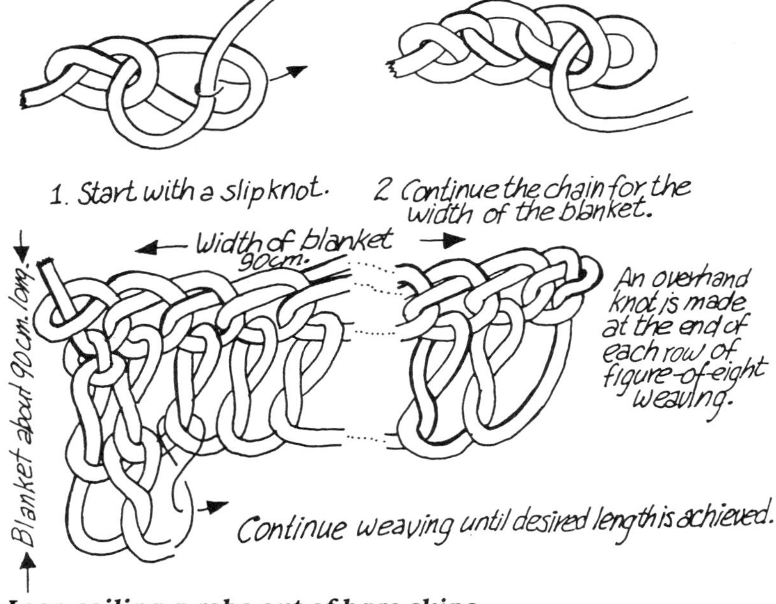

Loop coiling a robe out of hare skins.

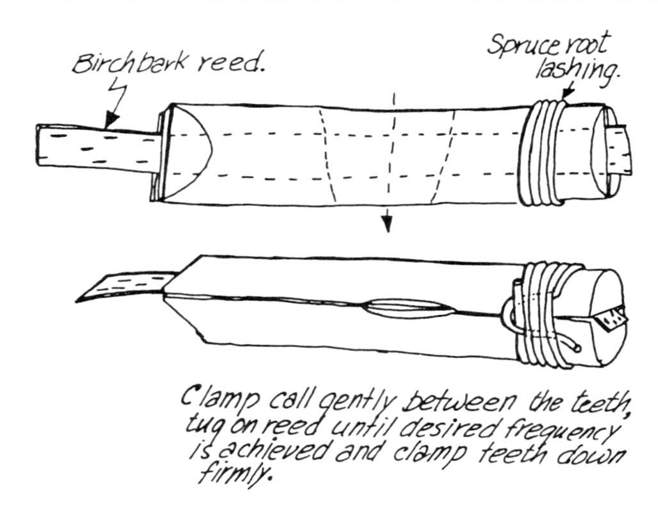

A predator call that sounds like a hare in distress.

to provide a more effective way to attach strips together by means of a sheet bend.

The strips are wrapped in balls or stored by wrapping on a metre long stick and kept frozen until 60 or 70 are collected to make a robe of the desired size. The robe has to be made before the skins dry.

A simple method of fashioning the robe begins by making a loose chain or monkey chain sinnet that acts as the foundation for the plaiting and determines the width of the blanket by its length. At the end of each row the cord is anchored with an overhand knot. At most, the mesh should allow two fingers to be poked through it. New strips are either tied or sewn on. When the blanket dries, the loops should hold their shape and stay in place. If the robe is to be made into a sleeping bag it is made wider at the top so that it will fit over the shoulders better. The robe weighs about three to four kilograms and can be rolled into a bundle about 25 centimetres thick and 50 centimetres long. This type of robe continually sheds hair so that you are likely to find hair in everything you own and in your food as well. Should the hair get in the eyes, it will cause an irritation. This can be averted by sewing an inner and outer shell made of cotton or nylon.

NOTES

NOTES

NOTES

NOTES

INDEX

COLOUR PHOTO SUPPLEMENT

This section, new to this second edition of *Northern Bushcraft*, is a series of photographs by outdoor educator and Wilderness Living Skills instructor, Henry Madsen.

Each photograph, with its explanatory text, illustrates a concept which is developed in the body of the original work. The supplement may be enjoyed on its own, or may be used in conjunction with the preceding text. Page numbers have been appended to each photo entry to facilitate reference to the main section of *Northern Bushcraft*.

The true tinder fungus

This fungus must be taken from a living tree to be usable. The interior of the fungus is crumbled, dried and used like regular tinder.

Shown cut open (*centre*) to expose the light-brown interior. The interior material of the fungus has been crumbled into a tinder box. This may be used with tobacco or medicinals that are inhaled as a smoke, to help sustain the ember in a pipe. Burning pieces were applied to the joints to reduce the intensity of arthritic pain. The fungus has a long list of medicinal uses in the herbal folk medicine of many Russian native peoples. The fungus is soaked in boiled warm water or powdered and taken as a tonic, and was touted as a remedy for many internal conditions including cancer. The part of the fungus that is corky in texture is best used for tinder while the harder part is best used for brewing tea. *See also p. 16.*

The false tinder fungus

This fungus is found on dead birch and occasionally on aspen. The outer skin is removed to reveal a thin layer of cottony material that is sliced off and processed into tinder. In the live fungus the cottony material can be teased into a soft chamois-like fabric. The smoldering dry fungus is a mosquito repellant and is also used to carry fire. *See also p. 16.*

Common kindlings of the Northern Forests
Balsam poplar outer bark (*top left*) is easily sliced down to dry material, no matter how wet the surface. Birch bark (*top*) Black poplar inner bark (*right*) Dry grass (*bottom*) Old man's beard (*left*) Resin-saturated bark or wood (*centre*) *See also p. 28.*

Old man's beard
(*Usnea* or *Alectoria*)
Although old man's beard burns furiously when dry, it is at its worst when you need it most. It absorbs moisture from the air and is too damp to use in wet weather. Usnea was fermented and then roasted to make it edible. It was also thought to be useful in curing athlete's foot. Alectoria was boiled for three hours and then dried for later use as a thickener in soups or stews. *See also p. 31.*

The red-needled pine bough
A very important fire starter in pine country are the red-needled pine boughs found lying on the forest floor. Most other kindlings are scarce in a pine ecology. *See also p. 29.*

△

Twig bundle sizes
The three sizes of twig bundle that may be commonly used in the Northern Forest are: the small handful for everyday fire lighting purposes; the survival bundle when it is critical not to loose a match; and the hug-sized bundle for making a signal fire or for quickly warming a large group. *See also p. 31.*

Arranging feathers ▷
A minimum of two good feathers and four poor ones will ensure a good start to a fire if arranged as shown. When the fire has a good start, change to a parallel configuration. *See also p. 37.*

△

Cooking fish

A grill being used for cooking fish over hot coals. The fish has been cut along the backbone instead of the belly so that it may spread out better, and to reduce the thickness that has to be cooked through. *See also p. 62*

◁ **Using resin-saturated wood**

A form of candle is made by splitting a pencil- to finger-sized splint into quarters and wedging chips in the splits to provide a slight separation. *See also p. 33.*

Combustible conifer resin
The hardened resin found in injuries of spruce and pine is very combustible. It is the most important material for use in augmenting a match flame in the spruce-moose forest. The red form of the resin is esteemed as a chewing gum. It is bitter at first, causing considerable spitting. *See also p. 33.*

A resin blister
A blister from the bark of the Porsild's white spruce has been cut open to reveal the liquid resinous material it contains. The blisters are rarely as prominent as this, but if the relatively smooth bark is observed, the tree is likely Porsild's and the hardly-discernable blisters will provide adequate resin for first aid purposes. The resin, like that of balsam fir, is a very useful antiseptic for cuts and burns. *See also p. 229.*

The blistered bark of balsam fir
See also p. 229.

Resin
The resin collected from the tree in the previous figure. Fifty blisters yielded about 5 cc. *See also p. 229.*

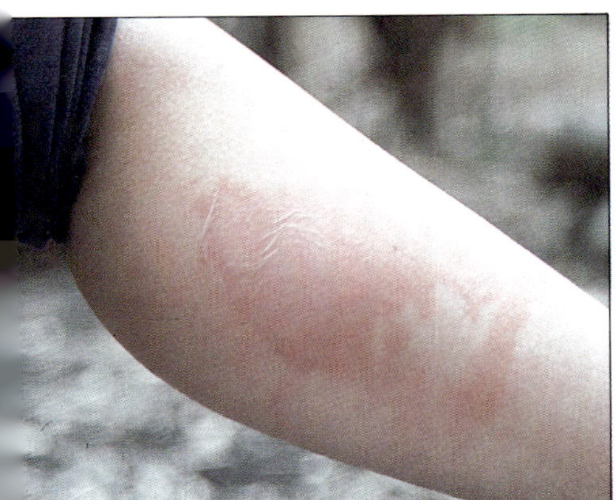

Scalds
This scald was sustained when a handle gave away on a pot of boiling water. The fabric of the pants held the heat against the skin, resulting in a burn that caused the epidermis to separate. The burn has been cooled with water. *See also p. 229.*

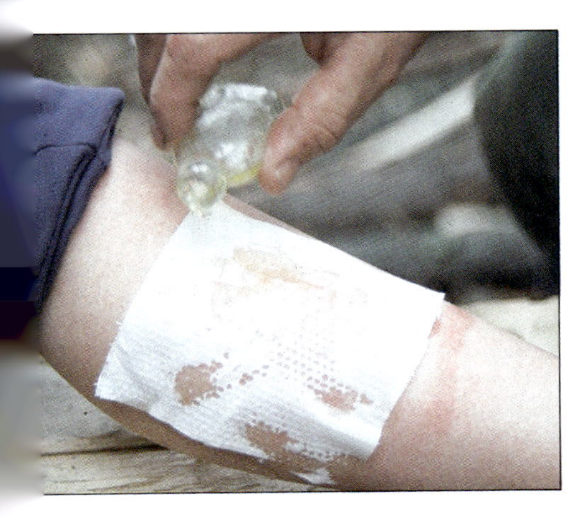

Burn treatment
Balsam fir has been poured on the burn, a layer of toilet paper (a substitute for the fluff of black poplar) applied and more resin poured on. The wound will heal under second skin without any puss formation. Initially the resin may produce a burning sensation, but afterwards there is very little pain associated with this treatment. *See also p. 229.*

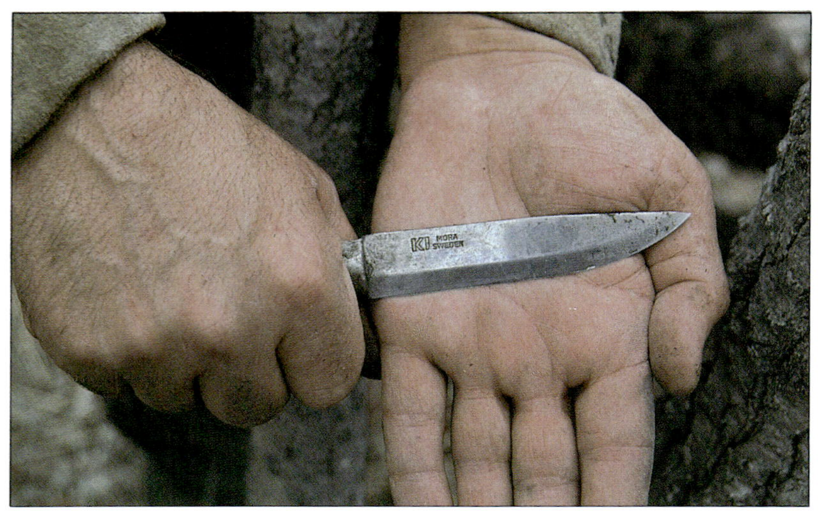

△
Mora knife
An approximate measure of the size of a general purpose bush knife where both the handle and the blade are as long as the width of the user's hand. This is the renowned Mora knife. *See also p. 110*

Carrying a knife ▷
One of the best methods in preventing the loss of a knife while carrying it is to use a deep sheath and wear it around the neck to be constantly aware of the knife's presence. When the knife is not in use the sheath is tucked in the shirt. *See also p. 110.*

△
Basket examples
Some common basket types that may be woven from spruce splints are shown. *See also p. 220.*

◁ **Birch bark basket**
A basket woven of birch bark strips in much the same way as with black spruce splints. Bark that is too brittle to be used in any other way still makes a passable basket if woven in this way. *See also p. 202.*

Labrador tea

Another associate of the spruces and pines is Labrador tea. The tea may be taken internally or used as a wash. An important use is as both a sedative and wash for burns, scalds and large abrasions. Besides being a sedative, the tea is a styptic which reduces the oozing of a wound, or causes the contraction of the lining of the intestine to help overcome both constipation and diarrhoea. This is an important plant in Native and Russian herbology. *See also p. 215.*

A wad of sphagnum moss

Black spruce and tamarack are often found growing in sphagnum bogs. Sphagnum is easy to identify, being quite different in appearance from all the other types of mosses. This moss makes a passable disposable diaper liner, compress for first aid, and sanitary napkin. It contains an antiseptic, whereas most other mosses do not. Bog cranberry grows only on sphagnum. *See also p. 215.*

△
Aspen bowls
The burls found on aspen were a favorite for making durable bowls that resisted checking or splitting. The interior of the bowl was hollowed out with the tool used to shave the hair off a hide being prepared for tanning. *See also p. 234.*

△
Conk
This conk, which is commonly found growing on the aspen, weakens the tree so that it is likely to come down in any strong wind. The fungus itself and the wood it attacked can make a superior board in the bow drill method of fire lighting. *See also p. 234.*

Peeling bark from the red-osier dogwood

(a) To peel the red outer bark from red osier dogwood, the first step is to cut the bark with a thumbnail or a knife.

(b) In late spring and early summer the bark is easily removed by unwrapping with the thumbs as shown. For the rest of the year it has to be laboriously scraped off with a knife or sharp stone.

(c) The inner bark is scraped towards the middle of the stick.

(d) The scrapings are left attached for drying in front of a fire. The fresh bark may be applied as a poultice on open wounds, as a styptic and pain killer. The dried bark makes a superior tobacco additive. *See also p. 246.*

A large basket woven from red-osier dogwood
See also p. 250.

▽

Black poplar
A medium-sized black poplar tree displaying the characteristic fluted bark. Trees three and four times this diameter can be found, especially on the island and flats of big lakes and rivers. *See also p. 236.*

Black poplar fluff
Black poplar is often called cottonwood on account of the cottony material attached to the seed. This can be used with the resin from the blisters of balsam fir or Porsild's white spruce to make effective dressings for cuts or burns. This fluff was added to buffalo berry juice and beaten into the confection known as Indian ice cream. *See also p. 239.*

Willow
Certain willows exhibit this long, fibrous fracture that indicates their suitability as bow wood. This particular fracture was caused by a moose in its attempt to reach the finer branches for browse. *See also p. 241.*

Tracking Moose
A good indicator of the presence of moose in the area is the grazed, contorted red-osier dogwood. *See also p. 252.*

Predator calls
The predator call is clamped between the teeth as the birch bark is tightened, in order to produce the desired frequency of sound to imitate a hare in distress. Take care in the use of this call as you may be attacked by an owl or hawk. *See also p. 280.*

THE AUTHOR

Bestselling author Mors Kochanski is widely known and well-respected for his years of experience in outdoor education in western Canada. His enthusiasm for wilderness recreation and his desire to learn everything there is to know about the wilderness have made him one of the foremost authorities on wilderness skills. He is especially familiar to outdoor enthusiasts in Alberta where he has worked and lived for the last 20 years. He is the former editor of *Alberta Wilderness Arts and Recreation*. He is currently an Assistant Professor in the Faculty of Physical Education at the University of Alberta.